The Phoenix Principle, Vol. 1

Forged in Ancient Fires

Myth and Meaning in Western Lore

Stephen H. Provost

All material © 2012, 2018 Stephen H. Provost

Previously published by the author as a single work, "The Phoenix Principle," under the name Stifyn Emrys.

Cover artwork: Public domain images
Cover concept and design: Stephen H. Provost
All interior images are in the public domain.

No part of this book may be reproduced, or stored in a retrieval system, or transmitted in any form or by any means, electronic, mechanical, photocopying, recording, or otherwise, without the express written permission of the publisher.

Dragon Crown Books 2018
All rights reserved.

ISBN: 978-1-948594-06-6

For Samaire, who had faith in me
when I no longer believed.

Contents

	Introduction	5
1	In the Beginning	11
2	The Migration	29
3	Esau's Fable	39
4	The Vizier	65
5	The Sun King	85
6	Trouble in Paradise	105
7	The Lawgiver	117
8	Queen of the South	139
9	Let My People Go	165
10	The Aaron Enigma	185
11	Bread from Heaven	215
12	The Phoenix Has Landed	231
13	Zion to Camelot	247
14	Son of the Dragon	267
15	In the Cards	285
16	Secret Identity	307
17	Gate of God	327
18	Nile to Nottingham	347
19	The Persian Messiah	373
20	Crisis in Jerusalem	383
21	Fish Stories	399
22	The Willow Queen	429
	Appendix: Timeline	469
	Bibliography	472
	Notes	479

Introduction

Who was Jesus?

This was the question that I set out to answer when I embarked upon this project. I was hardly the first to undertake this particular endeavor, nor will I be the last. The original idea was to find as much information as I could about Jesus and craft it into a sort of comprehensive biography, quoting directly from the original sources. Needless to say, this proved to be a mammoth undertaking. But as substantial as this task was, it gradually yielded to another, even broader concept. Instead of merely asking who Jesus was, my research gradually pulled me toward an even more intriguing question: What made him what he was?

Those who have read my book *The Gospel of the Phoenix* will find some material here that supports the conclusions of that work. Yet *The Gospel of the Phoenix* is a work of modern poetry and inspiration; it was intended as my personal contribution to the Jesus mythos. This present work is something entirely different: an attempt to look behind the veil that obscures what has made the myth of Jesus, and of western religion as a whole, what it is.

My first book is a tribute to the Jesus I admire. This volume is an examination of the Jesus I see in history — a product of the historical forces and mythic forces that molded him and many others who preceded and succeeded him. There is, indeed, some overlap, but there are a great many differences. Jesus appears to have urged his followers to love and accept one another but taken a much harder line with those who were outside his movement — who did not have ears to hear and would not make the sacrifices he called on them to make. He lived during a period of nationalistic fervor, and he was himself a claimant to the throne of David. There is every reason to believe that he was both a man of compassion toward his followers and a ruthless strategist toward those who opposed what he sought to accomplish — nothing less than the reinauguration of the kingdom of God on earth.

There is a tendency to believe that Jesus existed in something of a vacuum, that he burst upon the scene as an entirely original teacher and thinker. The world had never seen his like before, nor would it ever again. Such ideas were propagated by his followers, men (few women were involved) who wanted the world to believe that they offered something unique to the equation of life on earth. If Jesus had been, in any sense, a product of his times or his culture, or a student of any who had come before him, it might in some way diminish his authority as incarnate God — for certainly God was nothing if not original.

Yet the more I looked, the more I found that Jesus owed much of his message and even a good deal of his life story to those who had come before. And it was this realization that led me beyond the parameters of that story, into an investigation of the sources behind it as well as some of the diverse traditions that sprang from it. The result is a kaleidoscope of myth, history, political intrigue and spiritual questing. It began with a study of ancient Egypt, which in turn directed me to the famed "cradle of civilization" in Mesopotamia. From there, my queries drew me westward to the British Isles, where I found traces of the same traditions among the Celtic peoples preserved in the tales of King Arthur and Robin Hood. Other signs could be found in northern Europe, among the Norse and Germanic tribes. Indeed, echoes of this ancient story could be heard as far away as Persia, China and perhaps even

Australia and North America.

The story, at its core was remarkably simple. It involved three primary characters, whose likenesses still appear in, of all places, a modern deck of playing cards — the king, the queen and the jack. These three figures signified the eternal struggle for sovereignty between the aging king and his young heir apparent, with the winner gaining as his prize the land and its beautiful queen. But it was not merely a political struggle; it was, in truth, emblematic of the yearly battle of the seasons, pitting old man winter against the heroic champion of springtime. Even the prize for which they fought, the bountiful earth, corresponded quite well to the fertile queen and sovereignty over the land for which king and jack always grappled.

This struggle would be reproduced time and again in the rites of political succession as well as in religious rituals, myths, national chronicles and even faerie tales. The central theme remained constant, appearing in various permutations across centuries, cultures and continents. It surfaced in tales of gods and heroes. It can be glimpsed in the stores of pharaohs and patriarchs; in tributes to legendary architects and stealthy hunters; in medieval tomes chronicling the epic struggles of knights and dragons, damsels and wizards.

If you are reading these words, you are, in a very real sense, a wizard or "wise one" at least by ancient standards. To the largely illiterate cultures who lived at the dawn of history, the ability to write and to decipher what others had written was nothing less than magical. The scribal wizard had the ability to capture ideas in concrete form (by writing them down), then release them at his pleasure (by reading them). Even today, forms of writing such as Egyptian hieroglyphs and Norse runes retain a certain magical quality inherited from these ancient times, when the ability to read and write was regarded with a sense of awe and dread. The unlettered peasant did not know what power was contained in an imperial decree, but he knew that it empowered those who possessed it to carry out the wishes expressed therein. Only the educated priests knew the name of a god, and through this knowledge might wield his power.

Names and words contained the essence of power; to read or to utter them was to unlock that power. Prophets and poets laid claim to it through their sayings and writings, and so did the gods through inspired scripture. Is it any wonder that the greatest of the Norse gods, Odin, was master of the runes? Or that *The Gospel of John* describes Jesus specifically as the Logos — the Word of God? There were other scribal deities as well, figures with names such as Enki and Thoth with whom we shall become familiar in due course.

This book is, to a great extent, an exercise in rediscovering the power — in modern terms, the *meaning* — behind many of the writings left to us by the priests and prophets of an earlier time. Behind the symbols that recur so often over the landscape of history. The task may seem an exhausting one at times. It is often difficult to tell whether the scribes are dealing in history or poetry, whether they are chroniclers of history or spinners of sacred yarns. In fact, they appear not to have drawn such distinctions, and it is up to us to unravel these dual strands where we can. We must begin by admitting this is not always possible, but we must not allow this to deter us from the effort. Many authors have insisted that the accounts of Jesus' life are entirely historical, while others have recognized the pervasive element of myth therein and have declared the man himself a fiction. The truth is doubtless somewhere in between. Historical events that shake the foundations of our lives easily become myths, and these myths in turn attach themselves, in the form of archetypes, to future circumstances. It is in this way that a culture learns and evolves, yet remains secure in its foundations.

Jesus himself has much in common with figures such as King Arthur, Merlin and Robin Hood, whose stories shall likewise be examined in the pages that follow. He is both man and myth, a historical personage of some note whose story has become entwined with that of the archetypal man-god — perhaps at least partly as the result of his own conscious effort. Had Jesus himself never existed, those who later appropriated his message (and changed it to fit their own political agendas) would not have gone to such great pains to cover up his role as a revolutionary and his commitment to esoteric ideas that blended traditional Judaism with ancient Egyptian mystery rites. The author of *Luke* would not have — as we shall see — engaged in absurd historical distortions in order to place a Galilean in Bethlehem at the time of his birth. If Jesus were a mere fiction, such efforts would certainly not have been needed.

Yet this doesn't make it any easier to separate the man from the mythology that accrued to his story. To what extent did he purposely employ the potent symbols of ancient myth to enhance his own credibility, and which of these ideas were added by later authors? How did his story ultimately come together?

Exactly how that process unfolded is, to some extent, the subject of this investigation. It is not always easy to tell where myth ends and history begins, where heroes (and villains) acted purposely to fulfill their perceived destinies and where their chroniclers set them against mythic backgrounds long after their departure from this earth.

Many such questions are destined to remain a mystery. The best we can hope to do, in many cases, is come up with an approximation of what might have happened once we examine the political agendas, human impulses and the mythic underpinnings that make up our tales.

Our archetypal journey.

Our shared story.

It is, indeed, largely an investigation into words and symbols — and the meanings behind them. Such meanings are often hidden well beneath the surface, only to be revealed by roots a given word may share with others in its family. And these revelations can be surprising. The reader should be warned that many of the conclusions reached in this volume may be jarring to those who have grown up believing certain stories and particular meanings behind them. While it is not my intention to offend, neither is it my purpose to be constrained by the strictures of orthodoxy in my search for the truth — were I to consent to such limitations, my search would have ended prematurely.

    I do not pretend to have completed that search, nor do I consider it within the bounds of my limited ability to do so. This is but a beginning. Those who seek to embark on this journey are invited to read on. The route ahead is sometimes circuitous, a labyrinth filled with unexpected historical, political and mythological detours. Sometimes the way will be clearer, at others it will seem less so. The hope is that, when taken together, a cohesive and comprehensive picture emerges concerning the development of our common mythology. As we move forward, through and beyond this present volume, the destination will always remain ahead. There will ever be more to discover. Yet the endeavor of walking this maze is a rewarding one, and what you encounter on the way to that elusive destination is a spectacle guaranteed to astound you.

I

In the Beginning

The savior was dead, and the land was in an uproar.

Where was the king who had promised them so much, who had shown them the way to greatness?

Gone.

He was gone now, cut down in the prime of his life by his greatest adversary. And now, even the woman who had been most beloved to him in all the world couldn't find him, though she scoured the land in search of him.

He had been conquered by a tree, held captive there, altogether powerless. Yet still there was hope for redemption, for he would loose the bonds with which death enthralled him and ascend to the heavens, once more to watch over his people. God's people. He would, like the phoenix, rise again. And his symbol would be the cross, the emblem of eternal life from this time forward. His name would become legend — more than legend, it would be sacred. And throughout the land, nay, throughout the civilized world, men would utter that name in hope and reverence — reverence for what he had achieved and hope that somehow, by divine grace, they could share in that achievement.

The savior's name?

Those who recognize the elements of the legend will be quick to answer, "Jesus." The image of the humble yet victorious servant-king upon the cross is etched so deeply into our collective and individual consciousness that it is the only possible answer. The desperate cries of Mary Magdalene as she stood by his tomb seem still to echo resoundingly in our ears two millennia later. "They have taken my lord away, and I do not know where they have put him." [1]

And yet, these same cries were uttered long before, by another great woman mourning the loss of her beloved. The preceding account, you see, is not taken from the story of Jesus at all. It is more ancient — so much so, in fact, that more time elapsed between its original telling and the birth of Jesus than has passed in the two millennia since.

The savior in question was named Osiris, and his sacred story would serve as a model for the man named Jesus. More than a model, it would be to him his every hope. His inspiration. An all-consuming fire that would transform him until it became his very identity. This is the story of that transformation — of how and why it happened. It is a story of high myth and political intrigue, woven together to span five thousand years of human history. And it is a story that must begin with the myth that started it all — the myth of the enlightened king who sought to save the world, only to be betrayed and cut down at the height of his power.

This is the story of Osiris.

The legend tells us that he was the first great king of Egypt, a king of light whose birth, like that of Jesus, was accompanied by many wondrous portents. There was a voice from heaven that proclaimed, "The lord of all comes forth into the light." [2] It was an announcement that foreshadowed what would be said of Jesus: "The true light that gives light to every man was coming into the world." [3]

Osiris' birth was remarkable, to say the least. He was one of five divine children born on the five "extra" days of the year, the so-called epagomenal days.

These five days did not fit into the traditional Egyptian calendar, which had been divided into twelve months of thirty days. This particular calendar had the benefit of consistency but a significant drawback, as well — it was inaccurate. Earth took roughly three-hundred and sixty-five days to orbit the sun, five more than allowed for by the Egyptian calendar. As a result, the five lost days skewed the seasons more and more with each passing year, until what had once been summer months were being observed in the dead of winter. To adjust for this anomaly, the five extra days were created, and the Egyptians came up with a myth that explained their origin in terms of five great gods.

The Prophecy

As with so many myths, it was a story of personal betrayal, retribution and divine ingenuity. It all began with a prophesy by the wise scribe-god Thoth, who declared that "if Nut, the lady of the heavens, bears a son, he will one day rule in Egypt." [4] When word of it reached the ears of Ra, he was moved with jealousy and determined to prevent the oracle's fulfillment. He was, after all, the king of all the gods, the sun god whose majesty illumined all the heaven. And he was not about to permit a would-be rival to be born who might one day challenge him.

He therefore laid a curse upon the head of Nut, decreeing that she would be unable to give birth to any child on any day of the year.

Nut was heartbroken. But she had an advocate in Thoth, whose reputation as a prophet had been put at risk by the sun god's rash decree. He had a very personal stake in the matter, and he had another reason to intervene, as well: He was madly in love with the lady Nut. He therefore concocted a plot to circumvent the decree of Ra — a brilliant scheme that would allow him not only to save face, but also to impress Nut in the bargain. Approaching the heavenly goddess, he offered her this proposition: If she would reward him with her love, he would come up with a way for her to bear children without transgressing Ra's decree.

Nut readily assented to his plan, and Thoth went off on his way in search of the moon. His plan was simple but ingenious. He would challenge the moon to a game of draughts, with the stakes to be a portion of the moon's light. Being the wisest of the gods, Thoth knew that he would be able to outwit the moon — and indeed he did, in the end procuring enough of the moon's light to fashion five extra days.

These five days, which had not been covered in Ra's decree, then became available to Nut for bringing forth her children. The five born to her were:

- Osiris
- Horus
- Seth
- Isis
- Nephthys

Osiris, as the eldest, was destined to be the king of Egypt. He married his own sister, Isis, while Seth and Nephthys likewise married. And this became the basis for a custom that would be followed for centuries in Egypt: The king, or pharaoh, would marry his own sister or some other near relative, thus perpetuating a "pure" and royal bloodline.

But what of Horus?

According to the most popular version of the legend, he was the son not of Nut but of Osiris and Isis. To accommodate this tale, the storytellers concocted a fantastic idea. Isis and Osiris, they reasoned, must have conceived the child Horus while still in the womb *of their own mother*, Nut. Hence, while Horus appeared to have been born to Nut, he was in actuality the child of Isis and heir to the kingdom of Osiris.

This left Seth third in line to the throne — a situation with which he was hardly content. He chafed in his pride and vainglory as he watched Osiris and Isis receive the adoration of the Egyptian people. This adoration was much deserved. For together, Osiris and Isis did nothing less than transform the face of Egypt. Before, it had been a savage land of barbarians and cannibals, yet husband and wife set forth on an ambitious and ultimately successful crusade to make it instead the beacon of the civilized world. They taught men how to plant barley and wheat, how to grow fruit trees, and how to distill the fruits of their labors into the nectar that was wine; they made laws to guide their subjects, who had until then been brutal and lawless; they founded, in essence, the great kingdom that would produce the pyramids, the sphinx, the great library at Alexandria and the most magnificent temples of the ancient world.

And then, suddenly, it all came crashing down.

Osiris was in the prime of his life, at the height of his power when it happened. His brother Seth had grown jealous of his success and covetous of the throne Osiris occupied. So he gathered seventy-two conspirators, and together with the queen of Ethiopia, they hatched a plot to be rid of the one great king. At the heart of their plan was a beautiful chest of cedar and ebony, inlaid with precious jewels and adorned with gold and silver. This they fashioned so that its proportions matched exactly those of Osiris, in whose honor a great feast would be declared. The greatest men and women from throughout the kingdom would be invited to the celebration, at which the chest would be unveiled. Seth would then make a great show of offering the prize to whomever might fit inside of it — knowing all along, of course, that it had been designed specifically to accommodate one person and no other.

Osiris.

When the day of the feast came, all went according to design. The wondrous chest was unveiled to gasps of delight from the noble gathering, and each man present was eager to try his luck at Seth's competition. One by one, they stepped forward and attempted to fit into the chest. To their chagrin, however, each and every one of them failed, until at last only Osiris remained. He, like the others, was entranced by the bejeweled chest and eager to try his luck at this fine game, but it was no game to Seth and his co-conspirators — it was deadly serious.

As Osiris stepped into the chest, he found to his delight that it was a perfect fit. He lay down and luxuriated in its rich interior, beaming with pride that he should claim it as his prize....

Until, all at once, the lid slammed shut.

Seth and his cronies rushed forward, thrusting aside the astonished guests, and sealed the lid as muffled cries from the panicked Osiris issued forth from within. Paying them no heed, the conspirators nailed the chest shut, then produced a cauldron filled with molten iron, which they proceeded to pour over the whole container.

Soon the cries fell silent, and the party of onlookers could only watch in horror as Osiris' enemies carried the great chest that had become his casket away.

Isis was beside herself. Where had they taken her husband? How could they have done this? She had to find him!

Word quickly reached her that Seth had dumped the chest into the Nile River and that it had floated downstream toward the delta and the Mediterranean Sea. Isis longed to be away, but she had first to assure herself that her son Horus would be safe from the scheming Seth. Though Horus was the rightful heir to the throne, Seth had seized power for himself, and Isis knew that the usurper would never allow his nephew to challenge him. Horus' life, she knew, was in the gravest danger, so she set him on a magical floating island that sometimes appeared in the midst of the Nile and at other times was upon the sea itself, seeking to keep him from his uncle's clutches. She then cut her hair in mourning and set forth in pursuit of her dead husband's body.

But she had lost too much time. It was the season of the inundation, when the Nile's current was at its swiftest. It had carried the entombed Osiris inexorably forward toward the delta and from there into the Mediterranean. Isis followed in its wake until she reached the city of Tanis near the great sea, where she encountered a group of children who pointed her in the right direction: toward

Lebanon and its capital city, Byblos. It was there that the great chest had finally washed ashore, coming to rest in the branches of a tamarisk plant. In the course of time, this bush grew to become a great tree, encasing the chest in the hollow of its sturdy trunk.

The king of Byblos, catching sight of this impressive spectacle, ordered the tree to be cut down and instructed his servants to place the trunk as a pillar in the center of his palace. And there it remained — until Isis arrived.

The Nursemaid

She made her entrance incognito, pretending to be a nursemaid who had come to the palace to see the queen. It just so happened that the queen, Astarte, had an infant son of her own and was in need of a wet nurse. When Isis offered her services in this regard, she readily consented, giving the Egyptian goddess access to the palace — and her husband's tomb. In gratitude for Astarte's hospitality, she resolved to do her infant son a wondrous kindness: She would, by her magic, make him immortal. Every evening, she would shut the door to the chamber and offer the babe her finger to suckle instead of her breast. Then she would take him to the fire that was blazing on the hearth and pass him through its flames, fortifying him against the ravages of mortality. And she herself would be transformed into the aspect of a swallow, which would fly about the pillar of Osiris, bemoaning his terrible fate.

All this was, to say the least, very peculiar. And Astarte yearned to know what was going on behind the door to the goddess' chamber. What could be transpiring in the silence behind that door — a silence broken only by the faint chirping of a swallow? Astarte must have tried to calm her fears, for the babe appeared whole and well when again she saw him every morning. And yet, she asked herself, what could this strange nursemaid be doing? She wondered. As the child's mother, didn't she, the queen, have the right to know? How dare this total stranger lock her away from seeing her own child in her very own palace?

At last, her fears and curiosity got the better of her. Before Isis arrived, she managed to sneak into the room and position herself out of sight in a corner from which she could observe all that transpired. Needless to say, what she observed took her breath away. And when Isis took the babe to the hearth and began passing his tender body through the hungry flames, Astarte could not remain silent. Her baby! She leapt out from her hiding place and confronted Isis, snatching the infant from her arms — and in doing so robbed him of the immortality that the goddess would have conferred upon him.

Her secret discovered, Isis revealed her true identity and demanded that the pillar containing Osiris' remains be restored to her. This request was granted, and the Egyptian queen departed, returning to Egypt to arrange a proper burial for her husband.

This turned out to be no simple matter.

Upon setting foot once more in the land of her birth, she made straightaway for the floating island where she had left Horus in the care of the goddess Buto, taking her husband's casket with her. Though some versions of the myth held that Horus had been born of Nut along with the other four "epagomenal" gods, others maintained that Horus was born miraculously *after* the death of Osiris and was but an infant when Isis returned to Egypt to claim him. If so, his mother would have been even more concerned about his welfare. And upon arriving, she must have breathed a sigh of relief to find her infant son unharmed.

But as luck would have it, that sense of relief would be entirely too short-lived. For the very night after Isis arrived, she received an altogether unwelcome visit to the island. Seth, who was among other things an avid hunter, had set out on one of his nighttime forays and had stumbled across the very location where Isis had chosen to conceal her son.

Frantically, Isis snatched up Horus and concealed herself and her child and in the tall reeds that grew upon the island. But she was unable to conceal the chest in which the body of her husband remained encased. Seth, of course, recognized it at once as his own handiwork and seized hold of it and pried it open, removing the dead king's body from its resting place. In a frenzy, he hacked the body into fourteen pieces and made his escape, embarking on a journey across the length and breadth of Egypt, during which he scattered the pieces of the dead Osiris far and wide.

By his actions, Seth hoped to keep Osiris out of the Egyptian heaven.

Isis was devastated.

But she was not beaten.

Resolute, she enlisted the help of Anubis, the dog-headed god who was the offspring of Seth and Nephthys, to help her in her search. One by one, she managed to retrieve the pieces of her beloved husband's body — all except one, the phallus, which had fallen into the Nile and been consumed by a certain fish that dwelt there. Performing the appropriate burial rites, she at last laid his spirit to rest and thus thwarted Seth's attempts to keep him out of heaven. Arising to the skies, Osiris became identified with the constellation Orion, perhaps the most recognizable in the nighttime sky.

Isis had won one battle, but she had yet another, much more formidable challenge ahead of her. Seth the usurper still occupied the throne of Egypt, and she would not rest until it was transferred to its rightful occupant.

Her son.

The Battle

Seth was not about to let that happen. Newly determined to be rid of Horus once and for all, he appeared in the guise of a scorpion and crept into his crib while he slept, unbeknownst to Isis. Having done so, the ruthless usurper stung the baby as he slept and quietly departed, leaving his poison to do its deadly work.

When Isis discovered what had happened, she tried every kind of magic that she knew, but nothing seemed to have any effect against the toxin. It permeated the young boy's veins, infecting first his blood and then his heart, until he lay still and lifeless in his mother's arms. The image is a familiar one, recalling the portraits of the grieving Mary holding the body of her son Jesus, broken and bloodied, in her arms.

The images converge so neatly it is astonishing.

As do the stories.

Even the names of their adversaries are similar. Seth, also known as Set, most likely is the root name of Jesus' great nemesis, Satan. Both are depicted in legend as usurpers, and each appears to vanquish his enemy, only to watch as that enemy rises miraculously from the dead and embarks upon an apocalyptic war to reclaim his place upon the throne.

In the legend of Horus, the boy king appeared to be dead, but the scribal god Thoth visited Isis and assured her he would live again. His spirit had only been taken from him for a time, so that he might confer with the spirit of Osiris in heaven. In due course, he would return in the shape of the phoenix — the miraculous bird of the resurrection that came to rest, once every five hundred years on a magical obelisk in the ancient city of Heliopolis. There the phoenix would be consumed in the fire of the sun's rays, but in three days would be reborn from its own ashes.[5]

Jesus, like Horus, would relinquish his spirit so that he might confer with his father in heaven. And like Horus, he would return to life after the very same interval — three days — accorded the phoenix in Egyptian myth. Then, the legend said, he would lead the armies of heaven in a great assault on the forces of Satan, at last defeating him and uniting all the earth under his own beneficent rule.

This is exactly what happened in the myth of Horus.

Horus returned from the heavens and grew into a formidable prince, vowing that he would not rest until he had united Egypt under his rule. He made a habit of conferring with his father's spirit from time to time — just as Jesus would go away to a private place and pray to his heavenly father. And the advice Horus received during these consultations would prove invaluable. At the end of their final session, his father had asked him a single question to determine whether he was prepared for the challenge that lay before him: What creature would be most useful to take into battle?

Horus did not hesitate in providing his answer, naming a horse.

But Osiris pressed him: Would not a ferocious lion be of greater help?

It would if a man needed that kind of help, Horus answered, but a horse would be far more useful in cutting off a fleeing enemy and destroying him.

The answer pleased Osiris, who pronounced his son prepared to engage Seth in battle.

What followed was a series of epic struggles between the two sides. Horus retreated initially to the floating island to plot his strategy, only to be ambushed by Seth in the form of a wild boar. The great black pig caught him off guard as it rushed toward him, blinding him by a fiery flash that he sent forth like a bolt of lightning from a thundercloud. As a result, Horus was permanently blinded in one eye, leaving only one radiant beacon to shine forth — the beacon of the sun disc with which he became so closely associated.

The imagery associated with Seth in this encounter identifies him clearly as a storm god. The black boar appears like a storm cloud to block off the sun, represented by Horus, its white tusks flashing like lightning. It was this epic battle between sun and storm, the two greatest life-giving forces in the ancient Near East, that formed the thematic basis for the greatest epic myths of the period. The struggle never ended in victory for one side or the other — nor could it, for if either side were vanquished, it would leave the land without a vital element in the struggle for life. And so the struggle continued in perpetuity. In one version of the myth, the land was eventually divided between the two sides, with Horus taking half and Seth the other half. In other versions, however, the great battle eventually ended with Horus triumphant — reflecting the triumph of his cult in Egypt.

In the series of battles that followed the ambush on the island, Seth and his minions transformed themselves into creatures of the Nile — crocodiles and hippopotami — in an attempt to once again catch the forces of Horus off guard. But this time, they were ready for the onslaught. Horus had instructed his men to craft chains of iron, which they cast into the water, so that the beasts' legs would become entangled in them. Then, they could be pulled toward the boats, where they became easy targets for the iron-tipped spears Horus' men had made.

Seth himself, however, managed to avoid the trap and transformed himself into a great beast with a stinking head that roared violently and came at Horus in a fury. A great struggle ensued, from which Horus emerged the victor and exacted vengeance upon his hated enemy by hacking him into fourteen pieces — the same fate Seth himself had visited upon Osiris. At last, it appeared to be finished. But when dealing with gods, things are seldom as they might seem, for Seth's spirit had escaped the body of the dreaded beast and had taken up residence instead within the coiled from of a hideous black snake. It was merely the latest of many transformations, but a telling one. For the serpent was symbolic not only of Seth, but of his successor, Satan, who was said to have tempted the first woman and challenged the great god in the primordial garden known as Eden.

In this case, it was Seth who was challenging Horus. And, like Satan, he would wind up on the losing end.

Thoth alerted Horus to Seth's whereabouts, enjoining the son of Osiris to head south toward the island of Elephantine. It was there, in the midst of the Nile near the border of Ethiopia, that Horus found his adversary, standing defiant upon the island in the form of a red hippopotamus. Red was Seth's color, the color of the desert wastes over which he was said to rule. The men of Egypt saw him in the red hippopotamus that bellowed like thunder from the sky, or in the red donkey that was likewise his totem animal. Standing astride the island like a great behemoth, Seth sent forth a curse against Horus that unleashed a mighty tempest — a great wave that rose up and sent the boat of Horus reeling backward in a frenzy of wave and white foam.

The hero, however, was not to be beaten so easily. Miraculously, the boat righted itself, and Horus determined to sail straight into the jaws of his enemy. Seth stood there waiting for him, straddling the whole of the Nile River, resolved to end the great battle once and for all. And end it would — yet not in the way he imagined. For as Seth raged forward with a terrible roar, intent upon destroying his adversary, Horus took his harpoon and thrust it into the hippo's open maw, piercing the roof of its mouth and penetrating its brain.

And so it was finished, with Horus taking the throne of Egypt that was rightfully his. It was destined to be so, in a way, for shortly after Isis' return to Egypt, the gods had called a council to consider the matter of who was the rightful ruler of the land. Thoth began by presenting his case for Horus. It was a straightforward argument based on primacy of succession: Osiris had inherited the throne as the eldest of the gods, so Horus, as his eldest son, was his rightful heir. Seth countered that Horus was, at the time, still an infant and unfit to rule in his father's place.

Isis, however, argued so effectively before the assembly that she was on the verge of convincing them that they should rule in favor of her son. Seth, desperate to dissuade them from crediting her words, sought to smear her reputation by reminding them of some of her previous exploits. It seems that Isis, like Seth, had once hatched a plot of her own to seize power, having targeted the aging king Ra with her intrigues. Ra was the creator of all living things — all except one, that is: the dreaded Egyptian cobra, whose birth was the result of Isis' magic.

Ra had grown old and was battling the advances of senility when he chanced to walk by the place where Isis lay hidden. As he passed, a drop of spittle fell from his lips into the dirt. Seeing this, Isis hastened to the place where it had fallen. Taking the moist clay in her hands, she used her magic to mold it into the shape of a fearsome hooded serpent which she named Uraeus. It had a marking that looked like an eye on the back of its hood and venom in its curved fangs — venom that would prove to be the undoing of the great king Ra. For when Ra emerged from his slumber the following day, he stepped out into the grass and failed to notice Uraeus lurking there. By the time he had caught sight of the serpent, it had reared back and begun to strike, thrusting its gleaming white teeth into the flesh of his heel.

Howling in pain, Ra was both furious and incredulous in the same moment. This was no creature he had crafted. Where had it come from? And what was this pulsating fire that he felt so quickly infecting him, weaving its way through his veins and toward his heart? Because he had not created the beast that had inflicted this grievous wound, he knew of no cure for the affliction it had caused. There was only one hope for him: Isis, the greatest sorceress and healer in the entire kingdom, might be able to provide him with an antidote.

As if on cue, the goddess who had created the sun god's mortal quandary stepped forward with an offer that was more akin to blackmail than compassion. Her proposition was simple: She would apply her healing arts to cure Ra's ailment if — and only if — he would reveal to her his secret name. This was no trifling request. In the ancient world, whoever discovered the secret name of a god gained power over that god. It was for this reason that the Hebrew god Yahweh forbade that his true name be uttered or even written, except once a year by the high priest when he stood alone in the holy inner sanctuary. And it was for this reason that Ra hesitated, loath to reveal that which would be his downfall to the sorceress who sought to displace him.

He knew full well that if he were to disclose his secret name, Isis would gain power over him — and that she would use that power to elevate her own husband, Osiris, to the throne of the gods.

And yet, he had no choice.

His limbs were throbbing from the poison, and he was beginning to feel faint. Unless he had the antidote, and soon, the venom would overtake him completely and he would perish. Desperately, he attempted to preserve his secret name by revealing to Isis the various names by which he was known — Khepera at dawn, Ra at noontide and Tum at dusk. Yet none of these names was his secret name, and Isis was clever enough to reject such ruses out of hand. As the poison inundated his entire being, Ra knew he had no time to attempt any further deceptions. He would have to tell Isis what she wished to know, and he would have to do so without delay. Yet still, he laid down one condition: only one other person should know the sacred name that he would tell her, and that person would be Horus, the son of Osiris destined to rule over Egypt.

To this condition, Isis consented, and Ra leaned over and whispered to her the hidden name by which he was known.

Though the name itself was never revealed to anyone but Horus, it was embodied in the title Amen, which meant simply, "that which is hidden." [6] It was a mere substitute for the true hidden name, but that didn't stop the Egyptians from invoking it as a power name in spells. The Hebrew people, during their sojourn in Egypt, appear to have adopted this practice. They began to append the god's name to every praise and petition to their own "hidden" god, whose nature was likewise inscrutable and whose true name was in similar fashion known to only a single person — the high priest.

In the day that Ra revealed his sacred name, the legend went, he ceased to rule upon the earth but ascended to the heavens and relinquishing his terrestrial throne to Horus. Isis had accomplished her purpose. She had overthrown the greatest god's purpose with the aid of a crafty serpent, just as the cunning woman named Eve thwarted the purpose of the Hebrew deity in the garden known as Eden.

Anyone who wonders who got the best of the Eden encounter need only recall two assertions the serpent made to Eve during their conspiracy. The council of gods known as the Elohim (the name of the highest Canaanite god in its plural form) had forbidden Eve and her husband Adam to partake of the fruit from a single tree — the tree of the knowledge of good and evil. Were they to do so, the council warned them, they would surely perish that very instant.

The serpent, however, dismissed the warning as an idle threat. The truth of the matter was, the gods were afraid of them. "You will surely not die," the serpent declared. "For the Elohim know that when you eat of it, your eyes will be opened and you will be like the Elohim, knowing good and evil." [7]

In other words, the divine council didn't want the competition. The great god who had spoken for the council had blatantly lied to the human couple, knowing that as long as they believed the lie, they would remain under his authority. This was the serpent's contention — and it turned out to be entirely accurate. For the legend itself admits that Eve and her husband both partook of the fruit, yet did not perish for many years afterward. Moreover, the serpent's promise was fulfilled, and "the eyes of both of them were opened." [8]

As in the story of Ra and the serpent, the would-be king is given authority over the entire earth while the deity — who has heretofore walked in the garden with his creation — retires to the heavens. As in the tale of Isis and Ra, it is man who has triumphed and the deity who has fled. Only a gloss to the story, which depicts the Elohim as cursing the serpent and expelling the rebellious human couple from the garden, clouds its original nature. It was doubtless added to save the Hebrew scribes the embarrassment of having their hero thwarted by a mere human couple. Yet the true nature of the original tale is apparent in the serpent's words, which were not lies at all but indeed the essence of truth.

Though the names of the primary characters in the tale are all different, the roles they play are the same as in the Egyptian myth:

- Ra is recast as Elohim.
- Eve takes on the role of Isis.
- Adam plays the part of Osiris.
- The Edenic serpent replaces the cobra Uraeus.

The story of Ra and the serpent was what Seth referred to in attempting to discredit Isis before the assembly of the gods. How could she be trusted, when she had so blatantly deceived the great god Ra, extorting from him his secret name in exchange for his very life? The argument was persuasive — especially to the ears of Ra, who just happened to be presiding over the council. Having no wish to be embarrassed a second time by the crafty sorceress, he ordered the gathering to reconvene the next morning on an island in the center of the Nile. He gave explicit orders that Isis was not to attend this meeting, and he enjoined the ferryman who provided access to the island to prohibit her from crossing.

Such precautions, however, were hardly enough to deter the clever Isis. No sooner had Isis been escorted across than she began working on a scheme to secure victory. Her sister Nephthys had left her cruel husband Seth, and she had avoided the gathering of the gods for fear she might be compelled to reconcile with him. This gave Isis the opportunity she needed. Her appearance was similar enough to that of her sister that she could pass for her with a few modifications: a slight change in the tenor of her voice and the manner of her dress.

The story takes its cue here from Egyptian art, wherein the two sisters are frequently depicted as identical twins or mirror images of one another, with only their headdresses to distinguish them. Isis wore a stylized throne on her head, while Nephthys bore a hieroglyph for her title, "Lady of the Castle," that resembled a wide-based goblet. The two represented the tension between two opposing aspects of mortal existence: Isis was the great mother of all life, while Nephthys was associated with death and the underworld. Their resemblance indicated that they were, in a real sense, two sides of the same coin.

Isis' deception was therefore not difficult. Once she had disguised herself, she approached the ferryman and persuaded him to let her cross, tricking him into believing she was Nephthys. This accomplished, she had one more task to perform. Approaching

Seth's quarters, she let herself in and declared to him in the voice of Nephthys that she was his own true wife returning to him. She had wanted to reconcile with him all along, she declared, but the evil sorcery of Isis had prevented her from doing so. Now all she wished was to be in his arms again. She poured her "husband" a drink, and then another, plying him with liquor to make certain her ruse would be successful. Seth, intoxicated not only by the liquor but by the sight of such a beautiful woman standing seductively before him, could hardly resist her wiles. He was about to take her in his arms when she stopped him short and asked soothingly for a single favor. If he were to have her, he would have to promise her that her son would sit upon the throne of Egypt when his time came to rule.

It was a simple request to Seth's ears, for would not Nephthys' son also be his own?

He acceded to her demand, vowing that the woman's son would have the throne of Egypt when the time came. And no sooner had he done so than Isis cast off her disguise and revealed herself to him for the person that she was. Nephthys no longer stood before him, but the treacherous sister who had deceived Ra and now had done the same to him. He howled in a fury but realized that he had been undone. The oath had been sworn, and there was no taking it back. The woman's son would rule over Egypt. The woman was Isis. And her son was Horus.

When the other gods heard of the vow that Seth had taken, they had no choice but to endorse it and proclaim Horus the rightful king.

Isis had won. The phoenix was born.

II

The Migration

Ancient Egypt exercises a peculiar and potent influence upon the modern world, yet it does so quietly — like a whisper lodged somewhere just beyond the realm of consciousness. It is not tangible, but vaporous; a truth glimpsed from the corner of the eye that vanishes when one turns to face it directly. The pyramids and the treasures of the boy king Tutankhamen fascinate thousands each year, yet their significance is somehow lost in the recesses of time. We credit the Greeks and Romans as the progenitors of our secular traditions, the ancient Israelites as the fathers — the patriarchs — of our spiritual heritage. Yet each of these great civilizations owed a debt to the Egyptians, a debt greater than most realize.

It is not the Acropolis of Athens that appears on the back of the American dollar bill, but one of the great pyramids. Above its flattened top floats a smaller pyramid emblazoned with an eye, the sacred emblem of Horus, whose eye sends forth the sun's life-giving rays like a beacon over the Nile valley. It was this stone that was known to the Egyptians as the sacred benben stone, whereupon the magical phoenix was said to alight once every five hundred years in the ancient cult center of Heliopolis — the City of the Sun. The phoenix was the symbol of Horus, the god who embodied every bit of hope the Egyptians placed in their future, for it was Horus who had died and risen again to vanquish their greatest enemy, Seth.

One can almost hear the cries echo across the millennia. It is as if the Egyptian myth is proclaiming, "The king is dead! Long live the king!"

Every pyramid bore a benben stone at its apex, as did the tall and slender obelisks that dotted the landscape, crafted in the likeness of the pillar at Heliopolis. Such an obelisk is visible today in Washington, D.C., a monument to the first American president. Another stands in the courtyard of Saint Peter's Basilica at the heart of Vatican City. Still another was transported from Egypt to stand in New York's Central Park. Such symbols pass before our eyes almost unnoticed, so familiar that few bother to question their significance. And so it is with the symbols of our spiritual heritage, as well. It is easy to overlook the pervasive Egyptian influence upon the fabric of Judeo-Christian belief. After all, the Egyptian religion is a "dead" religion with a plethora of gods and goddesses, a confusing maze of animal-headed deities and overlapping traditions. Moreover, knowledge of Egyptian hieroglyphics had become so completely buried in the sands of time that no one remembered how to interpret the curious symbols until the discovery of the famed Rosetta Stone.

But the Egyptian religion is not, in fact, dead at all. It is merely hidden away like a pharaoh in the Valley of the Kings or a savior within a garden tomb, waiting to rise again to the heavens as the ancients have prophesied. We scarcely know it is there, and we mistake it for a corpse. Yet its legacy is as potent as the spirit that keeps the resurrected man-god alive and breathing at the core of our religion.

Should this somehow be surprising?

Not if we recall that Israel and Egypt are neighbors, kindred nations that share a border and so much more. Over the span of two millennia, Egypt and its rival to the east, Mesopotamia, would vie for influence in the narrow strip of fertile coastland that lay between them along the trading routes, a coastland known at various points in its history as Canaan, Philistia (or Palestine) and Israel. The two great powers would take turns ruling the "land of promise" famous for its olive trees, grapevines and abundant pastures for grazing. And though the men who lived there found themselves subject at various points to the Babylonian, Assyrian and Seleucid empires in the east, it was the land of the pharaohs to the southwest that left the greater imprint.

By the time of Jesus' birth, the world's largest Jewish population center lay not in Jerusalem, but in Alexandria, the great capital in the Nile Delta built by and named for Alexander the Great. By this time, there were not mere thousands but hundreds of thousands of Jews in Egypt, the better portion of whom lived in Alexandria. So numerous were they that they even had their own quarter of the city — which literally constituted about one-fourth of its geographic area.

This situation was the end result of countless migrations and cultural exchanges that had begun nearly two thousand years before. It was then that a group of nomads from Mesopotamia had undertaken a journey south and west in search of better grazing land for their flocks. The Egyptians called them *hapiru* or *habiru*, a word that meant simply "foreigners" and appears closely related to the name by which these people would become known: Hebrews.

But these were no simple nomads. Some of them were, in fact, noblemen from Ur, not far from the Persian Gulf on the shores of the Euphrates River. Ur was a grand city, site of a great step-sided ziggurat similar to the legendary Tower of Babel. It was from there that a man known as Abram set forth on a journey that would take him to the narrow strip of fertile land that would be his destiny. But he didn't stop there. Instead, he and his entourage continued their journey until they arrived in the Nile Delta, whereupon they received a greeting from the pharaoh worthy of princes.

And with good reason. Abram did not come alone, but at the head of a substantial army that would quickly earn a fearsome reputation. Not long after his journey to Egypt, Abram would venture north once again and lead his forces in a commando raid to rescue a nephew who had been captured by enemy forces. The battle would pit Abram and his men against four separate armies, yet Abram's forces would emerge victorious and succeed in rescuing his nephew.

Abram was clearly no simple nomadic herdsman, but a clan chief of some importance and an accomplished general. His title indicates as much. Abram was not, in fact, a proper name but rather a description. It meant simply "father," most likely indicating his position as patriarch of his particular clan. His wife, likewise, would be remembered not by her true name but by the role she played in history. Sarai, or Sarah as she would come to be called, meant "queen" or "princess."

So Abram was royalty — not a mere shepherd, but the chief of a roving band of nomadic raiders who probably claimed land for their flocks by force of arms more often than not. When they ran out of grazing land, they simply moved on to the next pasture and secured it in battle or by treaty. And at this particular point in history, they were running out of land all too quickly. Famine had enveloped the entire region, fueled by a drought that had left the usually verdant land dry and barren of grass. Without rain, no land could supply enough forage for the extensive flocks Abram had brought with him — no land except one, that is.

Egypt.

The Nile Delta retained its abundant pasturelands even during periods when no rain fell, because it gleaned its moisture not from the sky but from the great river herself. The rain that supplied the delta fell a thousand miles away at the river's headwaters, then meandered across the desert land of northern Africa until it reached the Mediterranean, supplying a narrow strip of land on either bank with its life-giving streams. Upon reaching the delta, it fanned out to embrace a broad cross-section of land, several branches tumbling past one another in a race to reach the sea. It was here that the land was most welcoming, and it was to this fertile oasis at the northern tip of the continent that Abram came seeking pasture for his flocks.

It was clear from the outset that he was a threat to the reigning Egyptian king, or pharaoh, who quickly hatched a plot to pre-empt any designs Abram might have on his kingdom by striking an alliance with him — an alliance that turned out to be far more complicated than the pharaoh had envisioned.

It seems Abram had been wary of the pharaoh's intentions and feared that if he presented Sarai as his wife, the Egyptian ruler would have him killed so he could marry her. Accordingly, he advised his wife to adopt a convenient pretense: She would pose as his sister, thus alleviating any need for the pharaoh to do away with the competition. There was only one problem with this plan, and it was a rather significant stumbling block, to say the least. If the pharaoh thought Sarai was his sister, he would be free to take her to his bed without fear that she was under any marital constraints.

And this is exactly what he decided to do.

Most likely, he was motivated as much by political concerns as any attraction he might have felt for the woman. If he were to forge a marital alliance with Abram's sister, it would force a military treaty and keep Abram from acting on any ambitions he might have to challenge the pharaoh and usurp his throne. He therefore took Sarai into his palace and "treated Abram well for her sake," bestowing upon him livestock, servants and beasts of burden. Given Abram's military prowess, this was not an unreasonable course of action. But given Abram's deception, it was one that would meet with disastrous results.

The author of *Genesis* discretely avoids any mention of whether the pharaoh actually took Sarai to his bed. But given the writer's description of Sarai as a "very beautiful woman" and the pharaoh's lavish gifts to Abram, one can be reasonably confident that he did. Such a union also would explain the plagues that immediately followed in the narrative, which led the pharaoh to suspect he had been tricked. In response, he brought Abram before him and demanded an explanation, not pausing long enough to receive one before he ordered the *habiru* prince expelled from Egypt for his deception.[9]

The pharaoh was extremely wary of Abram, whom he regarded as a threat to his sovereignty. And, as it turns out, he had good reason to be. For Abram's expulsion from the delta was not really an expulsion at all. Rather, he seems to have departed only after negotiating a treaty that gave him nothing less than sovereignty over Egypt. This is apparent from the fact that he did not leave the land of the Nile empty-handed. On the contrary, he departed with "everything he had" — an inventory that included a wealth of livestock, servants and beasts of burden that had been bestowed upon him by the pharaoh himself. Had Abram been a simple commoner, the pharaoh would no doubt have executed him on the spot for his audacity at pretending that Sarai was not his wife, but his sister.

But he didn't.

He didn't even try to confiscate the lavish presents he had given Abram, but instead allowed him to keep everything. He certainly wouldn't have done so unless he was afraid of him somehow — unless he needed to *bribe* him to leave. Abram did, after all, have a substantial army under his command, substantial enough to rout an army of four kings shortly after his encounter with the pharaoh, and perhaps substantial enough the threaten Egypt as well. In this context, the pharaoh's gifts to Abram take on the appearance of tribute paid from a vassal to his patron ruler, and this is doubtless exactly what they were. Most likely, Abram wasn't kicked out of Egypt at all — he probably went voluntarily, embarking upon a campaign to add to his territory by challenging the four kings of southern Palestine.

All this happened toward the end of the so-called Middle Kingdom, when the native Egyptian dynasty that had been ruling for centuries was in decline. The center of Egyptian power had long been southern or Upper Egypt, so named because of its relatively elevated terrain. As the pharaoh's power waned, more and more immigrants from the east began descending upon the fertile Nile Delta in the north, seeking pasturelands for their flocks. Their numbers quickly multiplied, and they began to band together under chieftains who had no allegiance to, or love for, the ruling house of Upper Egypt.

Abram was one such chieftain — and, it seems, the most powerful of them. He succeeded in consolidating power in the delta and then decided to challenge the Egyptian pharaoh, who had grown too weak to oppose him. The pharaoh responded to this challenge by seeking an alliance with Abram, loading him down with gifts and suggesting a marriage with his "sister" Sarai to cement the deal.

At first, Abram seems to have consented to the arrangement. He may have questioned whether he was powerful enough to challenge the pharaoh and decided it was better to surrender his wife to him. But then, at some point, he changed his mind. Perhaps the pharaoh seemed a little too eager to strike a deal. Perhaps Abram had received reports that the once-powerful Egyptian empire was not what it used to be. But whatever his reasoning, he suddenly revealed that the alliance was off — Sarai was *his* wife and would not be given in marriage to the pharaoh. Emboldened, he further demanded that he be allowed to keep the presents pharaoh had given him, perhaps as a dowry in exchange for Sarai's hand.

Abram and the pharaoh would not be allies. They would be lord and vassal, with Abram in the former role. He would be the first of the Hyksos, a term used by the Egyptian historian Manetho to describe the men he called "shepherd kings." It was certainly an apt description for Abram, who had come to Egypt in the first place seeking pastureland for his flocks. Another proposed meaning of the word Hyksos, however, is "foreign rulers" — an equally appropriate designation for Abram and those who would come after him. They were, to the native Egyptians, quite foreign, with their lighter skin and bearded faces. But now they were masters of the Nile, ruling from the delta and relegating the once-proud dynasty of Upper Egypt to the status of tribute-paying underlings.

Abram is remembered to history as Abraham, a title that he

probably gained upon ascending the throne of Egypt. It means "exalted father." But its roots are, in fact, Egyptian. To the natives, he was

Ma'abra Sheshy. The latter name meant something like "wanderer," a meaning also related to the word "Hebrew." Ma'abra could be translated as "true heart of Ra," a name that honored the ancient sun god and bore a striking resemblance to that of the famous patriarch. By simply transposing the first two letters and placing them at the end rather than the beginning, one comes up with the name Abra'am.

Abraham.

For the next two centuries, the Hyksos would be rulers of Egypt. The native dynasty and its successors would continue to exercise a measure of authority in Thebes, but they would be subordinate to the delta kings who had invaded their land. These foreign kings' names were preserved on scarabs, amulets in the shape of the sacred Egyptian beetle that was credited with propelling the sun across the sky. It was an allegorical legend based upon the beetle's habit of rolling a ball of dung into a hole and therein laying its eggs. The offspring would later emerge and, eventually, repeat the process. They therefore became symbols of death and rebirth, sunrise and sunset.

It was upon these scarabs that the pharaohs left their mark. The amulets then would be scattered far and wide, throughout Egypt and into Palestine — sometimes beyond — indicating, perhaps, the scope of the monarchs' influence. The Egyptian form of Abraham's name, for example, has been found on a large number of scarabs in Egypt, Nubia and Palestine.[10] The names of other Hyksos kings have been similarly attested on the scarabs, often carved out of gold or precious gemstones.

Among these is a name as familiar as that of Abraham. It should perhaps come as little surprise that this name belonged to another Jewish patriarch, who appears in the Hebrew scriptures as Abraham's grandson.

The Egyptian form of the name, as it appears on the scarabs, is

Yakob-har. The second half, *har*, probably refers to Horus — the god said to be synonymous with the living king. The first half, though, was not Egyptian at all but clearly Semitic. This was, after all, a Hyksos king.

And his name was unmistakable: It was Jacob.

… III

Esau's Fable

No one should wonder that the ancient Hebrews borrowed their myths from the Egyptians. The Hyksos had made themselves masters of the Nile — they had triumphed through force of arms. But superior military might was one thing; culture was quite another. And in the latter regard, the Hyksos were little more than barbarians compared with the high civilization of their neighbors to the south.

Mythology was central to that situation. The Egyptians explained their existence in terms of the myths, the foremost of which was the myth of Seth and Osiris. This myth illustrated how the land had become divided, with the kingdom of Lower Egypt to the north and the realm of Upper Egypt to the south. One portion was allotted to Seth, while his rival's son Horus reigned over the other.

To Horus belonged the fertile regions alongside the River Nile, while Seth's domain was the desert wilderness that lay beyond. Seth's color was red, like the scorching sands of the desert. He was embodied in the storms that flash across the arid desert, his thunderheads threatening to obscure the sacred eye of Horus — the solar orb. Thus their eternal battle was waged not only on the ground but in the heavens. This celestial battle between the forces of light, led by the sun god Horus, and the minions of shadowy darkness under the command of Seth would make its way into Hebrew lore. Seth was renamed Satan, literally "the adversary," and the battle was resumed against the Hebrew god Yahweh or, more correctly, his anointed champion.

His messiah.

As it was with the Egyptians, so it would be with the Hebrews: Every earthly situation was a mere reflection of some greater heavenly truth. For the Egyptians, the heavens even contained a celestial Nile, the Milky Way. According to one theory, the great pyramids of the Giza plateau are even laid out in a pattern to reflect a heavenly constellation. These pyramids were not only tombs, but sacred temples to the gods reflecting a design handed down from the heavens. And it is far from coincidental that the Hebrew temple in Jerusalem was said to be patterned precisely after a heavenly temple.

It was only natural that the Hyksos should absorb these traditions during their two centuries of sovereignty over the Nile Delta — and that their kings should follow the Egyptian example and cast themselves in the role of Egypt's mythic hero: Horus. Each pharaoh was considered the personification of Horus on earth, and the Hyksos were no exceptions. Jacob even seems to have incorporated the god's name (*har*) into his own, following the custom of native Egyptian pharaohs who consistently honored various gods in this manner.

So closely did Jacob identify with Horus that a myth grew up around him and his brother that closely paralleled the Egyptian myth of Horus and Seth.

In the Hebrew version of the story, Jacob's brother Esau takes on the role of Seth — and he is perfect for the part. When he is born, he is covered from head to toe in red hair, the color sacred to Seth. And his name, which is said to mean "hairy" is phonetically similar to the braying sound made by a donkey — one of Seth's totem animals.

According to the legend, Esau and Jacob were twins.

At first, this might seem to be at variance with the story of Seth and Horus, who were uncle and nephew. But according to one version of the tale, the two Egyptian gods were also brothers, Horus having been conceived while his parents were still in the womb and born at the same time. It was an odd birth, to be sure. And the birth of Jacob and Esau was also unique. Esau, the elder, was born with his younger brother grasping at his heel. As a result, the latter earned the name Jacob — meaning "supplanter." Just as Horus had supplanted his elder brother/uncle Seth on the throne of Egypt, so Jacob would supplant his elder brother as heir to his father's estates and claimant of his blessings.

Thus began the story of Jacob and Esau.

As it continues, elements of the Horus legend surface time and again.

The two brothers grow to adulthood as rivals for their parents' favor. Esau succeeds in winning the good will of his father Isaac, while Jacob is the apple of his mother's eye. Her name is Rebekah, a thoroughly Egyptian name meaning something like "soul and spirit of Ra." This could well indicate that the Hyksos king Isaac married a native Egyptian princess in a political move to consolidate his hold over the entire land.

He was not the first Hyksos ruler to do so, nor would he be the last. Indeed, Abraham himself had forged an alliance (probably an arranged marriage) with an Egyptian "servant" named Hagar. And although she was a servant, it seems likely that this was not meant in the sense that one might normally use the word. She was, more likely, a member of the Theban royal house and therefore also a vassal to the Hyksos overlords. In other words, a servant. The marriage was a strategic one. Abraham had been unable to sire an heir by his first wife, Sarai (or Sarah) and it was imperative that he do so. He was no longer a young man, and Sarah herself was past child-bearing years. She therefore consented to have him take Hagar to his bed for the purpose of producing an heir to the throne — and not just any heir, but one who could command the loyalty of both the Hyksos and Theban factions.

And indeed she did, conceiving a child named Ishmael who became next in line to the throne of Egypt.

The plan seemed to be working perfectly, until the unexpected happened.

Sarai, too, conceived a child.

Suddenly, things weren't quite so cut and dried. Ishmael was the eldest, but Isaac had been born to Abraham's first and favorite wife. The situation precipitated an instant power struggle as supporters lined up behind one or another of the two potential claimants to the throne. Ishmael appeared to have the better claim and apparently flaunted it by mocking his younger brother openly. But he had not counted on Sarah's influence. She did not take kindly to having her son made sport of and responded by demanding that Ishmael be disinherited: "Get rid of that slave woman and her son, for that slave woman's son shall never share the inheritance with my Isaac." [11]

Abraham is depicted in the account as somewhat sympathetic to Ishmael and reluctant to grant his wife's request. Nonetheless, he would eventually comply, sending Hagar and Ishmael into exile in the desert wilderness — the realm of Seth. It was a symbolic re-enactment of the Horus myth. Isaac was being chosen as the new Horus, the king of Egypt. But Ishmael would have his own realm, that of Seth. Just as the two great gods had divided the land between them, so now too did the sons of Abraham. Ishmael would be "a wild ass of a man," a clear reference to the totem animal of Seth.[12] He would gain renown as an archer, a profession closely identified with Seth, who likewise had a reputation as a hunter. Storm gods were often depicted as archers, drawing back their bows and sending arrows of fiery lightning down upon the earth. It is for this reason that Yahweh, another storm god who eventually became the national god of Israel, vowed to set his bow in the clouds after inundating the earth with a violent rainstorm.

Ishmael and Isaac would each become the patriarch of a great nation.

Just like Seth and Horus.

To this day, Jews and Arabs both trace their cultural history back to the great Hyksos king Abraham — Jews through Isaac and Arabs through Ishmael.

But no sooner is this fork in the genealogical road laid down than another is created a few steps further along the path. In moving through the biblical narrative, it is almost as though the reader is taken on a roller-coaster ride from which the operator is not about to let him off. This is the genius of *Genesis*. The narrator never lets up, introducing new characters and conflicts at a frantic pace that leaves the reader breathless in admiration. Yet he does so by repeating the same themes time and again, allowing his audience to absorb the main thrust of his narrative despite the rapid series of transitions from one generation to the next.

This frenetic approach grew out of a process foreign to most writers today. Most works of modern literature are composed by a single author, and even anthologies are a succession of works, each following neatly upon the last. But *Genesis* was not composed this way at all. It was the work not of one author, but of several. At least four streams of tradition have been identified in this one book, streams that were ultimately woven together by an editor with a daunting task before him. On the one hand, he was charged with crafting several divergent accounts into a coherent package; on the other, he could not simply delete two strands of tradition that had lingered on the lips of storytellers for generations — simply because they seemed to be at odds with one another. Ancient audiences were less concerned with reconciling contradictions than they were with drawing some deeper meaning from a story. Even the high culture of ancient Egypt contained myriad contradictions, including the contention that Horus was both brother and son to Osiris.

Because of this hesitance to simply strike contradiction from the record, many seemingly irreconcilable statements found their way into the Genesis account. One of the best-known examples occurs at the outset, when the author (actually the editor) includes not one but two distinct accounts of creation, one right after the other. In the first, the land produces vegetation on the third day and man does not emerge until the sixth. But the second version of the story reverses this, declaring that man was formed from the dust of the ground when "no shrub of the field had yet appeared on the land and no plant of the field had yet sprung up." [13]

This is a blatant contradiction. One clearly cannot have it both ways.

But the editor's aversion to simply excising material in forging a common tradition also led to another element commonly found in the text.

Repetition.

This can create quite a problem for the modern scholar, causing no end of confusion about which version of a story to believe. But it is also a blessing in disguise, with each story reinforcing patterns of belief that were integral to the culture in question and providing new facets of the core legend to explore. One example of this repetition involves the story of Abraham deceiving the pharaoh by introducing Sarah as his sister rather than his wife. This motif occurs in the course of *Genesis* not once or twice, but fully three times. In one instance, Abraham is once again the protagonist, echoing the tale of his sojourn in Egypt as he once again pretends that Sarah is his sister. This time, however, he does so not with the pharaoh, but during his dealings with a different monarch, Abimelech, whose kingdom lay in the Negev desert that separated Egypt and Palestine. In the third version of the story, Abimelech is once again involved, but this time it is Isaac who deceives him into believing that his wife Rebekah is actually his sister.

The similarities suggest that all three stories stem from a common source. During oral transmission, as is wont to happen, certain discrepancies emerged and became embedded in separate strands of tradition. Each version of the story became so well known among its constituent audience that it could not simply be discarded without offending a large segment of readers. Hence, all three stories were retained, despite their similarities, and conveniently employed to reinforce one of the editor's themes: Lying doesn't pay.

This tendency toward repetition surfaces in the story of Esau and Jacob, the next fork in the genealogical path. Jacob would become the father of the Israelite people, while Esau would be revered as patriarch to the neighboring Edomites. (The name Edom means "red," a reference to the sacred color of Seth.) The story of these two brothers, in many ways, recapitulates that of Isaac and Ishmael.

Just as Sarah had defended, Isaac, the younger of two sons, against his elder brother Ishmael, Rebekah now defended her younger son Jacob against Esau. And just as Seth and Ishmael had been renowned as hunters, so now was Esau. In fact, it was this skill as a hunter that got him in trouble. On one occasion, after a particularly exhausting hunt, he returned home to find Jacob cooking some red lentil stew — yet another allusion to Seth's sacred color. Famished from a day in the wilderness (Seth's domain), he demanded that his brother give him some of the stew he was preparing. But Jacob, seeing an opportunity in Esau's desperation, was not about to be so obliging. Instead, he insisted that his brother first swear to relinquish his birthright. Esau must have been starving, for he agreed to do so, thus transferring his inheritance to his younger brother.

But this was not the end of Jacob's scheming. In order to confirm his status as true heir to his father's estate, he would have to somehow obtain the old man's blessing. To this end, his mother devised a scheme that would allow him to trick her ailing husband into bestowing his sanction upon Jacob. This would be no simple matter, for Isaac favored Esau and would not willingly shun him in favor of his rival. Jacob would therefore have to deceive him into relinquishing the blessing he so coveted.

Rebekah's plan was to take advantage of Isaac's failing eyesight to trick him into mistaking Jacob for Esau. She instructed her younger son to go out into the fields and bring her two young goats so she might prepare just the sort of meal her husband enjoyed. Then, he was to take it to Isaac and present it to him in hopes of obtaining his blessing.

Here, the author repeated the motif of offering food in exchange for an inheritance. But this time, there was a catch. Jacob knew that his brother was "a hairy man" and that Isaac, despite his poor eyesight, would discover the ruse if he happened to feel Jacob's smooth skin.

His mother therefore agreed to fashion a disguise for him, using the skins of the goats she had just cooked. These she spread out across his hands and forearms, so that Isaac might mistake them for the hairy arms of Esau.

It sounded like a good plan. But even with this precaution, there were some anxious moments when it appeared the plan would fall to pieces, for although Jacob could disguise his skin, he could not do the same for his voice.

"The voice is the voice of Jacob, but the hands are the hands of Esau," Isaac remarked.[14]

But the old man was probably too tired to put much energy into deciphering this apparent contradiction. Instead, he merely asked for some reassurance that his son was, in fact, Esau — assurance that Jacob was only too happy to provide. He then supplied the blessing that Jacob had sought, only to find out when Esau returned that he had blessed the wrong son. But by this time, the words could not be taken back. The blessing had taken the form of an oath, and as such was irrevocable.

All Isaac could do was give Esau a sort of consolation prize, a "blessing" that decreed he should live in the wilderness "away from the earth's richness."

In the realm of Seth.

The legend's barely veiled identification of Esau as a Seth-type figure connects it clearly to Egyptian myth. And there are other similarities, as well, particularly to the story of Isis and the council of gods. In that tale, Isis had sought to secure for her son Horus succession to the throne in the face of a rival claim by Seth. But the father of the gods, Ra, had favored Seth, just as the family patriarch Isaac favored Esau in the Hebrew legend. So, in both cases, the doting mother resorted to a form of deception in order to obtain the inheritance for her son.

In both stories, the woman fashions a disguise as means of attaining her goal: Isis impersonates her sister, Nephthys, while Rebekah creates a guise whereby Jacob can pretend to be his brother. Both stories also involve an oath that is given in ignorance, yet cannot be taken back. In each case, the person receiving the pledge is not who he or she appears to be. And, moreover, both vows involve an inheritance. Seth pledges to Isis that her son shall ascend the throne of Egypt, while Isaac similarly grants his blessing to Jacob. There is even a reference to soup or stew in both stories. In the Egyptian version, Isis offers a bowl to the ferryman when she asks him for passage.

Such similarities were not accidental. They were designed to reinforce Jacob's identification with Horus and, hence, his status as rightful king of Egypt.

But the story of Jacob does not end there.

Stairway to Heaven

Esau understandably holds a grudge against Jacob for cheating him out of his inheritance and vows to kill him. Jacob, fearing for his life, packs his belongings and flees in the hope of finding refuge with his uncle in northwestern Mesopotamia. On his way, he stops for the night and experiences an odd dream: He envisions a stairway stretching from earth to heaven, with angels ascending and descending before his eyes. Then, a voice from heaven proclaims:

"I will give you and your descendants the land on which you are lying. Your descendants will be like the dust of the earth, and you will spread out to the west and to the east, to the north and to the south. All peoples on the earth will be blessed through you and your offspring." [15]

This is nothing less than a declaration of kingship. Jacob is to be at the head of a line that would bless all the peoples of the earth — a royal line of kings. And these kings are destined to expand their territory in all directions. Egypt will come under his sway, as will Mesopotamia in the east. According to one version of the story, Jacob ends up returning to the very spot of the heavenly stairway sometime later, where he experiences a historic transformation. No longer is he to be called Jacob, but by divine decree is thenceforth known as Israel.

The name is a fascinating one, for it embodies the promise made to Jacob at the foot of the ladder. He is to rule over all the earth — a region defined at that time by the border of southern Egypt at one end and eastern Mesopotamia on the other. The father of the gods in Egypt was Ra, the ancient sun god whose Palestinian counterpart, by way of Mesopotamia, was El. Each of these two great deities presided over a council of the gods, the group known in Palestine as the Elohim. Jacob was to be favored by both, the royal vessel through which their combined power would flow. He would be the "power of Ra and El" — in Egyptian, Userael.

Israel.

Was Jacob in fact fleeing his brother, or was he embarking on a campaign of diplomacy or conquest as his grandfather Abraham had done? The latter seems at the very least a distinct possibility.

But a crucial question remains to be answered: Just what did the dream mean?

The answer lies in the ancient Egyptian pyramid texts. The pyramids themselves were, of course, tombs. As a result, much of the material in the pyramid texts were concerned with the spiritual journey from earth to heaven. For the pharaohs, this journey entailed a transformation from the living king, symbolized by Horus into the departed king of heaven, embodied by Osiris.

The pyramids themselves were crucial to this transformation. The earliest of them was not a smooth-sided structure like the great pyramids on the Giza plateau. On the contrary, it was indented on its sides at regular intervals to create the impression of stair steps leading up to heaven. This was the step pyramid of Imhotep at Saqqara, similar in many ways to the ziggurat temples of Babylon.

Suddenly, the stairway to heaven in Jacob's dream makes a little more sense. And a text found in the tomb of the fifth century pharaoh Unas clarifies the symbolism further. It declares that Horus had set up a ladder for his father Osiris, which the dead god-king might use to ascend into heaven. Horus and Seth served figuratively as the ladder's two posts, with the dead pharaoh Unas between them.[16]

What could this have indicated in regard to Jacob?

The symbolism might, at first glance, seem to indicate that Jacob has died. But this is clearly impossible, as the narrative continues for some time after this with an account of his various exploits. In addition, Jacob does not ascend the stairway himself. He merely watches "angels" ascending and descending. It is therefore obvious from the symbolism that someone has died. Yet it is equally apparent that the someone in question is not Jacob.

But who?

The answer can be inferred from the circumstances surrounding the story. Before Jacob set off on his journey, his father had been bedridden. Isaac was old and frail, and he must have felt he was close to death, for he took the opportunity to impart his blessing to his sons. This is the sort of act one does not generally expect unless death is imminent. The narrative is somewhat confusing in this regard, probably because it was assembled from more than one source. On the one hand, it seems to indicate that Isaac was already dead before Jacob fled to Mesopotamia.[17] Yet afterward, Isaac inexplicably calls Jacob to him, entreats him not to marry a Canaanite woman and instructs him what to do on his journey![18]

The second account is the fuller of the two, indicating that the first reference to Isaac's death is simply misplaced. It appears, on the contrary, that Isaac was still alive — though gravely ill — at the time of Jacob's departure. It is therefore only natural that he should have passed away during the course of Jacob's journey. And his death would certainly explain the vision of the stairway to heaven. It was Isaac, the old pharaoh, who was taking on the role of Osiris and ascending into heaven — and Jacob, by way of the vision, was watching him go.

Jacob — the Yakob-har of the Hyksos — thereafter received a new name (Israel), as pharaohs did when they succeeded to the throne. The blessing he received from the divine presence standing at the top of the stairway was really no different than the blessing his father had given him: "May nations serve you and peoples bow down to you."[19] This is because the divine presence is none other than his father Isaac, transformed through death into the image of the god Osiris.

Just as Horus spoke to his dead father Osiris and received his blessing after the god's death, so now Jacob did the same.

He was the new Horus — the king of Egypt.

But he had work yet to do. As he set off to expand his influence into Mesopotamia, he knew he was leaving behind a rival determined to have the throne for himself. Esau had vowed to kill him, just as Seth had vowed to destroy Horus in the ancient myth. And it was inevitable that the next stage of the myth be re-enacted as well: Jacob would have to confront his brother and defeat him on in battle.

It was only a matter of time.

The Beanstalk Variation

The legend of Jacob's ladder, incidentally, appears to have formed the basis of the familiar faerie tale of Jack and the Beanstalk. The hero of this story is Jack — whose name was but a nickname for "Jacob" and will turn out to be highly significant in the course of this investigation.

Jack, of course, ends up climbing a magical beanstalk to the sky in much the same way that Jacob's angels ascend his ladder to heaven. But first things first.

The tale begins with an important bit of information, revealing that Jack is the son of a widow (hence, his father has died). Their prize possession is a cow named Milky White, whose milk apparently provides the boy and his mother with their sole reliable source of income.

One day, however, her milk dries up and they are forced to seek a buyer for the animal in an effort to procure enough money to start a business. Jack takes the task upon himself and sets out to market with the intention of selling Milky White for a handsome sum, only to be accosted on the road by an odd-looking old man who inexplicably knows his name. The man offers him a handful of magical beans in exchange for the cow, asserting that the beans will spring up overnight in the form of a stalk reaching up to the sky.

Our hero takes the man's word for it and pockets the beans, giving up Milky White in the bargain. His subsequent adventures include various trips up the beanstalk, during which he confronts a giant and his wife who live in the clouds. On successive trips, he manages to steal several bags of gold, a goose that lays golden eggs and finally a golden harp. On the final trip, the giant tries to chase him down the beanstalk but is thwarted when Jack grabs an axe and chops it down.

The theme of stealing treasure from heaven parallels that of Prometheus, who stole fire from the father god Zeus and brought it to earth for the enrichment of mankind. This parallel raises the intriguing possibility that the giant is, similarly, a father god of sorts. Perhaps he is even *Jack's* dead father. This would make perfect sense, given that the father in question has died and presumably ascended to heaven in the very same manner that the father-god Osiris did, leaving his heir, the prince Horus, to rule in his stead. Such symbolism is heightened further by the name Jack, which is the name given to the playing card that pictures a prince. The riches Jack obtains at the top of the beanstalk must therefore be his inheritance, which gains only after outwitting his dead father through deceit and trickery.

One should recall that the patriarch Jacob similarly uses deceit to outwit his father Isaac to gain his blessing in the incident with the stew.

The similarities are adding up, and it is becoming quite plain that the beanstalk tale is closely related to that of Jacob's ladder. And yet another parallel (perhaps an intermediate version of the legend) is contained in an Arab tale of a calf left by a father to his son. His mother instructs the boy to sell the animal for three gold pieces, but he meets an angel along the road who offers him six pieces of gold instead. The boy, however, demurs, insisting that he must talk the matter over with his mother before striking a deal.[20] In this detail, the story deviates from the classic version of Jack and the Beanstalk, but everything else is consistent:

- The father's death
- The cow left as inheritance
- The decision to sell the cow
- The sudden appearance of a magical man/angel in the road
- The stranger's desire to trade for the cow

The death of the father marked a turning point for Jack and the hero of the Arab tale, just as it did for Jacob.

But much more lay ahead for the patriarch in his quest to claim the kingdom.

Stolen Gods and Supermen

Jacob's stay in Mesopotamia was an eventful one. Preferring diplomacy to military action, he sought to forge an alliance by marriage. Dynastic ties between Egypt and Mesopotamia seem to have already existed, for the Mesopotamian clan leader is described as Jacob's maternal uncle. Family ties, however, clearly meant little to the man, whose name was Laban. He was older and more experienced in the art of negotiation than Jacob — and it showed.

Jacob sought his younger daughter's hand in marriage, but Laban was not about to simply oblige him without some sort of compensation. And his was no simple request. He demanded that

Jacob stay there and keep watch over his flocks for seven years. Although Jacob may well have worked as a shepherd, the reference might just as well have been allegorical. Jacob was agreeing to accept vassal status and administer Laban's realm on his behalf. Clearly, he could not claim the same sort of military advantage as Abraham had enjoyed during his incursion into Egypt. Had Jacob had sufficient force of arms at his disposal, he would never have agreed to such an arrangement.

But agree he did. And he opened the door for Laban to double-cross him. For when the seven years were up, he got Jacob drunk and tricked him into marrying his older daughter instead. Jacob was understandably livid. The marriage was to symbolize a political alliance, and how could Jacob trust an ally who deceived him so readily? And there were other considerations in play, as well: Jacob had fallen in love with Laban's younger daughter, Rachel, and had no desire to be stuck with her older sister instead. Yet thanks to Laban's trickery, he was. Jacob the deceiver had himself been deceived, and there was nothing to do but remain in Laban's service for another seven years to secure Rachel's hand in marriage.

And so he did — it would give him time to plot his revenge.

If Laban could play dirty, he could too. And he proceeded to hatch a plan whereby he could challenge Laban's supremacy. He asked Laban for permission to keep every speckled sheep or goat under his care as his wages. He then arranged to breed Laban's goats in such a way that their offspring all came out speckled. The story is clearly superstitious and perhaps, once again, allegorical. The likelihood is that we are not dealing with goats at all, but people. It is interesting to find that the name Rachel means "ewe," who joined with Jacob to produce offspring. And not just any offspring, but *speckled* offspring. This would seem to be confirmed by the name Laban, which means simply "white." The implication is that Jacob, a darker-skinned man from Egypt, and the light-skinned Rachel produced offspring that were in some sense speckled. The fact that these offspring became the property of Jacob indicates that he had managed to usurp Laban's position as patriarch of the clan.

Understandably, Laban was not about to simply accept such a turn of events without a fight. And Jacob, sensing the storm clouds building, instructed his wives to make a choice: They could remain with their father Laban, or they could accompany him on his journey back to Palestine. They chose the latter course, perhaps swayed by promises of a life as queen in a pharaoh's court. Knowing they would need all the help they could get, Rachel managed to steal her father's "household gods" as an added measure of protection. The rationale was simple: Jacob was no monotheist. No Egyptian monarch was. Like most men of his day, he believed that events on earth were a mere echo of what transpired in the spiritual world. If an army won on the battlefield, it was because its patron god had prevailed in some heavenly conflict. This idea was so powerful it survived for centuries — indeed millennia. Even today, there are many who believe in a final, apocalyptic war that will be waged not on earth but on the clouds of heaven.

In Jacob's time, it was pervasive. If he managed to steal Laban's gods — probably carved idols that could be carried around in a small pouch — they would be bound to do his bidding in the war ahead of him. Laban himself would be powerless to stop him without them, and their power would provide him with just what he needed to confront Esau.

The narrator takes some pains to absolve Jacob for this theft, blaming his wife Rachel and asserting that she had stolen the idols without his knowledge. Regardless of who was responsible, however, Laban was understandably distressed to find his talismanic gods missing. He therefore pursued Jacob in earnest, finally catching up with him seven days later in the hill country of Gilead.

The prophet Jeremiah would speak centuries later of the "balm of Gilead," a source of healing for the nation of Israel. And still later writers would use Gilead as a basis for the name of the heroic Sir Galahad, knight of the round table *par excellence*. All this might seem rather odd and arbitrary, but it will turn out to be highly significant.

And Gilead was significant to Jacob, as well. It was a crossroads where he and Laban traded vicious accusations before finally reaching an accord of sorts, a treaty validated by the construction of a pillar that would serve to demarcate the border between their respective lands. It was thus that the spot supposedly earned the name Gilead, which meant nothing more than "heap of witness." It would serve not only as a border marker but as a physical testimony to the treaty between Jacob and Laban, a pact sealed with the utterance of various oaths. These oaths themselves are intriguing. They make repeated reference to the plural Elohim as their guarantor, confirming the fact that both men clearly venerated several deities — if they didn't, the theft of Laban's household gods would not have been such an issue.

Laban clarifies things by identifying this particular deity as "the Elohim of Abraham and the Elohim of Nahor, the Elohim of their father. But Jacob responds by offering an oath "in the name of the fear of his father Isaac." [21]

What on earth could this mean? Did Jacob somehow consider Isaac a god? In the context of latter-day Jewish religion, such a statement makes no sense at all. But the text in question was produced — at least in its original form — not by latter-day Jews, but by Egyptian polytheists. And if one considers the oath in light of Egyptian myth, its meaning becomes perfectly clear. The pharaoh Isaac had recently died, assuming the role of the dead king Osiris; Jacob, meanwhile, had become the personification of the living king Horus. He therefore *was* invoking the authority of a deity to validate his treaty with Laban.

Because the dead king *was* a god.

All this blurring of lines between men of flesh and blood and the gods they worshipped can be a bit confusing. Yet the clearly defined lines of monotheism would not be set in place for hundreds of years yet, and in the ancient world it was taken for granted that gods and men shared a great deal in common. The classical gods of high Greek civilization represent the epitome of this phenomenon. They were really more like supermen, with all the appetites, foibles and failings of their mortal counterparts. They were self-absorbed, greedy, envious and extremely prone to anger. Even the Jews depicted their deity Yahweh in this way, declaring him to be "jealous" and ever-poised to throw a temper tantrum if he found his followers cavorting with other gods. The reason was simple: To betray one's god was to betray the king himself and the motherland. This is the ancient origin of the popular rallying cry for "God and country" — the king was divine, and the king and the land were one.

Though the Romans deified their emperors upon their passing, they were hardly the first to do so. Such was a common practice in the ancient world, perhaps stemming directly from the Egyptian tradition of deifying the dead pharaoh as the embodiment of the great Osiris.

In ancient traditions, the gods appeared frequently in the guise of morals, often taking human women as their consorts and producing heroes and demigods from these unions. Examples in Greek mythology are too numerous to mention, but the most famous include Hercules, who was supposedly conceived when the great god Zeus took on the guise of a woman's betrothed and lay with her. A certain similarity between such stories and the account of Jesus' supposed divine conception can hardly be ignored. And the Jewish scriptures themselves contain an account in which "the sons of the Elohim" found themselves seduced by the daughters of men and fathered a super-race called the Nephilim: "the heroes of old, men of renown." [22]

In a world where gods not only took on the likeness of men, but even married and produced half-breed supermen, it is no wonder that the ancient accounts can be confusing. And the sense of confusion only intensifies as the story of Jacob and Esau continues.

Wrestling With God

Jacob must have returned from his sojourn in Laban's territory filled with mixed emotions. In some ways, he had succeeded. He had obviously managed to build an army of sufficient strength to obtain a treaty with Laban, and he had managed to make off with his kinsman's household gods without being discovered. Yet what had it cost him? He had spent a full two decades in Laban's service and had failed to obtain the alliance he had originally sought. He had left with Laban's daughters as his wives, but the man was obviously in no mood to declare Jacob heir to his kingdom. Instead, he had erected a pillar between them and forced the younger man to take a series of oaths that would bring grave consequences down upon his head should he violate them. Jacob was not welcome in Laban's territory, and there was nothing for him to do but return to Palestine, where his brother and rival Esau had established himself as ruler.

Whether Esau ever succeeded in setting himself up as pharaoh in Egypt proper is unknown. His name, unlike Jacob's, does not appear on any ancient amulets or stone markers, so it is possible that he never managed to consolidate his rule beyond its base in southern Palestine — a land known variously as Edom and Seir.

But even if he never earned the title of pharaoh, he was still a force to be reckoned with. That much is apparent from Jacob's reaction to the prospect of meeting his brother on the field of battle: He clearly had no stomach for it.

Fearing that Esau would assemble an army to assail him, he arranged to send a lavish gift of livestock and servants ahead of him in an attempt to placate his brother. He also split his entourage into two camps, reasoning that if Esau attacked one, the other would at least be able to take flight.

Why was Jacob so worried? He had no reason to believe Esau would be expecting his arrival — unless, of course, somebody had tipped him off. And, in fact, the biblical account *does* refer to a potential source of such information. After concluding his treaty with Laban, it states, "Jacob also went on his way, and the angels of the

Elohim met him." [23]

What these angels told him is not recorded. But the manner in which Jacob responded to them reveals a great deal. He immediately "sent messengers ahead of him to his brother Esau in the land of Seir." [24] They bore with them an implicit promise of bountiful gifts from among Jacob's livestock, beasts of burden and servants, an obvious attempt to placate Esau and convince him of Jacob's peaceful intentions. It seems reasonable to conclude that the angels who visited Jacob had somehow warned him that Esau was in the vicinity and was aware of his presence. And such a scenario becomes even more likely when one realizes that the word translated as "angels" is the same word used to identify the "messengers" Jacob sent out to Esau.

The variant translations obscure what really happened. The "angels," it seems, were not supernatural beings at all, but flesh-and-blood messengers sent to inform Jacob of his brother's presence in the region. Most likely, they came from Esau himself, who plays the role of the Egyptian god Seth throughout the narrative. This would explain their identity as messengers from the divine council, of which Seth was a member. Esau must have judged his forces to be so clearly superior to those of Jacob that he had no need for the element of surprise. Under such circumstances, he probably hoped to avoid a costly battle by simply announcing his presence, confronting his rival and demanding that he capitulate.

In response to the news from these messengers, Jacob dispatched his own group of envoys, who confirmed upon returning that Esau was in fact coming to meet him — along with four hundred men. Jacob's reaction shows that Esau had good reason for his confidence: His younger brother was in a panic. Fearful that he was unprepared to meet Esau's forces, Jacob scrambled desperately to put his own men in order. It was at this point that he split his men and possessions into two groups, reasoning that if Esau attacked one group, at least the other would be able to flee. Having done this, he arranged for the gifts he had promised to be sent ahead of him and secured his camp as best he could. There was nothing more to be done now but wait, so Jacob settled down to a night of fitful sleep.

What follows might appear, at first blush, to be a rather awkward break in the narrative. But to anyone who has ever gone to sleep worrying about some impending crisis, it will doubtless seem perfectly natural.

Jacob, it seems, had a nightmare.

Having sent his family away to safety across a nearby waterway, he found himself suddenly confronted by a mysterious stranger who proceeded to engage him in a fierce wrestling match. The two antagonists grappled with one another all through the night, with neither able to overpower the other. This midnight battle, though condensed by the author into a few short paragraphs, nonetheless calls to mind the epic confrontations between Seth and Horus in Egyptian myth. In both legends, the two combatants throw everything they have at one another, gaining perhaps a momentary advantage but unable to deliver the decisive blow that will end the eternal struggle.

In the account of Jacob's dream, he once again plays the part of Horus. During the course of his struggle with the mysterious stranger, his opponent manages to lock him in a treacherous hold and succeeds in jarring his hip loose from its socket. From that point on, the narrator reveals, Jacob would walk with a limp. This is no idle reference. Indeed, it is extremely significant, for one Egyptian tale makes plain that Horus — like Jacob — was lame and walked with a limp.

Despite the injury, however, Jacob refuses to give up his struggle. Incredibly, he manages to keep his opponent in a stranglehold from which he is unable to free himself. Finally, despairing of his chances to prevail, the stranger beseeches Jacob to "let me go, for it is daybreak." [25] It is a curious plea, to say the least — the sort of thing one might expect to hear from a vampire. In the midst of such a fierce struggle, one has to wonder why either of these combatants should have bothered to notice the sunrise. And yet, they do.

Moreover, it seems to provide a sudden, altogether disproportionate sense of urgency on the part of the stranger to end their battle. The question is, why? Certainly, no vampires are involved in this account. We are, however, squarely in the realm of myth, where signs and wonders from on high play the kind of dominant role they rarely assume in modern culture.

And the myth in question, in this particular case, is the myth of Horus and Seth. Horus was the god of the solar orb, the shining eye that stared down from the heavens and traversed the daytime sky on the wings of the celestial falcon. Seth, by contrast, was the nighttime hunter and storm god who shrouded the sun with his menacing thunderheads. Their epic battle was the eternal struggle between night and day — the very same struggle in which Jacob and the stranger were now engaged. If Jacob played the part of Horus in his dream-fight, the stranger took the role of Seth. In this context, it is no surprise that the sunrise should have alarmed Jacob's assailant. During the night, he had held the advantage, but the arrival of morning would turn the tables in favor of the sun-god's avatar.

This he could not allow.

But Jacob was not about to simply oblige the stranger and surrender his advantage at the drop of a hat. He had a price: "I will not let you go unless you bless me!" [26]

This is a recurrence of the same theme already touched upon twice in the course of Jacob's story. In both instances, he had found himself pitted against his brother Esau. First he had forced Esau to surrender his birthright, then had compounded his victory by robbing him of their father's blessing. Throughout the narrative, Esau appears as a sort of alter-ego for the Egyptian god Seth, who in Jacob's dream is represented by a mysterious, unnamed stranger.

With the theme of the blessing surfacing once again, it becomes apparent that the stranger in fact represents Esau himself. Jacob, like so many of us, is using his dream world as a stage upon which to enact his worst possible fears. Terrified that Esau is about to attack him, he drifts into a nightmare in which such an assault actually occurs. But unable to fully face his fears, he fails to recognize them — and the mysterious stranger — for what they are. Desperate, he demands that the stranger identify himself. But the stranger refuses, instead inducing Jacob to reveal *his* name. Having done so, he declares that his name shall henceforth be changed to Israel.

This declaration is crucial, for it reveals the dream as something more than a psychological wrestling match. Indeed, the ancients were much more interested in dreams as arbiters between present and future, conduits for signs and omens of what was to come. Indeed, Jacob would have his name changed to Israel — more precisely, the Egyptian throne name Userael ("power of Ra and El"). The stranger's recognition of this was doubly significant. First, it indicated that Jacob would indeed occupy the throne of the Nile Delta. And moreover, it indicated that Esau — the mysterious stranger in the dream — would recognize his right to that position.

The whole episode appears in the narrative as something of a jumbled blur, just the sort of picture one would expect to emerge from a dream. The mysterious stranger appears initially as a man, but Jacob subsequently accords him the status of a deity, proclaiming that he has seen a god "face to face." [27] Once again, the god in question cannot be Yahweh, who will not arrive on the scene for several centuries. Moreover, his cult will make it quite clear that no one is permitted to view him in such a manner — i.e. "face to face" — and survive. This is a god-man, whose identity can be no other than Seth/Esau. This is confirmed immediately following the dream episode, when the narrator declares that "Jacob looked up, and there was Esau...." [28]

It seemed that Jacob's worst fears were coming to pass.

But his dream had assured him that Esau would recognize him as the rightful heir to their father's fortune. And indeed, this is exactly what happened. When Jacob offered his brother the gifts he had assembled as a peace offering, Esau attempted to rebuff him: "I already have plenty, my brother. Keep what you have for yourself." [29] Here was implicit recognition of Jacob's claims. Yet Jacob was, understandably, still wary. This could well be a ploy on the part of his brother to catch him off his guard. He therefore insisted that Esau accept his offerings and balked at the idea of accompanying his brother on his journeys. After all, he must have reasoned, Esau had vowed to kill him. It would be quite easy for the man to refuse his gifts if he planned to have Jacob murdered along the way and claim everything for himself. He therefore proposed that Esau go on ahead of him.

His brother, however, was not so easily discouraged.

"Then let me leave some of my men with you," he proposed.[30]

This must have confirmed Jacob's suspicions, for he blurted out the obvious question: "Why do that?" He was not about to accept a group of spies or assassins into his company. So he held his ground, leaving Esau little choice but to accept the gifts his brother had given him and go on ahead, trusting that Jacob would follow him to his stronghold in Seir as he had promised. But Esau was dealing with a man whose name was "the deceiver," and it must have come as no surprise that the man reneged on his pledge, avoiding Seir altogether and making instead for a place called Succoth.

This is the last we hear of the conflict between the two claimants to the throne of Egypt, but it does not mean that their rivalry ended there. Far from it. One might have expected these two brothers to continue their feud for some time to come, and in fact there are indications that they did so. The narrator makes a passing reference to a group of people called "Horites" who lived in Esau's domain of Seir. This clan is not further identified, but the name itself is revealing — rooted, it would seem, in the name of the Egyptian god Horus.

Throughout the Jacob saga, it is the protagonist who plays the role of Horus while Esau is the embodiment of Seth. Could it be, therefore, that the Horites were men loyal to Jacob who settled in Esau's lands, at least for a time, either as spies or as rival claimants to the territory stationed there at Jacob's behest? Such a scenario seems quite likely, and even more so when it is revealed that Esau married a woman named Oholibamah the daughter of Anah — a Horite clan chief. [31] This marriage was likely an attempt at an alliance between Esau and Jacob via his followers the Horites, perhaps as part of a treaty of non-aggression. Whether it succeeded in preserving the peace between the two men is debatable, but one thing is certain: Though each man retained sovereignty over at least some portion of Palestine, it was Jacob who eventually succeeded in establishing himself as pharaoh of Egypt.

Jacob of Horus.

Yakob-har.

IV

The Vizier

In Jacob's day, the Hyksos invaders had become the dominant force in the Nile Delta. They had driven the native dynasty back to Thebes and reduced it to the status of a vassal state, forced to pay tribute to its Semitic overlords — these "shepherd kings from foreign lands." Yet successful conquerors do not always prove the best administrators, and so it appears to have been with the Hyksos. Having vanquished their enemies, they might have turned their attention to establishing a measure of domestic stability. Unfortunately, however, they were far too preoccupied with squabbling and infighting to pay more than passing notice to the people they governed.

The feud between Jacob and Esau is a classic example of what the Hyksos period must have been like in the Nile Delta and southern Palestine. Though the most famous, they were actually but two of many clan chiefs to stake a claim to some portion of this territory during the two centuries of Hyksos rule. Their uneasy agreement, granting Jacob sovereignty over certain areas and Esau dominion over other designated regions, was typical of the deals that must have been struck. Jacob's treaty with Laban is another example.

Various Egyptian sources list several dozen rulers during a

Hyksos era that spanned less than two centuries, from about 1720 to 1550 B.C.E. — far too many to have reigned consecutively over such a short period of time. The prevailing theory is that only six of these rulers succeeded in consolidating their rule over the entire delta, with the others being identified as regional chieftains who reigned concurrently over different regions and fought among themselves for supremacy more than they did against any external enemy.

Just as Esau and Jacob did.

Out of this chaotic mixture, one man would emerge as the unifying force the Hyksos so badly needed. Though never elevated to the position of pharaoh, he would become without question the most important man in Egypt, his name echoing in memory after most of the great kings were long forgotten. He would become a vizier or head administrator in the mold of Imhotep, the great high priest, sage and architect who had lived a millennium earlier. It had been Imhotep who had designed the first of the pyramids, the step pyramid of Saqqara. Such was his fame that he eventually became elevated to the status of a deity and became equated with the Greek physician god Asclepios.

Joseph, like Imhotep, would become known for his ambitious and innovative and public works projects, as well as for his wisdom. It was said that he could interpret dreams, leaving no doubt of his stature as one favored by the gods. Imhotep had been high priest of the god Ptah; Joseph married the daughter of a priest in the ancient Egyptian city of On — known to the Greeks as Heliopolis. It is therefore not unlikely that he, too, was a high priest.

Heliopolis was, of course, the City of the Sun and birthplace of the legendary phoenix, symbol of the god-king Horus. Could it be that although there is no record that Joseph was ever formally acknowledged as pharaoh, he was in some sense recognized as the true Horus?

Certainly, at the very least, he was the power behind the throne.

According to the *Genesis* account, he was one of twelve sons of Jacob Israel. This would have made him an heir to one of the six great Hyksos kings, a fact that was not lost on his rivals. It was clear early on that he was his father's favorite and therefore the most likely to succeed him as ruler of the land. Jacob even bestowed upon him a richly ornamented robe — probably a symbol of his status as chosen heir to the throne. The *Genesis* legend never makes mention of a kingdom, per se, but the language it uses makes clear that Joseph's brothers knew the stakes involved: "Do you intend to reign over us? Will you actually rule us?" [32]

Unless they took action, they knew, Joseph was indeed destined to become a ruler. He was even arrogant enough to tell them of a dream in which the sun, the moon and eleven stars bowed down to him. The images plainly referred to Joseph's father, mother and eleven brothers. The fact that his father was depicted as the sun may well indicate Jacob's status as the sun god Horus — pharaoh of Egypt. If so, it indicated that Joseph would become even more powerful than the pharaoh.

And indeed, he would.

But Joseph miscalculated in sharing his dream with the others. Even his father, who had designated him as heir, rebuked him, perhaps wondering whether his son's blatant ambition might spur him to patricide. His brothers, incensed at Joseph's audacity, also felt threatened and believed it was imperative that they act against their brother before he moved against them. They therefore devised a plan to seize him while he was out in the fields and do away with him, bludgeoning him and blaming his unfortunate demise on a wild animal. One of his brothers, however, argued against such a rash act. Bloodshed was serious business, he said, and it would be a simple matter to rid themselves of Joseph without actually killing him. He managed to persuade the others, who laid hold of their brother and, stripping him of the robe his father had given him, deposited him in an empty cistern. This they sold to a band of passing Midianite traders bound for Egypt, who in turn found a buyer for him in the person of a certain Potiphar, the captain of the pharaoh's guard.

Here once again is evidence that there was no single ruler of the

Nile Delta at the time. While Jacob was clearly recognized as pharaoh in some circles, there were other Hyksos leaders who likewise claimed the title. In addition, there was still the native Egyptian dynasty ensconced at Thebes. Perhaps Joseph's brothers even knew that the Midianite traders would deliver him to a rival monarch's household. If so, they might have been counting on this rival to do what they lacked the fortitude to do themselves.

Kill him.

If this was their plan, it failed miserably — but not before Joseph came uncomfortably close to losing his life. The story of how he managed to escape this fate is contained in a section of *Genesis* that owes more than a passing nod to a famous Egyptian legend — a legend that in turn bears notable similarities to the tale of Seth and Osiris.

His Master's Wife

It is a classic tale of sexual tension, deceit, loyalty and betrayal. Joseph proves himself to Potiphar, who rewards the young slave by placing him in charge of his entire household. Such a degree of trust must have been hard-won, especially for a man who hailed from the land of a rival pharaoh. Potiphar would have been on his guard against such an individual, expecting him to betray that trust. Yet Joseph never did. In everything, he proved himself a capable and devoted servant, eventually proving himself to the point that his master "left in Joseph's care everything he had — with Joseph in charge, he did not concern himself with anything save the food he ate." [33]

Everything. Including Potiphar's wife.

And this could only mean trouble. Joseph was a good-looking, athletic young man, and the woman was something of a seductress. It was only a matter of time before enough sparks flew between the two of them (at least in one direction) to ignite this volatile combination. Joseph resisted the woman's advances, declining her brazen invitation to "come to bed with me." [34]

But the woman was nothing if not persistent. Despite his repeated refusal, she continued to press him, until she at last grew weary of the game and decided to take things to the next level. The narrator presents the somewhat comical picture of this lustful shrew grasping at Joseph's cloak and literally ripping it off his back as he flees from her advances. This was the last straw for the would-be adulteress. No doubt throwing one final scornful look at Joseph's back, she gathered up his cloak, hurried to one of her servants and cried rape.

This account has been widely recognized as dependent upon an ancient Egyptian story called *The Tale of Two Brothers*. The basic elements of the story are the same, though the main characters in the Egyptian tale are not master and slave but (as the title indicates) two brothers. The younger of the two, Bata, lives with his elder brother Anubis and the man's wife — a woman whose character bears a striking resemblance to that of Potiphar's shameless spouse. Bata, like Joseph, is responsible for the bulk of the work and basically manages his brother's household. Not only does he have charge of Anubis' cattle and plow his brother's fields, he even cooks and makes the man's clothes for him. The arrangement between them is clear: The elder brother is the master, and his younger sibling serves at his behest.

The story unfolds as follows:

When the time of sowing arrived, the two men went out together to plow the fields. After a time, however, they ran short of seed and Anubis directed his younger sibling to go back into the village and replenish their supply. Returning to their house, however, he was waylaid by Anubis' wife, who was busy doing her hair — a theme that will recur more than once along the vein of myth that winds its way from ancient Egypt to medieval Christianity. Such symbolism was a sure tipoff to whomever might read or hear this particular tale: The woman was a harlot, a seductress; in fact, the narrator later quotes Bata condemning her as a "filthy whore." [35]

What happened next, therefore, would come as no surprise. The woman began to flatter the young man, admiring the amount of grain he was able to bear upon his shoulders. The grain was a symbol of fertility, accentuating the idea that the woman viewed Bata as a desirable mate. "There is strength in you!" she enthused. "Now I see your energies every day." [36]

If this wasn't a come-on, nothing was. But still the text itself loses no time in stating the situation plainly for those who somehow might have missed the point: She wanted to know him as a woman knows a man. Having declared her intentions, she stood and sauntered over him, pulling him close to her and inviting him to share her bed — even offering to weave fine garments for him in return for his affections. (This reference to fine garments may have found its way into the story of Joseph, who left his cloak behind upon fleeing Potiphar's wife.)

But the young man, like Joseph, was appalled at the notion of betraying his master and spurned her advances. And the woman proceeded to follow the exact course adhered to by Potiphar's wife. Consuming a measure of fat and grease to make herself sick, she retired to bed and waited for her husband to return from the fields. Upon his arrival, he naturally asked her how she had come to that state, and she replied that his brother had forced himself upon her.

Anubis, like Potiphar, flew into a rage and vowed to kill the disloyal Bata.

From this point on, *The Tale of Two Brothers* diverges from the path followed by the legend of Joseph. But during this particular section, the two narratives so closely parallel each other that there can be little doubt they are related. Moreover, as the Egyptian tale continues, it becomes increasingly clear that the legend is a variation on the story of Seth and Horus, with the elder brother taking on the former role. Indeed, the name Anubis was also that of Seth's son in Egyptian lore. One of Seth's most prominent totem animals was a sort of wild dog (sometimes identified as a jackal), and the god Anubis was frequently depicted with the head of this same dog.

As the story continues, Anubis arms himself with a sharp lance and rushes to the stable, where he conceals himself behind a door in hopes of catching his brother by surprise. Bata, however, is warned of his presence by a fortuitous and astonishing turn of events: As he returns from the fields near sunset, one of the cows he has been keeping watch over enters the stable, catches sight of Anubis and turns to warn Bata in an all too human voice. "Here's your elder brother waiting before you, carrying his lance to kill you. Run away from him!" [37]

The scene conjures up the biblical image of the prophet Balaam and his stubborn donkey, refusing to proceed along the road for fear that an angel would strike them down. The donkey, like the cow, would admonish her master in a human voice not to proceed because an adversary lay waiting in ambush.

In Bata's case, however, it takes two animals to convince him, for the second cow to enter the stables repeats the warning issued by the first. The young man does not need to be told a third time. Taking the animals' advice, he turns tail and runs, fleeing from his brother's wrath. (It is intriguing to consider the possibility that this story, in which Bata the cowherd beats a hasty retreat rather than face his brother, may be the origin of the term "coward.")

Anubis naturally pursues him, and Bata, fearing for his life, sends up a prayer to Ra-Harakhti. This is significant because Harakhti was another name for Horus, the god with whom Bata is to be identified. As a sun god, Horus was often equated with the more ancient sun deity Ra, their identities becoming blurred and even fused at certain points. Specifically, Ra-Harakhti was the god of the sun as it rested upon the horizon. As Bata returns from the fields it is, after all, near sunset — the time at which darkness is poised to descend. In but a few moments, the lord of darkness, Seth, will ascend his throne. Then, Anubis, Seth's avatar, will have the advantage.

Bata knows, therefore, that there is no time to waste. His prayer is one of desperation, directed at the final fleeing rays of light flaring out across the distant horizon. It is enough.

The god causes a great body of water to spring up between Bata and his pursuer, its depths teeming with vicious crocodiles to turn aside any thoughts Anubis might have of crossing. This is perhaps meant to explain the appearance of the great expanse of water called Lake Moeris in the central district known as the Fayyum — the "land of lakes." The natural reservoir, like the lake in *The Tale of Two Brothers*, was known as a haven for crocodiles. So famous was it in this regard that a city established a short distance away was known to the Greeks as Crocodilopolis.

Lake Moeris formed a natural boundary between Upper and Lower Egypt, dividing the land ruled by Seth from the realm of Horus. Now, it formed a boundary between their respective avatars in *The Tale of Two Brothers*.

Standing on one shore of the lake, Bata calls out to his brother, appealing once again to the sun god: "Wait here until dawn," he commands him. "When the sun disc rises, I shall be judged with you in his presence, and he will turn the wicked over to the just. For I will not be with you ever again. I won't be in a place you can go — I shall go to the Valley of the Cedar." [38]

If this sounds familiar, perhaps it is because these words would be echoed by Jesus nearly two millennia later: "Where I am going, you cannot come." [39] These words were spoken in reference to Jesus' impending death and ascension to the heavens. And indeed, their meaning appears to be the same on the lips of Bata. His words are steeped in what would seem to be Christian symbolism. There is the reference to an ascension (the sun disc rising), talk of a journey to some great beyond and the promise of a final judgment. Did Jesus know these traditions and draw upon them? This seems at the very least a strong possibility.

What is all but certain is the fact that Bata is speaking of his own death, whereupon he will no longer be identified with the living king, Horus — but with the dead king, Osiris. From this point forward, the imagery leads the reader increasingly in this direction. Bata's assertion that he will find refuge in the Valley of the Cedar is a clear reference to the coast of Lebanon, famous for its cedar groves. And it was in Lebanon, specifically in the city of Byblos, where Osiris' casket was said to have washed ashore after its journey down the Nile to the Mediterranean.

When the sun does rise again the next morning, Bata castigates Anubis for believing the lies of his shrewish wife and rushing to judgment against his innocent brother. Furious at this betrayal, Bata takes out a reed knife and turns it on himself, slashing off his penis and flinging it into the newly formed lake that stands between them. A fish immediately swallows the severed flesh. And Anubis, unable to reach his brother because of the great expanse of water that separates them, mourns as he watches Bata smear himself with dust — a reference, perhaps, to his burial — and depart for the Valley of the Cedar.

Here more than anywhere else, the identification of Bata with Osiris is apparent. In the Osiris myth, as in *The Tale of Two Brothers*, the hero's phallus is severed and cast into a body of water, where it is likewise consumed by a fish.

The Cup

So, it would appear that at least the story of Potiphar's wife was borrowed from Egyptian lore. But what of the rest of Joseph's story? Is it all just myth?

As the narrative continues, the scene shifts to the prison where Joseph has been confined after the false accusation against him. It soon turns out that he is not the only prisoner of note, for the pharaoh — angry at some undisclosed transgression — has decided likewise to incarcerate both his chief cupbearer and his baker. Shortly after their imprisonment, each man is visited by a dream and, knowing Joseph's reputation as a soothsayer, asks him for an interpretation.

Joseph has good news for the cupbearer — within three days, the pharaoh will lift up his head and restore him to his former position.

The baker's dream, however, is less propitious. Joseph tells him that he, too, will experience a profound change of circumstance in three days' time — his head will likewise be "lifted up" by the pharaoh. But, in contrast to the cupbearer, that change will not be for the better. Indeed, he will be hanged upon a tree, where he will become food for the birds of the sky.

Once again, the imagery is familiar from Christian tradition.

Would not Jesus proclaim that he must be lifted up? [40] And was not the period of time involved three days, just as in the Joseph story? Would Jesus not also claim the role of both cupbearer and baker, declaring the fruit of the cup to be his blood and the loaf formed from the baker's dough to be his body? And would he not both be slain and exalted? It seems entirely possible that Jesus knew this story intimately and sought to emulate it in dramatic fashion, the entire process culminating with him — like the unfortunate baker — hanging on a "tree."

In the *Genesis* account, Joseph entreats the cupbearer to remember him to the pharaoh when, in due course, his interpretation of the man's dream finds fruition. This, too, echoes Jesus' admonition to his disciples in presenting them with the wine and bread: "Do this in remembrance of me." [41] Jesus' followers would take his directive to heart. Joseph, however, is less fortunate: The cupbearer, in his elation at being set free, neglects to do as Joseph has asked, leaving the unfortunate prisoner to languish a bit longer in confinement.

Indeed, it is not until two years later that Joseph receives another chance at freedom. As before, it comes to him courtesy of his reputation for interpreting dreams. The person visited by this particular dream, however, is just a tad more influential than the cupbearer. Indeed, it is the pharaoh himself. It seems the man has imagined seeing seven fat cows emerging from the waters of the Nile to graze on the reeds by the riverbank. This, however, is not all. These healthy cows were followed by seven others — each of them gaunt and bony, yet somehow capable of devouring the seven fat beasts that had come before them.

This dream he reports to his servants (together with a similar night vision involving heads of grain), hoping that one of them might succeed in deciphering its meaning. His wisest counselors, however, are stumped, and it looks as though he will have to do without an interpretation — until, that is, the cupbearer suddenly remembers Joseph's skill at making sense of his own dream and informs the pharaoh of his prowess. Hearing this, the monarch orders Joseph to be brought before him and listens as the man informs him of the dream's meaning: Egypt will experience seven years of abundance, followed by seven years of drought and famine.

The pharaoh is so impressed by Joseph's powers of discernment that he appoints him to administer the entire kingdom. He dresses him in robes of fine linen — the garments of a high priest — places a golden chain around his neck and even grants him the privilege of riding in a chariot, an innovation brought to Egypt by the Hyksos.

Joseph's return to prominence therefore parallels the restoration of the cupbearer two years earlier.

This is no accident.

For the *Genesis* narrative is not the only source of information available about the life of Joseph. The Greek commentator Herodotus, who has earned a reputation as the first true historian, tells a story so similar that it is evident we are dealing with another version of the *Genesis* account. The hero of his tale has a different name — Psammetichus — but the chain of events Herodotus relates closely parallels those that are said to have befallen Joseph.

The story begins, fittingly enough, with the fragmentation of the once-mighty Egyptian empire into a series of rival petty kingdoms. This situation mirrors that faced during the most chaotic period of Hyksos rule, when any number of competing chieftains were vying for supremacy in the Nile Delta and to the north in Palestine. But Herodotus doesn't mention just "any number" — he is very specific. And the number is highly significant: twelve.

This is, of course, the same figure used to enumerate the sons of

Jacob, each of whom, like the twelve kings mentioned by Herodotus, sought to emerge as pre-eminent in a complicated struggle for power.

According to Herodotus, the twelve kings sought to protect themselves by entering into a series of marriage alliances with one another. They even embarked upon a joint project to construct a wondrous edifice as a lasting memorial to their sovereignty. Though there is no trace of it today, Herodotus lauded the resulting work — a great labyrinth — as more impressive even than the pyramids. "The pyramids, too, are astonishing structures, each one of them the equal to many of the most ambitious works of Greece; but the labyrinth surpasses them." [42]

High praise indeed.

But more revealing, for our purposes, than the plaudits Herododus heaped upon the project was its location: on the shores of Lake Moeris in the heart of the Fayyum district. It was this lake that played such a pivotal role in *The Tale of the Two Brothers* — providing a clear link to Joseph, one of the twelve brothers in the *Genesis* account. But that is not nearly all.

It turns out that a certain industrious pharaoh hit upon the idea of using the lake as an overflow basin for the nearby Nile. In wet years, the river would overflow its banks, causing chaos in the fertile valleys on either shore. This particular pharaoh wanted to preserve these lands from such inundation, and to this end set out to construct a canal approximately ten miles long that would divert the river's excess waters into the Fayyum basin. It was a massive project that required a monumental effort, both in terms of architectural planning and physical labor.

This canal passed right by the labyrinth whose construction Herodotus attributed to the twelve rival princes.

Its name?

Bahr Yussef — the "Waterway of Joseph." [43]

The name indicates that, at least in some tradition, this canal was associated with the Jewish patriarch Joseph — one of the twelve sons of Jacob who appear to corresponded so well to Herodotus' twelve princes.

These twelve princes were understandably wary of one another — all the more so because an oracle had declared that one of them would eventually reign supreme. This one, the oracle proclaimed, would become master of all Egypt. And this is how he would be known: He would be seen pouring forth a libation from a bronze cup during ceremonies in a certain temple.

Upon hearing this, the twelve rivals naturally took immediate steps to thwart the oracle. They could not very well discontinue the sacred temple ceremonies. But they could ensure that the cups used were anything but bronze. Instead, they went to great pains to stock the temple with cups fashioned only of pure gold. Such safeguards, however, were no match for destiny — not to mention a forgetful high priest. For on one occasion, he neglected to supply the proper number of gold cups, bringing in one too few. Unwilling to simply be left out of the sacred ceremony, Psammetichus removed the helmet he was wearing and held it out to receive the wine. This bit of ingenuity allowed him to make the required libation, but it also had much more far-reaching consequences. For as it turned out, the helmet in question was made of...

Bronze!

Unwittingly, Psammetichus had fulfilled the oracle.

His eleven rivals were understandably quite distressed at this turn of events and apparently considered putting him to death then and there. But he managed to convince them that he had acted without any sort of malice, and they agreed to spare his life. Instead, they decided to strip him of the bulk of his power and banish him to the marsh country, prohibiting him from having any contact with the rest of Egypt.

If all this sounds more than a little familiar, it is probably because Joseph's brothers likewise considered killing him but ultimately decided against such a severe penalty and instead chose to sell him into exile.

But Psammetichus, like Joseph, was destined for bigger things.

During his exile, he received word from yet another oracle — this one proclaiming that he would be avenged against the other princes and that his deliverance would come in the form of "bronze men" from the sea. The oracle was indeed fulfilled, and Psammetichus struck an alliance with these sea raiders against his rival princes, defeating them and gaining control of Egypt as a result.

This is, of course, what happened to Joseph as well (though in his case without the benefit of bronze-clad sea raiders). He, like Psammetichus, was a master of oracles.

And like Psammetichus, he would be elevated to become the supreme power in Egypt, over and above eleven rivals.

In Herodotus' account, it is the cup that identifies Psammetichus as the one destined for power. So it is, likewise, in the Joseph legend. In the cupbearer's dream, he finds himself holding the pharaoh's cup in the palm of his hand. Joseph interprets this to mean that the cupbearer will be released from his bondage and elevated to a position of honor in the court of Egypt — the same fate that awaits Joseph himself a few short years later

Joseph, it appears, is in some sense a cupbearer himself.

One destined for power.

This suspicion is confirmed later in the Joseph legend, when the focus shifts to the hero's reunion with his estranged father and brothers. The circumstances of this reunion were hardly pleasant. The famine predicted in the pharaoh's dream had come to pass, spreading beyond Egypt and throughout the Middle East. Pastureland dried up, no longer yielding the plentiful grasses needed to support the flocks of migrating herdsmen such as Jacob and his family. The Nile Delta, bathed in the river's many branches as they fanned out across the marshy lowland, was among the few regions to successfully withstand the onset of the drought. So it was natural that Jacob and his family should be drawn to this fertile land in the north of Egypt. There, unlike in Palestine, grain was still plentiful. It was not a question of whether Jacob would send his sons into Egypt, but when — it was, quite simply, a matter of life and death: "I have heard that there is grain in Egypt," he announced matter-of-factly. "Go down there and buy some for us, that we may live and not die." [44]

Ten of Jacob's sons were chosen to make this journey, with only Benjamin remaining behind with his father. Jacob had a good reason for not sending his youngest son: "He was afraid that harm might come to him." [45] It is natural to assume that Jacob was afraid that Benjamin was simply too young to make such a journey safely. And, indeed, it is possible that this was a factor in Jacob's decision. But with his ten older brothers to protect him, would he not be safe enough? One would think so — unless those brothers could not be *trusted* to protect him. After all, had they not sold Joseph into slavery? And was not Benjamin, like Joseph, a son of Jacob's favorite wife and therefore a strong contender to claim the family inheritance? If the ten brothers had disposed of Joseph at their first opportunity, there was every reason to believe they would do likewise with Benjamin if given the chance.

And Jacob was taking no chances.

He therefore kept Benjamin behind with him while dispatching his other sons to do their business in Egypt.

While all this was going on, Joseph was busy dealing with the famine in his capacity as vizier of Egypt. Having been warned by the pharaoh's dream of the approaching famine, he had spent the past seven years storing up grain throughout Egypt. Taking advantage of the land's abundance, he had built great storehouses in the major cities and used them to stockpile huge amounts of grain, "like the sand of the sea." [46] This would, for one thing, enable the people to withstand the famine that he knew was to come. But it would accomplish something else, as well: It would put Joseph in charge of the country's very lifeblood. Without grain, the people would wind up starving. And if Joseph controlled the grain, he would control the people.

Thousands of men from within Egypt's borders and beyond flocked to the storehouses to buy grain, and the money they used went directly into Joseph's coffers. Eventually, they ran out of money and began to give him their herds and livestock in exchange for precious sustenance. Finally, when they exhausted this resource, they returned and, in desperation, sold off their land to Joseph. The *Genesis* account puts it bluntly: "Joseph reduced the people to servitude." [47] He instituted what amounted to a feudal arrangement, allowing the people to remain on the land and giving them seed to plant. For their part, however, they agreed to provide twenty percent of the land's yield to the pharaoh's storehouses, thus perpetuating Joseph's monopoly over the grain trade. If they refused, he could simply confiscate their lands and give them to others who would abide by his conditions.

Joseph's plan was a brilliant piece of proto-capitalist opportunism. His grain monopoly enabled him to consolidate the power that had been so badly fragmented under the twelve rival princes. It was probably the single biggest factor in the Hyksos' ascendance to a position of undisputed mastery over the Middle East. Not only did Joseph control the grain stockpiles, he also stood at the gateway to one of the region's most important trade routes. No one from the north could gain easy access to Egypt without passing through the Nile Delta, and no one from the south could enter Palestine over land except by following the same route.

This strategic position would have enabled Joseph to charge anyone wishing to pass through his territory a tribute fee — something that a person with Joseph's instincts almost certainly would have done. Not only did people come to the delta from the north, in Palestine, but representatives of the southern Theban dynasty undoubtedly traveled there, too. The lands in Upper Egypt were desert, a far cry from the fertile lowlands of the delta. The Hyksos had claimed nominal control over them since Abraham's regime, based primarily upon their superior military strength. Whether they had actually exerted that control — by invading Theban territory and establishing an active military presence there — is open to debate. Now, however, their control was anything but nominal. Hunger can be an even more powerful motivator than force of arms, and the Thebans were in the midst of the same famine that had spread throughout the rest of the region. Under these dire circumstances, they had no choice but to seek aid from their sworn enemies, the delta Hyksos. They were, literally, at their mercy.

It was into this atmosphere that the ten brothers from Palestine stepped during the height of the famine, seeking to buy grain from the only source available.

From the Hyksos.

From Joseph.

Upon their arrival, they asked to purchase grain and were told that they would have to present their petition to the vizier. As might be expected, Joseph was not about to welcome these particular supplicants with open arms. They had, after all, consigned him to a slaver's caravan in an attempt to rob him of his inheritance. They had succeeded in the short term, but he had persevered — and now here they were asking *him* for assistance. The irony of it would not have been lost on a shrewd man such as Joseph, who responded to their petition with a firm rebuke.

Who were they to ask him for help? More than likely, he reasoned, they were spies intent upon somehow usurping his power and position — just as they had attempted to do in denying him his inheritance. And now he was in a position to tell them so to their face: "You are spies," he declared. "You have come to see where our land is unprotected." [48] There is no reason to think he was playing games with them. He was deadly serious. He had struggled too hard to attain the position to which he had risen, and to hold the fractious Hyksos movement together. He was not about to let these men ruin everything he had worked to achieve.

So he gave them an ultimatum: He would hold one of their number in custody and allow the rest to return to their country with the grain for which they had come. But they would not be allowed to visit Egypt again — and they would never again see their imprisoned brother — unless they met one condition: They would have to bring their youngest brother, Benjamin, back with them. At first glance, it might seem like an odd requirement. Until one recalls that Benjamin was Joseph's full brother and most likely next in line to claim his father's inheritance.

Joseph certainly knew this.

He had his own sons, but they were still no more than young children. It seems reasonable that he should have wanted someone of his own blood to designate as heir to his own position. And if so, Benjamin was the natural choice. But how would Joseph go about announcing his selection? If he and Psammetichus were one and the same — and the parallels between their two stories seem to indicate that they were — he had discovered his destiny in the reflection of a shiny cup. He was the cupbearer. And his chosen heir would be the same.

The cup was that which held the sacred red wine, symbolic of the lifeblood that maintained a single dynasty. In passing it to his heir, he would symbolically place the bloodline in his hands.

When his brothers returned with Benjamin, he therefore hatched a plan to reveal his choice in an appropriate manner. Having welcomed his brothers back from their homeland, he treated them to a lavish feast and arranged for them to take home more of the grain they had come to purchase. In filling their bags with the precious commodity, however, he arranged to add a little something extra to the mix: He instructed his servants to take his own personal cup and place it in the young man's sack. Then, once his brothers had departed and traveled a short distance, his servants were to follow and overtake them. And upon doing so, they would demand to know what had become of their master's cup — it had turned up missing, and there was reason to suspect someone in the visiting party had made off with it.

They followed Joseph's instructions to the letter, catching up with the party and confronting them with the accusation their master had charged them to deliver. The brothers, unaware that the cup had been planted in Benjamin's sack, were understandably perplexed and insulted by the suggestion that they might have stolen anything from

Joseph's palace. So certain were they of their innocence that they calmly declared: "If any of your servants is found to have it, he will die, and the rest will become my lord's slaves." [49]

Confident of their innocence, they lowered their sacks one by one and allowed Joseph's men to look inside. But their confidence gave way to despair when at last they came to Benjamin's sack, wherein the stolen cup — much to their astonishment — was discovered.

In this manner, Joseph not only brought them under his power as accused thieves, he also announced to the world that Benjamin was his chosen heir.

If Benjamin did in fact succeed Joseph as ruler of Egypt, one would have reason to look for his name among those of the Hyksos pharaohs. Was he, perhaps, one of the six great Hyksos kings listed by the Egyptian historian Manetho? The question is a good one. Yet no name resembling Benjamin is to be found on that particular list — or so it would appear at first. Yet a closer look at the matter reveals that Benjamin was the name the boy's father had given him. Before he had done so, however, his mother had bestowed upon him a different name.

Ben-Oni.

This is quite significant, for it turns out that one of the six great Hyksos kings on Manetho's list bears a name that is all too similar.

Bnon.

This is not an Egyptian name at all, and it appears obvious that it is nothing more than a truncated version of Ben-Oni. This identification, remarkably, allows us to identify three of the six great Hyksos kings with significant patriarchal figures from the book of *Genesis*:

- Ma'abra Sheshy = Abraham the wanderer.
- Yakob-har = Jacob
- Bnon = Ben-Oni (Benjamin)

The other three kings on the list present more difficulties, though the identity of the last great Hyksos monarch is perhaps the most astonishing of them all. This pharaoh, however, shall be unmasked in due time. For the moment, it must suffice to say that he was considered the greatest of all the Hyksos monarchs — the one who managed to build Joseph's tightly run bureaucracy into a kingdom so lavish and full of wonder that it would be remembered and celebrated down through the ages.

The Hyksos golden age was about to dawn, complete with a monarch whose radiance would outshine that of any before or after him. This new Horus would ascend to the height of glory, very much like the solar orb that was his symbol. He would be the sun king, the prince of peace, the very image of god on earth. And he would establish a reign that was nothing like any other.

Yet, at almost the very moment his power reached its zenith, it would all come crashing down.

V

The Sun King

History has known any number of flamboyant rulers, men whose egos have driven them to dizzying heights — and often to abysmal depths. Alexander the Great subdued the whole of the known world, only to contract a foul affliction that cut him down while still a young man. The Roman emperor Nero feasted on a steady diet of debauchery and excess until at last his enemies caught up with him, forcing him to commit suicide rather than face the executioner.

Pride, it has been said, goes before a fall.

Perhaps no man exemplifies those fateful words than the man who was credited with uttering them, the famed King Solomon of Judah.[50]

He was, in a sense, the Alexander of his day, creating an empire that was said to have spanned the whole Near East. And he was also the prototype for Nero, amassing a legendary trove of wealth, the extent of which is hard to imagine. According to one account, he took in no fewer than twenty-five *tons* of gold each year from merchants, traders and vassal states. And the same narrative contains the astonishing assertion that "nothing was made of silver, because silver was considered of little worth in Solomon's day." [51]

Solomon was rich in other ways, as well. Even Nero's famed

libido would have been hard-pressed to match that of the wise king, who is said to have assembled a harem that included no fewer than seven hundred wives of royal birth — not to mention three hundred concubines.[52]

But Solomon, unlike Nero, did not yield completely to a life of self-indulgence. He knew that to maintain power, one had to be an able tactician fully disciplined in the art of war. And so he was. In fact, it is safe to say that Solomon's armed forces were without peer during his day. On land, he boasted an army that included fourteen hundred chariots and twelve thousand horses. (Compare this, for example, to the mere four hundred men Esau used to intimidate his brother Jacob.) And he ruled the seas with a grand fleet of ships, which he used to import exotic cargo such as precious metals, ivory, apes and baboons.[53] With such military might at his disposal, he was able to bend lesser rulers to his will, collecting tribute from them in exchange for non-aggression treaties. One such ruler, the king of the city-state of Tyre, reportedly supplied him with vast amounts of cedar from the forests of Lebanon along with laborers and craftsmen for Solomon's use in his great temple.

This wondrous tribute to his patron deity would rank as the great king's premiere achievement. But it was far from his only one. He also built great palaces for himself and his favorite wife, the daughter of an Egyptian pharaoh, and fortified the city with a citadel and embankments. At the height of his power, his biographer enthused, "King Solomon was greater in riches and wisdom than all the other kings of the earth. The whole world sought audience with Solomon to hear the wisdom God had put in his heart. Year after year, everyone who came brought a gift — articles of silver and gold, robes, weapons, spices, horses and mules." [54]

To hear his annals speak of it, Solomon built for himself the single greatest empire the world had ever known.

And yet, there is something missing.

There is no archaeological record of it.

According to his biographer, Solomon built his capital city of

Jerusalem into a shining city on a hill — a bustling metropolis that was home to any number of architectural wonders and served as nothing less than the Mecca of the ancient world. Yet archaeologists paint a very different picture. They insist that during the time of Solomon's supposed reign, at the dawn of the first millennium before Jesus' birth, the city we know as Jerusalem was little more than a sleepy outpost with a population scarcely in the thousands. A few potsherds and a single retaining wall are the only signs that the site was even inhabited during that period.[55] There is no trace of the grand palaces, temples or citadels described by Solomon's chronicler.

The obvious question, then, is what happened to it all. It is reported that Solomon's remarkable temple was destroyed, yet what of all his other works? Surely there would be some sign of them. An entire city could not simply vanish, foundation and all — especially a city as wondrous as Solomon's Jerusalem is supposed to have been. Certainly, archaeologists would find *some* sign of it.

Yet they have not.

And that strongly suggests a stunning possibility: It was never really there in the first place.

Cities do not simply vanish. But on the other hand, it is equally hard to believe that the man who chronicled Solomon's reign could have simply dreamed up, in such exquisite detail, a description of a city that never existed. Though undoubtedly a work of propaganda, it could hardly have been a complete fiction — which leaves only one possibility to consider: that the events described in the chronicle did not take place in Jerusalem at all, but in another time and/or place.

The question is when, and where?

Odd as it may seem, the answers to those question lie a good five hundred years before the time of Solomon's supposed reign, in a city a couple of hundred miles to the southwest.

In Egypt.

There would be no city of regional — let alone international — consequence in Palestine for another two centuries. Indeed, the only major city controlled by a Semitic ruler up until that time was the

Hyksos capital in the Nile Delta. It was, at the time, not only the focal point for the region, but for the entire civilized world. The Egyptians had named it Hut-Waret or Hawara; it would be known to the Greeks as Avaris.

The city's original name may have meant something like "great foundation" or "founded upon the water." Either name would have fit well, for Avaris was indeed a great city, and it stood at the heart of the watery delta region. Interestingly, it shared its name with another site well to the south for which the name was equally fitting. This second Avaris was the site of a pyramid and famous labyrinth on the shores of Lake Moeris in the heart of the Fayyum. Significantly, both the delta and the Fayyum were closely associated with the vizier Joseph, who laid the foundation for Hyksos dominance of the region with his economic program.

But the full fruits of his labor would not be realized until a few generations later.

It was then, at the height of the Hyksos period, that a new king came to the throne — a king unlike any who had come before him. This was the greatest of the Hyksos kings, a man whose vision was matched only by his wealth and ambition.

His name was A'ausere Apophis, and its flamboyance was a perfect match for the ostentatious pharaoh who wore it. The first name meant "great and powerful one of Ra," while the second was an homage to an ancient serpent god Apophis. According to legend, this great serpent dwelt in the heavens and made it his business to halt Ra's daily trek across the sky in his solar bark. Whenever a bank of clouds began to roll across the desert skies, the Egyptians feared Apophis was about to succeed in his purpose and overwhelm the great sun god. And in the event of an eclipse, they despaired that the sky serpent had in fact managed to devour the solar ship and Ra along with it.

Apophis was, clearly enough, a storm god and "lord of darkness" who commanded not only the thunderheads that gathered overhead but also the very essence of midnight. In this regard, he was a form of Seth, and his conflict with Ra mirrored the struggle between Seth and another sun god, Horus. Indeed, the latter struggle was probably nothing more than a variation on the same familiar tale, with only the gods' names changed to reflect a new generation of mythic culture.

Apophis became Seth.

Ra became Horus.

It should therefore come as no surprise that Apophis' namesake pharaoh was a devotee of Seth, also known as Sutekh. According to one ancient account, "King Apophis took Sutekh to himself as lord and served not any god which was in the entire land except Sutekh. And he built a temple of fair and everlasting work by the side of (his own palace), and he arose every day to make the daily sacrifice to Sutekh." [56]

So Apophis, like Solomon, dedicated himself to the worship of a single god and made it his business to construct a temple in his honor. And Apophis, like Solomon, extended his rule across a broad expanse of territory — a swath of land that extended from an outpost south of Thebes north into the heart of Palestine. If Solomon's chronicler describes his master in glowing terms, another scribe is even more emphatic about Apophis, hailing him as "stout-hearted in the day of battle, with a greater name than any other king, who protects strange lands that have never seen him." The scribe concludes by saying, "There is not his peer in any land." [57]

There are other similarities.

If Solomon's wealth was legend, so was Apophis'. Joseph had put everything in place during the famine to ensure a steady stream of income for the delta kingdom as long as an able administrator was at the helm. Apophis definitely fit the bill. One fragmentary account declares that while Apophis was lord of the delta, "the entire land paid tribute to him in full, as well as with all the good things of (Egypt)." [58] This sounds very much like the arrangement instituted by Solomon, who divided his realm into twelve districts and demanded that each provide supplies for the royal household during one month out of the year. Once again, the number twelve surfaces. Could it be that these twelve districts were actually in *Egypt*, perhaps corresponding to the twelve petty kingdoms unified under Psammetichus/Joseph?

And could it be that Solomon and Apophis were one and the same person?

Certainly, they sound quite similar. Solomon's chronicler makes a point of mentioning his vast number of chariots — an innovation that was crucial in establishing the Hyksos' domination of Egypt. The native Egyptian rulers knew nothing of this new weapon, and their reliance upon foot soldiers put them at a severe disadvantage against a mounted cavalry. The Hyksos forces used their cavalry and chariots to overwhelm the Egyptian defenders. And it appears Solomon was quite capable of doing the same. Given his extensive inventory of horse and chariot, Solomon would have made a fine Hyksos indeed.

There were similarities at sea, too. One of Apophis' enemies marveled at the "hundreds of ships of fresh cedar, which were filled with gold, lapis, silver, turquoise, bronze axes without number, not to mention the moringa oil, fat, honey, willow, box-wood, sticks and all their fine woods — all the fine products of Syria." [59] Apophis' fleet of merchant ships bears more than a passing resemblance to that of King Solomon, as do his trading connections. The cedars of the Lebanese-Syrian forests, mentioned in connection with Apophis' merchant ships, were the primary resource Solomon used to build his temple.

Even the account of Solomon's great harem, with is vast numbers of wives and concubines, finds a parallel of sorts in an observer's description of Avaris. In it, he describes lofty walls topped with harems. Passers-by could gaze up at the windows high above and see the faces of women staring out at them.[60] It does not seem farfetched to surmise that at least a few of these "kept women" were members of Apophis' (or Solomon's) entourage.

Solomon's penchant for collecting women like so many trophies or possessions was, in the view of his chronicler, his greatest failing. On the one hand, the king was a pious man, having vowed to worship his patron god to the exclusion of all others. Yet he was also a practical man. No monarch could have endured long in that age (or any other) without being so. And Solomon was nothing if not a shrewd politician. His seven hundred wives were all of royal birth, meaning these marriages were no doubt arranged to further various political alliances. As part of the bargain, Solomon was expected to show a certain degree of respect for their gods as well as his own. He therefore did the politically prudent thing and constructed altars in his kingdom to any number of foreign gods.

A'ausere Apophis, in like manner, was said to have worshipped Seth alone. Yet his very name paid tribute to the ancient sun god Ra. And he bore an elaborate and self-congratulatory title — one that paid homage to Seth, Horus and Ra in the same breath: "Horus, he who pacifies the two lands, the good god, the son of Ra, Apophis, beloved of Seth." [61]

Clearly Apophis was no true monotheist. He was, like Solomon, a realist who put the quest for power well before any concern over piety. By paying tribute to both the storm god and his mythical archrival who personified the solar orb, Apophis could claim sovereignty over northern and southern Egypt. He was truly "he who pacifies the two lands," having subdued the territory of Seth as well as that associated with Horus. Solomon in like manner pacified two lands, bringing northern and southern Palestine under a single rule. It was a union that would collapse upon his death, just as Apophis' unified state would crumble at the end of his reign.

And a long reign it was. Estimates vary from a little more than three decades to as long as sixty-one years, but it most likely spanned a little more than forty years.[62] It is probably no coincidence that the duration of Solomon's reign was said to have been equally impressive: "Solomon reigned over all Israel forty years." [63]

These four decades were a time of unprecedented peace and prosperity. Indeed, the name Solomon comes from a root word that means just that. It is a familiar greeting even today in Jewish culture: Shalom. Peace. "Solomon" was probably not the man's name at all, but yet another of his many majestic titles. He was, in the truest sense of the phrase, the prince of peace. And indeed, his great capital was known by the name Jerusalem — literally, the city of peace. No one dared attack this city with its high battlements and majestic fortifications. It was a fortress whose walls no enemy could breach.

For many years, no enemy tried.

With all external threats to the throne subdued through force of arms, economic blackmail or treaty, the king could turn his attention to his ambitious public works projects and to further stocking his already massive treasury. The story of King Solomon's mines is well known, and the extent of his wealth was legendary. So it was, too, with Apophis. Indeed, his prosperity was such that it is not hard to imagine the name of his capital city passing into the Latin lexicon as a synonym for voracious greed.

Avarice.

But there was more to Solomon than his drive to accumulate wealth and territory. He was among the most contradictory figures portrayed in the Hebrew scriptures. On the one hand, he was perhaps the most arrogant, self-serving ruler depicted therein; on the other, he is depicted as the wisest king who ever lived, a peerless philosopher whose reputation for solving riddles and mediating disputes had spread far and wide. Rulers and nobles from across the region came to visit him at court, bringing with them various questions and conundrums for him to solve. But Solomon didn't confine his wisdom to these encounters; indeed, he is said to have recorded his sayings in any number of books. A collection of such aphorisms attributed to him is contained in a book known simply as "the proverbs," and he also is credited with writing a proto-existential work known as Ecclesiastes. But his fame would lead other writers to use his name as well, thereby lending prestige to their works.

Writings emerged fast and furious, most of them well after Solomon's day. A collection of psalms was written in his name, and another author produced a book of odes he credited to the wise king. Given Solomon's fame as both a thinker and philosopher, it is hardly surprising to find that Apophis had a similar reputation. In one inscription, he is described as "a scribe of Ra, taught by Thoth himself" who is capable of reading "all the difficult (passages) of the writings." [64] Thoth was, it may be recalled, revered as the inventor of writing and the wisest of all the gods. In describing himself as the protégé of this particular deity, Apophis was in effect claiming to be the wisest of all men — just as Solomon was.

Indeed, Solomon was said to have received his wisdom from an esoteric source. According to one tradition, secrets from before the great flood had been inscribed on tablets of clay and stone. Since the deluge, many eyes had gazed upon these marvelous tablets but none had been able to interpret the words inscribed thereon. Until the time of Solomon, that is.

Like Apophis, he was able to read all the difficult passages of the ancient writings, and the tablets were no exception. But what makes this legend even more interesting is the author of the tablets, identified as one of the early patriarchs.

His name? Seth.

This was the son of Adam and Eve, who shared his name with the god to whom A'ausere Apophis owed his first allegiance. According to the legend, these tablets were inscribed "by the finger of Seth." [65] If this expression sounds vaguely familiar, it is probably because the author of *Exodus* describes another event in quite similar terms. This is, of course, the account of the Ten Commandments. "When Yahweh finished speaking to Moses on Mount Sinai, he gave him the two tablets of the testimony, the tablets of stone inscribed by the finger of God." [66]

There is no dismissing the similarities between these two traditions. A couple of possibilities present themselves: Either one is dependent upon the other, or the two share a common source. In each account, a set of sacred tablets is inscribed by the finger of a certain god; only the name of the deity changes. In one case it is Seth, in the other Yahweh — the gods worshipped by Apophis and Solomon, respectively.

And even this discrepancy is not so glaring as it might seem at first, for the two gods played virtually identical roles in the ancient cultures that revered them.

Gods of Thunder

Seth was, of course, a storm god.

And so was Yahweh. Anyone who doubts this has only to read between the lines of the great traditions in Hebrew lore. Among the most revealing accounts is the legend of Noah and the flood, arguably the most familiar tale in the entire canon of scripture. In it, Yahweh appears as the epitome of the storm god. Enraged at the lawlessness of creation, he resolves to destroy all that lies before him, sparing only a single man who has remained true to his vision for humanity. In a fleeting moment of compassion, he warns that man and his family to build a giant ark wherein he will be able to ride out the terrible storm.

Although the word "ark" has come to be equated with a large boat, it originally meant nothing more than a box. The baby Moses was said to have been placed in an ark during his childhood and cast adrift upon the Nile, and one would hardly need a gigantic ship to bear a single newborn infant. The famed tablets inscribed by the finger of God were likewise placed in an ark — not a ship at all, but a box that was entrusted to the care of King Solomon.

As the reader has probably surmised, these connections will turn out to be quite significant.

But for now, suffice to say that the ark in the legend of Noah does serve very nicely as a sea craft. And it is a good thing, too. For having warned Noah of his intentions, the storm god proceeds to carry through with his terrible threat. Raging through the clouds like a madman, he buffets the earth with a relentless downpour and sends shafts of white lightning down upon the roiling waters from the string of his celestial bow. Forty days and forty nights it rains, until at last the siege is lifted and the storm god dispenses with his fury.

Repenting of his vile deed, he pledges never again to flood the earth, setting his multicolored bow among the clouds as a sign that he will keep his promise.

This is hardly the only evidence of Yahweh's identity as a storm god, as testified by the prophet Nahum when he declared that "his way is in the whirlwind and the storm." [67] The psalmist adheres to this same theme, at one point calling upon Yahweh to "pursue them with your tempest and terrify them with your storm." [68] And the prophet Jeremiah more than once declares that Yahweh's wrath will be manifest in a storm and driving wind.[69] Another prophet, Zechariah, in his work, declares that Yahweh is the maker of storm clouds.[70]

In the book of *Job*, Yahweh twice speaks to the title character "out of the storm." [71] And a paean to Yahweh in this same text reads as follows:

He draws up the drops of water
Which distill as rain to the storms
The clouds pour down their moisture
And abundant showers fall on mankind

Who can understand how he spreads out the clouds?
How he thunders from his pavilion?
See how he scatters the lightning about him
Bathing the depths of the sea

He fills his hands with lightning
And commands it to strike its mark
His thunder announces the coming storm
Even the cattle make known his approach [72]

After the Hebrews' flight from Egypt, Yahweh would take up residence on a particular mountain, whence he would deliver the sacred tablets to Moses. It was only natural to think that the storm god might dwell in the highest recesses of some great mountain. Many an ancient traveler must have gazed up from the foot of such a mountain, only to find the summit in a ring of clouds. These clouds were evidence enough of the storm god's presence, keeping watch over the valley below. Now a benevolent deity who sent rain to thirsty crops, now a menacing demon threatening to inundate them with his fury, he was neither predictable nor particularly beloved. But he was feared. Oh, yes, always feared.

"The fear of the lord," Solomon is said to have written, "is the beginning of understanding." [73]

Such a statement makes perfect sense from one who served the storm god. If the men who worshipped such a deity failed to placate him, such a god might respond by withholding precious moisture from a farmer's fields, causing his crops to shrivel up and die. Or he might be moved to anger, lashing out against the offending mortal with a storm so violent that it would not only ruin his croplands but destroy his very habitation. No one who has seen a bank of angry gray clouds rolling in on a strong wind will wonder at the ancients' fear of evoking the wrath of such a god. Dozens of times in the Hebrew scriptures, Yahweh's anger is said to have burned fiercely — often because he has been aroused or provoked. The results could be catastrophic.

Earthquakes.

Pestilence.

Leprosy.

Infestation.

All are said to have been visited upon helpless men and women by an angry or vengeful Yahweh in the midst of a celestial temper tantrum. But if Yahweh was capricious, it was only because the thunderheads that blew across the Near Eastern plains and deserts were equally so.

It is worth noting that Yahweh's intense and bitter rivalry throughout much of the Hebrew scripture with another god, known as Baal. Time and again, Yahweh's followers are warned against any dealings with the cult of Baal. Whenever they ignore these warnings, they are vigorously chastened for "prostituting themselves to the Baals." [74] And whenever their kings come to ruin, the blame is placed squarely upon their allegiance to Baal and other foreign gods.

This was not so much a matter of piety as nationalism. By the time the Hebrew scriptures were put to paper, Yahweh was a national god who represented the entire Jewish people. He was their champion, leading them into battle against their enemies and protecting them from invaders. In this context, it makes perfect sense that the scribes of Yahweh should have inveighed against Baal, whose center of worship was to the north in Syria. To exchange the worship of Yahweh for that of Baal was tantamount to treason, a betrayal of one's own people and culture for a foreign tradition. A foreign god. A foreign nation. This was the situation as it existed at the time the scribes committed their thoughts to paper.

But it was not always so.

In the beginning, Yahweh was not a national deity at all, but one of several members seated on a council of the gods. Such councils were enthroned throughout the land — in Egypt, Palestine, Syria, Arabia and Mesopotamia. The names of the gods were different, but their functions were remarkably similar from one region to the next. In almost every case, three deities emerged as the most powerful on the heavenly council:

- The mother goddess, often equated with the earth.
- The sun god.
- The storm god.

The fact that these three gods assumed places of such prominence should come as no surprise given the character of those who worshipped them. Although they had attained a higher level of civilization than any who had come before them, these were still, first and foremost, tillers of the soil. They were dependent upon three things: the fertility of the earth, the life-giving rays of the sun and the nurturing moisture from heaven. These qualities became personified in gods and goddesses such as the nurturing earth mother Isis, the majestic sun falcon Horus and the terrifying thunder god Seth.

These were their names in Egypt.

In other lands, they were known by other names.

Yahweh was the storm god of southern Palestine; in Syria and northern Palestine, Baal reigned supreme; and Zeus hurled down thunderbolts from Greece's Mt. Olympus. Yet before the advent of nationalism, the names mattered little. A devotee of Baal who found himself in the Nile Delta could offer his sacrifice to Seth with full assurance that he was paying tribute to his native god. Yahweh and Baal were similarly interchangeable. To the nationalist scribe writing hundreds of years later, such a practice was anathema. Yet such a scribe's aversion to the cult of Baal only served to betray his ignorance of its original character. Like those who worshipped Yahweh, the servants of Baal were merely paying homage to the storm god — only under a different name. The pious Yahwist would certainly have been chagrined to find that, in condemning his ancestors for honoring Baal, he was in fact condemning their worship of Yahweh without realizing it.

The writer of *Exodus* describes the sight of "thunder and lightning, with a thick cloud over the mountain" of Yahweh.[75] If such imagery does not conjure up thoughts of a storm god, nothing will. And there are other examples, as well. One of the oldest pieces of literature in the Hebrew scripture, a song of celebration attributed to the prophetess Deborah, also paid tribute to Yahweh as the great storm god: "When you went forth from Seir, when you marched from the land of Edom, the earth shook, the heavens poured, the clouds poured down water. The mountains quaked before Yahweh, the one from Sinai." [76]

Similar language was used to describe Baal, who was known to his adherents as the rider on the clouds and whose full name was Baal Hadad — literally, Lord of Thunder. "Then Baal opened a slit in the clouds," one of his followers declared in a manuscript that has, mercifully, survived. "Baal sounded his holy voice; Baal thundered from his lips ... (and) the earth's high places shook."[77]

Zeus was Yahweh.

Yahweh was Baal.

Baal was Seth ... and so on.

Each had his own special mountain from which he sent driving rains, peals of thunder and bolts of lightning down upon the populace below. Zeus reigned atop Mt. Olympus, while Yahweh was enthroned on a mountain in the Sinai desert and Baal's seat of power was Mt. Zaphon in Syria. Even the psalmist acknowledged that Yahweh and Baal were interchangeable, metaphorically placing Yahweh's own sacred city in "the utmost heights of Zaphon." [78] When the Hyksos invaders came to Egypt, they brought the cult of Baal with them — and quickly exchanged his worship for that of his local counterpart, Seth. This was no contradiction. Nor is it any accident that numerous portrayals of Seth uncovered in the Nile Delta bear a striking resemblance to traditional depictions of Baal.

The two gods were one and the same.

It was only natural that, with the advent of nationalism, each nation should nominate its own particular storm god to serve as its heavenly "champion." With his menacing aspect, booming voice and flashing thunderbolts, the storm god was the obvious choice as to symbolize any nation's armed forces — the driving force behind their military conquests. If the deity depicted in the Hebrew scriptures sometimes appears as little more than a schoolyard bully endowed with frighteningly devastating super powers, this is the reason.

Despite the storm god's prominence in many parts of the ancient Near East, he was never able to dislodge his greatest rival in one particular locale: Egypt.

Here, on the northern threshold of the great Sahara Desert, the storm god was an infrequent guest, now and again sending wicked sandstorms across the arid plains but seldom deigning to provide the life-giving rain so essential farther to the north. Egypt did not rely on the storm god for its nourishing moisture, but upon the seasonal inundation of the Nile. It was then that accumulated snowmelt from far upstream would make its way toward the mouth of the great river, saturating the lowland fields along its banks and preparing the earth for the coming harvest.

In such a region as this, it was the sun god who reigned supreme, first in the guise of the great Ra and later in the form of his successor, Horus. When the Hyksos came to Egypt, they maintained their allegiance to their storm god Baal (or Seth), but they also adopted the native custom of paying homage to the great solar orb. The pharaoh was the sun god manifest — Horus incarnate. And this did not change under the Hyksos, who were careful to abide by the first rule of ancient political correctness in the ancient world:

When in Rome, do as the Romans do.

Or when in Egypt....

Despite his allegiance to Seth, Apophis was quick to embrace Egyptian tradition by casting himself as the embodiment of the sun's glory on earth. The first word to appear on monuments dedicated in his honor was "Horus," leaving no doubt that he considered himself the sun god incarnate. The kings of Israel likely inherited this tradition, though it was effectively suppressed in later years by devotees of Yahweh's national cult.

Effectively, but not thoroughly.

An oracle attributed to the great King David declared that "when one rules over men in righteousness … he is like the light of morning at sunrise on a cloudless morning, like the brightness after rain that brings the grass from the earth." [79] The righteous ruler was Horus in the flesh, bringing prosperity to his kingdom just as the sun's rays breaking across the horizon nourished the fertile ground. The analogy could not have been any clearer. The good monarch shone forth upon his people, who basked in the warmth of his benevolent rule.

And no one shone more brightly than King Solomon. Many long centuries after his death, the famed king's glory remained the standard against which all else was to be measured. Jesus marveled at the natural beauty of the wild lilies by comparing them favorably to the radiance of Solomon: "Not even Solomon in all his splendor was arrayed as one of these." [80] If the lily in question was the *lilium candidum*, a flower native to Jesus' homeland, this comparison would have made perfect sense. Its white petals of spread out majestically from a yellow center, perfectly simulating the majesty of the white-hot desert sun. And perfectly symbolizing the splendor and radiance of the man who was the sun king.

Anyone who doubts that Solomon filled this role need only consider one description of his fabled throne, its magnificence surpassed only by that of the temple itself. This was no simple chair upon a dais. It was, rather, an elevated platform that could be reached only by ascending an ornate staircase. The entire structure was covered in gold and jewels, capturing both the sun's rich color and its radiance. The platform itself was round, simulating the spherical appearance of the sun. And above the monarch's head was a golden candlestick, golden lamps and censers — the combination of which, when lit, would have created a brilliant glow above the monarch's head in the likeness of the sun itself. Seated on each of the six steps leading up to the throne were two lions; perched alongside them were two eagles.[81]

No two animals were more closely associated with solar imagery. The lion, with its golden coat and flaring mane, was universally recognized as a creature of the sun. Lions were said to stand watch at the gates of dawn and, according to legend, served as faithful escorts to the solar ship during its passage across the sky. They even had their own cult center in northern Egypt, which the Greeks would call Leontopolis in their honor. This site, which would later come to be of great significance to the Jewish cult, stood only a few miles from the ancient City of the Sun itself — Heliopolis. There, lions were actually kept in the temple compound itself. And elsewhere, where living beasts were less than practical, images of the regal creatures were carved from stone and placed at either side of entrances to palaces, tombs and temples. One named "Yesterday" and the other

"Tomorrow" kept eternal watch over the passage of day into night into newborn day — the companions of Ra and the avatars of Horus.[82]

Horus' most famous avatar, however, was not the lion but the falcon, whose passage across the sky mimicked that of the sun itself. The hawk and eagle served a similar function, the latter often taken as a model for the mythical phoenix that symbolized Horus' death and resurrection. And it was the eagle that stood perched with the lion on the staircase that led to Solomon's throne.

Yet there is more.

According to legend, perhaps the most important feature of the throne was a single eagle that appeared when Solomon took his place upon the dais. As soon as the king was seated, this majestic bird would ascend to the apex of the throne and place a golden crown upon his head.[83] This symbolism can only have been derived from an ancient Egyptian coronation ritual. Time and again, statues and engravings depict one or another of the pharaohs seated upon his throne, his expression serene and his ceremonial headdress firmly in place. Behind him, its wings outstretched to embrace that headdress, is a falcon symbolizing the god Horus. In these representations, it almost looks as though the falcon is crowning the seated monarch.

Just as the eagle crowns Solomon in the Jewish legend.

Anyone who doubts the Egyptian symbolism associated with Solomon's throne need only look to the site known as Saqqara, where a pharaoh named Zoser is entombed in the first of the great pyramids. The shape of the structure, tapering as it rises, is familiar, yet also quite distinct. For unlike the great pyramids of the Giza plateau, its sides are jagged, rising in stair-step fashion toward its apex. Indeed, the sides of this particular pyramid are carved out to form six distinct steps, leading to a platform on top — just as six steps led to the platform where King Solomon was enthroned. The intriguing possibility therefore presents itself that Solomon's so-called "throne" wasn't a throne at all, but a pyramid prepared in the ruler's honor after his death.

The number of steps plus the platform in each case equals seven, long held to be a mystical number by the ancients. When they looked to the night sky, they saw the stars in their fixed positions. But they also saw seven other lights that did not conform to the pattern of the heavens, wandering instead from place to place against the constant backdrop of the celestial fabric. These rogue vagabonds were the five planets visible to the naked eye — Mars, Venus, Saturn, Jupiter and Mercury — along with the sun and the moon. The ancients believed that each of these guarded a particular sphere through which one must pass on the way to eternity. Anyone who has ever uttered the phrase "seventh heaven" is, probably unwittingly, calling upon symbolism that has its origins in this belief.

Each step of the Zoser pyramid — and each step of Solomon's throne — most likely represented a heavenly sphere the occupant must pass through on his way to the platform that represented the seventh heaven.

But whatever the nature of Solomon's marvelous throne, it was only one of many wonders associated with his long and prosperous reign — a reign that archaeology suggests could not have occurred in Palestine, but which bears an uncanny resemblance to that of the Hyksos king Apophis in the Nile Delta. Built on the foundation of Joseph's innovative programs, it marked the apex of Hyksos civilization. Yet in the end, even Joseph's shrewd planning could not support the lavish excess of Solomon's reign. It was only a matter of time before this excess caught up with the fabled monarch, breeding resentment both within his own kingdom and abroad. Among the men upon whose backs he had built his great public works. Among the traders whose caravans he taxed to pay for his extravagances. And, perhaps most notably, among the native Egyptians he had reduced to second-class citizens — the nobles of once mighty Thebes, whose pride had been trampled by the Hyksos chariots.

Trampled, but not destroyed.

Those who belonged to the royal house of Thebes did not look kindly upon this Hyksos lord flaunting his wealth and power so brazenly in the heartland of Egypt. This was their land, not his. And it was only a matter of time before they set forth on a mission to reclaim it.

VI

Trouble in Paradise

Seqenenre Tao was livid. The Theban monarch had just received a communiqué from the court of the delta pharaoh making what — by an measure — appeared to be an outrageous demand: "Get rid of the hippopotamus pool at the east end of your city. I cannot sleep for them. Night and day, the noise of them rings in my ears!" [84]

The audacity of Apophis!

Thebes was several hundred miles from the delta capital. There was not even the remotest possibility that the sound of a few hippopotami (no matter how loud they might bellow) could have reached the ears of Apophis, much less kept him awake. Such a notion was the height of absurdity. But Apophis was not given to making absurd statements. This was, after all, a ruler renowned as the wisest man in the civilized world. He was a master politician, and he did not speak without a purpose.

In this case, that purpose was thinly veiled behind what appeared — on the surface at least — to be nothing more than a frivolous complaint about some noisy hippos. In fact, the message was packed with symbolism. The hippopotamus pool on the eastern edge of the Theban metropolis was no simple zoological garden. Like most such animal holding places in this deeply religious region, it was a site of profound spiritual significance. Here it was that men carried out the daily ritual of re-enacting the ancient conflict between Seth and Horus. The hippo was one of the totem animals of Seth, who had taken the form of a giant hippopotamus and lain in wait for Horus as he took to the river in his majestic boat. But Seth's plan had gone awry, for Horus and his party had caught sight of Seth and his minions — disguised in the form of hippos and crocodiles — before they could spring their ambush. Seizing the initiative, Horus and his men had thrust their spears into the open maws of the fearsome beasts, killing many and setting the rest to flight.

It was a great victory. And it was this victory that was ritually re-enacted on a regular basis in the Theban hippopotamus pool.

The ritual sent a message that, quite naturally, offended the Hyksos. Seth was, after all, Apophis' patron god. In carrying out these re-enactments of the great legend, the Thebans were directly and not too subtly challenging the power of the Hyksos. The ceremony was, moreover, thought to protect the health and well-being of the pharaoh. To the Thebans, their prince was the true pharaoh, the true embodiment of Horus on earth, who was therefore destined to defeat Seth and his minions — the usurper pharaoh Apophis and his Hyksos armies.

Apophis was, indeed, a wise man. Such a message would not have been lost on him for a second. Seqenenre had made sure he "heard" the bellowing of the hippos loud and clear. It was a direct challenge to Apophis' reign as lord of Egypt, and there was no way he could allow it to go unanswered. For this reason he dispatched his courier to the southern city with clear instructions for the upstart Theban prince: Close down the hippopotamus pool. If this horrific din was the sound of the Theban nobles inciting revolution, it would have to stop. Now.

Apophis' response appears to have caught Seqenenre off guard. Perhaps his advisors had told him that the Hyksos king would be too distracted, too supremely confident to care about a little saber-rattling. This appears to have been what the Theban nobles had counted on. They had believed Avaris was vulnerable and had issued his not-so-subtle challenge with the full expectation that Apophis would simply dismiss it. Had he done so, the Theban suspicions — that the Hyksos king had become complacent — would have surely been confirmed.

But instead, Apophis called their bluff. His prompt response to the Theban provocation, in the form of the letter regarding the hippopotamus pool, caught Seqenenre entirely unprepared. Scrambling, he sought to stall the courier who had delivered the letter, putting him off by pledging that Apophis would "hear about this pool." Such an answer was ambiguous in the extreme. Was it meant as an attempt to buy time, or as a threat further buttressing the initial Theban challenge? In all likelihood, it was both. But whatever the case, the courier was not about to accept it. He had received strict instructions from Apophis to settle for nothing less than full capitulation on the issue, and he was not about to cave in to the Theban prince's doublespeak. He put it to Seqenenre plainly: "This matter about which I have been sent must be dealt with."

Feeling himself being backed into a corner, Seqenenre resorted to that time-honored means of political persuasion: the bribe. He made sure the courier was "supplied with good things — with meats and cakes." But even this proved ineffective, perhaps because the courier knew that his own master had the capacity to offer him far more extravagant rewards. He was no fool. And he would not leave until he had extracted from Seqenenre the promise for which he had come.

Seqenenre must have known at this point that he was out of options. There was nothing to do but tell Apophis what he wanted to hear. The Thebans' first gambit had backfired, but at least now the prince knew where his rival stood. Apophis was not complacent — far from it. But that did not mean he would remain forever vigilant. Perhaps if Seqenenre were to take a new tack. ... Perhaps if he were to distance himself from his nobles' boastful challenge and declare the whole thing a colossal misunderstanding. ... Perhaps if he were to cast himself once more in the role of loyal subject — perhaps then he could succeed in lulling the Hyksos to sleep. This, therefore, was the message had for Apophis via his courier: "All you have told me to do, I shall do — tell him that!"

Once the man had gone, Seqenenre dutifully relayed Apophis' command to his own top officials, "then one and all remained silent for quite a while." [85] All of whom? It would seem that the sentence refers to the Theban officials. It appears that these men — not the sacred hippos — had been the ones making all the noise, counseling Seqenenre rather loudly to rise up against the delta pharaoh. If it was their intention to test Apophis' resolve, he had passed with flying colors. Catching wind of the Theban boasting, the Hyksos king had reacted quickly and decisively, determined to quell any designs on his kingdom before they could evolve into full-fledged revolution.

Now, the Thebans backed down.

They silenced their hippos — and their boasting.

And they waited.

It was only a matter of time, they believed, before Apophis diverted his attention to other matters.

And when he did, they would destroy him.

The Avengers

Unfortunately for the Thebans, things didn't quite work out that way. The account of Seqenenre's battle of wills with Apophis breaks off before revealing the final resolution of this simmering conflict. We can be sure, however, that Seqenenre's capitulation to Apophis' courier was not the end of it. Not by a long shot. The mummy of Seqenenre Tao, the proud prince of Thebes, has been discovered and offers the evidence needed to write at least a tentative conclusion of this story. And a sad conclusion it is — at least from the Theban point of view. For Seqenenre's corpse bears the scars of battle, and these were not the sort of scars a man could have survived. His face is contorted in agony, bearing witness to the final, excruciating moments of his proud life. He was apparently brought down by multiple assailants, attacking him with heavy battle weapons such as an axe, sword, spear or mace. His forehead has given way to a crushing, bone-shattering blow. Another weapon seems to have caught him in the back of the head, reverberating from his left ear down to the top of his spine. And a third strike must have fractured his right eye socket, his nose and his cheekbone.[86]

From the nature of his wounds, it would seem that Seqenenre fell in battle. And while there is no direct evidence implicating Apophis in his death, the Hyksos pharaoh clearly had both the means and the motive to carry it out. As the showdown over the hippopotamus pool aptly demonstrated, tensions were running extremely high between the Thebans and the Hyksos, threatening to escalate into a full-scale conflict. Seqenenre's death would seem to indicate that this is exactly what occurred. It would seem that the man known to us as Solomon had once again demonstrated his famed wisdom by nipping a potential problem in the bud before it could destroy him. Not only was Seqenenre dead, it appears that the Hyksos king made a grisly example of the man. This was what happened to those who dared oppose him. They would not simply die, they would be humiliated. They would be obliterated from the face of the earth, so that even in the afterlife they would bear their hideous scars as reminders of their folly in opposing him.

It was a masterful piece of intimidation.

There was only one problem: It didn't work.

If Seqenenre and the Theban nobles had underestimated Apophis' vigilance, he had underestimated their pride. This was a people whose ancestors had virtually introduced civilization to the planet. They were the sons of the gods — at least that is how they saw themselves. Yet these usurpers, these Hyksos "foreigners," had come along and robbed them of their inheritance. And now, in their brutal slaying of the rightful pharaoh, they had added insult to injury. Instead of discouraging the Thebans from future rebellion, Apophis has only succeeded in hardening their resolve. They would avenge the death of their leader. They would throw off the chains of the Hyksos despot. They would restore their kingdom to its former glory.

This was the objective — indeed, the all-consuming purpose — of Seqenenre's son and successor, a man named Kamose. His father's death had left the kingdom in disarray, humbled once again by the Hyksos. Cowed back into submission by Seqenenre's death, the Thebans had signed a treaty with the Hyksos giving each side access to the other's land and commodities.

This treaty, however, would not last. There was a short interlude of peaceful relations immediately following Seqenenre's demise, as the nation mourned his death and Kamose became accustomed to his new position. But it was not long before the new prince turned his attention from grieving his father to thoughts of breaking the treaty and exacting his revenge.

In the third year of his reign, Kamose called together his advisors and posed the following question:

"I should like to know," he began, "how my strength is served — when one chieftain is in Avaris and another is in Ethiopia. Here I sit between an Asiatic and a Nubian, each of us in possession of his slice of Egypt! ... No man has any rest from the devastation that is wrought in the service of Seth. My desire, therefore, is to deliver Egypt and smite the Asiatics!"

Bold words.

Too bold, it would seem, for his advisors, many of whom seem to have valued peace above vengeance. They had apparently been duly chastened by Apophis' response to their most recent attempts at sedition. And as they surveyed the continued Hyksos strength, they were hardly encouraged.

"See," they warned Kamose, "all are loyal to the Asiatics as far south as Cusae." The reference was to a city on the Nile about midway between the Fayyum and Thebes itself. Hyksos support was solid to this point, leaving only a narrow strip of land scarcely three hundred miles long between Cusae and Elephantine under Theban control. Farther south than this river island outpost lay the kingdom of Cush — ancient Ethiopia, which was allied at the moment with the Hyksos. Kamose felt as though he were being squeezed in a vise between two enemies. His counselors, however, preferred to look on the bright side of things.

"We are tranquil in our part of Egypt," they told him. "Elephantine is strong, and the middle part of the country is with us as far as Cusae. Men till for us the finest of their lands. Our cattle pasture in the papyrus marshes. Corn is sent for our swine. Our cattle are not taken away." [87]

The argument was clear: Apophis had the power to confiscate Theban cattle if provoked. The counselors' argument seemed to indicate that Joseph's program of controlling the grain trade remained in full force. It was his successor, Apophis, who held the keys to the grain silos and could release or withhold their contents at his discretion. If Thebes were to attack Avaris, the delta pharaoh would hardly be inclined to share this crucial commodity with a sworn enemy.

Kamose's advisors had some good points. But it was Kamose who had the last word, and his wounded pride overrode any inclination he might have had to play it safe. As far as he was concerned, Thebes and Avaris were already at war — and they had been ever since the foreign invasion nearly two centuries earlier. Just because some were willing to accept the status quo, that didn't mean it was right. Or just. Egypt was still an occupied territory as far as Kamose was concerned, and he was determined to finish the job his father had started. He would confront the great Apophis and expel the Hyksos once and for all.

He would break the vise that held him fast.

The first indication that he might succeed in doing so came from the south — from Ethiopia. The kingdom of Cush had been a staunch ally of the Hyksos regime. But despite this, Kamose somehow managed to persuade an elite group of Ethiopian scout troops known as the medjay (who would in later years become Egypt's official police force) to join him in his campaign. The medjay were a light infantry force that had earned a reputation for stamina during long journeys across the great desert expanse. Employed primarily as scouts and spies, they were nonetheless also regarded as fierce fighters. They were known to station themselves on the front lines of battle and rush forward, engaging the enemy in fierce hand-to-hand combat.[88]

The medjay's first assignment? They were dispatched to attack a Hyksos official named Teti, the son of Pepi, who had barricade himself in a fortress on the Nile. Nothing more is known about this particular official, but his name provides an intriguing possibility. Pepi is a variation on the name "Apophis" — could it be, therefore, that this particular official was a son of the Hyksos pharaoh himself? Unfortunately, there is no way to confirm this hypothesis. Pepi was, after all, not a unique name, and the person in question could just as easily have been someone else altogether. But the very fact that the father's name was mentioned at all suggests that, at the very least, he was someone of significance. And it is certainly not beyond the realm of possibility that Solomon Apophis, with his hundreds of wives and concubines, might have fathered a son and given him charge of such an outpost.

Whoever this Teti was, he was in the wrong place at the wrong time. Having sent the medjay to bring him word of his enemy's vulnerabilities, Kamose himself spent the night contented in his warcraft on the Nile. But at first light, having received word back from his scouts, he lost no time in launching a full-scale attack against Teti. "When the earth became light, I was on him like a hawk," he would recall. "I overthrew him, I razed his wall, I slew his people and I caused his wife to go down to the river bank. My soldiers were like lions with their prey, with serfs, cattle, milk, fat and honey, dividing up their possessions." [89]

Kamose had struck the first blow, and now he exulted in his victory. But the outpost he had taken was a long way from his ultimate goal, the Hyksos capital of Avaris. And it was a sure bet that Apophis would not let such a strike go unanswered. How he responded, however, is not recorded. Kamose's account of his campaign against the Hyksos breaks off, and the narrative is picked up on a different inscription from a much later date.

What actions did Apophis take to counter Kamose's initial strike? Probably he did just as the Theban counselors had feared and cut off the grain supply to southern Egypt. This would have limited Kamose's ability to feed his soldiers and added a sense of urgency to the campaign. It would be natural to surmise that Apophis also launched an offensive of his own against Theban positions, though there is no evidence of what specific action he took. But whatever he did, it obviously wasn't enough — for the next time we meet Kamose, he is laying siege to Avaris itself.

Kamose had cut a swath of destruction that spanned the length of the Nile river valley — from Thebes to the doorstep of the Hyksos capital. In his path lay cities once loyal to Thebes that had submitted to the foreigners' yoke. And these cities were shown no mercy. "I razed their towns and burned their places, transforming them into red ruins forever on account of the damage they did within Egypt," the Theban prince exulted. "For they had made themselves serve the Asiatics and had forsaken Egypt as their mistress." [90]

Apophis had a fight on his hands. And it was becoming apparent that despite the great lengths he had gone to in fortifying Avaris, his capital was in danger of falling to his most hated rival. Something had to be done. There was no guarantee that the troops could hold the city against a Theban siege — Apophis would need help from another quarter. That quarter, he decided, would be Ethiopia. Although Kamose had managed to recruit the medjay to his cause, the kingdom of Cush remained allied with the delta pharaoh. If the Ethiopians could send reinforcements from the south, they could sandwich the Theban troops between the advancing army and the walls of Avaris. They would then be the ones under siege, ripe for the slaughter.

With this in mind, Apophis dispatched a courier with an urgent message to Ethiopia: "I, A'ausere, the son of Ra, Apophis, greet my son the chieftain of Cush. Why have you arisen as chieftain without letting me know? Have you seen what Egypt has done against me — the chieftain who is in it, Kamose the Mighty, ousting me from my soil? And I have not reached him." [91]

This final admission would seem to indicate that Apophis had, in fact, launched a counteroffensive against the Thebans. But the initiative had failed, for Apophis had been unable to reach Kamose. Amazingly, he found himself outmatched and outmaneuvered by this upstart Theban prince, who was now on the verge of avenging his father's death by expelling the Hyksos from Egypt altogether.

Apophis was frantic.

"Come, face north at once!" he pressed his Ethiopian allies. "Do not be timid!" Kamose had reached Avaris, he told them, vowing: "I will not let him go until you arrive." Then, he promised, "we will divide the towns of Egypt between us." [92] Despite Apophis' assurances that he would keep Kamose occupied in the interim, his words left little doubt as to the urgency of the situation. Here was the man who had ruled most of the civilized world promising to divide Egypt on an equal basis with one of his vassals. Only desperation could have led him to make such an extravagant offer. It was the kind of proposal that was hard to refuse.

But the Ethiopians did not take him up on it. Indeed, they never got the chance.

Apophis' missive never reached Cush — it never even got close. En route, the courier was intercepted at an oasis by men loyal to Kamose, men who dutifully delivered the letter to their master. Kamose was on the verge of completing his mission. One can easily picture him laughing euphorically and shaking his fist at Apophis as he boasted from the foot of Avaris' high battlements: "Your heart is undone, base Asiatic, who once used to say, 'I am lord, and there is not my equal from Khmun to Pi-Hathor all the way to Avaris!" [93]

Yet once again, it was Apophis who would have the last laugh. Though Kamose would return to Thebes in triumph, Avaris did not fall. And within a short time, the prince of Thebes had followed his father to the grave. The prince's death so shortly after the siege of Avaris raises the question of whether he might have been forced to withdraw after being wounded in battle. Whatever the cause of his demise, he was still a young man at his death. He left no sons to succeed him, forcing the succession onto his brother — a man known to Egyptian lore as Ahmose, but whose name passed into the Hebrew scriptures slightly altered.

Both traditions celebrated him as the founder of a new era.

Both knew him as "The Liberator."

And he has come to be recognized as one of the most celebrated and influential men in the history of the world: Moses.

VII

The Lawgiver

There has never been any question that Moses' name is Egyptian. The suffix *-mose* was a common feature of many names, meaning "born of." The question was, born of whom? The prefix generally provided the answer — often one or another of the great gods. The pharaoh Tuthmose was "born of Thoth," and the great pharaoh Ramases was "born of Ra."

But in Moses' case, there is no prefix.

What happened to it? The Hebrew scribes, seeking to establish Moses as a champion of monotheism, would certainly have been embarrassed by a reference a pagan god in his very name. It is not hard to imagine them conveniently dropping such a reference, especially if it were short and easily dispensed with. *Ah-* was just such a prefix, identifying Moses with the Egyptian symbol for the moon and its guardian, the god Thoth.

Moses was literally born of the moon.

Interestingly, he is most closely associated with the Sinai Desert, which took its name from the Mesopotamian moon god, Sin. But his true roots lay not in Mesopotamia but in Egypt.

The connection with Thoth, the wisest of all Egyptian gods, is worthy of note, for Moses was lauded as the wisest of all men. A learned Egyptian Jew named Philo, who lived in the first century, described Moses in glowing terms: "Everyone who knew him marveled at him ... inquiring what kind of mind had taken abode in his body."

They wanted to know, Philo continued, "whether it was a human mind or divine intellect, or some combination of the two." [94]

Another writer went even further.

Artapanus, writing perhaps two centuries before Philo, elevated Moses to virtual godhood. According to his account, Moses:

- Invented boats and "devices for stone construction."
- Supplied the Egyptians with arms for warfare.
- Contrived implements for drawing water more efficiently.
- Excelled in philosophy.
- Virtually founded and organized Egyptian religion.
- Served as the mentor for the legendary Greek hero Orpheus.

Such was his reputation among the people, that the priests declared him divine and equated him with Hermes.[95] This particular god was recognized far and wide as the Greek equivalent of the heavenly scribe Thoth. He was regarded specifically as the messenger of the gods and was said to have inscribed his wisdom on tablets fashioned out of emerald. All this sounds very much like Moses, who was specifically chosen to serve as a divine messenger to his people — and to receive the sacred tablets inscribed by the finger of Yahweh.

Hermes also carried a staff known as a caduceus, which doubled as a magic wand.

The caduceus is familiar to most today as a symbol associated with medicine — another area for which Thoth was renowned. Its shape is quite distinctive, being formed from the bodies of two snakes entwined around a pole. Interestingly enough, Moses was likewise closely associated with a magic staff — one that would transform itself into a living snake when cast upon the ground.

Another item linked to Hermes was the lyre, an instrument he was credited with inventing. This explains Artapanus' assertion that Moses was the teacher of Orpheus, for the latter was renowned as a master of this particular instrument. Indeed, his command of the lyre was such that he was said to have calmed the waves and silenced the deadly Sirens during the legendary voyage of Jason and the Argonauts.

Though Moses himself is never specifically associated with the lyre, he is credited with an uncanny control over the seas — parting them to create a path for his followers and then commanding them to swallow his enemies.

All by simply raising his magic staff.

His caduceus.

Horus Reborn

But if Moses was often equated with Thoth/Hermes, he was also closely associated with Horus.

His birth is a case in point.

The Hebrew scribes, seeking to distance Moses from his Egyptian heritage, created a legend that reinvented him as a Jew. Yet in doing so, they had to explain how their hero had been universally acknowledged, not merely as an Egyptian, but as a royal son of the pharaoh's household. This was a tall order indeed. They could not very well deny the historicity of Moses' connection to the royal house, but neither could they admit that their divine messenger was in fact a full-blooded Egyptian.

To get around this obvious contradiction, they fashioned a story in which Moses was secretly born to Hebrew parents but — through a series of events — came to be raised by the pharaoh's daughter.

According to this tale, the pharaoh had become troubled by the large number of Hebrew children being born and had begun to fear they would pose a threat to him. He therefore contrived to enslave them, using their forced labor to build cities and till the fields. "But the more they were oppressed, the more they multiplied and spread," the Hebrew scribes related. "So the Egyptians came to dread the Israelites and worked them ruthlessly. They made their lives bitter with hard labor in brick and mortar and with all kinds of work in the fields." [96]

The pharaoh therefore resorted to more drastic measures, decreeing that all infant boys born to Hebrew mothers should be slain. This, of course, put the as-yet-unborn Moses in mortal danger. Growing frantic as the time of her delivery drew near, his mother conceived a plan whereby she hoped to preserve him from the pharaoh's wrath. It was a desperate plan, to say the least, but it would offer the babe at least a chance — though a slim one — of survival. Seeing no other alternative, the Hebrew woman resolved to place him in an "ark" and cast him adrift upon the mighty Nile.

In the end, her gambit paid off.

Shortly after the baby Moses was set upon the waters, his basket came to rest in a bed of reeds near the banks of the river. About the same time, a certain woman happened to be making her way to the Nile for a bath. And she, of course, chanced upon the infant floating in the tiny ark that had borne him thence. But this woman was no commoner: She just happened to be a princess — the daughter of the pharaoh himself. Taking pity on the child, she returned home with him and decided to care for him as a sort of surrogate mother. Yet she, not having given birth to a child, was in need of a new mother to provide him sustenance from her breast. In a further twist of fate, she happened upon Moses' natural mother (whose breasts were, of course, full of milk) and called upon her to serve as his wet nurse.

All this is, to be sure, much too convenient. But the scribe has succeeded in his purpose. He has managed to transform Moses the Egyptian into a Hebrew child without anyone being the wiser.

Yet in doing so, he has retained the framework of an older myth — one created by the Egyptians themselves to laud their hero Ahmose. This myth is, once again, a variation on the myth of Horus. The latter tale, one might recall, involves a scene in which Horus' mother, Isis, seeks to conceal her son from the wrathful pharaoh (Seth) amidst the reeds of the Nile, casting him adrift upon a "floating island" that is meant to keep him safe from harm.

Other elements of the Horus story made their way into Jewish lore, as well. One legend, not included in the Hebrew scriptures, tells the story of an incident said to have occurred one evening at the pharaoh's palace. The king's daughter was seated next to him at the dinner table, with the 3-year-old Moses in her lap. As 3-year-olds are inclined to do, the boy became playful and got into a bit of mischief. Reaching over when the king was not looking, he plucked the crown from the sovereign's head and set it squarely on his own. This, of course, was seen as an omen that Moses would one day displace his grandfather as king of Egypt.

The pharaoh, in a quandary about how to react, asked the advice of his counselors. One responded that the child had certainly acted with malice, and the king would be well advised to order his execution on the spot. Otherwise, he warned, the boy would grow up to carry out the "threat" he had just made against the pharaoh.

But before the king could act upon this counsel, an angel disguised as a court official intervened with a suggestion: He would place two objects upon the table, an onyx stone and a coal of fire. If the child were to stretch forth his hand toward the stone, it would confirm that he had acted with malice toward the king. If, however, he were to grasp for the coal, it would prove that he was merely a simple-minded youth and that snatching the crown had been about nothing more than a childish game. Of course, the act *had* been an omen, and Moses was clearly smart enough to steer clear of the coal and favor the onyx stone. Yet where angels are involved, things have a way of working out in their favor. And in this case, the angel silently guided the little boy's hand toward the flaming coal.

Upon seeing this, the pharaoh breathed a sigh of relief — even as little Moses howled in pain.

Seeking relief from the searing heat, he instinctively brought his burned hand up to his lips and sought to cool it in his mouth.[97] This seemingly innocent act further identifies Moses as an avatar of Horus. In one inscription after another, the child Horus is almost universally depicted with one hand lifted to his mouth and pressed against his lips.

Another passage from Jewish legend describes Moses in the following terms:

"He was slender like a palm tree, his countenance shone like the morning sun, and his strength was equal to a lion's." [98]

The imagery is overwhelmingly that of a Horus king. Horus was the god of the sun disk, whose guardians were the mighty lions. And the date palm was also known, significantly, as the *benu* — the same word used for the sacred benu bird or phoenix. It was this great firebird that was the symbol of the risen Horus.

Such imagery made it clear that Moses was no common man: He was one born to be king. And though he is never formally recognized as such in the Hebrew scriptures, it is nonetheless clear that he *did*, in fact, reign over his people. Indeed, the imagery of kingship — specifically, the Egyptian variety of kingship — is everywhere.

Perhaps most telling is the story in which Moses ascends a great mountain to receive the eternal law from Yahweh. In this role, Moses has been likened to the great Mesopotamian king Hammurabi, whose legal code preceded the Mosaic law by a few centuries. A famous inscription discovered upon a diorite stele (a stone tablet) not only conveys Hammurabi's code itself, but also shows him receiving the code from the sun god Shamash.

Yahweh, of course, was not primarily a sun god but a storm god. But it is likely that, as Yahweh's cult drifted inexorably toward monotheism, he absorbed many qualities of the other gods he superseded. Including the sun god. This synthesis is evident in the legend of Moses and the law, wherein Yahweh exhibits certain characteristics of a sun god. Consider, for instance, Moses' appearance when he returns from the sacred mountain: "His face was radiant because he had spoken to Yahweh." [99] In fact, his countenance was so bright that he had to wear a veil in order to avoid blinding his countrymen. All this makes little sense in its present context. A storm god, whose menacing clouds were known for obscuring the light of day, was hardly apt to impart such a radiant glow. But a sun god, on the other hand, was likely to have just such an effect. Indeed, this warning is placed in the mouth of Moses' patron deity: "You cannot see my face, for no one may see me and live." [100] This is precisely the sort of warning one might expect to hear from a sun god, whose heavenly "face" is so brilliant that no one may look upon it for more than a few seconds without risking blindness.

What is happening in this episode?

It is apparent that, having ascended the mountain, Moses has taken on the aspect of the deity himself. His face has become as brilliant as that of the god he worships. He has, in effect, become the manifestation of the god on earth — just as every pharaoh did upon ascending the throne. And, of course, the god in question for the pharaohs of Egypt was none other than the sun god Horus.

In Egyptian myth, the world had emerged as a single hill rising out of a primordial ocean at the site which would become Heliopolis. This hill was associated with the god Atum, the ancient sun god who came to be associated, in latter times, with Ra. According to Egyptian myth, this god had existed before all the others and was the author of all creation — just as Yahweh was in the Hebrew myth. In effect, Atum *was* the hill that rose forth from a primal sea. This concept of a swirling, watery void will sound familiar to anyone with knowledge of the *Genesis* account — an account that speaks of creation in similar terms. As the author of *Genesis* would tell it, "the earth was formless and void, and darkness was upon the surface of the deep." [101] The similarity between these two accounts is plain on this point and is no less so as the tale progresses. According to the Hebrew scribes, creation became manifest at a word from God. Each time he spoke, something new came into being. Light. The sky. The birds of the air, the fish of the sea and the living things that roamed the face of the earth. In like manner, Atum was said to have spoken *his* creation into being. An inscription relates the process according to the priests of Memphis, who proclaimed that Atum had created the gods by "the teeth and lips in his mouth, which pronounced the name of everything." [102]

This is an amazing statement, because it links Atum not only to the Hebrew god in the *Genesis* account but also to another pivotal character in that narrative.

Adam.

The first man.

It was Adam who was given the privilege of naming all the animals, a role reserved for Atum did in the Egyptian myth.[103] Could it be that the god Atum served as the basis for the sound-alike character of Adam in the later myth? It certainly would seem possible, especially when one considers that Atum was the father of the gods, just as Adam was the father of the human race. Atum rose up like a hill out of the primal sea, indicating that he was in some sense synonymous with the earthen soil. And so, too, was Adam, whose very name was said to be a play on the Hebrew word for earth. According to *Genesis*, Yahweh "formed man (*adam*) from the dust of the ground (*adamah*)." [104] All this seems to indicate that Adam was not originally a man at all, but a god who found himself demoted by a group of scribes determined to make him subservient to their own patron deity, Yahweh. Such a move was not without precedent: The priests of Memphis themselves had adapted the old myth of Atum to their purposes, subordinating him to their own god, Ptah. According to their mythic cycle, Atum was merely the agent sent to do Ptah's bidding.

This relationship sounds an awful lot like that of Adam and Yahweh.

But despite all this theological sleight of hand, a prayer uttered by the priests of Heliopolis makes it clear that Atum was originally revered not as a human being, but as the creator himself:

O, Atum!

FORGED IN ANCIENT FIRES

When you came into being,
you rose up as a high hill
You shone as the benben stone
in the temple of the phoenix at Heliopolis [105]

This hill was central to the Egyptian faith.

When a pharaoh died, his subjects performed an elaborate ceremony in his behalf inside his tomb. They would place a heap of sand on the floor, upon which they would set a statue of the king. When this was done, the doppelganger would receive a crown signifying the king's royal stature. It was a ceremony meant to symbolize the king's ascension of the primordial hill — signified by the pile of sand — where he would be recognized by his heavenly father, the great sun god Atum.[106]

The ritual itself typically took place inside one of the pyramids, those oddly shaped structures that served as the monuments to the pharaohs. Yet on second glance, their shape is not so odd after all, for the pyramid is nothing more than a stylized mountain, meant to represent the primordial hill that rose in Heliopolis. It is even crowned with its own benben stone, upon which the phoenix came to rest. The oldest of the pyramids, the so-called step pyramid of Zoser, as previously noted, stands out because its sides are notched at regular intervals to convey the impression of a staircase. This was no doubt intentional, an effort on the part of the builders to provide the departed pharaoh with an easy path to the top of the great hill. The pyramids of Mesopotamia were constructed in similar fashion, which seems natural given Hammurabi's communion with his own sun god, Shamash. The imagery also brings to mind Solomon's magnificent throne, as well as the story of "Jacob's ladder" — the great stairway to heaven.

Is it therefore possible that Moses' ascension of the great sacred mountain is symbolic of the pharaoh Ahmose's death? Was the mountain in question actually a pyramid?

The answers to these questions seem apparent, and become even more obvious as further evidence is uncovered. It is noteworthy, for example, that the mountain where Moses receives the commandments is referred to as Horeb.[107] In Egyptian, this name meant simply "the heart of Horus" — a fitting name indeed for the pharaoh's final resting place. This was the "mountain of God," the primordial hill that had risen from the great watery void at the beginning of time.

It is also interesting to note that the Moses of Hebrew legend dies before he reaches the so-called promised land. This would have been only natural if Moses was, in fact, Ahmose. For it is well known that Ahmose did not die in Palestine, but in Egypt. His tomb has even been discovered and his mummy removed from its resting place in Thebes, raising the intriguing likelihood that we actually have in our possession the actual body of Moses.

The corpse was laid to rest ringed in purple-blue flowers known as delphiniums. It shows Ahmose to have been a man of moderate stature, slender of frame with healthy teeth and a prominent chin. Though he was not an old man at his death — having passed away in his forties after ruling a quarter-century — his limbs were bent somewhat by the effects of arthritis and scoliosis. And, most strikingly, he does not appear to have been circumcised.[108] This is a bit of an anomaly, considering the Egyptians are regarded as the originators of this practice. And it is even more significant considering the Hebrews adopted it as the very symbol of their covenant with God. Surely the initiator of that covenant, Moses himself, would have been circumcised, would he not?

Surprisingly, the answer is no.

The Hebrew account of the *Exodus* includes a rather odd vignette in which Yahweh actually seeks to kill Moses. The incident is all the more peculiar because it occurs immediately after Moses has received a divine commission. As a result, Yahweh appears to be thwarting his own purpose — attempting to slay the very instrument he had chosen to use in accomplishing it. Such an act would seem to make little sense, exposing Yahweh as something of a capricious buffoon.

But this makes the tradition no less authentic. Indeed, its very nature seems to indicate that it was not only reliable but widely known. Why else would the editor of the work have included such an embarrassing incident in his narrative?

Certainly, it does little for Yahweh's credibility. Not only does he seek to frustrate his own intentions, but he attempts to do so by violating his own prohibition against murder. The act is worse than foolish — it is, in fact, both hypocritical and immoral. And to cap it all off, Yahweh ends up being unsuccessful in his endeavor, turned aside from his purpose by a single woman armed with a knife.

This is how the narrative unfolds: Moses and his wife Zipporah had stopped for the night during a journey when Yahweh came upon them. Moses himself was apparently asleep, but his wife was alert to the divine presence and — realizing Yahweh's intent — took quick action to prevent her husband's demise. Snatching up a flint knife, she moved swiftly to cut off her son's foreskin and then touched the bloody mess to Moses' feet. Strangely enough, this was sufficient to dissuade Yahweh from completing his task, and he departed without having accomplished his purpose.[109]

Moses was safe.

On the surface of it, the story appears to leave at least one key question unanswered: Why was Yahweh so angry — angry enough to strike out against his own chosen messenger?

But the answer is contained in the story's climax. Somehow, by circumcising her child and touching the foreskin to Moses' feet, Zipporah was able to quell the divine wrath. It was this action that had saved Moses' life. But why? The most reasonable answer is that Moses himself was not circumcised. According to legend, Abraham had been commanded to follow this ritual, and it had been passed along to the generations that followed. Moses' failure to keep this covenant himself evoked the wrath of Yahweh, which was only assuaged by Zipporah's quick action. The fact that she circumcised her son and touched the foreskin to Moses' feet indicates that the ritual was being performed in her husband's behalf. The youth was, in effect, a proxy for Moses himself. The net result was that Moses got credit for being circumcised — *even though he never was*. Hence, both Ahmose and Moses were uncircumcised, even though each man's culture demanded that he submit to the ritual.

This coincidence is too great to ignore.

Another coincidence can be found in a more well-known passage involving Moses, the tale of the burning bush. According to the *Exodus* account, the angel — or messenger — from his patron deity appeared to Moses in flames of fire from within a bush. And Moses was struck by the fact that, although the bush appeared to be on fire, it was not consumed.[110]

Just who was this messenger? The location of the event in question provides the first clue. The bush, it turns out, was at the base of Mount Horeb — the "heart of Horus." One could therefore surmise that the messenger, in the original version of the myth, was a messenger of Horus. And not merely a messenger, but *the* messenger. As it turns out, Horus had one specific messenger who appeared on his behalf: the benu bird or phoenix. This bird was considered not only Horus' courier, but a manifestation of the god himself — which would explain why the so-called "angel of the lord" mentioned in the Hebrew scriptures is sometimes confused with God himself. The sacred Egyptian Book of the Dead contains a so-called spell for becoming the benu bird, in which this mysterious creature declares in no uncertain terms, "I am Horus, the god who gives light by means of his body." [111]

The burning bush was, therefore, an aspect of the sun itself. Just as the sun's flame could not be extinguished, neither could the flame Moses saw emanating from the bush. This peculiar plant, according to the *Exodus* narrative, was not consumed by the fire that enveloped it. If it had been, the flame — deprived of its fuel source — would have eventually died out. But because the bush was *not* consumed, the flame could continue burning indefinitely.

It was, therefore, a symbol of eternal life and continual renewal. Just as the phoenix was.

The connection with the sun is made plain in a coffin text wherein the soul of the deceased proclaims: "I come from the Isle of Fire, having filled my body with the divine word (literally, *hike*), like that bird which filled the world with that which it had not known." [112]

The bird in question is obviously the phoenix, and the isle of fire is the sun as it rests on the horizon. This isle of fire was considered the eternal abode of the gods, whence they were sent into the world. This sort of vivid imagery would provide the inspiration for a much later writer whose work would likewise extol the virtues of the divine word. Indeed, each line of the famously poetic preamble to his greatest work is steeped in the language of the phoenix myth.

In the beginning was the word
And the word was with God
And the word was God
Through him all things were made
Without him, nothing was made that has been manifest
In him was life
And that life was the light of men
The light shines in the darkness
But the darkness does not comprehend it [113]

The "word" (Greek: *logos*) was, like the phoenix, a source of light who functioned on the one hand as a divine messenger and on the other as the deity himself. He was with God, and he *was* God. Just as the mysterious bird had filled the world with "that which it had not known," so also had the light had radiated forth into the darkness — a darkness that could not comprehend it. There can be little question that the writer was drawing upon the imagery of the phoenix to introduce his own great hero, Jesus — a man who many considered to be a sort of new Moses. Jesus himself even is quoted as saying, "If you believed Moses, you would also believe me." [114] Both men were considered divine messengers, just as the phoenix was. And the phoenix was, in turn, equated by the Egyptians with the divine word or *logos*.[115]

But the *logos* was also embodied in another member of the Egyptian pantheon, one who — like Horus — was closely associated with the legend of Moses. This was none other than Thoth, the messenger god who was also patron of the written word. Given his reputation for wisdom, it is natural that he became known as the very personification of divine speech.[116]

It was, in a way, natural that Thoth and Horus should have become somewhat confused. Thoth was, like the phoenix, both a messenger from the gods and a god himself. He was with god and he *was* god. He was there from the beginning with the highest of the gods, the sun god Ra, and it was his divine tongue that gave utterance to the great god's decrees.

He was also, like Horus, most often depicted in the form of a bird. The phoenix was portrayed at times as a hawk or a falcon, at times as a heron-like creature. And Thoth's most common epiphany was in the form of an ibis — a wading bird with a long neck and beak not unlike those of the heron.

It should therefore come as little surprise that one story associated with Moses should portray him as the master of just such a bird. Indeed, according to this story, the ibis would be instrumental in making him a king.

An Inside Job

The Hebrew scriptures contain no reference to Moses ever being crowned king. But that doesn't mean that no such reference exists in Hebrew literature. Indeed, the Jewish historian Josephus and a popular tradition passed down from the rabbis agree that Moses did, in fact, ascend the throne. One might expect that these accounts would portray him as a king of the Hebrews. What makes both accounts intriguing, however, is the fact that this is *not* the case.

According to these parallel traditions, Moses was chosen as monarch of a different kingdom altogether.

The kingdom of Ethiopia.

It is worth recalling that Ethiopia was a key player — perhaps *the* key player — in the conflict between the Kamose and Apophis. The former had managed to enlist the help of the elite medjay troops in his march toward the Nile Delta, but the latter still considered the Ethiopian kingdom his ally. He had dispatched a courier to Ethiopia in the full expectation that the new king there would send reinforcements for his battle with the Thebans. Unfortunately for him, this courier was intercepted by Kamose's men, and his message never reached its intended recipient. Be that as it may, however, its very existence is proof enough of the pivotal role Ethiopia was playing in the unfolding Egyptian civil war.

According to tradition contained in the Hebrew scriptures, Moses grew up in the court of the pharaoh.

This would have been Apophis.

How Moses came to be in such a position is a matter for conjecture. As the younger brother of the Theban prince, he might well have been sent to the delta as part of the peace treaty between the two sides. Kamose had struck such a deal after the death of his father, and it would have made sense for Apophis to demand that his enemy offer a pledge of good faith to seal the agreement. What better pledge than a member of the royal family? With his younger brother under house arrest in Avaris, Kamose would never have dared to attack the city.

Or would he?

For while Moses remained a "hostage" of sorts at the delta court, he appears to have been treated more like an honored guest. This would have made sense from Apophis' point of view. The delta king would not have wanted to risk goading Kamose into an invasion by mistreating his brother, so it was natural that Moses should have been given a great deal of freedom within delta capital and its environs. According to the Hebrew scripture, he was treated as a full-fledged member of the royal household and was allowed considerable latitude in his comings and goings. But the situation cut both ways.

Although he was certainly under constant scrutiny, the relative freedom he enjoyed might well have enabled him to stay in contact with his brother's regime. If this were the case, he would have been privy to Kamose's plans to invade the city — and he would have been able to develop a coordinated response from inside the walls to coincide with that invasion.

This may have been exactly what happened. Once Moses received word that an invasion was imminent, he would have begun looking for an opportunity to spark an uprising in the delta. And with thousands of maltreated conscripts toiling in the delta quarries (a.k.a. King Solomon's mines) to provide material for the pharaoh's extravagant building projects, conditions were ripe for a just such a revolt. All Moses needed was the proper excuse to turn these slaves into a potent weapon for his cause.

It was not long before just such an excuse presented itself — in the form of an incident Moses witnessed involving one of the pharaoh's agents. This man, an overseer for the pharaoh's work crews, was mercilessly beating one of Moses' countrymen who had been conscripted to work on the king's projects. Indignant at such treatment, Moses lashed out and slew the heartless overseer. The Hebrew scripture makes it appear as though he simply acted in the heat of the moment, but one is left with the nagging suspicion that he had a broader purpose in mind. Moses was not naïve. He must have known that such a brutal attack would be discovered, and that when it was, it would inflame violent passions on both sides of this volatile situation.

And if so, he was probably counting on it.

Indeed, the Egyptian historian Manetho confirms that Moses *did* incite conscripts from the delta pharaoh's labor crews to revolt in Avaris. Though he makes no specific mention of the assault on the overseer, this would have been just the sort of event to ignite a full-scale uprising. According to Manetho, Moses then sent for reinforcements from among his countrymen beyond the walls of Avaris, and they answered his call to descend upon the city.

This response suggests a coordinated effort involving Kamose's invasion.

It was an invasion that was destined to fail.

In fact, Moses' assault on the overseer left him in a particularly vulnerable position. Though his elder brother succeeded in marching all the way to the walls of Avaris, he ultimately failed in his attempt to breach those defenses. After a siege of indeterminate length, Kamose's forces were obliged to withdraw from the delta and return to Thebes, having failed in their objective to take the city from Apophis. In the meantime, Moses had become a marked man. The delta pharaoh, furious at Moses' attempts to incite an uprising against his throne, immediately put out orders to have him captured and killed.

Moses, however, was too quick for him. Somehow managing to evade the pharaoh's agents, he quit the city in short order and headed for one of two destinations. According to the author of *Exodus*, he headed to the land of Midian. Here, he came upon a group of seven women at a well, daughters of a Midianite priest, who were being harassed by a group of shepherds. Moses responded by chasing the shepherds away and subsequently married one of the seven women, Zipporah. According to tradition, Zipporah was a black woman, whose name meant "swallow." This identifies her firmly as the embodiment of Isis, who was known to transform herself into a swallow and has been depicted as black.

When the women's father asked them why they had returned so soon from the well, they responded as follows: "An Egyptian delivered us out of the hands of the shepherds." [117] This not only reaffirms Moses' role as deliverer, it is clear confirmation of Moses' identity as an *Egyptian* (not an Israelite). And not just any Egyptian, but one sent to liberate his people from the shepherds. These are none other than the Hyksos or "shepherd kings," the Semitic invaders who had maintained the native Egyptian dynasty at Thebes in a state of subjugation for several generations. This single sentence serves as stunning confirmation that later Jewish scribes, seeking to transform Moses into an Israelite hero, obscured his true identity by making him the liberator *of* the Semites rather than *from* the Semites. This role-reversal has, for centuries, made it nearly impossible to identify Moses convincingly with any known figure from history.

Until now.

But what, one may ask, was Moses doing in Midian, on the Arabian peninsula? The fact is, he probably wasn't there at all. The name "Midian" likely means nothing more than "the middle place," perhaps referring to a borderland area between two major political entities. And certainly there were other borderlands, including one to the south of Egypt, separating it from Ethiopia. The fact that Zipporah seems to have been a black woman would appear to make such an identification reasonable. And indeed, a separate tradition preserved by both Josephus and the rabbis states that this is exactly where Moses went next, eventually finding his way to the capital city of Ethiopia — a city known as Saba.

The Ethiopian Adventure

The story that follows is filled with romance and intrigue — and with clues as to what may have actually happened after Kamose's failed attempt to take Avaris.

Moses arrived in Ethiopia to find the city in turmoil. Regions to the east that had been subject to the Ethiopian monarch had risen up in rebellion, forcing the country's armed forces to march out and confront the insurgents. In their absence, the king placed one of his advisors in charge of the kingdom — a move that turned out to be a grave mistake. The advisor, identified in tradition as the villainous prophet Balaam, took advantage of the situation to seize power for himself and fortify the city. On two sides, he raised imposing battlements; on a third, he fashioned a network of canals; the fourth he guarded with a collection of poisonous snakes.

When the king returned from a victorious campaign in the east, he found himself unable to enter his own capital. The guards, acting under Balaam's instructions, denied them entry. The king lost more than a hundred men in the fracas that ensued, and subsequent efforts to breach the city's defenses only cost him more men. He then decided to lay siege to the city, no doubt hoping to starve the usurpers out. But the rebels stayed ensconced in their stronghold for a good many years before something happened that finally turned the tide.

That something was Moses.

Having fled the delta pharaoh's wrath, he came upon the Ethiopian camp in the midst of the siege. In short order, the king came to be impressed with this newcomer. He lost no time in appointing him commander-in-chief of his armed forces and charging him with the task of retaking the city. Before this could occur, however, the king fell ill and died, leaving Moses in charge of a military force bereft of its leader and flagging in its purpose.

The situation was grave.

But Moses was not about to abandon the Ethiopians to defeat. Instead, he took charge of the situation and accepted the mantle of kingship when it was offered him. He then set about fulfilling his pledge to the departed king, hatching a fanciful but ingenious plan to retake the city. The capital was well-fortified on three sides, and he therefore decided to attack from the fourth — the side that was guarded by the poisonous snakes. This obstacle was more easily addressed than high walls or deep water, he judged, and he had just the thing with which to combat this particular impediment.

The ibis. The sacred bird of Thoth.

Barking orders to his lieutenants, he instructed them to go into the forests on the fringes of the city and procure as many young birds of this species as possible. Each soldier was to raise one of the fledglings: "You shall rear them until they grow up, and you shall teach them to fly as the hawk flies." [118] When this was accomplished, he ordered his men to starve their birds for three days in preparation for an assault on the city. The men would then march forth toward the city and release their ravenous birds, which would fly forth and devour the poisonous serpents that guarded the city — thus clearing a path for the army to descend upon the usurpers.

The symbolism of this tale is not to be missed. The ibis is depicted as no mere bird, but a regal predator that is taught to fly like a solar hawk. If one is reminded of the royal phoenix, this impression is strengthened by Moses' instruction to starve the birds *for three days* before sending them skyward toward their prey. The phoenix, in like manner, was said to rise again from the ashes after three days in a legend that would also serve as the prototype for Jesus' resurrection. It is interesting in this context to recall that Jesus supposedly descended into hell and did battle with his serpentine adversary Satan after his death. This tradition closely corresponds to that of Moses, who went down to Ethiopia and sent forth the phoenix-like ibises to do battle with serpents appointed by a man named Balaam. The man's name is clearly derived from that of the god Baal, the same god seen by Egpytians as the counterpart of Seth.

The prototype of Satan.

Moses plan, of course, worked like a charm. The city was retaken. Moses was enthroned as monarch and took the old king's widow (or daughter, depending on the version of the story) as his wife.

This old king's name just happened to be Kikanos — a name suspiciously similar to that of Kamose. And the similarities don't stop there. In fact, many of the circumstances surrounding the two men's lives and deaths read like pages from the same book. The Theban monarch, like Kikanos, had laid siege to a city he wished to reclaim as his own. In each case, the city was heavily fortified. And in each case, the king in question died before accomplishing his purpose. Kamose was then succeeded to the throne by his younger brother Ahmose — none other than Moses himself. And Moses, in like fashion, succeeded Kikanos to the throne. Even Balaam the serpent master serves as a fitting stand-in for Apophis, who was named for a serpent himself. Both were seen as usurpers of the throne; moreover, Balaam's name associates him closely with Baal, the counterpart of Seth.

The patron god of Apophis.

It appears as though some ancient storyteller decided to uproot the siege of Avaris from its proper context and transplant it squarely in the soil of Ethiopia. The question is, why? One possibility is that the chronicler simply conflated two legends into a single story. During his reign, Ahmose would in fact journey to the Ethiopian frontier to put down an insurrection.[119] It is conceivable that the memory of this event intruded into the chronicler's account of the siege of Avaris. Moreover, Ethiopia *was* a crucial player in the conflict between the Thebans and the Hyksos, so it would have been easy to make such a mistake.

This conflict involved three key players.

The first was Solomon Apophis. The second was Moses, or Ahmose.

But the third was a woman, a beguiling enchantress who at one point shared the beds of both great monarchs. She was lauded for both her wisdom and her captivating beauty, and she is known to history as one of the shrewdest women ever to occupy any nation's throne. It was she who held the balance of power between Thebes and Avaris, and it was she who would decide the fate of both great cities. She occupied the throne in the city of Saba, the Ethiopian capital.

Otherwise known as Sheba.

She was its queen.

VIII

Queen of the South

She is one of the most celebrated women in history, yet little is known about her. The Hebrew scriptures have remarkably little to say about her — at least directly. The short passage that appears there tells the story of her visit to King Solomon's court, which she visited "to test him with hard questions." She came at the head of a great caravan loaded with gold and precious stones and spices, and talked with King Solomon about "all that she had on her mind." [120]

Just what did she have on her mind?

From all indications, the queen was on a diplomatic mission. Ethiopia had been allied to the Hyksos regime for some time, and the queen wanted to gauge whether such an alliance was still in her nation's best interests. Perhaps she had been approached by emissaries from the Theban court seeking to undermine the coalition and strike a deal of their own. And the queen, a shrewd negotiator, wanted to see if relations with Avaris still made good strategic sense. Hence, the need for "hard questions" directed toward the Hyksos king.

One can imagine an intense diplomatic negotiating session, during which the queen demanded that Solomon Apophis offer her guarantees of free trade and military protection in exchange for her continued support for his regime. In exchange, she was prepared to continue offering him the tariffs and tribute he demanded — an offer she backed up by the stunning display of riches she had brought with her.

By the time this north African summit meeting was concluded, the queen seems to have been duly impressed by Solomon's own wealth and wisdom. The Hebrew scriptures, written from Solomon's point of view, go so far as to report that she was overwhelmed by the grandeur of his court. Her words were filled with praise — but was that praise genuine, or was it a diplomatic ploy to put the king at ease? Before answering that question, one must remember that the queen was considered perhaps the canniest monarch of her day. This woman knew how to play the game, and it was entirely possible that she was trying to play Solomon for a fool.

A fool, however, is one thing Solomon wasn't.

He knew how to play the game as well or better than the queen of Ethiopia. And he wasn't about to let his guard down simply because she had arrived at the head of a great caravan, her lips dripping with praise. He would have needed assurance to back up her words, something more concrete than simple flattery. The Hebrew scriptures do not report the demand he made of her, though they acknowledge it indirectly in a work attributed to Solomon titled simply the "Song of Songs." The scroll is a poetic exchange between a bride and her husband, offering words of adoration in evocative — at times erotic — language. Solomon was widely acknowledged to be the bridegroom depicted therein, leaving the obvious question:

Who was the bride?

The opening verses of the poem place an essential clue on her lips:

> *Dark I am, yet lovely…*
> *Dark as the tent curtains of Solomon*
> *Do not stare at me because I am dark*
> *Because I am darkened by the sun* [121]

The tent curtains of Solomon were woven from black goats' hair, leaving little doubt that the woman in question was a dark-skinned African. And of all the African nations that had contact with the ancient Near East, by far the most accessible and cosmopolitan was Ethiopia. This raises the distinct possibility that the object of Solomon's affection in this poetic love play was, in fact, a woman from Ethiopia — most likely a woman of his station.

A queen.

If, indeed, Solomon did wed the Queen of Sheba, it would have made perfect sense from a political standpoint. A marriage agreement would have solidified the alliance between Avaris and Saba, providing the sort of guarantee that riches and kind words could not. If the marriage produced a son, the allegiance of Ethiopia to the Hyksos would only be strengthened by the presence of a common heir.

There are other indications that such a marriage did, in fact, take place. One lies in the scriptural account of Solomon's marriage to an Egyptian princess. This would seem, at first glance, to contradict the queen's identity as an Ethiopian woman. Yet Josephus provides the necessary link, referring to her clearly as "the queen of Egypt and Ethiopia." [122] Jesus, likewise, would refer to her by the more generic title Queen of the South — indicating that she perhaps ruled an area that included both regions.[123]

The title Queen of Sheba has led many to believe that she hailed from the southern Arabian peninsula, in a region populated by a sect known as the Sabeans. These people of Sabea were taken to be somehow connected with the dynasty that spawned the Queen of Sheba — or Sabea. And, indeed, such a connection may well have existed. For one thing, the legend of Moses and Kikanos makes mention of "nations to the east" that were subject to the Ethiopians.[124] Certainly the Arabian peninsula would have qualified as such, being directly east of Ethiopia and southern Egypt. Moreover, the Sabeans themselves trace both their ethnic origins and their religious beliefs not to Arabia but to, of all places, Egypt.[125] This would seem to place the Queen of Sheba squarely where Josephus said she was — in southern Egypt and Ethiopia, specifically in the capital city of Saba. Apparently, she not only held sway over Ethiopia, but also had dynastic ties to the Theban royal house. If so, this would have made Solomon's choice of her as a wife even more significant, from a political standpoint. Not only would it have strengthened his ties to Ethiopia, it also would have solidified his connection to Thebes.

This was one special woman.

So it is hardly surprising that, of the seven hundred women Solomon is said to have married, one was singled out for special attention in the Hebrew scripture. She was the only one for whom Solomon built an entire palace. And, not surprisingly, she was closely linked to the native Egyptian royal house, having been identified as no less than a pharaoh's daughter — perhaps born from a union with an Ethiopian princess.[126] Her name is not included in the Hebrew writings, but it is perhaps known to us through inscriptions that link a certain woman with Apophis.

The name recorded in these inscriptions is Princess Tany — a name with special significance. The Hebrew account reveals that Solomon built a palace in honor of his Egyptian bride, but the name Tany could very well indicate that he built an entire city. Not far from the delta capital of Avaris, the Hyksos constructed their second most important city.

Its name?

Tanis.

From Tana to Tanis

Tany's name is quite revealing.

Even today, it appears just possible that a lake in Ethiopia itself might have some connection to this famed Queen of the South.

Lake Tana, it is called.

It is, in reality, much more than a lake, covering a vast expanse of the Ethiopian central highlands six thousand feet above sea level. The huge natural reservoir covers some fourteen-hundred square miles. It collects water from several tributaries before releasing it into the Blue Nile, one of the great river's two main sources and the one that accounts for the great majority of its volume.

It is, in many ways, the mother of the Nile.

In the same way, the Queen of Sheba is considered, even today, the mother of the Ethiopian nation. According to legend, she conceived a son by Solomon who became the first king in a line of monarchs that extended forward to our own time. Yet that is only one of the many traditions that circulate about the famed queen in the land of Ethiopia. In one such legend, the unfortunate queen finds herself captured and tied in a tree, where she is left to serve as an offering to a dragon. Her tears, falling from the heights of the tree, chance to fall upon a group of seven holy men resting underneath. Taking pity on the queen, they not only rescue her from the tree but slay the dragon for good measure. In the process, however, some of the serpent's blood splatters on her foot, transforming it to the hoof of an ass. She therefore sets off for the court of Solomon to be healed of her deformity.[127]

The story is riddled with connections between the queen and Apophis, whose very name was that of a cosmic dragon or serpent. When the creature's blood disfigures her foot, it recalls Apophis' worship of the storm god Seth — whose totem animals included the donkey. Would it not seem only natural that a devotee of this god should be called upon to heal such an ailment?

The queen's journey to Solomon's court would have brought her to Avaris, near the site of its sister city, Tanis. It is here, far to the north of Ethiopia, that more connections are to be found. The name of this city was quite appropriate, given the structure of Hyksos religion. When the Hyksos had migrated to the delta, they had brought their ancestral traditions with them. And among those traditions was the myth of Baal and Anat, divine consorts who stood at the head of the pantheon in ancient Syria and Palestine. Though the Hyksos had exchanged their worship of Baal for that of Seth, they had really done little more than exchange one name for another. Still they worshiped the storm god. And still they depicted him in familiar terms, often representing Seth in the likeness of Baal.

The cult of Anat, likewise, became important in northern Africa with the spread of Syrian religion. The Hyksos were hardly the only conduit for this expansion, nor even the most effective. Indeed, a new, seafaring empire would arise several centuries after the fall of the Hyksos to disseminate the ancient cult even farther afield. These seafarers were, interestingly enough, known as the Phoenicians — a name that perhaps designated them as the people of the phoenix. Though they were not Egyptians themselves, it would seem that they had some connection to the nation and its religious traditions, particularly those of the Hyksos. One of their great kings, Hiram of Tyre, is even associated with Solomon in the Hebrew scriptures — even though he lived several centuries after the reign and death of Solomon Apophis. This would suggest at least some sort of connection between the two men.

Could it be that Hiram considered himself the new Solomon, a phoenix reborn to follow in the great king's footsteps by re-establishing his empire? Hiram lived slightly more than five centuries after Apophis, a span of time that becomes significant in light of the testimony provided by Herodotus. The Greek historian, who claimed to have spoken with a good number of priests and commoners during his visit to Egypt, subsequently included an account of the nation's history and traditions in his seminal work, *The Histories*. "Another sacred bird," he wrote, "is the phoenix. I have not seen the phoenix myself, except in paintings, for it is very rare and visits the country — so they say in Heliopolis — only at intervals of five hundred years." [128]

A period that roughly approximates the span of time separating Apophis and Hiram.

If it was Hiram's intention to resurrect the glories of the Hyksos empire, he failed in his mission. But though the Phoenicians never succeeded in conquering Egypt, they did establish a vast trading network that spanned much of the known world. Their ships ventured out into the Mediterranean and beyond, establishing port colonies at various locations along the coast. Among those colonies was the city of Carthage in north Africa, which would grow to become the first great rival of the expanding Roman Republic.

When they arrived at Carthage, the Phoenicians brought with them their own religious traditions, foremost among them the cult of Baal and Anat. Baal would remain the patron god of Carthaginian religion, but much of the focus would actually shift to his consort — the formidable goddess of love and war. Elsewhere, she was known as Diana, the huntress. But in Carthage, she was known by still another name: Tanit. It strikes a familiar chord immediately, being clearly related to that of Apophis' queen, Tany. It would appear that this Tany was a devotee (or perhaps even a priestess) of the goddess, which would have been quite appropriate under the circumstances. Apophis, after all, belonged to the cult of Seth — a.k.a. Tanit's consort Baal.

King and queen, therefore, mirrored god and goddess perfectly.

But all was not perfect in paradise.

The Betrayal

The stage was now set for a momentous series of intrigues, one that would shake the foundations of Egypt and reverberate across the centuries in various tales and legends. The Hyksos would be cast down from their lofty heights as masters of the delta and cast out of Egypt altogether. The Theban kings would be restored to their place as lords of the Nile. The nation would be left in tatters, but two new nations would arise from the ashes — a new and even more glorious Egypt in the south, and a people who would come to be known as Israel to the north.

All through the machinations of a single woman.

Her motives for doing so are not known, but one thing is clear — the Ethiopian queen abrogated her treaty with Apophis and threw her support behind the Theban house seeking to destroy him. If, in fact, she was a member of this house, her reasoning can be guessed at. In all probability, she had been forced into her union with Solomon Apophis to begin with and had resented it. She was, in all likelihood, a member of the Theban royal house, and as such would have maintained clear loyalties in that direction.

All she needed was an excuse.

If, as it seems, the legend of Kikanos' siege on the capital of Ethiopia is a veiled account of Kamose's siege of Avaris, this would have offered her the perfect opportunity to flee. And the queen was not one to let an opportunity slip between her fingers. The legend of Kikanos relates what happened next. When victory was finally secure, the Ethiopian queen ended up marrying the author of that triumph — the army general who had succeeded Kikanos to the throne.

Moses.

The Theban prince Ahmose.

The Hebrew scriptures confirm the fact that Moses married an Ethiopian woman, stating unequivocally: "He had married a Cushite." [129] This, of course, would have been Zipporah. None of this should come as any surprise. Nor should it be shocking that the Theban prince married a member of his own royal household. Incest was not only accepted but ritually encouraged for Egyptian rulers, so the practice was to be expected. And history in fact confirms that at least one of Ahmose's wives was his own sister.

But the legend of Kikanos is not the only tale relevant here. There is also an account in the Hebrew scriptures that, at first glance, would seem to have little bearing on the events in question. Set during the reign of the person said to have been Solomon's father, the equally famed King David, it is a favorite topic of moral instructors who cite it as evidence that even the most virtuous men can stumble. The account in question is the story of David and Bath-Sheba. It concerns David's infatuation with a certain fair maiden, who he happens to see bathing on a rooftop one day. He inquires about her, but to his chagrin finds that she is married to a certain soldier in his army, a man named Uriah the Hittite.

Undeterred in his lust, David beds the woman and determines to be rid of his rival. Summoning him for an audience, he instructs the man to return home, sending a "gift" after him. But Uriah is not about to take the bait. It is apparent that he suspects that the gift in question is not a gift at all — but an assassin lying in wait for him. He therefore ignores the king's instructions and passes the night in public view on the steps of the palace itself, in effect keeping himself out of harm's way.

Upon finding Uriah still alive the next day, David is beside himself. But he refuses to discard his plan altogether, reasoning that he might be able to grease the wheels with a little alcohol. The scenario then repeats itself, with David getting Uriah drunk and commanding him to return home. But Uriah is apparently not *too* drunk, for he once again has enough wits about him to avoid returning home.

This is too much for David. Having failed twice in his objective, he determines to plot a new course, ordering Uriah to the front lines where he is certain to be slain in the fighting. To ensure the success of his plot, he instructs the commander to pull back his forces at a signal, leaving Uriah alone and vulnerable to the enemy assault. In the end, this plan finally enables David to achieve his goal: Uriah is slain, leaving him free to wed the man's widow.

Bath-Sheba.

The story is intriguing on the face of it. For one thing, it implies that the object of David's lust earned her name simply because she was bathing when the king first spied her. The activity in which she engages is, in fact, quite significant. It seems to identify her as a mermaid of sorts, recalling the enigmatic Lady of the Lake who emerges from the waters in Arthurian myth. And her position on the roof could well signify her status as a celestial figure or queen of heaven, another significant archetype that will play a prominent role in our investigation. Yet leaving this aside for the moment, the name was probably also meant as a shrewd play on words. For *bath* in

Hebrew means nothing other than "daughter," and a slight variation in the prefix produces *beth*, which means "house." (Because the written language did not make use of vowels, either word might have been indicated.) Hence, the name might have meant either "daughter of Sheba" or "house of Sheba."

The inescapable conclusion: The woman in question was somehow connected with Sheba, or Saba.

The capital of Ethiopia.

The nature of the title seems to imply she was a person of some importance — a member of the nobility or the royal family. A queen, perhaps. All of which raises the question: Is it just possible that we have here another, albeit veiled, reference to the Queen of Sheba herself? It is fascinating to note that the Ethiopians to this day identify a certain reservoir in their ancient city of Axum as the Queen of Sheba's pleasure bath.[130] It seems tantalizingly possible that the Ethiopians were well aware of Bath-Sheba's true identity and applied the myth to this local landmark.

But Bath-Sheba is not the only person in the Hebrew narrative whose identity raises questions. Uriah the Hittite is similarly intriguing. At its height, the Hittite Empire encompassed much of modern Turkey and a portion of northern Syria. It enjoyed a spirited military rivalry with Egypt, and the two sides engaged in several inconclusive conflicts. By the time David is supposed to have ruled, however, the empire itself had been a memory for some two centuries. Although some of the city-states that emerged following the breakup of the great empire may have laid claim to its legacy, it seems more than odd that someone identified as a Hittite should show up — seemingly out of nowhere — as a member of the Israelite army. In fact, other than a dozen or so references to Uriah, only one other mention is made of the Hittites in the entire scriptural record of Israel's kings.

All this seems just a bit too peculiar.

Adding to the mystery is the fact that David seems to treat Uriah more as a negotiating partner than a subject. He throws a feast for him, offers him a gift and entertains him at the palace. Surely if Uriah were a mere subject, David would have dispensed with such niceties and simply ordered him executed on some trumped-up charge. As king, he had the power to do so and would certainly not have hesitated to use it under the circumstances.

It therefore it seems likely that Uriah was neither a Hittite nor a subject. But if not, then who was he?

The name Uriah provides the first clue. It seems closely related to the Egyptian term *uraeus*, which was used to describe the cobra that adorned the headdresses of every pharaoh. This terrible serpent was depicted rearing back, its hood flaring as it prepared to strike the enemies of Egypt. The cobra was symbolic of Horus in several ways. For one thing, it was the only creature that was not the handiwork of Ra, having been created instead by Isis using the old god's spittle. In a sense, therefore, it was her "only child" — just as Horus was. The cobra in ancient Egypt also symbolized the eternal eye of the sun god Horus, its fiery bite mimicking the heat of the solar orb. In this regard, it is probably not coincidental that certain species of cobra have markings on their hoods that resemble a pair of eyes or a single eye.

If the name Uriah is, in fact, based upon the word *uraeus*, it would have therefore marked him as an Egyptian pharaoh. Why, then, would he have been identified as a Hittite? The answer probably lies in the Egyptian language, which includes two words that appear pertinent here:

> ➤ H'ty = governor.
> ➤ Ity = sovereign.

If one were to run these two words together, the result would be h'tyity, a word meaning something like "sovereign governor" and sounding an awful lot like "Hittite." Certainly such a description would have been quite appropriate for a pharaoh, and it would explain the reference to the person in question as a Hittite. It appears that the problem was created by a scribe unfamiliar with the Egyptian tongue who, baffled as to the meaning of the word, chose to substitute the sound-alike appellation "Hittite" in its stead.

The next question that must be asked is, if Bath-Sheba was in fact the Queen of Sheba, who was the pharaoh in question?

But before that question is answered, another must be addressed: Namely, what is King David doing in this story? Or, perhaps more to the point, just who *was* King David in the first place. The answer that presents itself is somewhat shocking and would indicate that he is not at all who he seems to have been. The derivation of the name David has long been open to debate. But given the apparent origins of Uriah and Sheba, it seems appropriate to look along the banks of the Nile.

What one finds is not a king, but a god.

Once again, it is important to keep in mind that the original Hebrew name did not contain any vowels — the "a" and "i" in David had been added as placeholders. Moreover, the middle letter has been changed in the Anglicized version of the name. Originally, the whole thing was written out as simply *dwd* and pronounced either Dewed or simply Duud. This might in fact be related to the Celtic word "druid," used to designate the ruling priestly class in Gaul and the British Isles (where, according to one legend, the sword of David was said to have ended up after drifting there aboard Solomon's burial ship). Intriguing though this may be, the *dwd* construction seems to bring us no closer to an answer until we look a little more closely into another popular name of the time: Thoth. This was, in fact, a Greek corruption of the original Egyptian name Tehuti, spelled out — again without the vowels — as *dhwty*. It was pronounced as either Dewety or Duud(e).

The seeming assertion, which on the face of it appears preposterous, is that David was in fact the Egyptian god Thoth. Yet this idea is not so outlandish as it might appear. For another Hebrew hero was widely equated *with the very same Egyptian god*. That hero's name was Moses.

This raises the intriguing possibility that "David" was merely another name for Moses — which would make perfect sense. The more information that surfaces about the two men, the harder it is to ignore the parallels in their life stories. Moses stole the Queen of Sheba away from his rival Apophis, just as David stole Bath-Sheba from Uriah. And Uriah was the "sovereign governor" of Egypt who wore the sacred *uraeus*, just as Apophis did. What we have here is a story taken out of its original context, with the names changed just enough to conceal the characters' true identities to the casual reader — but not enough to eliminate all the vital clues.

Word of Mouth

Knowing how to read such clues is essential in any attempt to decipher ancient texts. This is because such texts are quite frequently patchworks made up of oral traditions from a variety of sources. It is difficult, from any current perspective, to understand the nature of the storyteller's craft. Modern society is steeped in the concept of "linear" history, assuming that each event follows neatly on the last in a timeline from the dawn of civilization to the present. Timelines adorn classroom walls, leading students obediently along on a symbolic leash from point to point.

But ancient storytellers had no timelines to restrict them. They were not yet muzzled by the leash of "accepted fact" and hence were free to embellish or rearrange their material if doing so would make it more compelling. Or if it served to further the cause of king and kingdom. Or if the storyteller simply got his facts confused. All these factors came into play in the telling and retelling of the Hyksos-Theban saga, creating a confusing tableau wherein someone named David came to be portrayed as King Solomon's *father* of all people. The mortal enemies Ahmose and Apophis would doubtless have shared a bitterly ironic laugh could they have seen what would become of their history.

And what a history it was.

One of David's most famous acts was the capture of the city perched atop a holy mountain known as Zion. This name, like so many others, is revealing when broken down into its component parts. The Hebrew prefix is *tsiyah*, meaning "desert," and the suffix is rendered as *on*. This latter also happens to stand alone during a handful of instances in the Hebrew scriptures. And wherever it does, it refers to another sacred city — the Egyptian city of Heliopolis. It was at Heliopolis that the primeval hill was said to have risen out of the waters of chaos at the moment of creation, identifying it therefore as the center of the earth. Likewise, Zion would come to be considered the center of the earth by the Hebrews who worshipped on their mountain. Each city was the center of a national cult, each housing a temple that was considered the holiest site in all creation by its adherents.

It is therefore no accident that the most significant Jewish temple ever to be founded outside of Palestine would be built within view of Heliopolis.

Just as David conquered Zion, Ahmose is known to have taken Heliopolis on his march northward to confront Apophis in the delta. The event is preserved by chance in the notes of a scribe who happened to record on the back of a papyrus leaf that, in the thirty-third year of Apophis' reign, "Heliopolis was entered" by "the southern prince." [131]

Moses. Or Ahmose. Or David. Take your pick.

Other Davids

Though some events in David's story were drawn from the life of Ahmose, others were culled from different Egyptian sources. In fact, it appears that David himself is something of a composite character, whose legend is based on the exploits of two different pharaohs as well as those of a heroic prince named Sinuhe.

The latter was a high-ranking member of the Egyptian court nearly a millennium before David is supposed to have lived. He begins his account by describing himself as "the hereditary prince and count." He was, furthermore, "judge and district overseer of the sovereign in the land of the Asiatics." [132]

Palestine.

Sinuhe appears, in some respects, to be a prototype of the judges spoken of in the Hebrew text — men who presided over the Palestinian region but who were not kings themselves. The implication is that they ruled at the behest of some greater power, having been designated to oversee that particular region on some ruler's behalf. And the ruler who dominated Palestine throughout this period in history was the pharaoh, the king of Egypt.

After his rather self-congratulatory introduction, Sinuhe launches into a lively narrative that relates a series of adventures. His lofty position does not protect him when, shortly after the pharaoh's death, he overhears word of some intrigue involving the succession. Fearing for his life, he flees and through the desert until he is at last overcome with thirst and collapses, on the brink of death. He is rescued, however, by a passing caravan of Asiatic cowherds who revive him and take him in. In exchange for their hospitality, these men apparently make Sinuhe a servant and subsequently pass him on to another Asiatic tribe.

He makes his way to Byblos and eventually winds up in the service of a chieftain by the name of Ammi-enshi, with whom he finds favor and who therefore bestows upon him a district of land.

Sinuhe calls this the land of Yaa and says unequivocally, "it was a good land." He then proceeds to describe it in glowing terms:

Figs were in it, and grapes.
It had more wine than water.
Plentiful was its honey, abundant its olives
Every kind of fruit was on its trees.
Barley was there, and ... there was no limit to all breeds of cattle [133]

Sinuhe tells of being fed the choices meals, dining on fresh-baked bread and roast fowl while quenching his thirst on an abundance of wine and milk. Indeed, his description of this land of Yaa bears a striking resemblance to the depiction of Yahweh's "promised land" in the Hebrew texts — the names Yaa and Yahweh being closely connected. This, too, was a land flowing with milk and honey, described by the spies who first saw it in the exact terms used by Sinuhe: "It is a good land." [134] When the Hebrew spies ventured forth to scout out the land, they found pomegranates, figs and grapes so large that it takes two men to bear a single cluster suspended on a pole between them.[135]

The great size of the grapes was par for the course in this land. It appeared that the *people* in the region were giants, as well: "All the people we saw there are of great size," the spies reported. "We seemed like grasshoppers in our own eyes, and we looked the same to them." [136]

Giants are mentioned infrequently in the Hebrew texts. It is therefore intriguing to find that the most famous account of a giant therein corresponds closely to a portion of Sinuhe's tale. This is, of course, the famous account of David and his gigantic Philistine nemesis Goliath, a nine-foot-tall behemoth who had established a fierce reputation in single combat. As it turns out, Sinuhe faced a similar opponent during his sojourn in the land of Yaa. He describes this fearsome enemy as a "hero without peer," a mighty man of Retenu — the same geographical area that would later be occupied by the Philistines.

The term "hero" or "mighty man" was used in the Hebrew texts to describe a race of men known as the Nephilim.[137] And it was this same race that the Hebrew spies encountered in their foray into the promised land — a race of giants who made them seem like grasshoppers in comparison.

Goliath, apparently, belonged to this ancient race, as did Sinuhe's opponent, whose prowess was such that Sinuhe's compatriots despaired: "Is there another strong man who could fight against him?"

It was a lament nearly identical to the boastful challenge issued by Goliath, who was also seen as invincible. "This day, I defy the ranks of Israel to give me a man and let us fight each other." [138] That man would be a shepherd named David.

Sinuhe, like David, would take up the challenge.

And the descriptions of the battles that ensued are strikingly similar. Both men use projectiles to defeat their enemy — David employs a sling, while Sinuhe makes use of a longbow. Both stone and arrow find their mark, with Goliath collapsing in a heap "facedown to the ground" and Sinuhe's foe falling "on his nose." David then runs over to Goliath, unsheathes the giant's sword and uses it to cut off his head. Sinuhe, in similar fashion, uses his enemy's own weapon (in this case, a battle-axe) to strike the killing blow.

As David is lauded for his victory over Goliath, so Sinuhe's defeat of the Retenu champion is celebrated. Sinuhe marries the Asiatic chieftain's eldest daughter, while David is likewise offered the hand of *his* king's daughter. Such uncanny parallels demonstrate a strong likelihood that the story of Sinuhe served as the inspiration for the legend of David and Goliath.

But there are other elements to the legend of David as well — elements drawn from yet another source. This source was the life story of the Tuthmoses, the third pharaoh to bear that name and the fourth to serve after the death of Ahmose. He was a warrior king who, like David, made his reputation as a great general, conducting a series of seventeen campaigns in Palestine over the course of two decades.

But in all these campaigns, a single battle stood out as by far the most extraordinary. It was extraordinary enough to be memorialized on the walls of the great temple to the god Amen at Thebes. And it was even extraordinary enough to serve as the model for one man's vision of history's climactic battle, known to him as the battle of Armageddon.[139]

This name referred to the ancient pass of Megiddo, where the forces of Tuthmoses earned a hard-fought and decisive victory over a coalition of Syrian kings and their armies. The description of this battle closely corresponds to that of David's most difficult campaign, his defeat of the Ammonites at the city of Rabbah bene Ammon. This ancient city is none other than the modern capital of the Jordanian kingdom, known today simply as Amman. It was to this city that David sent emissaries in hopes of completing a peace agreement, only to have them rudely rebuffed — sent back with their beards shaved off.

The Ammonites, realizing that such a move was sure to provoke David, enlisted the services of an army from Syria to help defend their city against the assault they knew was coming.

And come it did.

David sent an army under the command of his top general, Joab, to go against the city. But Joab arrived to find the defenders split into two contingents — the Ammonites themselves at the city gates and their Syrian allies in the open field. Finding himself suddenly hemmed in between the proverbial "rock and a hard place," Joab was forced to do battle on two fronts. Hastily, he assembled a company under the command of his brother to engage the Ammonites while he turned his attention to their Syrian allies. His rationale was simple: He hoped one group would prevail quickly and be free to aid the second company.

As it turned out, the strategy worked. Joab was able to rout the Arameans and turn back toward Rabbah, whereupon the Ammonites — sensing they were about to be outnumbered — abandoned their positions and took refuge inside the city walls. Unwilling to engage in a protracted siege, Joab left well enough alone and returned to David with news of the battle. In the meantime, however, the Syrians regrouped and sought to re-enter the fray, forcing David himself to march out and deliver the coup de gras. This he did, slaying the army commander and presiding over a convincing victory that left more than forty thousand of the enemy dead.[140]

Tuthmoses' army, like David's, found itself between a rock and a hard place during the siege of Megiddo.

Literally.

In order to reach Megiddo, the Egyptian army had to make its way through a narrow pass guarded by two high mountains. Alternative routes were available to the north and south, but Tuthmoses insisted upon advancing single file through the pass itself — even though, in doing so, he left his forces dangerously exposed. It was a daring maneuver.

And it was one the defenders were definitely not expecting.

There are several parallels between the battle that followed and David's campaign against Rabbah. As at Rabbah, the armies of Megiddo consisted of a Syrian coalition. And, as at Rabbah, these forces had divided themselves into two distinct contingents. In this case, one was stationed along the northern route to the fortress city and the other to the south, leaving the pass itself unguarded and allowing Tuthmoses to traverse this narrow canyon without meeting a single enemy. As he did so, he effectively split his own army, heading one company and leaving the other behind in Aruna at the other end of the pass.

When this second company arrived to join the fray, the defenders of Megiddo fled within the fortress walls — just as the defenders of Rabbah were said to have done when the two divisions of David's army combined their forces. Megiddo finally fell to the Egyptians seven months later, just as Rabbah eventually capitulated to David's forces and accepted his sovereignty.

Several names in the story of Tuthmoses also appear in the annals of David:

➤ The king that led the Syrian coalition against the Egyptians was the king of Qadesh, a word that means "the holy." This was a name of a Syrian city, but it was also often applied to Jerusalem itself, the so-called city of David. Indeed, the prophet Nehemiah would refer to it as Jerusalem ha Qadesh, or "Jerusalem the holy." [141] And this very slogan would appear on coins minted by the short-lived kingdom of Jerusalem during its ill-fated uprising against Rome more than a millennium later. [142]

➤ The city of Aruna, which the Egyptians used as a base before their assault on Megiddo, appears in the annals of David personified as a man named Arauna. This individual owns a threshing floor that David seeks to purchase "so I can build an altar to Yahweh, that the plague on my people may be stopped." [143] There is every reason to believe that this is a reference to Tuthmoses' decision to station his troops at the city of Aruna before launching his assault on Megiddo. For one thing, the Hebrew word most commonly translated as threshing floor is *goren* — a word that can refer to any smooth or open area and which is closely related to *garon*, meaning "mouth" or "neck." The city of Aruna fits both descriptions perfectly, being situated on a relatively flat plain at the mouth of the pass to Megiddo.

➤ Then there is the reference to the altar. According to the Hebrew tradition, David wished to purchase the "threshing floor" from Arauna in order to establish an altar there. This, too, is consistent with the account of Tuthmoses' campaign, for he appears to have traveled with a portable shrine or altar dedicated to his patron god, Amen or Amon.

This would explain why the Hebrew scribes mistakenly described the battle of Megiddo as taking place at Rabbah. The full name of that city was Rabbah bene Ammon, which literally means "children of Ammon." In the original version of the story, this term was not meant to describe the Jordanian city but the Egyptian forces — who viewed themselves in precisely these terms, as children of Amen.

This god was no stranger to Palestine. Three centuries after Tuthmoses' campaign at Megiddo, one of his successors on the throne of Egypt (the third pharaoh to bear the name Rameses) would establish a temple to Amen in the land.[144] And, moreover, the god's very name would make its way into the Hebrew canon of scripture in a supremely obvious way. Even today, prayers to the heavenly father are concluded with this single word.

Amen.

Indeed, Amen *was* the heavenly father, just as Osiris was. In fact, he appears to have been a form of Osiris. The connection is somewhat complicated, but worth exploring.

Like Horus, Amen was a sun god. He was often equated with Ra as the composite deity Amen-Ra, but in fact he performed a more specific function. His name meant "the hidden one," indicating that he personified the sun after it slipped below the horizon and began its journey through the nighttime underworld. The ancients viewed the daily sunset as the death of the sun, which would nonetheless be reborn the following morning in renewed glory. Osiris, likewise, died and was reborn in Egyptian myth. And as he awaited his new birth, he lay concealed in a sarcophagus, making him — like Amen — "the hidden one."

The pharaohs considered themselves the personification of Horus, the son of Osiris. And in the same manner, Tuthmoses appears to have viewed himself as the son of Amen. The account of his victory at Megiddo is replete with references to "my father Amen" and "my father Amen-Ra" whose presence stood guard over the pharaoh and helped ensure that he would emerge victorious.

And this was no mere spiritual presence.

It was *real*.

And entirely tangible.

The annals of David make it quite clear that he established a physical altar on the so-called threshing floor of Arauna. It should therefore come as no surprise that Tuthmoses carried with him a portable altar dedicated to Amen. In chronicling his campaign, he referred to the fateful day of his advance on Megiddo as "the awakening in the tent of life, prosperity and health at the town of Aruna." He then went on to relate how he set out that morning and proceeded northward at the head of his army, "carrying my father

Amen-Ra, lord of the thrones of the two lands, that he might open the ways before me."[145]

How could he have been *carrying* the god?

The only possible explanation is that the god was believed to be contained in the shrine itself — a box or sarcophagus made expressly to house the hidden one. This was probably a ritual casket containing a small stone statue or image of the old pharaoh, who upon his death had been transformed into the heavenly father Osiris or Amen. The ark was too small to contain the actual remains of the pharaoh, and it was customary to convey stone statues of the gods in such arks during a festival known as the Opet in the Egyptian capital of Thebes. This festival solidified the pharaoh's power by establishing him as the mystical son of Amen, the god whom the festival honored. During the celebration, a stone statue of Amen was carried in a boat-shaped ark from the temple of Amen at Karnak to its sister temple, dedicated to Amen's consort, across town at Luxor. The connection of the ark to Amen as the hidden Osiris cannot help but bring to mind the famous prayer that begins with the phrase "our father in heaven" and traditionally concludes with the word "amen."

Evidence suggests, moreover, that the Ark of the Covenant was likewise a vehicle in which the god (or more precisely his image) were transported from one place to another. The Hebrew scribes reported that "whenever the ark set out, Moses said, 'Rise up, Yahweh. May your enemies be scattered; may your foes flee before you. And whenever it came to rest, he said, 'Return, Yahweh, to the countless thousands of Israel.' " [146]

This ritual incantation reveals that the deity's movements mirrored those of his sacred ark or boat-casket. Why would this have occurred unless he was in some sense believed to be a *passenger* in the vessel? This conclusion is confirmed by the Hebrew scribes, who record Yahweh's command to "have them make a sanctuary for me, and I will dwell among them." [147]

The sanctuary in question was the tabernacle or tent of meeting, which contained the ark, the design for which was imparted to Moses immediately after the directive to build a sanctuary. It was there, on the mercy seat that covered the ark, that he would meet with Moses and impart to him the divine wisdom he needed to effectively govern his people.

On occasion, the ark is even referred to as the Ark of Yahweh.[148] The implication is that Yahweh somehow dwelt in the ark, which must have served as his vessel for traversing the gulf between heaven and earth. Such a journey was to have been expected, for who would construct a boat for himself and not go for a ride in it?

Certainly not Yahweh.

But this connection became embarrassing to later generations, who were appalled at the idea that the ark should have contained a statue — a graven image forbidden under their law. This was an obvious contradiction. To rectify it, they sought to obscure the ark's true purpose as a ritual vessel that bore the god's image across the gulf between the mortal world and the heavenly realm. Language connecting the deity himself with the ark was made more ambiguous, but the parallel was still visible to those who looked closely enough.

It can be no coincidence that David, like Tuthmoses, possessed a portable shrine that was housed in a tent (or tabernacle) and said to house the divine presence. Just as Tuthmoses carried his shrine forth onto the battlefield, so the armies of David paraded the so-called ark before them into combat. Just as the shrine of Amen was Tuthmoses' guardian, so the ark was the protector of David's forces.

This ark would be identified with David and even more closely with Solomon, whose name in Hebrew means "peace." In Egyptian, however, it may have meant something more. The Egyptian word *sah* signifies the constellation of Orion, the heavenly manifestation of Osiris. When combined with the divine name Amen (or Amon), it forms Sah-Amon, perhaps providing the basis for the famous title worn by the Hyksos pharaoh Apophis.

Solomon.

The Egyptian alphabet does not come equipped with an "L" sound, so it would have been natural for the Hebrews to insert a consonant sound — and this was probably as good as any — between the two "ah" sounds in *sah* and Amon. Hence, the name Solomon. The hieroglyph for *sah* was a divine figure seated staring at a five-pointed star (★).[149] It is likely no coincidence that this star, a variation of which adorns the flag of the United States, is traditionally known as the star of Solomon. This star, incidentally, would even end up making its way into the tarot deck as the suit known as pentacles, which later evolved into diamonds.

In light of all this, "Solomon" appears to have been a name for the dead king who had taken the form of Osiris/Amen. In this state, he was at peace in the heavenly realm; hence, he became the prince of peace. At least twice in the biblical tradition, a king's death is foretold as a promise of peace.

➢ "You, however, will go to your fathers in peace and be buried at a good old age" — a promise to the patriarch (Hyksos king) Abraham.[150]

➢ "Now I will gather you to your fathers, and you will be buried in peace" — a reference to King Josiah.[151]

In each case, the king's fathers were those who had occupied the throne before but was now at peace in death. These men had already undergone the mystical transformation from earthly Horus to heavenly Osiris, the "father of the gods." [152] This was a transformation of peace, accomplished through a spiritual journey to the place of the other fathers. If "Solomon" was the title applied to many kings who had undergone this process, for some reason it came to be applied specifically to a single Hyksos pharaoh.

As living king, he had been known as Apophis, and he had built his temple to Seth in Avaris.

Just as the Jews were said to have built a temple of Solomon in Jerusalem.

But neither of these sites served as the original temple of Sah-Amon. That honor belonged to a much more ancient structure, the great temple of Amen at Karnak in the Egyptian capital of Thebes. It was here that Tuthmose would inscribe the account of his great victory at Megiddo, an account that would make its way into the annals of King David. And just as the Jerusalem temple became the permanent resting place for the ark that preceded David into combat, so the temple at Karnak served as the permanent abode of Amen — the god whose shrine preceded Tuthmoses.

It is perhaps obvious why Tuthmoses and Moses should have both served as models in crafting the life story of David, for "Tuthmoses" is in fact a combination of the two other names. The suffix is, of course, moses. And Tuth refers to the god Thoth, whose name is rendered variously as Dhwty or Dwd.

In other words, David.

Final Connections

While the connection between David and Tuthmoses is apparent, another convoluted tale further cements the ties between David and Moses (or Ahmose). The narrative in question, preserved by the Hebrew scribes, recounts King David's success in quelling a revolt near the end of his illustrious reign. What makes this particular account significant is that the revolt was supposedly authored by a man named Sheba. Could this be a veiled reference to Ahmose's success in putting down a rebellion based in the Ethiopian capital of Saba, late in *his* reign? When one considers the fact that such a rebellion did, in fact, occur, it is hard to dismiss the similarities without admitting the likelihood that they are related.

Searching through such material for the hidden parallels needed to make sense of it can be difficult. The fluid nature of oral accounts meant that nothing was carved in stone, and oral traditions often appear to have been simply thrown together in creating early written histories. Legends were transported hundreds of miles — or years — out of context without a second thought. This is what appears to have happened with the story of the Hyksos-Theban conflict, which was not only removed from its proper time, but also transported over the vast stretch of territory that separated the Nile Delta region from Palestine.

Even within a single account, varying sources could be used to create a sort of composite character out of more than one historical figure. Solomon Apophis is a prime example. On the one hand, the life story of Solomon was obviously that of the Hyksos king Apophis, but the name itself was probably derived from Sah-Amon. And a variation on this epithet was worn, in turn, by a later Egyptian pharaoh. This particular pharaoh not only has a similar-sounding name (Siamun), he also reigned about the same time the biblical Solomon was said to have ruled in Palestine. Never mind that this was five hundred years after the reign of King Apophis.

Despite these hurdles, however, it is possible to reconstruct a fairly clear picture of the events as they most likely occurred. When the Queen of Sheba switched her allegiance from Apophis to Moses/Ahmose, those events began careening headlong toward a conflict that would set the course not only for the future of Egypt but for that of the entire civilized world. Confrontation was now inevitable. Kamose had very nearly brought the Hyksos empire to its knees, and now his younger brother had the means to finish the job. He led his army north from Thebes, single-minded in his purpose to take back what was rightfully his.

He would rip the kingdom of Egypt from the clutches of Apophis and the foreign usurpers. He would confront the false and arrogant "pharaoh" who had stolen it from him. And he would demand and end to the enslavement of his subjects, in a voice that would echo down across the centuries.

He would stand before Apophis and issue what would become his famous ultimatum …

IX

Let My People Go

Moses' push toward Avaris was relentless.

Following the same path taken by his elder brother a few short years before, he traced the Nile's course northward across Egypt. His forces came on foot, marching over land. They came in chariots, intent on turning the Hyksos' innovation against them. They came in ships borne upon the current of the river, ships with names like "Northern" and "The Wild Bull."

In midsummer, he took Heliopolis, then diverted his forces eastward toward the fortress of Tjaru on the Sinai frontier. Reaching it in less than two weeks, his forces took the fortress in a mere two days. It was a crucial strategic victory, for it put Moses in control of the narrow land bridge that connected Africa with the Arabian Peninsula. From there, his troops could effectively seal the delta off from the rest of the world — isolating Apophis from his holdings in Palestine. There would be no reinforcements from that quarter. Moses had made sure of that.

Things were starting to look bad for the Hyksos. Even the skies were ominous, according to one eyewitness: "On the birthday of Seth, a roar was emitted by the majesty of this god. On the birthday of Isis, the sky poured rain." [153]

The time had come.

From Tjaru, the Theban army turned back westward toward its ultimate objective: Avaris.

A member of Moses' company, a commander who served aboard the ship "Appearing in Memphis," left a record of what happened next. As the force advanced upon Avaris, it encountered fierce resistance from the Hyksos at a canal outside the city. The Theban commander, never one to shrink from reveling in his own achievements, managed to kill one of the defenders and capture another — deeds for which he was rewarded with something called the "gold of valor."

The fighting then spread to the towns south of Avaris, whereupon the commander took another prisoner and was honored yet again.

"Then," the commander wrote, "Avaris was sacked."[154]

The statement was blunt and to the point. The reality, however, wasn't as simple as that. Moses doubtless recalled how Kamose had lain siege to Avaris for an extended period, yet had been unable to breach its walls. Apophis had made this a heavily fortified city, and its residents were undoubtedly well stocked with supplies to withstand a prolonged offensive. Moses had gotten this far, and he wasn't about to put his mission in jeopardy by acting too hastily. If he could intimidate Apophis into surrendering, he could avoid a protracted siege — and the possibility that such a siege might fail.

He therefore arranged for a meeting with Apophis, who was certainly quite amenable to such an encounter. He was, after all, the man reputed to be the wisest king in the civilized world. And while he was clearly on the defensive in the current conflict, he would have been quite confident he could outmaneuver this Theban prince at the negotiating table. If nothing else, such a meeting would buy his forces some time to regroup so they could launch a counteroffensive against the Theban army.

Apophis' strategy was simple. He would stall for time by forcing Moses to place his terms on the table; he would listen patiently —

and then turn him down cold. If all worked as planned, this would give the Hyksos army the chance it needed to turn the tide against the Thebans.

And just what were Moses' terms?

They were simple: He would break off the attack if Apophis consented to free the thousands of Thebans he had put to work in his quarries.

Apophis, of course, was not about to do this. He recognized the terms for what they were — a thinly veiled attempt to trick him into releasing a group of men who would immediately side with the Theban army, swelling its ranks even further. With this advantage, Moses could feel free to turn his back on the agreement and attack Avaris anyway. The result, according to the Hebrew scribes, is that the pharaoh's heart was "hardened" and he refused to accept Moses' terms. In doing so, he was able not only to avoid a disastrous agreement, but he was able to buy time by continuing to haggle with his adversary.

This marathon negotiating session is portrayed in mythic terms by the Hebrew scribes, who present Moses attempting to intimidate his rival with a series of magic tricks and demonstrations of power. The key to these tricks was his magic staff or caduceus, which miraculously transformed itself into a snake when cast upon the ground, thus identifying Moses is the rightful pharaoh. When his rival's sorcerers succeeded in matching this amazing feat, Moses went them one better — his snake attacked the others and swallowed them up.

The pharaoh, however, was unimpressed, and Moses was forced to resort to sterner measures.

It was by this point clear that Apophis had no intention of negotiating in good faith. There was nothing left for Moses to do but to demonstrate his army's power to the pharaoh. And this he did in a series of "miracles" that probably represented, in semi-allegorical terms, the damage inflicted upon Avaris by the Theban forces

First, the Nile was turned to blood –the blood of the Hyksos forces being slaughtered by the southern army. Then, a plague of frogs was unleashed. This was to be expected, for the Theban campaign was punctuated by a powerful storm in which "the sky poured rain." Such a storm would have brought an abundance of the creatures out into the open. This was followed by a plague of gnats and flies, the winged pests gathering around the corpses of men fallen in battle.

And this, in turn, gave way to a plague on livestock. It was unique, however, in that it attacked only those animals belonging to the pharaoh's people and left Moses' livestock unscathed. Since there were no vaccines available to protect Moses' animals from such a disease, this report seems rather incredible — unless it was not a true plague that slaughtered the beasts. A more likely explanation is that it was a systematic slaughter at the hands of Moses' army.

Still, however, the pharaoh refused to surrender. So for Moses' next demonstration, he took a handful of soot from the furnace and tossed it into the air, producing festering boils on "all the Egyptians." Again, the allegorical nature of the text is apparent. Under Kamose, the Theban army had pursued a scorched-earth policy as it had advanced on Avaris, mercilessly burning every town that stood between it and its objective. In tossing soot into the air, Moses was threatening to renew this policy of destruction. Just as the soot rose from his hands, in the same way black smoke and ashes would rise from the cities of the delta as they burned.

Even this, however, failed to make an impression on the pharaoh, who next faced a plague of hail — another consequence of the powerful storm that was raging overhead. A plague of locusts followed, symbolic of the Theban army swarming Avaris, and shortly afterward, darkness covered the land.

It was now clear that Apophis could not escape the fate to which he had been consigned. Despite all his fortifications, Moses had succeeded in breaching the walls of Avaris, his men pouring in like locusts beneath a sky darkened by menacing thunderheads and clouds of smoke from a countryside set ablaze. The next thing Apophis knew, Moses' men had become "angels of death," looting the Hyksos' belongings as they rampaged through the streets of the capital, slaughtering the firstborn sons of every Hyksos family. Theban residents of the city, alerted to the impending assault, managed to avoid this fate by smearing the blood of a lamb on their doorposts — a prearranged signal to the invaders that they were friendly to the assailants' cause.

It was all over.

The Hyksos were defeated, and there was nothing to do but flee. Perhaps if the remnants of the army could fight its way through to Palestine, reinforcements would be waiting there to join them. Then, if all went well, they could regroup and turn back toward the delta with new resolve to recapture their land. This appears to have been their plan, but Moses and the Thebans were bent on making sure it did not turn out the way they hoped.

The Great Escape

The Hebrew scribes tell of a mass exodus from the delta led by Moses, with the pharaoh in pursuit. In fact, however, they got it backwards — it was the Hyksos king who had fled, with the Egyptian pharaoh Moses hot on his heels. Though badly depleted during its losing struggle with the Thebans, the retreating army remained a force to be reckoned with. The author of *Exodus* placed the number of refugees at no fewer than six hundred thousand, certainly a vast exaggeration but nevertheless an indication that this was no small contingent.

The army moved quickly to the northwest, in the direction of Palestine, stopping first at a place called Succoth. The name means something like "lair" or "den" or "pavilion of tents." It was apparently a way station slightly more than twenty miles from the delta capital that remained in the hands of the Hyksos. Most likely, it was the Egyptian frontier fortress known as Tjeku, a name that bears some linguistic similarity to Succoth. Here there was a small settlement, with two forts and pools for watering beasts of burden.[155] They lodged for a short time here before departing once more, this time for a place known as Etham whose name was most likely derived from the god Atum but whose location is unclear. It was, however, on the edge of the desert, indicating that the refugees had reached the farthest extent of the great alluvial marshland created by the Nile Delta.

Here, a decision had to be made: Would they go forward into Palestine at once in an effort to find reinforcements, or would they turn and fight the pursuing Theban army in an attempt to slow it down? It was a difficult decision. If they chose the latter course, they risked utter defeat then and there. Yet if they continued their flight, they ran the risk of being cut down from the rear by their pursuers in the desert. At least here, on the fringes of the delta wetlands, they retained something of an advantage: They knew the territory well, and perhaps they could use that knowledge to deal the Thebans a blow that would stop them in their tracks.

This was doubtless the rationale behind their decision to turn and fight. Leaving Etham, they turned back in the direction from which they had come, making for an encampment known as Pi-Hahiroth that stood between a place identified as Migdol — literally "tower" or "fortress" — and the sea. The name of the camp means something like "house of caves," indicating that the terrain near the fortress was pockmarked with gorges and crevices, suitable hiding places for men who did not wish to be found. Men such as the members of a retreating army.

There, they waited, hoping that their pursuers would think they were "wandering around the land in confusion, hemmed in by the desert." [156]

The trap was set. And the Thebans were walking right into it.

Most of those in the southern army were strangers to the wetlands of the northwest delta. They didn't know, for example, that the low-lying marshes near the seashore were subject to inundation at high tide. This made navigating them rather tricky. When the tides receded, the land dried out and the "reed sea" as it was known (often mistranslated and therefore confused with the Red Sea) could be crossed with relative ease, but when the tides came in, unwary travelers could find themselves trapped in a morass of mud and water.

This is what the Hyksos were counting on.

At a signal from their leader, the refugees broke from their hiding places in the caves of Pi-Hahiroth and fled across the relatively dry, reedy marshland that stretched away to the west. The pursuing army was caught off guard by this sudden tactic but rushed to resume its pursuit, encouraged by the fact that their enemy was now in sight but heedless of the danger that lay ahead of them. Before they could catch up to their fleeing adversaries, the tide abruptly turned. First, the wheels of their chariots became mired in the muddy sediment. Then, as they struggled to free themselves from the morass, water began to race in upon them, catching them by surprise and drowning many of them.

According to the *Exodus* account, the entire Egyptian army was washed away into the sea, leaving not a single survivor.[157] Unfortunately for the Hyksos, this was an exaggeration: The Theban army was hardly wiped out. But the "reed sea" maneuver was, nonetheless, a great tactical victory. The gambit had paid off. The Hyksos forces had bought themselves precious time and had managed to stave off defeat — at least for the moment. And they used this time not only to put some distance between themselves and the Thebans, but to devise a plan that would give them at least a fighting chance to turn the tide of battle, just as they had turned the tide of the ocean.

Split Decision

The *Exodus* account states that, following the reed sea victory, the refugees made their way east into the desert of the Sinai Peninsula. There, they spent the next forty years wandering in the wilderness before finally staging a series of attacks on various Palestinian strongholds. But the account preserved by the Theban ship commander tells a different story. According to his record, the fleeing army instead made its way north toward the fortress city of Sharuhen on the eastern shore of the Mediterranean. There, the Hyksos refugees endured a protracted siege of no less than three years before finally surrendering to the Theban army.

So what really happened?

Neither story can be dismissed out of hand, and it seems probable that both contain elements of truth. The Hyksos army remained a sizeable force, large enough to split into two separate contingents, and such a move would have made a good deal of sense under the circumstances. Sharuhen was a strongly fortified city that could be counted upon to hold off an invading army for an extended period. This would have been crucial if the Hyksos were planning the sort of countermove that their movements seem to indicate. Under such a plan, one detachment of the army to would make its way up the coast to the city, luring the Theban army in its wake. These troops would then settle in for an extended siege, offering just enough resistance to keep the Thebans from taking the city. Meanwhile, the army's second detachment would slip off unnoticed into the eastern desert, circle around and catch the Thebans by surprise as they were assailing Sharuhen. It would be a classic military pincer move, putting the unsuspecting southern force between two contingents of the enemy army. Had the Hyksos been able to carry it off, they might have been able to change history.

But this was not to be.

For the eastern detachment that marched off into the desert never returned to liberate Sharuhen. Inside that mighty fortress, members of the western detachment held out valiantly as first one year, then two, then three finally passed without any word from their estranged comrades. Finally, they could endure no more, and the city fell to Moses' forces. Once again, the Theban commander who had previously been aboard the ship "Appearing in Memphis" was in the thick of the action, carrying off two women as slaves and killing yet another member of the enemy contingent — once again receiving the "gold of valor" for his heroism.

The fall of Sharuhen effectively ended any hope of a Hyksos resurgence in the delta. But it left some nagging questions to be answered: What ever happened to the eastern detachment? And why did they fail to keep their appointed rendezvous in Sharuhen?

The answers to these questions can be found in the record left by the Hebrew scribes, a record that chronicles in detail the collapse of the Hyksos army's final remnants. This was an army ill prepared for a trek across the arid waste of the Sinai Peninsula. Though familiar enough with the delta marshlands to pull off the reed sea maneuver without a hitch, they proved less capable of confronting the realities of the desert. Food was in short supply, the sun beat down on them relentlessly, and their bodies were wilting in the desert heat. Given such conditions, it was not long before some in the company began to complain openly about their predicament. It would have been better to remain in Egypt and accept the sovereignty of the Thebans, they said, than to be marching through the desert on a mission that was probably hopeless in the first place. If they had died in Egypt, at least they would have died happy. "There," they told their leaders, "we had pots of meat and ate all the food we wanted, but you brought us out into this desert to starve the lot of us to death." [158]

The grumbling was checked to some extent when the company happened upon a flock of quail that served as a passable meal for one evening. But the extent of their hunger is revealed in the fact that they attempted to store away some of the meat for the future without preserving it. Predictably, it went bad and came to be infested with maggots. Though there would be other flocks of quail in the days to come, opposition to the leadership became more strident and it became clear that something more would be needed to rescue the company's badly deteriorating morale. Water was even scarcer than food, and members of the company openly confronted their leaders: "Why did you bring us up out of Egypt — to make us and our children and livestock die of thirst?" [159]

Clearly, something had to give.

And, finally, it did.

The continual protests of the malcontents provide a clue as to what it was, for their words sound the same theme time and again: If only we had not left Egypt.... It was becoming abundantly clear that a significant number of refugees wanted to abandon their mission altogether and return to Egypt, counting on the new pharaoh to grant them amnesty for their past resistance in exchange for a pledge of loyalty. This new pharaoh, of course, was Moses. And he would have been all too ready to accept a change of heart by these men who represented the final threat to his kingdom.

The leaders of the eastern detachment cannot have failed to recognize the growing discontent within their ranks, and it must have caused them no small amount of anxiety. As it turned out, however, they had even greater reason to be concerned. It seems that Moses had not been sufficiently distracted by the western detachment's march to Sharuhen. The decoy apparently had not worked, for while the Theban prince had pursued the western company north to the fortress, he had also dispatched a force of men — under the leadership of a certain Joshua — to harry the eastern detachment as it made its way across the desert.

The Son of Nun

It must have seemed to the Hyksos that Joshua and his men came out of nowhere, appearing on the horizon like phantoms from some netherworld. Appropriately, Joshua materializes out of nowhere in the Hebrew text as well, appearing without introduction as commander-in-chief of his nation's forces. This is, perhaps, an indication that the portion of the narrative which follows is out of context. But whether or not this is true, it must have only furthered the enigma surrounding the man referred to mysteriously as the "son of Nun."

The Hebrew scribes never explain who Nun was — perhaps because Nun wasn't a person at all, but rather a sort of divine presence. Once again, the reference is to Egyptian mythology, wherein Nun is described the primeval watery abyss from which creation was formed. It was out of Nun that Atum arose as the first hill, making him the only uncreated (or self-created) being in the universe. By referring to Joshua as the "son of Nun," the scribes were in fact equating him to the ancient sun god Atum. Joshua is, in effect, the second Atum — or Adam. It is perhaps no accident that another man would come to be referred to as the second Adam, the uncreated one by whom all things were created. This man's Hebrew name was also Joshua, though he is more commonly referred to by his Greek name.

Jesus.

For as in Adam all die
So in Christ, all will be made alive
The first man Adam became a living being
The last Adam, an eternal spirit [160]

Joshua's relationship with Atum would also perhaps explain one of the best-known folktales in the Hebrew writings, which describes a feat perhaps more impressive than any other in the scripture: Joshua commands the sun to stand still long enough for his forces to prevail in battle.

And it obeys him.[161]

If Joshua were considered the manifestation of Atum, this would only make sense. Of course a sun god could command his own blazing disc to stand still. And of course it would obey him.

Interestingly, this account is not original to the Hebrew scribes, who themselves admit having obtained it from a work called *The Book of Jasher*. This text has not survived, perhaps because it contained even clearer links to Egypt — links the Hebrew writers had no interest in preserving. Who was Jasher? The name has never been explained to anyone's real satisfaction. But there is one possibility worth considering: Perhaps it was a reference to Joshua himself.

Clearly, Joshua was more than a general. Hebrew lore plainly identifies him as Moses' chosen successor, which would have made him nothing less than a pharaoh. The question is, which one? The answer can be found by examining records of the Theban dynasty, which indicate the pharaoh Ahmose (Moses) was succeeded to the throne of Egypt by his son. This man is known to history as Amenhotep I, but like all pharaohs he had more than one name — in his case, he also was known as Djeserkare, meaning "holy spirit of Ra."

It seems entirely possible that later scribes corrupted this name by shortening it to simply Djeser. Or Jasher. Literally, the holy one. And it is certainly no coincidence that a similar-sounding Hebrew word, *yashar*, means "righteous." Once again, the Egyptian roots of Hebrew myth and culture are apparent if one only knows where to look. And they are confirmed by the fact that Amenhotep did in fact conduct a military excursion into Palestine during his own reign. Whether he also accompanied his father on an earlier campaign to obliterate what was left of the Hyksos cannot be determined from Egyptian sources. He would most likely have been quite young at the time. Yet the Hebrew scribes seem to indicate that he did, in fact, play a role in just such a campaign.

And a crucial role, at that — pursuing the eastern detachment in an effort to prevent it from circling back and coming to the aid of the refugees in Sharuhen. His army's appearance on the horizon must have shocked the Hyksos forces, already demoralized by their long desert march. Now, faced with this unexpected new threat, anxiety turned to panic as the Hyksos leaders were once again forced to decide between two alternatives: face the enemy head-on or flee. They had made the right choice before, using the reed sea maneuver to successfully escape their pursuers. But here, the situation was different. There was no reed sea to protect them, only a barren desert that was as hostile to them as it was to the enemy. Yet even so, there was only one choice that could be made. Morale was so low that, if they called a retreat, their leaders feared the army would disintegrate before their eyes, with deserters fleeing into the desert or rushing toward the enemy to beg for mercy.

The only option was to fight. So fight they did.

The Hebrew scribes recount the details of this epic confrontation as an attack by the so-called Amalekites on Joshua's forces. These Amalekites are a mysterious group, but their name provides a clue as to their true identity. At the root of it stands the Hebrew word *melek*, which means "king" and shares the same m-l-k consonant structure with *malak* — meaning angel or messenger. Since Hebrew words had no vowels, the two terms were essentially the same when written. In this context, it is fascinating to find a reference to the exodus among the Hebrew psalms that refers to a band of "evil angels" sent by Yahweh against the Egyptians.[162]

An evil angel in Hebrew is *malak ra*.

But this phrase is virtually identical to the Hebrew *melek ra'ah*.

Its meaning: king-shepherds.[163] Or, if turned on its head, shepherd kings. This latter was, of course, the very term the historian Josephus used to describe the Hyksos. Perhaps the psalmist's account even served as one of his sources in arriving at that appellation. Whatever the case, it is apparent that the Amelekites were none other than shepherd kings, the remnants of the once mighty Hyksos force now wandering the desert of the Sinai Peninsula.

Their desperate attack on the Thebans under Joshua's command resulted in a heroic battle during which neither side was quick to prevail. According to legend, Moses himself stood watching from a nearby hill, raising his magic staff over his head to direct his troops like an orchestra leader. Whenever he grew tired and lowered his arms, the battle would turn against him, so two of his lieutenants — Aaron and Hur — instructed him to seat himself on a nearby rock while they propped up his hands on either side. And when they did, the battle would turn once again in Joshua's favor.

This is a very vivid image.

Clearly, some sort of symbolism is in play. In this account, Moses' two companions act almost as pillars or beams holding up his tired arms. The picture recalls the image of the Jacob's ladder, with its two vertical beams representing two gods supporting the weight of the dying king as he ascends to his new heavenly home. Could it be that Moses' two companions were, in fact, gods supporting his enfeebled frame as he passed his authority to his successor, Joshua? Certainly their names seem to indicate that they were. On the one side stood Hur, an enigmatic character who is mentioned directly only in this account. His name seems to have derived from Hor, the shortened form of the name Horus. On the other side stood Aaron, an equally mysterious figure who seldom appears outside the company of Moses.

Two Pillars

Before going any further, it might behoove us to ask: Who was this Aaron?

And why does he play such a crucial role in the story of Moses and the exodus from Egypt?

In Hebrew lore, Aaron was the first great high priest and the model for all who are to follow. His link to the name Hur/Hor is solidified by the brief reference to his death: By divine decree, he is ordered to ascend a certain mountain and there to give his life. That mountain's name? Mount Hor, the mountain of Horus — the sacred pyramid wherein the dead king is entombed.

This only seems to confirm the purpose of Aaron's presence with Moses and a man named Hur on another mountain.

Moses was dying.

And to steady him as he ascended the stairway to heaven, he was accompanied by two godlike companions — one representing the royal office of king (Hur), and the other personifying the priestly office (Aaron). As in the text found in the tomb of the pharaoh Unas, one was Horus and the other was Seth. As we shall see, the figure of

Horus the falcon god consistently represented the monarchy in ancient myth, while that of the serpentine Seth corresponded to the high priesthood. It was upon these two pillars that the heavens were said to rest, and it had been thus for as long as anyone could remember. According to legend, the world rested upon two mountains that had arisen at the dawn of time, lifting up the dome of heaven and holding it steady above the earth. These two mountains were symbolized in two great pillars that stood at the entrance to many an Egyptian temple.

It is therefore hardly surprising to find that Solomon had two such pillars erected at the gateway to his great temple:

> *In the front of the temple, he made two pillars*
> *Each together were thirty-five cubits long*
> *Each with a capital on top measuring five cubits*
>
> *He made interwoven chains and put them on top of the pillars*
> *He also made a hundred pomegranates and attached them to the chains*
>
> *He erected them in front of the temple*
> *One to the south and one to the north*
> *The one to the south he named Jachin,*
> *The one to the north Boaz* [164]

Jachin meant "he establishes" — a reference to the priestly function of establishing the king upon his throne, of establishing the nation before its god(s). Boaz meant "strength," that quality most essential in a king as ruler and protector of the nation. The chains that united these two columns were interlaced with pomegranates, a fruit that symbolizes fertility and abundance. As long as the two pillars remained standing and united, such prosperity would be guaranteed; conversely, if either pillar were to collapse, the prosperity would come crashing to the earth.

In Egypt itself, two pillars were said to hold up the canvas of the heavens. The first was in Heliopolis — the ancient name of which was On or Annu, meaning simply "pillar." This was nothing other than the obelisk in the temple of the phoenix, upon which the great bird was said to alight. It was the priestly pillar of ancient Egypt, and it seems to have been paired with a royal pillar signified by the capital city of Thebes, which was known as the "southern pillar." [165] (Coincidentally, two massive obelisks in the Egyptian style may be found in two great capitals of the world today: One in the Vatican, headquarters of the Catholic priesthood at the heart of Rome, and the other in Washington, D.C., the center of secular power. While the former is a symbol of the priesthood, the latter pays tribute to the first American president, George Washington, who at one point was offered the office of king.)

The pillars of Solomon's temple stood united in supporting the eternal order of the kingdom, and the twin pillars of ancient Egypt performed the same function. Nothing signified order more fully than the heavens, which could be counted upon to provide eternal stability — in the sun's rising and setting, the waxing and waning of the moon, and the procession of the constellations. The pillars also united the two lands, whether they be Upper and Lower Egypt or the consolidated kingdoms of Israel and Judah.

From all this, it seems clear that the tradition of the two pillars was transported from Egypt into Palestine at some point. The most logical conclusion is that this happened following the end of the Hyksos regime, during the great mass exodus northward into the so-called land of promise. And indeed, the exodus tradition contains a legend that actually describes the symbolic conveyance of these two pillars. During their journey out of Egypt, the refugees were accompanied during the day by "a pillar of cloud to guide them on their way, and by night … a pillar of fire to give them light." [166] Here, the two great pillars of Egypt — the pillars of sunrise and sunset — are seen physically moving northeast with the refugees into Palestine.

It was only natural that these two pillars should come to be personified by the two most important men in the land.

The king and the high priest.

By positioning Moses on the mountaintop between Aaron the priest and Hur the king, the scribes appear to have been making a powerful declaration — that Moses embodied both holy offices *in a single person*. And in fact, tradition seems to indicate that he did. Not only was Moses remembered as pharaoh of Egypt and king of Ethiopia, he was also honored by some as a priest. And not just any priest, but a priest of Osiris.

Osiris himself was intimately associated with a pillar. According to the legend of his betrayal and death, his casket had come to rest on the shores of Syria, where it became encased in the trunk of a tamarisk tree. This tree was subsequently cut down and fashioned into a pillar, which the king of Byblos used to support the roof of his house.[167] Its purpose was therefore analogous to that of the two pillars in said to sustain the canopy of heaven.

Given the significance of the pillar to the myth of Osiris, it is no surprise to find that just such a pillar played an integral role in the rituals associated with his cult. Whether he was a king, a priest of Osiris or both, Moses would have almost certainly taken part these very rituals. They involved a detailed re-creation of the god's death and rebirth, culminating with a ceremony known as the raising of the pillar. By setting the pillar upright, the priest or pharaoh was declaring the god's return to life. The pillar itself was known as a *djed*, meaning "stability." This sounds virtually identical to one of the pillars that stood at the entrance to Solomon's temple.

Jachin, meaning "established."

This would seem to indicate that the temple of Solomon as depicted in the Hebrew scriptures had characteristics consistent with a temple of Osiris. (How much this portrayal of the temple owes to its actual character is open to question, considering the fact that Apophis' temple was dedicated to Seth.)

Moses was, according to the Egyptian historian Manetho, a priest of Osiris: "He was by birth of Heliopolis, and his name was Osarsiph from Osiris, the god of Heliopolis. But he changed his name and called himself Moses." [168]

Hence, Moses is connected with both pillar cities. As the pharaoh Ahmose, he is linked to the royal city of Thebes; as the priest Osarsiph, he is tied to the sacred precincts of Heliopolis.

Despite this, he was remembered primarily for his kingly role. It was in this role that he would reappear centuries later, in a dramatic re-enactment of the mountaintop scene from the exodus. This scene played out on a different mountain, with another man standing between two companions — one a priest and the other a king. The former was Elijah; the latter, none other than Moses himself. Just as Moses had, this man was claiming for himself the sacred offices of both priest and king. And just as Moses had passed his authority on to a man named Joshua as he stood on the mountain with Aaron and Hur, so now he was passing his authority to this other man — whose name was also Joshua.

Or, in Greek, Jesus.

The story is, of course, the famous account of the transfiguration, which is plainly modeled on the exodus event. Whether allegorical or actual, it is shown as a turning point in the life of Jesus, just as the exodus event had marked a turning point in the history of the refugees who would become known, collectively, as the children of Israel. For as Moses stretched out his hands above the desert battlefield that lay before him, the Amalekite (Hyksos) army began to give way. Eventually, at sunset, the ragged contingent grew too weary to stave off the continuing onslaught from the Theban army any longer. Many fell by the sword; others must have fled; still others likely sought refuge by surrendering and pledging their loyalty to the Theban king. However it finally ended, the magnitude of the triumph could not be understated — this was, in effect, the end of the Hyksos. The Hebrew scribes acknowledged as much, even going so far as to state that the memory of the Amalekite king would be completely erased from history.[169]

This, of course, was an exaggeration.

Though defeated, the remnants of the Hyksos army would not

easily forget the golden age they had left behind them. They would acknowledge Moses as their king and even hail him as their champion, but they would never repudiate the memory of their own great pharaoh Solomon Apophis. Over time, both men would become heroes and the fierce enmity between them would be forgotten. The scribes would transform Moses from a Theban prince into a great deliverer who had dared to defy an evil pharaoh, thereby claiming his heroic story as their own. And they would relocate Solomon's legend to a new time and place, the new capital city of Jerusalem several hundred years after his life had ended.

Thus, the two great legends of the Hyksos-Theban conflict were not only preserved, but consolidated into a single account more powerful and enduring than the history of the events as they occurred. It was the end of the Hyksos' golden reign in Egypt, left in ruins on the fields of the delta. But in many ways, it was the beginning of something even more glorious.

The Aaron Enigma

Aaron appears on the pages of the Hebrew text like a shadow on the face of history. Rarely does he act on his own accord, but almost always at the behest of the man identified as his younger brother, Moses.

He appears out of nowhere when Moses objects to confronting the pharaoh based upon the fact that he is "slow of speech." Aaron is therefore appointed as his spokesman and furnished with the miraculous staff — the caduceus — that can transform itself into a serpent when cast to the ground and serves as a catalyst for performing various other astounding feats. This would seem to make him a figure of some importance. Yet after teaming up with Moses, he seldom appears to be much more than a sort of conjoined twin or phantom lurking in the background. The phrase "Moses and Aaron" appears repeatedly. It is almost as though Aaron is not Moses' brother, but rather a sort of alter ego or appendage.

So who — or what — was Aaron?

The name's origins are not immediately clear, but it seems as though they are Egyptian.[170] It sounds a lot like the Greek name Orion, a mythical character who gave his name to the famous stellar constellation sometimes known as the hunter. The idea that a figure from Greek mythology should have been derived from someone with an Egyptian name is not so novel as it might appear. Indeed, Herodotus considered it quite natural: He stated plainly that the names of the Greek gods had been borrowed from their counterparts in Egypt.[171]

In Egyptian mythology, however, the constellation Orion was associated with a deity of a different name — one who also played a pivotal role in forming the legendary "ladder to the heavens" re-enacted in the legend of Moses, Aaron and Hur on the mountaintop.

That god was Osiris.

If Hur played the role of Horus in the mountaintop drama during the exodus, Aaron played the part of Seth. Yet he was also inextricably linked to the dying god, Osiris. A text found in the pyramid of the first pharaoh named Pepi (who ruled about 2300 B.C.E.) refers repeatedly to the ladder of Seth and Horus, on which the dead king ascended to heaven in the form of Osiris.[172] These two gods therefore seem to have been the instruments of his resurrection. And just such an event was being played out on the mountaintop in *Exodus*. Aaron and Hur were holding Moses upright, raising him up like a *djed* pillar so that he could ascend to the heavens as he made the transition from living monarch to dead pharaoh. Such a transition is also indicated at Jesus' "transfiguration" — so closely patterned after the exodus event. In this mythic account, Jesus appears first as a mere human but later is transformed into a glorified being, thus foreshadowing his resurrection. He would indeed be raised from the dead, just as the *djed* pillar that signified Osiris was set upright after the pharaoh's death.

But what of Orion? What was the nature of his myth?

In Roman legend, Orion was paired with the virgin huntress Diana. She was enamored of him and therefore invited him to join her on a hunt. But fate intervened in the form of Diana's rather protective brother, the sun god Apollo, who did not fancy the idea of Orion deflowering his virgin sister. He therefore told the earth goddess Gaia that Orion had boasted he could kill every animal on the face of the earth, an affront that provoked Gaia to send forth a scorpion to pursue him. Fearing for his safety upon seeing this creature coming after him, the great hunter jumped into the water and swam off. Unfortunately for Orion, Apollo's plan was not so easily thwarted. When the sun god saw that his quarry had escaped Gaia's scorpion, he came up with another plan to end Orion's amorous overtures toward his sister: He told Diana herself that the distant figure making its way through the water (Orion) was nothing more than a ne'er-do-well pirate who had ravished one of the goddess' devotees. Furious upon hearing this, Diana drew her bowstring and let fly with an arrow that pierced the helpless Orion through the head. Upon realizing her mistake, she mourned his death and placed him among the stars as the constellation to which he gave his name.

Though the story includes several novel details, its basic elements are much older than the Roman myth in which they are embedded. And these elements, not surprisingly, come directly from Egyptian and Palestinian lore.

Diana is none other than the virgin war goddess Anat or Tanit, who was depicted mourning the death of her hunter consort Baal. She also bears a certain resemblance to Isis, likewise revered as a virgin who mourned the death of her heroic consort — in this case Osiris, who was in turn associated with the constellation Orion. And these two myths have yet another point of contact, as well. In the Orion tale, the hero is slain as he moves through the water. In the case of Osiris, the god-man is trapped in a magnificent chest, which is then cast adrift on the waters of the Nile.

Across the River Styx

Crossing a body of water was no simple matter to the ancients. It was a task of momentous import. According to Egyptian and Hebrew myth, for example, the earth had arisen out of a great watery void. Water, therefore, marked the boundary between the land of the living and the kingdom of eternity — symbolic of the frontier that must be crossed at death.

In Greece, the dead were conveyed across the River Styx by a ferryman who brought them into the underworld. Relatives of the dead often buried them with a coin in their mouths, so they would have some payment to offer the ferryman in exchange for delivering them safely to their destination. Several tales depict Hermes as a guide of sorts on this journey to the land of the dead.[173]

The waters of the Styx had the power to render one immortal, as demonstrated by the case of Achilles. His mother, Thetis, sought to "wash away" his mortality by dipping his entire body in the sacred river — all save for one of his heels, which she held as she immersed him. It was, of course, this very spot where the great hero was fated to be mortally wounded.

In another version of the same myth, Thetis seeks to immortalize him by roasting his flesh in fire at night. This tale recalls the efforts of Isis to accomplish the very same purpose by similar means for the infant son of Queen Astarte. It was in this myth, so closely linked with traditions of Osiris, that Isis took on the guise of a nursemaid and secretly passed the infant's body over a blazing hearth at the same time every evening. She would then assume the form of a swallow and fly around the chamber, encircling the pillar wherein her dead husband was entombed. By flapping her wings, Isis was in effect guiding the spirit of her dead husband toward the body of the newborn babe, transferring the right of kingship from the dead king to an infant heir. This was the principle of royal immortality in operation.

"The king is dead! Long live the king!"

The motif of crossing the river also is familiar from the myth of Isis, who had been banned from speaking before the council of the gods in behalf of her son, Horus. The queen-goddess, however, was unwilling to take no for an answer. Desperate to present the case for Horus' accession to the throne, she disguised herself to fool the ferryman, who had been ordered to deny her passage across the waters. Her disguise proved effective, and she was therefore able to pass beyond the boundary between the world of men and the world of the gods.

Other echoes of Egyptian myth may be found in the Greek traditions. Just as Hermes served as a guide to the dead, so his Egyptian counterpart, Thoth, was said to oversee the soul's passage from this life to the next. In this capacity, he supervised a ceremony in which the heart of the deceased was placed upon the scales of justice. If the heart failed to tip the balance when weighed against a feather, the person was deemed to have lived a virtuous life and was considered worthy of entry into the heavenly realm of Osiris. It was Thoth who recorded the results of this great test, inscribing the name of the virtuous soul in a sort of Egyptian book of life. Meanwhile, it was the dog-headed god Anubis who performed the actual weighing.

(Much of this imagery would eventually make its way into Christian traditions concerning the so-called last judgment.)

It is probably no coincidence that a dog played a pivotal role in the Greek myth of the underworld, as well. It was this "hound of hell" that Hercules subdued on a quest that took him to the nether region, making him one of the few to survive this arduous journey. During this particular quest, he was forced to cross the waters of Styx and return again to the land of the living, abducting the fierce dog guardian in the process.

This was not the only time Hercules was compelled to take part in a symbolic crossing of the waters. In a related tale, he set forth on a quest to retrieve a herd of cattle kept under the watchful eye of a certain monster on an island to the west. To help him perform this task, the sun god gave Hercules a golden cup he used as a vessel that enabled him to navigate the ocean on his journey. In this story, interestingly enough, it is a chalice that serves as a sort of ark that allows Hercules to survive the harrowing trip to the netherworld. The importance of this connection will become apparent as our inquiry continues.

As a monument to this journey, the hero is said to have set up two pillars — the so-called pillars of Hercules that mark the Straits of Gibraltar at the western edge of the ancient world. Beyond these great rocky outcroppings that flank the entrance to the Mediterranean, dry land gives way to what must have seemed like an endless ocean. It was across this ocean, toward the sunset, that the mystic isle of eternity was said to lie.

Could these pillars have been based upon the pillars of ancient Egypt? The two great mountains that held up the veil of the sky? The pillars that were said to have guarded the temple of King Solomon — the pillars known as Jachin and Boaz?

The answers will become clear enough in due course. But leaving that aside for the moment, it is enough to say that the two pillars in question clearly marked the boundary between the world of the living and the vast expanse of water that had to be crossed to reach the world of the dead.

The Great Flood

Perhaps the most famous legend involving a hero who crossed a great body of water is that of the patriarch Noah. The story is so familiar that many can recite the details from memory. According to the Hebrew legend, Noah is instructed to build a great "ark" in preparation for a massive flood that was destined to inundate the earth. On the surface, it might not seem as though this story fits the pattern of the others. There is no river crossing per se, and no ferryman to serve as a guide for the beleaguered hero. Yet despite this, there is little doubt that the theme of death and resurrection lies at the very heart of this tale. God is quoted as saying he is sorry he has made the race of men and vows to sweep them all away in a raging torrent of water. Only the virtuous Noah and his family are deemed worthy to survive and become keepers of the new world that will supplant the old one once the floodwaters have receded. They are therefore given fair warning to prepare by building an ark in which to ride out the coming storm.

What exactly is this ark?

It is generally portrayed as having been a giant boat of some sort, but the Hebrew word used in this case means simply "box." Not boat. Not ship. Not even raft. It is, interestingly enough, the same word used to describe the vessel in which Moses was cast adrift on the Nile as an infant.

And this story of Moses was, in turn, modeled after the myth of Osiris — who likewise was cast adrift in a box upon the Nile after he was slain. In this case, of course, the box was nothing less than a casket, indicating that the journey down the Nile was in fact a passage into the mystical land of the dead. This was the journey of Osiris; it was also, apparently, the journey of Noah.

This is confirmed by the source of the Noah legend, which has long been recognized as the Babylonian epic of Gilgamesh. The similarities between the two accounts are far too numerous to be mere coincidence, and the details upon which they differ add the missing pieces to the puzzle of Noah's legend — exposing it as an allegory of life and death.

The tale of Gilgamesh is one of great tragedy. It is the struggle of one man, a heroic god-king, to reconcile himself to the senseless death of his dearest friend and come to terms with his own mortality. As with so many, this latter challenge is one he is loath to accept. So instead, still mourning the demise of his beloved comrade, he sets forth on a quest to cheat fate by somehow finding the secret to eternal life. And to this end, he resolves to find the one man who is said to have learned this secret, the legendary hero Utnapishtim.

This man lives beyond the so-called "waters of death" — yet another reference to the boundary that separates the world of the living from the hereafter. And once again, this boundary can be crossed only with the help of a ferryman, who agrees to escort the hero across the sacred waters.

What does any of this have to do with Noah?

In fact, it has *everything* to do with him. For once Gilgamesh has crossed the "waters of death," he finds himself face-to-face with the man he has so resolutely sought — Utnapishtim. Here was the man who had conquered death and could share with Gilgamesh the secret of doing so. After welcoming Gilgamesh, he recounts an epic saga of a great flood with which the gods had resolved to inundate all the earth. One of the gods, however, took pity on him and gave him the following instructions:

> *Tear down (this) house and build a ship...*
> *Aboard this ship, take the seed of all living things*
> *The ship that you shall build*
> *Her dimensions you shall measure*
> *Equal shall be her width and length*[174]

This sounds an awful lot like the legend of Noah, who was commanded to "bring into the ark two of all living creatures, male and female" — in other words, the seed of all living things.[175] Moreover, a ship of equal width and length doesn't sound so much like a ship as a box — the exact meaning of the Hebrew word that is used to describe the vessel in question. Utnapishtim therefore appears to have crossed the "waters of death" in a box, or a casket, and has arrived safely on the other side. Upon his arrival, things proceed along lines that closely parallel the Noah myth.

Utnapishtim's vessel, like that of Noah, comes to rest on the top of a mountain.

Events then proceed apace:

➢ Noah "opened the window he had made in the ark and sent out a raven, and it kept flying back and forth until the water had dried up from the earth." Utnapishtim "set free a dove. The dove went forth and came back. Since no resting place for it was visible, she turned round."

➢ Noah then "sent out a dove to see if the water had receded from the surface of the ground. But the dove could find no place to set its feet because there was water all over the surface of the earth; so it returned to Noah in the ark." Utnapishtim "set free a swallow. The swallow went forth, but came back; since no resting place for it was visible, she turned round."

> Noah "waited seven more days and again sent out the dove from the ark. When the dove returned to him in the evening, there in its beak was a freshly plucked olive leaf. Then Noah knew that the water had receded from the earth." Utnapishtim "set free a raven. The raven went forth and, seeing the waters had diminished, he eats, circles, caws and turns not around."

> Noah "built an altar to Yahweh and, taking some of all the clean animals and clean birds, he sacrificed burnt offerings on it." Utnapishtim "let out to the four winds and offered a sacrifice." [176]

From the numerous parallels, it is obvious that either the two stories have a common origin or one is based upon the other. The Gilgamesh legend, being the older of the two, is the logical candidate as the more primitive form of the tale. Ultimately, Gilgamesh pleads with his host to share with him eternal life. In response, the old man presents him with a challenge: If he can go without sleep for six days and seven nights, he will be adjudged worthy to live forever. This, of course, proves to be an impossible task, and Gilgamesh quickly falls into a deep sleep.

In ancient circles, sleep was often used as a euphemism for death. The moral of the story?

No one lives forever — not even great heroes like Gilgamesh and Utnapishtim. All must sleep and cross the "waters of death" to partake of the eternal kingdom that lies beyond the boundaries of life. Utnapishtim's crossing of the waters in his square boat implies a journey in a coffin across the sea. Noah's passage in a box from the old world swept away by a great flood to a brave new world symbolizes the very same sort of journey.

The Egyptians seem to have recognized this, for near one pyramid, they buried six large, wooden boats. And on the Giza plateau itself, a cedar boat measuring more than one hundred and forty feet in length was discovered in a pit just south of the Great Pyramid itself. [177]

Could this be Noah's ark, or at least a representation of it?

The Ziggurat

The driving behind the Great Pyramid of Giza is a shadowy figure of a man. A pharaoh who lived forty-five centuries ago, he left scant record of his reign beyond a few paragraphs preserved by much later historians. His name was Khufu, though he is referred to more commonly as Cheops or Suphis — perhaps a nickname earned from his apparent obsession for stonework. The name would survive in a slightly altered form centuries later, when it would be worn by a man named Cephas.

Or Peter.

Literally, "the rock."

No one would have deserved such a name more than this particular pharaoh, who directed what remains to all accounts the most ambitious stone construction project ever undertaken. It involved thousands of tons of rock, hauled large distances and arranged with exacting precision in a shape of a stylized mountain. It is a shape that brings to mind the legend of Noah, whose ark supposedly came to rest on a high range of hills known as the "mountains of Ararat." [178] The location of this particular range has long been disputed, but the text probably refers to a mountainous region in modern Armenia that was known in ancient times as Arrata or Uratu.

This is, needless to say, a long way from Egypt — several hundred miles in fact. But the connection between the two regions is more concrete than their geography might suggest. Abram, for one, is said to have traveled from the city of Ur in Mesopotamia to Egypt, where he settled and founded the Hyksos dynasty. Yet the pyramids predate Abram by a good seven centuries, indicating that the connection between the two lands stretches back much further. In tracing that connection, a good place to start is the ancient epic known as *Enmerkar and the Lord of Arrata*.

The principal character in this drama, Enmerkar, is a king of Uruk, a city on the floodplain of southern Mesopotamia that also happened to be the home city of Gilgamesh.

Uruk was a thriving metropolis in ancient times, and was well enough known to make an appearance in the Hebrew texts under the name "Erech." [179] It is one of the most extensive ancient sites in Mesopotamia, a fortified metropolis whose walls extended nearly seven miles and enclosed the city.[180] At the time of Enmerkar, its power was waxing, and the monarch was eager to test his growing might and expand the bounds of his kingdom. Yet to do so, he knew, he would need the blessing of the goddess of love and war Inanna — the Sumerian counterpart of Ishtar and Isis — whose statue resided in the mountain kingdom of Uratu to the north. To this end, he proceeded to remove the statue from Uratu and transport it to his own city, where he then constructed a temple to house the divine image. This temple he made in the likeness of the mountains whence she came, set upon one of three main hills at the center of the city. Its grandeur must have been such that it appeared to be a mountain itself, one of many such temples to be built around the region.

Such symbolism was entirely natural considering it came from Uratu, a lofty district of high plateaus and snowy peaks whose very name meant "mountain" in the language of the day. And was equally natural that the ancient skyscraper should be dubbed a mountain — specifically a high mountain. This is the meaning of the word ziggurat, which stems from two roots in the ancient Sumerian tongue:

Zig = rising.
Uratu = mountain.

Perhaps the first great ziggurat was the temple to Inanna erected by Enmerkar in his capital city of Uruk. This was the structure that passed into legend as the Tower of Babel, a title that was mistranslated by the Hebrew scribes as meaning "confusion" or "chaos." According to these scribes, it was derived from the word *balal*, which indeed carries this connotation. But there is something less than convincing about this assertion. First of all, the Hebrew word is hardly an exact homonym for the famous tower. Second, and even more significantly, it is a *Hebrew* word. The scribes who wrote of the great tower were well aware that the events they were relating had transpired not in Palestine but Mesopotamia, and they should have known to look for the roots of any such title in the language of that region. Had they done so, they would have certainly found the explanation they sought. In point of fact, the title Babel had nothing to do with confusion; it was based upon a Babylonian word with a decidedly more positive connotation: *bab-ili*, meaning "gate of God."

Why should the Hebrew scribes have erred in their understanding of this particular term? And why should they have associated the raising of this particular tower with a myth in which a seemingly paranoid divine council of the Elohim passes the following resolution: "Come, let us go down and confuse their language, so they will not understand each other"? [181]

Actually, they had a very good reason for doing so.

As it turns out, the same Sumerian epic that tells of the tower's construction also contains a reference to just such an event. In a brief aside, the author of *Enmerkar and the Lord of Arrata* refers to an episode in which the god Enki changed the speech of men's mouths, substituting contention and confusion where there had once been harmony. The Hebrew scribes seem to have simply latched onto this passage and assumed it had something to do with the construction of Inanna's ziggurat temple, which lies at the heart of the narrative. The supposed similarity between the Hebrew word for confusion and the tower's name only served to transform the link from assumption to solid conclusion — at least in the minds of the scribes.

It was a stretch, but few have questioned it since.

As to the tower itself, it was one of several ziggurats to have been erected on the Mesopotamian floodplain. Their builders gave these artificial mountains such exalted names as the "Temple which Links Heaven and Earth" in the city of Larsa and the "Temple of the Stairway of Pure Heaven" in Sippar, the center of the sun cult. Such titles expressed the ambition of their builders to bridge the chasm that separated the temporal world from the mystical land of the gods, an ambition preserved by the Hebrew scribes in describing the Tower of Babel: "Come, let us build ourselves a city with a tower that reaches to the heavens." [182]

The steps that ascended the temple indeed formed a stairway to heaven.

Or, as the title Babel signified, a gateway to god.

This was the central function of the ziggurats, artificial mountains that were the precursors to the pyramids. The Egyptians faithfully preserved the concept of a stairway to heaven by crafting a ritual in which the dead pharaoh ascended his heavenly throne, a ritual that eventually found its way into Hebrew tradition as the legend of Jacob's ladder. But they did not stop at retaining the symbolism of the ziggurat; they retained its form as well, faithfully reproducing it in the nation's first great synthetic mountain, Imhotep's step pyramid at a site known as Saqqara. One does not have to be a linguistic expert to notice the resemblance between the name of this site and the term ziggurat, the more ancient spelling of which was *ziqquratu*.

Within a few years of its construction, pyramids had become all the rage in Egypt, with the step-sided form giving way to the more stylized version employed by Cheops. But despite this variation, he remained true to the original myth by burying a boat or ark at the foot of his mountain — just as Noah's ark had landed on the mountains of Ararat or Uratu. It had been there that the image of Inanna had been housed before its removal to Uruk, site of the first ziggurat. And thus the name remained sacred for millennia to come, though the reason for such reverence was apparently all but forgotten.

If the pyramids were stairways to heaven, what could the ark have been but a vessel to carry the deceased across the waters of death to his brave new kingdom? Egyptian literature contains numerous references to such "arks" or "barks," which were designed for just such a purpose. Among them was the so-called bark of Osiris, which no doubt represented the sacred casket in which the god-king was encased and cast adrift on the waters of the Nile.

The fact that just such a boat was found in the Giza pyramid complex is interesting. The Giza plateau is adjacent to the Nile, indicating that the boat was meant to traverse the great river. It was, in fact, meant to be used by the dead king, whose mummified remains were entombed in the pyramid itself, and who was fated to re-enact the journey of Osiris.

As he himself *became* Osiris.

Yet there is even more symbolism here than at first there might appear. Independent researchers have noticed that the three pyramids on the Giza Plateau were sized and aligned deliberately to reflect the positioning of three stars in the evening sky. And not just any three stars, but the three stars that make up what we know today as Orion's belt.[183] This was the very constellation that, to the ancient Egyptians, represented Osiris himself. And beside it, running like a starry current bisecting the black of night, was the serpentine concentration of stars we know as the Milky Way. A river in the sky to mirror the great River Nile on the earth — a river which the dead king might navigate by means of a bark.

Or ark.

Which brings us back to the person of Aaron, a.k.a. Orion.

There is one notable reference to an ark in the Hebrew writings that has yet to be addressed. Though not as famous as Noah's boxy vessel, it is nearly so. This is, of course, the Ark of the Covenant — the container Moses supposedly built to carry the stone tablets upon which were inscribed the divine commandments. It must be pointed out that Hebrew word for ark, in this case, is different than the one used to describe the ark of Noah. But its meaning is virtually the same: a box — specifically, a chest or coffin. And the Hebrew word itself removes any doubt as to its relevance to this particular line of inquiry: It was called, quite simply, an *aron*.

This chest supposedly contained not only the tablets of the covenant, but also the magical staff of Aaron.[184] On one occasion, it was said, this staff had actually sprouted forth with buds, blossoms and even almonds.[185] One need not look too hard to find the obvious phallic symbolism at work here. The fact that the staff of Aaron bore fruit — even almonds, a kind of seed — indicates all too clearly what the imagery was meant to convey. This was the sacred principle of procreation in action.

And procreation was crucial to the Egyptian cycle. It was by this means that the spirit of kingship passed from one pharaoh to the next, traversing the generations from dead Osiris to living Horus as the process repeated itself continually through all eternity. To the Egyptians, the three stars at the heart of Orion were not his "belt" at all, but his staff or phallus — by which he impregnated his celestial queen Isis, symbolized either by the bright star Sirius or by the virgin constellation of Virgo. The result of their union was the new king, or Horus, god made flesh and sent to earth as benevolent ruler of the two lands.

As the pyramid texts proclaimed:

> *Your sister-wife Isis comes to you*
> *Rejoicing for love of you*
> *You have placed her on your phallus*
> *And your seed issues into her*
> *She being ready as Sirius*
> *And Horus-Sopd has come forth from you*
> *As Horus who is in Sirius* [186]

Such language leaves nothing to the imagination. And neither did the Egyptians. They had to make certain that the eternal cycle of Osiris-Horus-Osiris continued unbroken from one generation to the next. To do so, they had to make sure the dead king was buried in proper fashion. The bark of Osiris was prepared and placed alongside the pyramid to bear him across the "waters of death." And the pyramid itself was constructed to unite his spirit with the heavenly realm for which it was bound. Indeed, a long and narrow shaft led from the king's chamber in the Great Pyramid to the exterior, angled toward the expanse of heaven. The builders seem to have intended this as a gateway to the stars, for it points directly at Orion's belt. In like manner, a similar shaft leading from the queen's chamber is set at an angle that takes direct aim at Sirius.

Everything appears to be coming together:

- Aron = a chest.
- Osiris = dying king who was buried in a chest.
- Orion = constellation that embodied the dying king.

It would appear, then, that Aaron must have been a dead king? But which one?

It would be easy to conclude that he was, in fact, King Kamose. After all, Aaron is portrayed as Moses' older brother — just as Kamose was Ahmose's elder sibling. Yet there is one sticking point here: The mummy of Kamose has been discovered, and it seems clear that the ark or casket bearing the remains of this particular king was carried about from one place to another. Why would this have been so? Why would the dead king not have been given a proper sendoff to his celestial haven from a chamber in the heart of some great pyramid or temple?

Perhaps because there was no time for such a grand burial.

Perhaps because the pharaoh in question was forced to flee by some great crisis.

Perhaps because his people were refugees.

All these things point squarely to the very real possibility that the remains carried in this particular ark were those of none other than Solomon Apophis, who appears to have lost his life at some point during the Theban uprising. In the midst of such a conflict, there would have been no time for an elaborate burial ceremony. The king's attendants would have been forced to improvise, and they seem to have done so by sealing the pharaoh's body in a mobile sarcophagus that accompanied them as the trekked across the desert. It is even possible that the pharaoh did not die in Avaris at all, but met his end at some point during this journey. There is evidence of this in the Koran, which contains an account of the pharaoh's departure from Egypt and maintains that he died in an attempt to cross the Red Sea (actually the *reed* sea).

The theme of crossing the "waters of death" is strikingly apparent in this narrative, for these waters do indeed prove deadly for the unfortunate pharaoh. As they prepare to engulf him, however, he cries out for divine mercy and receives the following response: "This day we shall deliver your body, that you may be a sign to those who come after you." [187] The implication is that the pharaoh's life was taken, but that his body was somehow delivered or spared. The question is, what was done with it? The obvious answer is that it was deposited in a golden chest or ark until such time as it could be placed in a proper setting, a temple or pyramid that would serve as the final resting place for the great king Solomon Apophis.

Such a time would eventually come.

Centuries after the expulsion of the Hyksos from the delta, a temple would be built in the Palestinian city of Jerusalem that came to be known as the great temple of Solomon. As time passed, a legend would develop that Solomon himself had ordered the construction of this temple, but this can hardly have been the case. He was, after all, long dead by the time it was erected. The truth of the matter is, the temple was named for Solomon not because he had ordered it built, but *because it housed his remains*. This was the express purpose for which the temple was constructed: to house the sacred reliquary known as the ark.

The ark that contained the remains of king Solomon.

This was doubtless a modest structure for, as we have seen, archaeologists have failed to discover any trace of it. For many years, the ark was actually housed in something no more substantial than a tent or tabernacle. Whether the temple actually ever took a more permanent form than this is unknown, but it was certainly not the grand and imposing structure suggested in the Hebrew scriptures. It took on this aspect only when it came to be confused, at some point, with the great temple to Seth built by Solomon Apophis during his own actual lifetime.

As to the ark itself, however, it was far more than a simple sarcophagus. It was altar, throne and good luck charm all rolled into one. Its appearance was quite distinctive: Fashioned from acacia wood and covered completely in gold, it was crowned with a so-called "atonement seat" that was itself flanked by two impressive looking figures. Each was identified as a *karuwb* or cherub, but these were not the baby-faced, angelic cherubs depicted in paintings from a much later age. They were most likely representations of the twin sisters Isis and Nephthys, two goddesses often represented as winged women. Symbolic of life and death, they were commonly depicted as attendants of Osiris in the funerary inscriptions of the pharaohs. So it would have been natural to include representations of them on the mobile reliquary that housed the remains of Solomon Apophis in his role as Osiris.

As to the word cherub, its origins bear closer examination. Like so many others, it appears to stem from an Egyptian composite. In all likelihood, it did not originally refer to the two winged figures by themselves, but to the ark as a whole. And it seems to have been derived from *kher heb*, a name for the Egyptian high priest, a designation that would make sense considering that Aaron was the prototypical high priest according to Hebrew tradition.

And this *aron* was his resting place.

Another possibility is that it stemmed from two other Egyptian roots:

- *Khrw* = voice
- *Ib* = heart

This, too, would make sense. In latter days, when the ark was placed the temple of Solomon, it was housed a sanctuary at the very *heart* of the tabernacle. It was here that the *voice* of Yahweh could be heard. Indeed, the sanctuary itself was called the *debir*, a word that appears to stem from the Hebrew root verb meaning "to speak." (Hence, the Hebrew prophetess Deborah's name meant "Ra speaks.") But only one person was privileged to hear this voice: he who held the office of high priest. And this high priest had to be a direct descendant of Aaron.

Once each year, on the Day of Atonement, the high priest would enter the sanctuary and purify it with a the blood of a goat. This was to be a sacrifice on behalf of all the people. Before he could offer it, however, he was required to make a sacrifice on his own behalf — not of a goat, but of a bull. This sacrifice, first performed by Aaron himself, reflected a celestial encounter involving Orion and its neighboring constellation, the bull Taurus. This parallel only serves to further reinforce the identification of Aaron with Orion.

Or Osiris.

All this was part of an elaborate atonement ritual that was perhaps the central rite of Judaism. Having sacrificed the bull for his own sins, it was now the high priest's duty to sacrifice the goat for the sins of the people. In fact, however, this ceremony involved not one, but two goats, chosen by lot to perform very different functions. One was to be sacrificed on the atonement seat that covered the ark, while the other was to be sent off into the desert. The symbolism here is nothing less than astounding. The two goats seem to represent the two archetypal brothers Osiris and Seth, the first of whom was slain and entombed in a floating chest or ark, while the second survived and became lord of the desert wastelands.

Confirmation of this can be found in the legend of Esau and

Jacob, two brothers whose saga mirrored the ancient battle between Seth and Osiris/Horus. Recall that in this tale, Jacob's mother instructs him to impersonate Esau in an attempt to steal his older brother's blessing from their ailing father. The ruse depends upon Jacob first going out and killing two goats, which he uses to prepare a favorite meal for the bedridden patriarch Isaac.

This motif, interestingly, mirrors that present in another Seth-Horus conflict — this one between two brothers in *Genesis*. In this tale, Cain prepares a grain offering for the Elohim but is spurned in favor of a sacrifice from the flocks of his younger brother Abel. As in the legend of Jacob and Esau, the younger brother wins a blessing by offering a lamb or goat to a father figure (the Elohim); Cain subsequently kills Abel, just as Seth murders Osiris and Esau seeks to kill Jacob.

Each story is merely a variation on the same theme, dating back to the archetypal Egyptian myth and doubtless much earlier in oral tradition. Osiris was the key figure in this myth, and it was for this reason that a son of Aaron was the only person permitted to enter the inner sanctuary of the Hebrew temple: He was the only one fit to re-enact the death and rebirth of Osiris.

When Solomon had died, he had *become* Osiris. Or Orion. Or Aaron. It was therefore only appropriate that "a son of Aaron" should take part in this most solemn of ceremonies. His function? To assume the role of Osiris himself, who had been slain but had been miraculously raised to life. The temple was the perfect setting to re-enact this epic tale because it was, like the pyramids, a tomb. And the inner sanctuary was nothing less than a burial vault, containing the ark. Just as the king's burial chamber stood at the heart of the ancient pyramids, so the inner sanctuary stood at the heart of the temple. When the son of Aaron entered this sacred vault, it was as though he were symbolically dying himself. When he emerged once more, he ritually rose from the dead — just as Osiris had done.

A similar ceremony seems to have taken place in the pyramids. Upon the death of the old king, his body would be mummified and placed in a funeral vault at the center of the pyramid. The *kher heb* priest would then enter and oversee the ritual slaughter of a bull.[188] This, of course, mirrors the Jewish high priest's act of sacrificing a bull on the altar in the temple of Solomon. At this point, the dead pharaoh's son or a priestly representative would step forward to perform a ritual known as the opening of the mouth. For this task, he would use an axe-like tool with a curved blade to physically pry open the dead king's mouth.

A passage from the pyramid texts contains the formula that was recited during this ceremony:

> *O, King, I have come in search of you*
> *For I am Horus*
> *I have struck your mouth for you*
> *For I am your beloved son*
> *I have split open your mouth for you* [189]

What was the purpose of this bizarre ceremony? The idea was to reanimate the corpse by opening its mouth, along with its eyes. The most common reasons to open one's mouth are to eat and to speak. It is therefore reasonable to conclude that new king was parting his father's lips to "feed" him and hear his spiritual voice. Just as the high priest would enter the inner sanctuary to hear the voice of God the Father, so the new king or Horus would enter the pyramid vault to hear the voice of god *his* father. In the great mythic cycle, Osiris had given counsel to his only son from beyond the grave in preparation Horus' epic battle with Seth. This would seem to indicate that the next step in the ritual would have been a re-enactment of that battle, and there is evidence to suggest that this was, in fact, the case.

Before considering the nature of this ritual, however, it is important to answer one question: How did the figures of Solomon Apophis (a.k.a. Aaron) and Moses, mortal enemies on opposite sides of an epic conflict, come to be viewed as allies in a common cause and even brothers?

In addressing this incongruity, it must be remembered that the writings of the ancients are equal parts history, myth and political propaganda. And the Hebrew scribes were adept at interlacing strands of fact with details that were purely symbolic. Long after they surrendered to the Theban forces, the remnants of the Hyksos army still clung to their memories of a golden age under the wise king Solomon. This great, compassionate ruler remained a shining example to them, and history demanded that he be accorded his due. Yet on the other hand, Moses had prevailed by force of arms, and now *he* likewise had to be duly acknowledged. Such a situation might seem impossible to reconcile, but the Hebrew scribes — unconstrained by the modern historian's obligation to linear chronologies — managed to pull it off. By rewriting history to portray the two as allies rather than enemies, they were able to harmonize these two conflicting aims in a manner worthy of the wise King Solomon himself.

Even so, however, they were not able to erase the memory of what had actually happened — not entirely. Even after they had completed their synthesis, the echoes of enmity could still be heard at places within the text. Indeed, on more than one occasion, Aaron is explicitly depicted not as Moses' ally but his adversary. At one point, Aaron and his sister conspire to oppose Moses *because of his Ethiopian wife*.

This seems like a rather trifling matter on the face of it. But this Ethiopian wife was, in fact, no one to be trifled with. She was none other than the Queen of Sheba, who held in her hands the balance of power between the Hyksos and the Thebans. Unwittingly, the scribes seem to have preserved a dim memory of the rivalry between Apophis and Ahmose over this woman — a woman who at some point during their conflict deserted the Hyksos pharaoh to forge an alliance with the Theban king.

The Hero and the Bull

And this is not the only apparent example of discord between Aaron and Moses. Their mutual antagonism seems to come through just as strongly in the famous legend of the golden calf, an idol forged in Moses' absence on the express instructions of Aaron. The situation was this: Moses had lingered at the top of the mountain after receiving the sacred tablets, causing his followers to fear that he had disappeared for good. They therefore called upon Aaron to "make a god" to go before them as a sort of substitute for Moses himself.

Not only did Aaron fail to object, he was in fact more than ready to comply. Taking the bull by the horns, so to speak, he instructed the people to remove their earrings and hand them over to him. He then presumably had them melted down and recast in the shape of a golden calf.

It was natural that he should select this particular creature as the inspiration for his idol, for the bull was a sacred symbol of Egyptian kingship. Indeed, the so-called Apis bull was considered a manifestation of Osiris himself and was so closely identified with the god that the two were actually merged in later antiquity under the cult of "Serapis" (a conflation of the names Osiris and Apis). In hindsight, it seems almost inevitable that these two figures should have become linked. Their origins were in the stars, and their constellations stood adjacent to one another in the night sky — the mighty king poised for battle and the "bull of heaven" that shadowed him across the sky.

Orion and Taurus.

These two constellations were inextricably linked in the minds of the ancients. The Egyptians may have merged them in late antiquity, but they were originally seen as mortal enemies, often depicted as two rivals engaged in a ritual combat. In Persia, for example, the heroic god Mithras was lauded for having slain a mythic bull. And Orion himself appeared to be holding up a shield or bow to protect himself from the wrath of the charging sky bull.

Even the Babylonian hero Gilgamesh, so closely linked with the "waters of death" and the original story of the ark, was said to have done battle with the great bull of heaven. The story is fascinating, for it or some story like it appears to have served as the basis for the opening of the mouth ceremony practiced by the Egyptians. In this account, Gilgamesh incurs the wrath of Ishtar, the queen of heaven, by spurning her advances and impugning her reputation — basically calling her an unfaithful whore. The goddess, quite understandably, flies into a rage and appeals to her father, the sun god Shamash, to unleash the bull of heaven against her accuser.

(Here again, a point of contact should be noted with the legend of King Solomon, who is said to have built a "high place" dedicated to this very god.)[190]

In the Babylonian myth, Shamash is at first reluctant to grant his daughter's request. But when she throws a huge tantrum and threatens to unleash the dead on the world of the living, he at last consents. There ensues a heroic battle pitting Gilgamesh and his comrade Enkidu against the fearsome creature, a struggle described in vivid language on a series of tablets from Mesopotamia:

> *With his third snort, he sprang at Enkidu*
> *But Enkidu parried his onslaught*
> *Up leaped Enkidu*
> *Seizing the bull of heaven by the horns*
> *The bull of heaven hurled foam in his face*
> *And brushed him with the thick of his tail*

Shortly after this, the text becomes mutilated and unreadable, but when it picks up Gilgamesh is finishing off the dreaded beast: "Between neck and horns he thrust his sword." This imagery is almost identical to the numerous depictions of Mithras that have survived in ancient engravings and sculptures. In these, the hero is portrayed half astride the great bull, grasping the animal by the nostrils and jerking its head back as he thrusts a sword into its neck. The celestial character of this struggle is confirmed by the presence of a zodiac framing many of these engravings. Such parallel imagery would seem to indicate that the stories of Mithras and Gilgamesh are, in fact, one and the same.

Having defeated the great bull, Gilgamesh and Enkidu glory in their victory, gloating to no small extent before Ishtar and her father. Standing before the great sun god, they make a show of ripping out the slain bull's heart and placing it before him in a grisly display. This sends Ishtar into an even greater fury, and she announces a curse against Gilgamesh: "Woe unto Gilgamesh, for he has insulted me by slaying the bull of heaven."

Enkidu, however, is having none of it. Far from being intimidated by her ranting, he responds in kind with an overt threat. Tearing loose the dead bull's thigh, he flings it insolently in the goddess' face, proclaiming rashly: "If I could only get at you, I would do the same to you as I have done to him. His entrails I would hang at your side." [191] This bit of bravado is meant to explain the presence in the night sky of yet another constellation, our Big Dipper, which the ancient Egyptians identified as a thigh. This constellation rotates once around the Pole Star every twenty-four hours, giving the impression that it is flying through the air — having been flung at the enraged goddess by the boastful Enkidu.

In the Babylonian myth, however, the goddess is to have the last laugh — as is usually the case with gods and goddesses. For shortly after the battle, Enkidu falls ill and dies, perhaps from wounds inflicted by the bull of heaven. It is this great tragedy that impels Gilgamesh to embark on his journey across the waters of death in his ultimately futile search for the secret of eternal life.

This myth (or an Egyptian version of it) appears to have served as the basis for the ritual re-enactment undertaken by the priests of Egypt at the opening of the mouth. During this ceremony, a bull was slain. And, as in the Gilgamesh epic, its heart was torn from its chest and one of its legs severed.[192] Two priests were present for this ritual, the *kher heb* who served as the counterpart to Gilgamesh and an associate known as the *sem* priest who represented Enkidu — two men described as "brothers" in the Babylonian tablets.

Flash forward to the legend of Aaron and Moses.

These two brothers seem to enact a similar ritual in the story of the golden bull or calf. Aaron oversees the creation of this golden sculpture, which Moses subsequently dashes to bits. The Hebrew scribes interpreted his reaction as an expression of divine wrath against a profane idol. Yet it seems more than a little odd that Aaron should have maintained his esteemed position as high priest after indulging in this apparently gross act of idolatry. Unless, of course, the creation of the golden calf wasn't idolatry at all. Unless it was, in fact, part of an elaborate ritual re-enactment similar to the opening of the mouth. Indeed, this appears to have been precisely the case: The bull was created not to serve as an idol, but for the express purpose of being slain by the hero, Moses, who is cast in the role of Mithras, Gilgamesh, Orion and Osiris.

This was the whole point of the ritual. Without the golden bull, it could not even take place. In order for one to stage an epic battle, a hero is certainly needed — but an adversary is also essential. They are, in a sense, two sides of the same coin, as inseparable as the two constellations of Orion and Taurus in the night sky. This would explain why the Apis bull is seen as a manifestation of Osiris himself on the one hand, while at the same time playing the part of his mortal enemy.

One would almost expect the bull to be seen as the embodiment of the great god's nemesis, Seth.

And indeed, this was the case.

It turns out the star cluster known as the Hyades — at the heart of the bull constellation — was in ancient times associated with this very god.[193] Just as these two twin gods were at enmity with each other in the world of myth, so they likewise stood ever poised to engage one another in combat on the celestial battlefield. The names and symbols involved in this great eternal struggle between good and evil tug at the back of the mind, longing to be recognized for what they are.

> Seth (Set) = Satan, the demon with horns like those of a bull.
> Hyades = Hades, his heavenly domain.

This great celestial struggle was carried out each year on earth as a "son of Aaron" entered the inner sanctuary and slaughtered a bull. It was part of the belief, deeply ingrained in the Egyptian psyche, that everything on earth was a mere reflection of the heavenly realm. The stars in Orion's belt found their terrestrial expression in the pyramids of Giza. The Nile River was but a mirror of the great celestial river known as the Milky Way. And Solomon's temple itself was said to have been modeled after a heavenly temple, down to the very last detail.

All this was embodied in the greatest teaching of Thoth, a single saying that, legend had it, could be found on a set of emerald tablets: "As above, so below." This saying would live on in the teaching of no less a person than Jesus, who would utter such words as "on earth as it is in heaven" and would give his followers the keys to the heavens, promising them: "Whatsoever you bind on earth shall be bound in heaven, and whatsoever you loose on earth shall be loosed in heaven." [194]

What was it that was bound?
Could it, perhaps, have been a bull?

Solomon's Ship

In light of all this, one might even expect to find an account linking Solomon with a great ship or ark.

And ideed, one does.

It is a later legend, but one that preserves all the symbolism that must have been crucial to the development of a far older tradition.

According to this story, Solomon's wife (the Queen of Sheba?) noticed that he was despondent and approached him to offer some advice. As it turned out, the counsel she offered was anything but mundane: "Tomorrow morning, call together all the carpenters in your kingdom. When they are assembled, command them to make a ship so that it can never rot, neither from sea water nor from any other cause ...." [195]

In other words, an ark.

This ship was to contain an object variously described as a bed or altar, the king's final resting place. At its head was placed the crown of King David; at its foot a marvelous sword, its hilt inlaid with precious gemstones and its blade sharper than any other. But the ship's most important cargo was to be something else: a branch cut from the crimson tree of life. According to Hebrew lore, the Elohim had planted a tree in his garden that endowed whomever might partake of it with eternal life. The first human couple, however, were restrained from tasting its fruit by certain celestial guards armed with a flaming sword.

These guards were none other than cherubs — the same figures depicted on the ark that contained Solomon's remains. The implication is that Solomon was somehow able to get past these two cherubs and partake of the tree of life, rendering him immortal. And this was only natural, for immortality was the lot of Osiris. Indeed, the symbolism of the Osiris myth permeates the story of Solomon's ship, especially in the narrative that follows. For when Solomon's wife orders her servants to sever a limb from the tree of life, they are loath to comply with her. She assures them that she will not hold it against them if they refuse her order, but in the end persuades them to carry out her wishes. When they begin to cut into the tree, however, they watch in astonishment and horror as the tree begins to bleed. It is as though they had cut into human flesh and severed a man's arm from his body.

All this recalls clearly the myth of Osiris, whose casket (or ark) had landed at Byblos and become encased in the trunk of a great tree.

If one were to have cut into this tree, one would have unwittingly cut into the flesh of Osiris himself.

It is also worth recalling that it was around this tree-pillar that the winged Isis circled, in the form of a swallow, during the bizarre ritual in which she sought to grant the infant king immortality. In like manner, a representation of the winged Isis in the form of a cherub stood facing her winged sister Nephthys on the ceremonial lid of the Ark of the Covenant.

The ship of Solomon.

In this way, the gift of eternal life was passed from the dead king to his son, the young Horus. Initially, this son of Aaron/Orion was both king and high priest, but Ahmose's victory over the Hyksos put an end to the line of "shepherd kings" that had ruled in the Nile Delta. These once-proud nobles were now subject to the Theban dynasty and could not be permitted to have their own king. Yet they could retain their ancient rituals of kingship in veiled form, transferring them to the care of the high priest who would keep them alive for generations to come.

Even if their meaning was lost on all but a select few.

One such ritual was the symbolic death and resurrection of the high priest on the Day of Atonement.

Another was the ceremony that followed, a ceremony that might be best described as the wilderness ritual.

XI

Bread from Heaven

The great combatants Seth and Horus/Osiris were the yin and yang of ancient Egypt, neither capable of existing without the other.

They were twin brothers who personified the opposite extremes of reality.

- ➤ Seth was the night sky, Horus the day.
- ➤ Seth was the storm, Horus the sun.
- ➤ Seth was the wilderness, Osiris the fertile earth.
- ➤ Horus was the hero, Seth his eternal adversary.
- ➤ Seth was the hand of death, Osiris the god of life.
- ➤ Seth ruled one half of Egypt, Horus the other.

And the king who succeeded in uniting the two lands must therefore exhibit the qualities of both great gods. Solomon Apophis was studious in this regard, worshipping Seth as his patron god but also acknowledging the sun god with a high place of his own. Indeed, Solomon himself was known as the sun king and worshipped the "most high god."

This title can only be a description of the noontime sun.

Like Apophis, the scions of the fallen Hyksos regime recognized the need to acknowledge both these great warring gods. This is why, on the Day of Atonement, the high priest would sacrifice one goat on the ark, the tomb of the fallen sun king Solomon/Osiris, and send the other off into the desert — the domain of Seth.

This very same journey into the wilderness was undertaken time and again by the biblical patriarchs, who were really kings of Egypt. Even the very first man, Adam, had to venture forth into the wilderness after being expelled from the primordial garden. This garden was the fertile earth, the realm of Osiris and Horus represented by the lush and fruitful delta lowlands. The first man had been given this as his domain, to till and tend the soil. But in order to unite the two lands he also to conquer the domain of Seth, the harsh barren desert wastes of the southern interior. And he could not return to the garden until he had done so.

Only then could he truly rule the land.

This theme would continue with Adam's son, Cain, who was likewise banished to the wilderness — in this case after killing his brother Abel in a story clearly modeled on the conflict between Seth and Osiris: "When you work the ground, it will no longer yield its crops for you. You will become a restless wanderer on the earth." [196] Though this is said to be a curse, it is only so in the *ritual* sense. Cain is in fact being challenged to go forth and subdue the wilderness, thus proving himself worthy to become a king. That he succeeds is evident from the fact that he eventually founds a city, implying that he has established himself as a ruler.

In these legends, the fertile ground and the garden represent life; the wilderness connotes death. In overcoming the wilderness, therefore, Cain can be said to have overcome death. This is the goal of the entire process, a goal made evident by Cain's single overriding concern at the outset: He is afraid of dying.[197] But Cain is, in fact, all but assured of success. Not only does he receive a mark that keeps anyone from killing him, he is further promised that "if anyone kills Cain, he will suffer vengeance seven times over." [198]

Cain's royal status is confirmed by the etymology of his name, which in Hebrew denotes a spear and which is furthermore closely related to the place-name Cana, which means "reed." The reference to the reed recalls the story of the two Egyptian brothers, in which the younger is forced into exile (i.e. the wilderness) after cutting off his own male member with a *reed* knife. It also brings to mind once again the story of Jesus, who was pierced with a spear and offered vinegar on the end of a reed at his crucifixion.[199] And this is not to mention the fact that Jesus was associated with the village of Cana, where he is said to have turned water into wine at a wedding.

Jesus is elsewhere himself identified as the "bruised reed" whose coming was foretold by the prophet Isaiah.[200] The Hebrew word employed by the prophet in this oracle was *qaneh*, pronounced cana. This would seem to be an odd term to use in such a description until one realizes that a reed staff was often used as a symbol of kingship in the ancient world. It was nothing less than the phallic staff of Aaron, which bore fruit and thus ensured the continuance of the royal bloodline from one generation to the next. This royal blood was the wine that Jesus produced at Cana, where it is no coincidence that a wedding was taking place. The coupling of male and female, after all, was what perpetuated the line of kings.

This coupling, as we shall see, took place in a sacred house such as the temple at Luxor. There must therefore be some significance to the fact that the Persian word *khana*, which denoted a house or dwelling, is so similar to the place-name Cana. It also serves as the root word for "khan," the familiar title bestowed on the famed Mongol conqueror named Genghis and those who followed him. This word sounds a bit like "king" and in fact denoted the holder of just such an office, who typically ruled over a dominion known as a khanate.

The relationship between the words for "king" and "house" seen in the Persian tongue is hardly unique. Even today, we speak of a royal house when referring to such matters. And the ancient Egyptians similarly called their leaders pharaohs, a term that originally meant "great house."

Even the English word "king" itself can be traced back through the old Anglo-Saxon word *cyning* and the middle English *kynge*, each of which probably can be traced to the old word for reed. If this is the case, the prophecy attributed to Isaiah suddenly makes a bit more sense: Jesus was not seen merely as a bruised reed, but a bruised king. And he was, in fact, identified by a sign over his cross as king of the Jews.

Beyond this, it is interesting to note that the Hebrew word for jealousy is *qana* and that the description of Yahweh as a jealous god may have more than this simple meaning.

He was also the god of the reed.

The god of kings.

Just as Cain is afraid of dying as he is sent out into the wilderness, so Jesus is afraid of death as he approaches the cross. Yet just as Cain succeeds in founding a city and thereby becoming a king after his wilderness ordeal, so Jesus firmly believes that he will establish a new kingdom through his ordeal on the cross. As we shall see, the symbolism of the wilderness ritual occurs time and again in the life story of Jesus, not to mention the legends associated with other great men in Judeo-Christian tradition.

In its original form, the wilderness ritual clearly constituted a period of time during which the new king was consigned to the realm of death. This period nearly always seems to have been associated with the number forty. In some cases, it is defined as forty days. This is, of course, the exact length of time Noah is said to have endured the deluge as he traveled in his "ark" — or casket — across the waters of death. And it is also, notably, the length of time the Egyptian physicians needed to embalm the patriarch Jacob upon his death.[201] Jacob was, as we have discovered, much more than a patriarch. He was a pharaoh, one of the famed shepherd kings who ruled the delta lowlands, whose name has been preserved on various scarabs as Yakob-har. And the length of time required for his embalming appears to confirm the nature of the wilderness ritual.

It embodied the continuing cycle of birth, death and rebirth that was central to the Egyptian sacred tradition.

One king had just died.

Another was to take his place.

The dead king had been mummified and sent on his way to heaven in the form of the god Osiris. This heaven was no abstract wonderland off in some other dimension. It was the *literal* heaven. The night sky. From which "god the father" looked down upon the land of the living — a land now governed by his heir, the "son of god" — from his place in the great constellation Orion. Once again, Osiris was dead. And once again, his son was destined to avenge him by going forth and doing battle with Seth, the personification of mortality itself.

His son Horus.

The new pharaoh.

God incarnate.

This was the essence of the wilderness ritual. It was not just a re-enactment of the ancient epic myth of Seth and Horus, it was a direct and audacious challenge to death itself.

Another pharaoh, Moses, also seems to have issued such a challenge. Legend has it that he spent forty days and nights on a mountain in the wilderness, during which time he ate no bread and drank no water.[202] The wilderness, of course, was Seth's domain, and the mountain stood at the very heart of it. Seth was, after all, a storm god whose menacing thunderheads seemed to gravitate toward the heights of the mountain. In climbing the mountain, Moses was going to meet death on its own turf, and its own terms, for a corpse neither eats nor drinks.

Neither did he.

These were the rules of the wilderness ritual.

At times, this rite of passage involved venturing forth into the desert or climbing a forbidding mountain. At others, it entailed ritually crossing the waters of death. This appears to have been the case with Solomon, who was placed on his father's mule and escorted to a place called Gihon.[203] This was one of four sacred rivers known to the Hebrew writers, who described it as traversing the entire length of Ethiopia.[204] Only one river fits this description: the mighty Nile. It was to the banks of this river that Solomon was taken for the express purpose of being anointed king. One can imagine him crossing the waters of death, or perhaps even being immersed in them. Could it be that such a ceremony was the precursor to the later practice of baptism, likewise regarded as a symbolic death and resurrection?

During this ceremony, Solomon was anointed with oil from a horn kept within the sacred tent. In fact, this oil may well have been fat from a "dragon" or crocodile, the substance traditionally used to anoint the pharaohs of Egypt. This creature was known as a *messeh*, providing the likely origin of the term messiah, meaning "anointed one." [205] The word may also bear some relation to the Egyptian *msi*, meaning "to give birth." If so, it would confirm the nature of the ceremony as a rebirth ritual following the king's sojourn in the land of death.

It would also explain Jesus' famous and enigmatic saying: "Truly I say to you, no one can see the kingdom of God unless he is born again." [206]

Who is more fit for a kingdom than a king? A messiah? An anointed one?

In Egyptian tradition, it was just such a rebirth ceremony that accompanied the coronation of the pharaoh. It followed the wilderness ritual and celebrated the new king's conquest of Seth and his realm of death. In this regard, the mule on which Solomon rode was particularly significant. It was apparently customary for the new king to make his triumphant entry into the capital astride a mule or donkey, the totem animal of Seth. This signified that the wild god had been reined in. The wilderness ritual was complete, and the king had conquered the god of the desert — indeed, he had conquered death.

The prophet Zechariah would refer to this ceremony in stating, "Behold, your king comes to you righteous and bearing salvation, gentle and riding a donkey." [207]

There followed a great celebration, during which a trumpet was sounded and the people of the nation acclaimed their new sovereign. "Long live the king!" they shouted. And they went up after their king, rejoicing greatly as they played their flutes, making such a commotion that the noise of it shook the ground.[208] It is interesting to conjecture that this description may have provided the basis for one particularly vivid detail in the story of Jesus' resurrection, which was said to have been accompanied by a major earthquake.[209]

Certainly, Jesus' return was a cause for celebration, as was Solomon's coronation. And it seems the people had more than one reason to celebrate: Not only was the king being lauded for having emerged reborn from the wilderness ritual, he was also being congratulated on his sacred union with his new queen. There is every reason to believe that such a marriage ceremony followed immediately upon the conclusion of the wilderness ritual. Perhaps the most prominent clue is the age of at least two biblical patriarchs at the time of their marriage:

Forty.

This is the very same number used to measure the length of the wilderness ritual itself. Just as the wilderness ritual ended after forty days, so several figures were either recognized as leaders of their people or married at the end of forty *years*. Among the examples from the Hebrew writings:

- Isaac was forty years old when he married Rebekah.[210]
- Esau was forty years old when he married Judith.[211]
- Moses was the same age when he became leader of his people.[212]
- Caleb was forty when he was deputized by Moses.[213]
- Saul's son Ish-bosheth was forty years old when he became king.[214]

Still other monarchs reigned over Israel for the same period of time. Indeed, this particular span seems to have been reserved for particularly successful rulers, men who managed to lead their nation through the "wilderness" without falling prey to the terrible death that was the consequence of war and idolatry. Two prominent judges, Othniel and Gideon, ruled for forty years apiece.[215] And Asa, king of Judah, likewise died after forty years on the throne.[216] The same period of time was allotted to the legendary David and his equally famous "son" Solomon.[217]

According to tradition, Solomon himself appears to have been wed on the very day of his coronation. One Hebrew scribe invited the daughters of Jerusalem to come out "and look at King Solomon wearing the crown, the crown with which his mother crowned him on the day of his wedding."[218] This would seem to indicate that, at least for Solomon, the two ceremonies were one and the same.

The reason for this was quite simple, given the origins of the Osiris cult.

Osiris had been, from the beginning, a fertility god. His green face stands out on ancient tomb paintings and inscriptions, identifying him as a keeper of the harvest. The tamarisk tree that grew up around his casket was another clue to his identity. From death sprang life. It was the way of things, the natural cycle, of which Osiris was the ultimate expression. This was why Osiris was depicted in legend as teaching men to plant wheat, barley and fruit trees. It was even the custom, around the period that Ahmose ruled Egypt, to fashion a mummy of Osiris from a linen bag filled with wheat. This bag was then watered, so that the corn would sprout through the meshes in the sack, signifying the god's resurrection.[219]

This sort of symbolism served as a precursor to many of Jesus' ideas. He seems to have drawn directly on the Osiris myth when he told his disciples a story about a kernel of wheat: "Verily I say to you, unless a kernel of wheat falls to the earth and dies, it remains but a single seed. But if it dies, it produces many seeds."[220] This was the law of the harvest. Unless the stalk (or reed) of wheat itself was killed in the cutting, its seed could never bear fruit and provide life to the people. The connection of the harvest with this great paradox is echoed forth time and again in the words of Jesus. In one parable, it is at harvest time that the tenants of a vineyard conspire to kill the landowner's son.[221] In another, workers eager to separate the wheat from the chaff are urged to wait until the harvest.[222] This was the appropriate time of judgment, after death. For the Egyptians, it was the time when a pharaoh's heart was weighed to determine whether he was worthy to be taken into heaven.

It appears to have meant something quite similar to Jesus.

Within the Egyptian pantheon, it was Osiris who stood as lord of the harvest.[223] It is therefore revealing that Jesus should refer to his patron deity as "lord of the harvest."[224] This could have been none other than Osiris. It was he who embodied the power of new life emerging from the apparent finality of the grave. It was he who was the resurrection and the life. One of the Egyptian coffin texts illustrates this in graphic language depicting the shoot of a new plant springing forth from the bones of Osiris himself:

I am the plant of life
Which comes forth from Osiris
Which grows upon the ribs of Osiris
Which allows the people to live
Which makes the gods divine…

Now Isis is content for her Horus, her god
She is jubilant in him,
Her Horus, her god
I am life appearing from Osiris [225]

This text equates Horus himself with the plant of life that springs forth from the decomposing body of Osiris. Jesus made the same claim for himself, declaring: "I am the vine, and my father is the gardener."[226] Jesus knew the language of the times. He knew that the cult of Osiris had grown extremely popular, and he knew that Osiris was the god of the vine — he always had been. Not only had

Osiris taught his people to tame the wild grape, but also how to distill it into wine. This was, according to the historian Diodorus of Sicily, one of his great passions. Diodorus, writing a few generations before Jesus' birth, said Osiris *"had an especial liking for fine wines"* and made a particular point of *"teaching mankind the culture of the vine, as well as the way to harvest the grape and to store the wine."* The Greeks had seized on this idea and made it the basis for a cult of their own, venerating a vine god named Dionysus who has been widely recognized as based upon the figure of Osiris.

In declaring himself to be the vine, Jesus was seizing on this symbolism. Not only did he associate himself with Osiris by declaring himself to be the sacred vine, he even went so far as to identify his father as "the gardener." This was the very essence of Osiris' identity. He was the vegetation god with the green face who taught men how to raise the crops they needed to sustain life. More than anything, he came to be associated with the fruit of those crops, the grain that could be pounded into bread and the grapevine that yielded up its wine.

Bread and wine were at the heart of the Osiris myth. And they would likewise be essential components of a ritual honoring another risen god-king, one who would claim his mantle: Jesus.

Tree of Life

All of this points back to the original Hebrew myth of beginnings, wherein another deity, the spokesman for the Elohim, plants a garden and creates a man to tend it. This man is Adam — Atum to the Egyptians. The tale is a familiar one. It is one of intrigue, deception is one of divine paranoia.

Having created Adam, the Elohim began to view him as a potential rival. Carelessly, they had placed him in the midst of a garden that was home to some rather magical trees — powerful weapons the man could conceivably use against them. Instead of uprooting the trees, as might be expected, the gods decided to let the man remain in the garden. But they attempted to cow him into submission by issuing a rather ominous threat. He would be permitted to eat of any tree in the garden save one, the tree of knowledge. In the day you eat of it, they warned him, he would surely die.

This turned out to be nothing more than a rather heavy-handed bluff, and another resident of the garden was all too eager to expose it as such. This was the serpent, who approached Adam's consort with the truth of the matter: "You will surely not die," he declared. "For the Elohim know that when you eat of it, your eyes will be opened and you will be like the Elohim, knowing good and evil." [227] The serpent turns out to be right on both counts. When the woman partakes of the fruit, she does not die. And her eyes are, in fact, opened to good and evil.

The man then follows suit.

The Elohim, realizing their deception has been exposed, act quickly to prevent any further damage. Immediately they turn their attention to a second tree in the garden, which has the power to grant eternal life. Losing no time, they summarily dismiss the man and his consort from the garden — not as punishment for their disobedience, but out of fear that they might challenge the gods' supremacy: "He must not be allowed to reach out his hand and take also from the tree of life, and eat and live forever." [228] Not content with simply expelling the pair, they appoint some cherubs with a flaming sword to stand guard over the tree itself.

The appearance of the cherubs, or priestly *kher hebs*, in this story exposes its Egyptian origin. Here they guard the tree off life, just as the cherubs guard the sacred ark in the temple of Solomon. At first, it might appear that these two stories have little to do with one another.

In fact, however, they are intimately related.

The ark and the tree symbolize exactly the same thing. Just as the ark is at the heart of the temple, so the tree of life stands at the center of the garden.[229] The setting of the creation story in the garden identifies it with Osiris, the green-faced god of vegetation and fertility. This was his domain. And the tree of life that stood at the center of the garden was, in fact, Osiris himself. It was the tree in which Osiris' casket had become encased after it washed ashore in Syria.

This very casket was associated with the ark of King Solomon, who had become identified with Osiris upon his death. It was therefore natural to find the Egyptian high priests known as *kher hebs* (or cherubs) standing guard at both sites, for they were really one and the same. The center of the garden with its tree of life was nothing more than the mythic counterpart of the temple's inner sanctuary with its ark. Ark and tree both contained the body of the dead Osiris. And this would explain why Solomon's wife thought it necessary to procure a branch from the tree of life and place it in her husband's great ship.

His ark.

What remains to be considered is the nature of the tree itself: Just what kind of a tree was it?

There are at least two answers to this question, each of which further connects the myth of Osiris with the Hebrew legends.

According to Egyptian myth, the chest containing Osiris' body came to rest in the branches of a tamarisk, a deciduous tree that can grow to twenty feet in height. It produces pink flowers and can be found in places where moisture is abundant, for it consumes a large volume of water. But it is perhaps most noteworthy as the likely source of the mysterious edible substance known as manna, which sustained the Hebrews during their wanderings in the desert. The word manna probably stems from the Egyptian word *mennu*, which means simply "food." [230] This particular food may have been produced by the tamarisk itself in the form of a gum resin, or it may have taken the form of secretions left by insects associated with the tree.[231]

Either way, it produced a substance that also was known as bread from heaven.[232]

This description appears to link the manna directly with Osiris, who was in fact a god of the heavenly realm. According to Diodorus of Sicily, it was he who "introduced the Egyptians to agriculture, in particular to the cultivation of wheat and barley." Such grains were integral to the production of bread. And it could therefore be said of Osiris that he provided his people with bread from heaven. But there is even stronger evidence to connect Osiris with the mysterious manna. According to Hebrew legend, Aaron collected a jar of manna to be kept for posterity and placed it alongside the sacred tablets *inside the ark itself.* [233]

In the ritual burial casket of Solomon as Osiris.

The *aron.*

This would seem to imply an intimate connection between the bread from heaven and the body of Osiris. And in fact, such a connection did exist. One has only to recall the imagery of corn sprouting from the linen bag filled with grain — a bag designed to simulate the mummy of Osiris — to see the relationship.[234] From death came life. From the sacred casket encased in the tamarisk tree issued forth bread from heaven. The grain was the living offspring of Osiris. It is a connection long forgotten by most, but it was certainly remembered by Jesus in his day:

"Verily I say to you, it is not Moses who has given you the bread from heaven, but it is my father who gives you the true bread from heaven. For the bread from God is he who comes down from heaven and gives life to the world. ... I am the bread of life." [235]

In this extraordinary statement, Jesus was doing nothing less than equating himself with the manna in the ark. He was the nourishment that sprang forth from the dead body of Osiris, his father who had sent forth the bread from heaven. This goes a long way toward explaining the enigmatic — and ostensibly grotesque — command, which he delivered at the end of this same discourse: "Verily I say to you, unless you eat the flesh of the son of man and drink his blood, you have no life in you. Whoever eats my flesh and drinks my blood has eternal life, and I will raise him up on the last day." [236]

Just as the pillar of Osiris was raised up on the final day of his ritual.

In time, Jesus would be honored with a ritual of his own. His followers would celebrate his death and resurrection by partaking of bread, revering it as the bread from heaven and regarding it as his actual physical body. This was, however, but one half of the ceremony. The other half involved drinking the blood of the fallen god-man, represented by a chalice of wine. And it is this second aspect of the ceremony that points toward the second plant associated with the tree of life — a plant that is not really a tree at all, but a vine.

The ancients viewed the grapevine as a source of life. On the one hand, it had certain medicinal qualities that made it useful in combating mortality. It was, in this sense, the original "lifeblood" that coursed through the veins of all who partook. But it was something more than this, as well. Its intoxicating qualities produced an ecstatic state that seemed to indicate a union with a greater spirit — the spirit of a god. This was certainly the case for the followers of Dionysus, the Greek alter-ego of Osiris, who were known for their drunken rituals. And it may well have been the case for the followers of Jesus, too. They were, after all, dismissed as drunks who had swallowed too much wine during a particularly noisy celebration shortly after his death.[237]

The vine was intimately associated with Osiris. In one papyrus, a vine bearing numerous clusters of grapes extends from the banks of a pool toward the green-faced god, who sits enthroned nearby. In another, from about the time of the Hyksos-Theban conflict, the god is seen sitting upon a shrine (the ark?), with clusters of grapes hanging from the roof. [238]

The vine was clearly a symbol of kingship, and not just to the Egyptians. In Hebrew lore, when the clan of Judah is set apart as the royal house of Israel, it is set forth in the following terms:

> *The scepter will not depart from Judah*
> *Nor the ruler's staff from between his feet...*

FORGED IN ANCIENT FIRES

He will tether his donkey to a vine
His colt to the choicest branch [239]

The symbolism of the vine as a royal plant is apparent, and the presence of the donkey seems to refer back once more to the wilderness ritual. All this is clear enough. But amid all these allusions and allegories, one rather glaring question remains: How could a vine be confused with a tree?

Anyone who has driven past a vineyard knows the answer. Vines are not left to simply grow upon the ground, they are supported — usually by wooden crosses that look something like trees. This practice is very old. Indeed, it is so old that Osiris himself was credited with teaching men not only to prune the vines and extract juice from the fruit, but also to grow grapevines on poles.[240] In doing so, he created the appearance of a tree, although in reality only the vine itself was alive and the wood used to support it was dead.

Just as the body of Osiris was dead, but the plant that sprang forth from his skeletal remains was alive and vital. This was the plant of life which came forth from Osiris, which grew upon his ribs, which allowed the people to live, and which made the gods divine. To the ancients, the plant said to impart divinity was none other than the vine with its healing and intoxicating qualities. It is for this reason that Jesus would describe himself as the vine. Like it, he would be hung upon a piece of dead wood — at which point he would be offered wine, the fruit of the vine, to drink. And like it, he would rise again from the dead.

It is perhaps for this reason that the cross itself has been worshipped consistently throughout the centuries. It is identified not merely as a piece of wood, but as the father himself. In at least one legend, the cross itself is even pictured as walking and talking. *The Gospel of Peter*, an ancient manuscript uncovered just over a century ago, tells of a cross that follows the risen Jesus out of his grave before a crowd of onlookers: "And they heard a voice from the heavens saying, 'You have preached to those who sleep.' And a response was heard from the cross: 'Yes.' " [241] This incredible passage depicts the cross as echoing heavenly father, as though the two are one and the same.

Both are Osiris.

And Jesus was his son. He was flesh and blood, bread and wine — the bread of life that grew from the fallen seed of grain and the vine that sprang forth from the dead body of his father. Osiris was the father, and he was the son. Horus. The anointed one who, like King Solomon, was the rightful heir to the throne of Egypt. He was the phoenix, the great benu bird who emerged from the ashes of his fallen father, just as the vine emerged from the bones of dead Osiris.

"Benu" was not just the name for the phoenix but also for the date palm. This tree, known to botanists as *phoenix dactylifera*, rose like a giant pillar above the desert and was crowned with palm leaves fanning out in all directions like a giant sunburst. The pillar being the symbol of Osiris and the sun disk that of Horus, this imagery made perfect sense. But it should also be pointed out that the palm tree is called something else in Hebrew. And its name bears a close relationship, linguistically, to that of the tamarisk tree in which Osiris' ark became encased.

That word is *tamar*.

The Phoenix Has Landed

It fell from the sky like a bolt of lightning, piercing the heavens with its fiery presence and streaking toward the earth. One can imagine the people of Egypt turning their heads skyward while uttering something akin to that famous comic-book exclamation: "Look! Up in the sky!" And asking what, exactly, *it* was. To some, it must have seemed like a piece of the sun hurled down from heaven. Others viewed it as a bird of flame; still others as a fire-breathing serpent — a dragon.

Whatever it was, there was no mistaking one thing: It was important, as though a god were arriving from heaven. The Greeks held that this god was Prometheus, who stole fire from heaven and conveyed it to earth as a benefit to mankind. The Egyptians believed he was Horus descending in the form of the phoenix to alight on the sacred date palm symbolized by the obelisk at Heliopolis. And the Hebrews saw him as Lucifer, the "morning star" cast down from heaven after an unsuccessful challenge to the most high god.[242]

This latter story is, of course, the most famous today. It stems from an oracle of the prophet Isaiah — or one of several writers who appear to have made use of that name — who would exult in the failure of Lucifer's subversive plot and chasten him for his presumption:

> *How you have fallen from heaven,*
> *O morning star, son of dawn*
> *You have been cast down to earth,*
> *You who once laid low the nations*
>
> *You said in your heart:*
>   *I will ascend to heaven*
>   *I will raise my throne above the stars of El*
>   *I will sit enthroned on the mount of assembly*
>   *On the utmost heights of Zaphon*
>   *I will ascend above the tops of the clouds*
>   *I will make myself like the Most High*
>
> *But you are brought down to the grave*
> *To the depths of the pit* [243]

If this was meant to be an oracle, it was hardly original — either to Isaiah or to his people. El was the supreme deity of ancient Syria, and Zaphon was the domain of its patron god of thunder. This was the home to Baal, the rider on the clouds who brought rain and sustenance to those who dwelt in the shadow of his mountain. When the rains did not come, these people naturally began to wonder what had happened. They therefore wove an elaborate tale to explain his absence and the search for someone to take his place.

According to this myth, Baal has "died," leaving his throne in the heights of the mountain vacant. This is hardly an acceptable state of affairs, so the supreme god El asks the goddess Asherah (mentioned dozens of times in the Hebrew scriptures) to name a successor. After rejecting her first candidate as inadequate, he agrees to appoint a certain Athtar the Awesome to the lofty post. This decision, however, turns out to be a disaster, and events proceed from this point along the exact same course described in the prophecy of Isaiah.

> *Then Athtar the Awesome went up*
> *To the peaks of Zaphon*
> *He sat on Baal the Conqueror's throne*
> *His feet did not reach the footstool*
> *His head did not reach the headrest*
>
> *And Athtar the Awesome spoke:*
> *"I cannot be king on the peaks of Zaphon."*
> *Athtar the Awesome descended*
> *He descended from Baal the Conqueror's throne*
> *And he became the king of the underworld*
> *The god of it all* [244]

The parallels of the two stories include the presence of El as the supreme deity, the reference to Zaphon, the unsuccessful attempt by a usurper to claim a mountaintop throne, the usurper's subsequent descent and his transformation into lord of the underworld. Furthermore, Athtar was associated with the planet Venus, often identified as the morning star because it is the brightest of all celestial bodies and remains visible even as the sun begins its ascent. The epithet "morning star" was likewise used to describe Lucifer in Isaiah's oracle.

But this was not the only legend to focus on Lucifer. Over the years, other myths were created to embellish upon Isaiah's words. One such story maintained that, when Lucifer fell from heaven, he did not fall alone. A jewel came loose from his crown and fell to earth along with him, a precious emerald that later came to be revered as a sacred object.[245] Can it be an accident that Thoth was said to have inscribed his wisdom on heavenly tablets of emerald? And can it be mere coincidence that a sacred stone from the sky was associated with the phoenix myth? This latter was, of course, the benben stone upon which the phoenix was said to alight. It stood at the apex of the obelisk in Heliopolis and served as the symbolic capstone to each of the pyramids, having the shape of a miniature pyramid itself.

Descriptions of this stone as an emerald probably refer to its life-giving power. Green was the color of vegetation, the ultimate source of life in the ancient world. It was for this reason that Osiris was depicted as a green-faced god, and the same sort of symbolism was probably at work with the stone. Indeed, an early medieval legend confirms that just this sort of vital force was said to have emanated from the stone. According to the author, it seems to have contained nothing less than the secret of immortality: "However ill a mortal may be, from the day on which he sees the stone, he cannot die for that week, nor does he lose his color." This was quite a statement. But the author went even further, asserting that if anyone were to gaze on the stone for a prolonged period — even two hundred years — the person would remain as vibrant as he had been in his prime, save only that his hair would turn gray.[246]

These are the very sort of properties that one might expect to issue forth from a stone associated with the phoenix, the symbol of immortality. But despite the descriptions of the stone as an emerald, it is much more likely that it was made of an altogether different substance.

Iron.

This was the stuff of stones from heaven, otherwise known as meteorites. The Egyptians knew this all too well, proclaiming in their pyramid texts that the bones of Osiris had been forged of iron, his limbs fashioned from the stars.[247] And the meteorite itself was the seed of Osiris, plunging toward the womb of mother earth to produce his offspring, Horus. The new king. In its rapid descent, such an object might seem like a fiery bird or sky-born serpent streaking across the heaven. But when those who beheld its glory raced to welcome its arrival, they were greeted instead by a dark metallic stone. Such an object might have taken on a conical or even loosely pyramidal shape, its face having been seared to a near point during its rapid descent through the intense heat of the atmosphere. Hence, it would serve as a fitting model for the stylized capstone at the apex of the pyramids, the nesting place of the phoenix.

The medieval writer would refer to it using the odd Latin phrase *lapsit exillis,* probably a corruption of *lapsit ex caelis,* meaning simply "stone from heaven."[248] This writer would reveal that "by virtue of this stone, the phoenix is burned to ashes, in which it is reborn. Thus does the phoenix molt its feathers, which when done, it shines dazzling bright and lovely as before." [249]

Once again, the stone is depicted as the essence of eternal life. By the act of molting, the phoenix shed its feathers and thus appeared to become a whole new creature. In this, it had something in common with the snake, which in shedding its skin likewise appeared to be reborn. And indeed, the phoenix seems to have been something of a composite creature — part bird, part serpent. When the ancients looked to the skies and saw a comet or a shooting star, this is what they believed they saw. The Aztecs called one such marvel Quetzalcoatl, a name that means simply "feathered serpent." And later generations would identify these celestial wonders as nothing less than fire-breathing dragons, winged serpents that ruled the sky.

As with everything else, the Egyptians believed this heavenly phenomenon had its counterpart below. It took the form of an earthbound serpent which, nonetheless, appeared to be equipped with "wings." The flaring protrusions on either side of the Egyptian cobra looked every bit like spreading pinions. And the venom from its bite sped like wildfire through the veins, just as the flaming winged serpent sped across the evening sky.

According to legend, the cobra was Isis' only creation — in a very real sense, her "son."

Just as Horus was her son. And Horus was the phoenix.

Horus had a Greek counterpart in the sun god Apollo, who was venerated at a temple in the city of Delphi. In can hardly be a coincidence that this temple housed a stone known as the *omphalos* —

literally, the "phallus of the sun." Like the benben stone, this was a conical or egg-shaped object placed on a rectangular base to create an obelisk shaped like the male sexual organ. And like the benben, it was said to have come down from heaven. According to this legend, the god Cronos sought to preserve his position as king of the universe by devouring the earth goddess' children as she bore them. She deceived him, however, by placing a stone in *swaddling cloth* and pretending it was her son Zeus.

The child eventually grew up and dethroned Cronos, who expelled the stone and sent it hurtling to earth.

Cronos was associated with one of the solar system's largest planets, the name of which was also *his* name in Roman lore.

Saturn.

The relationship between the names Saturn and Satan has long been recognized. And the chain of evidence reveals quite clearly why the figure known as Lucifer came to be associated with Satan. Both were associated with stones cast down from heaven. And each was a ruling figure deprived of his throne. The two myths obviously stem from a common origin. And when one begins to consider the parallels, it becomes clear what that origin is: the ancient tale of Seth and Horus. Isis (who was also an earth goddess) had hidden her son Horus from the devious Seth, just as Zeus was hidden from Cronos/Saturn. And Horus had grown up to depose the villain who had sought his life as an infant, just as Zeus did in the myth of his accession.

The stone in these stories was shaped either like a cone or an egg. And the ancients seem to have viewed it as the egg of this mystical phoenix, fertilized by fire from heaven. Those who called this creature a dragon would depict it guarding a cache of golden eggs, stones from heaven still glowing from the heat of their descent.

Those who called it a phoenix would adopt the egg as a symbol for their great springtime celebration of the resurrection — Easter. This connection would be obscured by later writers seeking to distance their faith from this myth, but early followers of Jesus were not shy about equating their hero with the phoenix. On the contrary, they seemed eager to draw this comparison. One writer, for example, recounted the phoenix legend in detail and then asked why it was so difficult to believe in the resurrection: "Shall we then think it to be any great or strange thing for the lord of all to raise up those that religiously serve him ... when even by a bird he shows us the greatness of his power to fulfill his promise?" [250] The writer in question was, by tradition, said to be no less a personage than Peter's successor as to the papal throne. His letter to the residents of Corinth, a city in Greece, was deemed canonical in some quarters but was later discredited — in part because of his reference to the phoenix.

Such connections were simply too embarrassing to later writers intent upon stressing the originality of their beliefs. In fact, however, there was very little original about them. The Easter holiday, with which the "egg" of the phoenix became most closely linked, appears to have drawn its name from the goddess Ishtar or Astarte. This was, of course, the same Astarte whose infant son lost his chance at the immortality Isis wished to bestow upon him by passing him through the fire — just as the phoenix "passed through the fire" on its way to earth.

This queen-goddess made an appearance in the Hebrew scriptures as well, under the name Esther. The book that bears her name has long been one of the most controversial works in the canon, mostly because it is the only one that fails to mention the Hebrew god, either as Yahweh or in the plural Elohim. There is, it turns out, quite a good reason for this: The book has nothing to do with late Hebrew mythology, but rather is an adaptation of a much older myth involving deities from a different cycle altogether. The names of the main characters have been altered only slightly.

> Esther is Ishtar/Astarte, the ancient goddess of love and war. In the Hebrew adaptation, she is known for both her physical beauty and her courage, the qualities most widely associated with the

goddess. As the embodiment of love, she seduces the king of Persia with her beauty and sensuality. As the uncompromising war maiden, she stands up to the king in condemning her archenemy. She is also made queen, just as Ishtar is queen of heaven.

> ➤ Haman is Baal-Hammon, which means something like "roaring lord" — a clear reference to his identity as god of thunder. In the Hebrew text, Haman is elevated to a position of supremacy over all the other nobles, mirroring the god's preeminent status within the pantheon. He is depicted as a prince, the position also held by Baal. All the officials at court kneel before him at the king's gate to pay him homage, treating him very much like a god. Only Esther's adoptive father Mordecai refuses to bow down.

> ➤ Mordecai is Marduk, the father of the gods in Babylonian tradition and the adoptive father of Esther in the Hebrew tale. He alone stood above Baal in the divine pecking order, and it is for this reason (not because he is a monotheist) that he refuses to bow down to Haman. The story makes it clear that Haman is bent on assassinating Mordecai and his followers for this insult; in the original story, he doubtless sought to kill the king and take his place. Vestiges of this earlier myth cling to the edges of the Hebrew text in slightly altered form, with Mordecai thwarting an assassination attempt against the Persian king.

In the end, Esther thwarts the plot on Mordecai's life and turns the tables on Haman, persuading the king to invoke against him the very penalty the scheming prince had planned to carry out against her father. The villainous Haman is hanged to death on a gallows seventy-five feet high. Mordecai, by contrast, is dressed in a royal robe and placed upon one of the king's horses to be publicly hailed as he rides through the city streets. This episode identifies Mordecai without a doubt as a king himself and suggests the original form of the story. Though he is mounted on a horse instead of a donkey, the scene is otherwise reminiscent of the new king's triumphal entry following completion of the wilderness ritual.

The new king has conquered Seth — or Baal, symbolized by Haman.

The Capstone and the Grail

Having overcome death through the wilderness ritual, the new king became the keeper of the mysterious stone from heaven. But he was more than its guardian; he was its very embodiment. He was the phoenix, the mystical bird synonymous with the sacred benben stone that stood at the apex of the pyramids.

There is stunning evidence that Jesus thought of himself in terms of this very stone. This much became apparent during an encounter in the temple courts. When his adversaries — members of the temple priesthood and their allies — stepped forward to challenge his authority, he responded with his parable of the vineyard. This was the story of the unscrupulous tenants who conspired to murder the vineyard owner's son. Jesus wasn't pulling any punches, implicitly equating the villains of the tale with the temple priesthood. He, meanwhile, played the part of the vineyard owner's son. And the temple itself was the vineyard, the house of life.

Jesus must have been well acquainted with the temple's original purpose as the final resting place for King Solomon in the form of Osiris. Though it was not a pyramid, it served the same function, and it therefore seems quite likely that its design preserved a special place for a replica of the benben stone. The capstone. It was this very symbolism that Jesus drew upon to drive home the point of his parable, quoting the psalmist: "The stone the builders rejected has become the capstone."[251] There is little doubt from the context that he identified himself as that capstone. Just as the tenants had slain the vineyard owner's son, now these same "tenants" — the temple priests — were seeking to destroy him.

And he considered himself the temple owner's son.

The temple belonged to the god he identified as his father, Osiris, the king of heaven. This was the god whose very name *meant* father. To the Greeks he was known as Osiris. But to the Egyptians, he was Asir, an appellation that supplies the linguistic root for a term that describes both the act of insemination that defines fatherhood and a title of address for a king.

Sire.

The related Hebrew verb *suwr* means to rule or govern.

Jesus wasn't being vague at all in referring to his father. He was in fact naming him as none other than the Egyptian god of fertility and the resurrection. In claiming to be the son of this god, Jesus was identifying himself with Horus. He was the capstone. The phoenix. The incarnate god destined to reign as pharaoh of Egypt and ruler of the civilized world. These were the traditions he called upon in making his claim to be the messiah, a claim that understandably met a good deal of resistance from the Roman emperor and his allies. This was a direct challenge to their authority, and they were not about to let it stand.

Jesus *was* claiming to be god in the flesh.

But he wasn't claiming anything new or original. The same status had been asserted for Moses, Solomon and a long line of kings dating back virtually to the dawn of civilization. He was simply the latest to appeal to that tradition — a tradition that would in fact continue long after his death. More than twelve centuries later, a German writer would set pen to paper and create the first of what would come to be called the "Grail romances." These tales, diluted into little more than fairy tales through centuries in the telling, were originally quite a bit more. The names of the key figures in this mythic cycle are deeply embedded in popular lore.

- King Arthur.
- Merlin.
- Queen Guinevere.
- Mordred.

- Sir Galahad.
- Sir Percival.
- Sir Gawain.
- Sir Lancelot.

Each would have a prominent role to play in a long series of myths and legends that would be produced over the course of about three centuries. Yet in the beginning, the stories weren't really about any specific figure — mythical or historical. They concerned themselves primarily with something called the *gral* or *graal*, identified by one early author as the stone from heaven. And this same author, a man named Wolfram Von Eschenbach, made it quite clear that this stone was nothing less than the ancient benben stone. It was through its efficacy, he asserted, that the phoenix was reborn. "Such powers does this stone confer on mortal men that their flesh and bones are soon made young again," Von Eschenbach declared in his masterwork *Parzival* (named for the figure who would come to be known years later as Sir Percival). "This stone," he continued, "is called 'the Gral.' " [252]

Not only did the so-called grail confer upon those who beheld it life and vigor, it also was capable of producing a sumptuous feast. This is hardly a surprise, for food *was* life in the ancient world. Starvation was a constant and near universal threat, and the next meal was seldom taken for granted. Flooding, drought or a plague of insects might wipe out vast populations. It was therefore natural that life-giving talismans should have been linked with the fruit of the earth.

Talismans such as the grail stone.

It not only served a symbol of continued vitality, but more specifically as a guarantor of lasting fruitfulness fit for a vegetation god such as Osiris. In this capacity, it was often depicted as something more than a stone — as a slightly curved platter piled high with various delicacies. The term for such a platter in old French was *gradale*, a word known to have been slurred in common discourse as *greal*.[253] Hence, the origin of the term.

But why should the benben stone have been described as a platter? The association makes a certain amount of sense in the context of the grail feast. It is, after all, simply more natural to associate food with a platter than with a stone. But even so, it is hard to shake the nagging suspicion that there is something more going on here. And indeed there is. The author of the earliest grail romance in our possession, writing a few years before Von Eschenbach, claimed to have received his version of the tale from another source altogether. This author, one Chretien de Troyes, modeled his work after a book his patron had obtained during a crusade in Palestine. The crusades were a series of holy wars sponsored by the church for the express purpose of recapturing the ancient land of Israel from its Muslim overlords. Though initially successful, the invaders who took part in these enterprises only managed to regain the holy land in the short term before eventually relinquishing it once again. In the interim, however, they managed to produce a rich literary tradition that helped inspire a series of chivalric tales. It was during one such crusade that Chretien's source supposedly came to light. Along with this text, which itself has been lost, the crusading knight brought back a green platter supposedly *fashioned from an emerald*.

Even more astonishing, this platter was said to have been a gift from the Queen of Sheba of King Solomon.[254]

The grail as a platter is a powerful image, but it would not be an enduring one. As the years passed and troubadours spread the popular tale across the breadth of Europe, it became customary to describe the grail in different terms. No longer was it a stone or even a platter — but a chalice. And to this day, this is how it is most frequently depicted, often sending forth streams of brilliant light from the hands of a beautiful maiden known as the grail bearer.

Why?

The simplest explanation is that it was meant to represent the cup used by Jesus at the so-called "last supper." And there is something to this explanation. By partaking of the fruit of the grape, Jesus was symbolically joining himself to his "father" Osiris. He was the vine, and this was his blood to be given as a sacrifice. When the sacrifice was complete, he would truly be united once more with Osiris, his father in heaven. He would, like the pharaohs of old, *become* Osiris.

According to the grail legends, this cup passed into the possession of a man named Joseph of Arimathea, who stood at the foot of the cross when Jesus was pierced by a Roman soldier's spear. As blood and water flowed out of the wound in his side, Joseph collected it in this sacred cup, thus preserving the royal bloodline in symbolic fashion as Jesus himself was dying. In doing so, this Joseph the cupbearer followed in the footsteps of the original patriarch Joseph (a.k.a. Psammetichus) whose status was likewise defined by his possession of a sacred cup.

This is one explanation of the cup's significance. But as it turns out, another tradition was just as important in identifying the grail as a chalice, a tradition based less upon the nature of the grail itself than upon the character of its bearer. This was the beautiful maiden known as Repanse de Schoye, a name that translates as "spreading of joy." The sexual imagery with reference to the female genitalia is quite apparent, and in this regard it should also be noted that the maiden bore the grail just as a woman might "bear" a child. In Egyptian lore, the stone and the phoenix were one — and each represented the new king. Is it just possible that the same sort of imagery is in play here? Is it conceivable (so to speak) that this enigmatic grail bearer also bore the king's heir?

This was, in fact, the essence of eternal life. The birth of a new king was a cause for great joy because it ensured a continuation of the royal bloodline, a sacred unbroken chain often dating back centuries. In Ethiopia, a line of kings claiming direct descent from Solomon himself ruled until more than three millennia after his death. One of Jesus' biographers traced his lineage back through this same Solomon; another took things one step further and went back to Adam, the original god-king and father of all mankind. Such unbroken bloodlines, though clearly legendary, confirmed a given ruler's legitimacy by linking him to the legendary heroes of old. But they served another function that was just as crucial: They preserved the immortality of the fathers or patriarchs, literally the "sires" or Osirises. This concept was crucial to the Egyptian belief system, and it was just as crucial to the grail myth. Some commentators have even gone so far as to suggest that the French phrase for holy grail, *san greal*, was a play on *sang real*, meaning "royal blood."

The grail bearer also was known as the Lady of the Castle, for she dwelt in the enigmatic Grail Castle. As it turns out, this is a vital clue, for a certain Egyptian goddess was known by exactly the same epithet. The goddess in question is Nephthys, whose name in Egyptian was expressed as *nbt-hwt*.

Nbt = lady.
Hwt = castle.

The first syllable is expressed as a hieroglyph in the shape of a shallow dish or platter. The second syllable is a narrow vertical rectangle engraved with two smaller symbols, giving one the impression of a castle or enclosure. When used in concert, however, the two symbols lose their individual identities and take on a new appearance altogether. The dish is placed directly on top of the rectangle, creating the clear impression of *a chalice*. This, it would seem, is the ultimate origin of the chalice as a symbol for the grail.

Nephthys was the perfect model for the grail bearer. As goddess of the dead, she was the special protector of Osiris — the dead king. With her sister Isis, she stood guard in the sanctuary of the great temple that was also a crypt. And so it was also in the grail legend, where the "lady of the castle" likewise served as protector for the master of the house. This latter, enigmatic figure lay wounded on the brink of death, yet something prevented from him leaving the world of the living. And that something was the absence of an heir.

The tradition must be maintained.

A new king must be placed upon the throne.

There must rule over the land of the living a new incarnation of the immortal god-made-flesh. His spirit lived on from one generation to the next. Call him Horus. Call him David. Call him Solomon. Call him Jesus. All shared the same great spirit of the god who ruled mankind as king of all the earth, the mysterious figure known to history as the once and future king.

Zion to Camelot

King Solomon's ship sailed over the waves to a faraway land, finally washing up on the shores of a mist-shrouded island far removed from the searing sun of the Egyptian desert. This was one writer's way of linking perhaps two of history's most enduring legends. Separated by hundreds of miles and two millennia, one would hardly think to associate two of the world's most famous monarchs, Solomon and the mysterious King Arthur. Yet this is exactly what the storytellers did, even casting Arthur as a scion of the royal house and rightful heir to the ancient "prince of peace."

Why would they have done so?

The times certainly had something to do with it. The Arthurian tales enjoyed their greatest popularity during the era of the crusades, when the kings and religious leaders of Europe united in a drive to recapture the holy lands from their "heathen" masters. At the heart of this ostensibly noble — but in truth bloody and savage — effort was a campaign to conquer Jerusalem, the presumed site of Solomon's legendary original temple. Once the conquest was complete, the guardians of this site would even take their name from it: the Knights Templar. The paramount importance of the ancient temple and the raised plateau on which it once rested set off a scramble for legitimacy among the European nobles jockeying for position in the rapidly changing political milieu. The prospect of conquest meant new lands to rule, and someone would be needed to rule them. There would, presumably, be a king of Jerusalem. And the candidates would do well to have a bona fide claim to the throne based, if possible, on a bloodline stretching back to Solomon himself.

The Arthurian romances may have provided a basis for such a claim, but that hardly precludes a more ancient origin for the tales. If the medieval storytellers hearkened back to the time of King Arthur for material, there was nothing to prevent them from making use of even more time-honored legends — legends that might, in fact, reveal a historical link between the Egypt of the pharaohs and ancient Europe.

One such legend was that of the Tuatha de Danaan, a group of invaders who had traveled a great distance in antiquity to settle on the westernmost of the British Isles. Given the widespread association between Solomon and the sacred emerald, it is perhaps fitting that this green and fertile land of Eire would come to be known as the "emerald isle." And that the name Eire itself meant "peace" in Greek, just as *shalom* — the root of the name Solomon — did in Hebrew. This was the paradisiacal garden at the edge of the world, and the Tuatha de Danaan would, in many ways, become synonymous with it.

The word Tuatha is interesting because it appears to be of Egyptian origin. As the letters T and D are used interchangeably, it seems likely that the prefix *tuat* referred to the afterworld known as the Duat. The suffix *ha*, meanwhile, is represented by a hieroglyph depicting the head and forepaw of a sphinx that carries the meaning "beginning." [255] The word, therefore, may be translated as "beginning of heaven," a gateway or entrance of sorts into the afterworld. This concept will be extremely important as things begin to unfold.

The sphinx that guards the Giza plateau similarly serves as the gateway to the afterworld symbolized by the pyramids.

The Tuatha took the latter portion of their name from their chief goddess and were known as the "people of Dana," whose consort was named Beli or Bile. The resemblance of these names to Tanit (Diana) and Baal, the divine king and queen of the Phoenicians, can hardly be coincidence. Indeed, as the Phoenicians were the premier seafaring nation of their time, it is not only possible but nearly certain that their trading network included the British Isles. And with their goods, they brought their religion.

In Irish lore, Bile took the form of a giant oak tree that was nourished by the waters of Dana. This symbolism is quite familiar, being reminiscent of the biblical tradition, in which a single great river watered a sacred garden surrounding the tree of life. According to Irish myth, Bile *was* that tree of life. In fact, in the language of the island, the word bile means nothing less than "sacred tree." It was this tree's union with the waters supplied by the goddess Dana that produced a son called the Dagda — literally "the good god" — who served as chief of the Tuatha. The Dagda thus played the part of god incarnate, ruling the Tuatha as their chieftain just as Horus ruled the Egyptians.

Bile was clearly a fertility god, whose chief holiday was celebrated on the first day of May. This remained a popular festival into modern times, with youths still dancing around a maypole that represents both the sacred tree and the divine phallus. Moving in circles around this ancient fertility symbol, they would wrap it in strands of colorful material. All this seems very much like a sort of ritual mummification, such as would have been undertaken in ancient Egypt on the dead king. And mummification was an integral part of the ritual that transformed the pharaoh from the living Horus into the god Osiris.

Like Bile, Osiris was seen as the original tree of life.

Both were fertility gods.

And both, it would seem, had some connection to ritual mummification.

It is true that in Egypt, Baal was equated not with Osiris but with the villainous Seth. Yet this is not as odd as it might seem, for it should be remembered that these two deities were inextricably linked. They were, after all, brothers — and twin brothers at that. Seth was the storm god, who replenished the earth with new waters from heaven; Osiris was the god of the inundation, who guided the snowmelt from the Nile's headwaters safely downstream to fertilize the valley below. Thence he passed his scepter to his son Horus, whose blazing solar "eye" sent down the warming rays that called for new life from the earth.

Seth might struggle against Horus in the myth, the one sending forth a violent flood and the other striking back with a withering drought. But ultimately, both were needed to ensure the continuance of life. This is why their struggle could never truly be decided. It is also one reason the pharaoh, though considered the incarnation of Horus, also claimed to be the chosen one of Seth. Apophis even went so far as to make the latter his patron deity. The land of Egypt was really two lands: one the domain of Horus, and the other the land of Seth. To rule both lands, the pharaoh needed to court the favor of both gods.

These are the traditions that were transferred across the sea on Phoenician ships, vessels that may well have been considered, in some sense, ships of Solomon. According to the Hebrew writings, Solomon had an entire fleet of ships at his disposal. And these same writings linked his empire closely with the port of Tyre, the most powerful city in the Phoenician confederation. Here dwelt the "people of the phoenix" who seem to have considered themselves heirs to the Hyksos tradition and their kings successors to the great Solomon. These were also the greatest shipbuilders in the ancient era, traveling to the ends of the known world and establishing several colonies in the process. Most prominent among them was the famed city of Carthage on the coast of northern Africa, roughly halfway between Tyre and the British Isles. By tracing the course of this journey, one can also follow the spread of the ancient fertility rites they practiced — rites associated at every step with the very same god and goddess under slightly different names.

- Tyre — Baal and Anat.
- Carthage — Baal and Tanit.
- Ireland — Bile and Dana.

The Phoenicians visited many other ports as well, their ships crisscrossing the Mediterranean and establishing a network of trading posts unrivalled in their day. At the height of their power, they controlled not only their homeland in Syria but also the entire northwest coast of Africa, the islands of Sardinia and Corsica, a portion of Cyprus and virtually the whole southern coast of Iberian Peninsula. No one could pass between the famed Pillars of Hercules that formed the gateway to the great western ocean without leave from the Phoenicians. They were, indeed, the doorkeepers to the uncharted waters of the Atlantic.

This vast network of trading posts facilitated the quick spread not only of the seafarers' religion, but also of their myths and legends. Among these was a version of the great Hyksos exodus from Egypt that contained an interesting twist: As one might expect in a mariner's tale, the flight did not take place over land but on the ocean. This myth later gained currency among the Greeks, who retold it as the myth of twin brothers named Aegyptus and Danaus who fought for the right to rule the Nile. This is yet another story that appears to recall the archetypal struggle between Osiris and his evil twin Seth.

In this case, however, the two brothers are said to be descended from a pharaoh named Epaphus — a virtual homonym for Apophis.

This alone would seem to provide at least a tenuous link to the exodus traditions. But as it turns out, other names surface in the tale that are equally intriguing. Belus, for example, is a mentioned as an Egyptian ruler — one whose name recalls that of the god Bile. This deity's consort was Dana, an echo of which is preserved in Danaus, a male figure whose true feminine nature is revealed in the fact that he becomes the father of fifty *daughters*.

These fifty daughters are at the heart of the myth in question.

As Danaus' quarrel with his brother grows more heated, he fears for his life and begins to plot his escape from Egypt. This he accomplishes by building the world's first boat, in which he and his daughters set sail for Greece. They eventually land and settle in the city of Argos — the name of which is closely related to the word "ark." This connection makes sense in light of the story's reference to the world's first ship. In a related myth, fifty other mariners set sail on a series of adventures that would be told and retold for generations.

The name of their ship?

The Argo.

Could the *argo* at the root of all these myths have been the sacred ark that bore the remains of a certain pharaoh to a land of promise? Could it have been the fabled Solomon's ship? In the end, these two vessels were one and the same. Both were meant to convey the dead king across the waters of death to the realm of immortality. As such, they belonged in part to the realm of myth. But history played an equal role in the creation of these tales, for there can be no doubt that real mariners piloted real ships across the seas of the ancient world. And it is very possible these mariners did, in fact, consider themselves the "people of Dana" or Danaus — known to the Irish as the Tuatha de Danaan.

The Tuatha were in fact the fifth wave of invaders to conquer Ireland, supplanting those who had arrived before them and enduring as masters of the island for some time. Their undoing turned out to be yet another band of settlers who arrived by way of the Iberian Peninsula. The Tuatha initially repelled these rivals, under the command of a certain Milesius, driving them back to the European mainland. But as it turned out, they had not seen the last of them. A second expedition was dispatched some time later to the emerald isle, and this contingent fared better than the first, defeating the Tuatha in their initial engagement.

Unwilling to concede defeat, however, the Tuatha rallied under the command of a woman named Eire, wife of the Tuatha chieftain Mac Grene. The counteroffensive succeeded to a certain extent, and the Tuatha even managed to make the wife of the enemy leader — an Egyptian woman named Scota — a casualty of war. In one version of the story, Eire sat on top of a mountain hurling balls of mud at the enemy. When these hit the ground, they burst into thousands of pieces that magically transformed themselves into warriors. These fighting men flew at the enemies of the Tuatha and engaged them in a fierce battle. In the end, however, the invaders regained the upper hand and claimed ultimate victory over the defenders.[256]

In this latter portion of the tale, the narrator has clearly entered the realm of myth. The account of the mud warriors is quite fantastic. Moreover, the names Eire and Scota are clearly symbolic of two realms, Ireland and Scotland (though it is interesting to note that the latter is identified as an *Egyptian*).

Mac Grene, meanwhile, means simply "son of the sun" and sounds equally like "son of the green." This mythical character may have been the predecessor of jack-in-the-green, a character associated with the first of May celebration. In these festivities, the jack-in-the-green is portrayed by a man or youth enclosed in a wicker pyramid covered with leaves. This character probably derived from the original Mac Grene, an ancient solar fertility god-king along the lines of the sun god Horus and the green-faced Osiris. (The tradition that made Osiris the personification of the nourishing grain is noteworthy in this respect, for the word "grain" may stem from a common root as well.)

As Mac Grene's consort, Eire personifies mother earth in all her beauty and fury. One poem describes her transformation from an emaciated, gray-haired old hag during wintertime into a gorgeous maiden with a stunning green mantle in springtime.[257] This drastic change is intended to illustrate the yearly cycle of the seasons in highly anthropomorphic terms. And Eire is not the only goddess to exemplify this theme. The same sort of imagery is used to depict Anat, for example, as the Phoenician goddess of love and war — on the one hand beautiful and seductive; on the other hand harsh and forbidding.

After relating the fall of the Tuatha de Danaan, the legend continues on its mythical track. It relates that after their defeat, the Dagda took them to live under the hollow hills — the distinctive barrows or burial mounds scattered across the British Isles. As time wore on, they would earn renown as the faerie folk, beings from the spirit realm whose handiwork is revealed on occasion in land of the living, but who themselves remain elusive and are seldom seen. They remain, nonetheless, alive and vibrant, their youth sustained throughout eternity by the Dagda's magical cauldron, the contents of which are never exhausted.

This cauldron, constantly filled with victuals, sounds very much like the life-giving grail in its form as a serving platter. It was one of four treasures associated with the Tuatha, along with a magical stone, a sword and a spear. Each of these objects plays a major role in the grail stories, which repeatedly mention a bleeding spear as a key component of the so-called grail procession, the central ritual in the myth. The legend also refers to several mystical swords, including the sword on Solomon's ship and the famed sword of King Arthur known as Excalibur. But perhaps the most interesting of the four objects is the stone, which would seem to correspond to the benben stone of the phoenix. If so, one might expect it to be associated with royalty. (The phoenix was, after all, a personification of Horus, the Egyptian king.)

And as it turns out, this turns out to be precisely the case.

The Stone and the Throne

The Stone of Destiny, as it was called, was actually used in ancient times during the coronation of Irish kings. During this ceremony, the candidate for the throne would literally stand on top of the stone and wait for its approval. If he was deemed a fit candidate for the high honor, legend said the stone would cry out its approval.

In some traditions, the stone was associated with the place where Jacob rested his head on the night he received his vision of a "stairway to heaven." This stone had, according to this legend, been taken from Egypt on a long and arduous journey that finally came to an end in Ireland. It appears the storytellers went to a great deal of trouble in their effort to transport (in a literary sense) this particular stone to the emerald isle. The question is, why should they have done so? And why should they have chosen to associate this particular stone with the coronation of a new king?

The answer is, quite simply, because Jacob's vision had been about precisely this. Jacob was an Egyptian pharaoh, so it was natural that the story of his ascension to the throne should have been told using ancient Egyptian symbolism. In this context, his vision conveyed a very specific message — that his father Isaac was dead and had ascended to heaven on a sacred ladder in the form of Osiris. In doing so, he had passed the mantle to his successor, who became the new Horus. This very process is laid out in Egyptian funerary ritual, which describes a headrest or pillow that exemplifies the word of truth. The so-called Chapter of the Headrest contains the following admonition:

Awake from your sufferings
You who lie prostrate
The gods watch over your head in the horizon

You are lifted up
Your word is truth
In respect to the things you have accomplished

Ptah has cast down your enemies headlong
This work was ordered to be done for you

You are Horus [258]

One can imagine these words being uttered to Jacob as he awoke from sleeping on the stone pillow.

His father was dead.

He was Horus, who was lifted up. And as Horus, it was his duty to prepare his father to ascend to heaven as Osiris. This is why Jacob promptly took the stone upon which he had lain his head and "set it up as a pillar." [259] Again, the Egyptian symbolism is apparent, for this was exactly the sort of ceremony conducted upon the death of a pharaoh. A pillar, or *djed* column, was set up to represent the dead god, Osiris. This signified that the king was no longer reclining, a position associated with death. On the contrary, he was now in fact upright, a position signifying life. The pharaoh was, in other words, "risen" from the dead or resurrected.

It appears that Jacob, upon hearing of his father's death, was carrying out just such a ritual with the stone upon which he had rested his head.

This was, indeed, a special stone. It was as though it had spoken the "word of truth" to him during the night, informing Jacob of his father's death and confirming his legitimacy as heir to the throne. Even in this myth, it seems, the stone acted as a sort of coronation stone, serving to authenticate the rule of the new pharaoh. And this would remain its purpose throughout the centuries. It was eventually taken to Scotland, where it became known as the Stone of Scone. Later, it was captured by the English, who took it south to serve as the coronation seat for that country's kings — the seat on which they are still crowned to this day.[260]

The stone was, in its capacity as the benben, serving as the guarantor of Egyptian kingship. The phoenix might die but would ever be reborn. One king might ascend to heaven, but his heir would ascend the throne. And so it was that the line of kings would remain unbroken, and Horus — in one incarnation or another — would always sit upon the throne.

This was exactly the sort of promise contained in the divine pledge made to Jacob during his vision. It is a promise of kingship, not only for Jacob but his descendants: "I will give you and your descendants the land upon which you are lying," the Hyksos pharaoh was told. "All peoples on earth will be blessed through you and your offspring." [261]

There was only one conceivable threat to this promise.

What happened if the king died without an heir?

The Fisher King

The Egyptian pharaoh was more than a monarch; he was a symbol of life and its ultimate protector. As Horus, the living shoot that sprang forth from the bowels of death, he epitomized the fertility of the land itself. In a very real sense, the king and the land he ruled were one. And so it was only natural that the pharaoh's ability to produce an heir should serve as a reminder of life's enduring power and a reason to hope for a bountiful harvest.

This sort of symbolism could be quite comforting to a people who faced the near-constant threat of war, drought and pestilence. Such events were hardly extraordinary in the ancient world; they were facts of life, and the gods provided the only defense against them. The king, as a god himself, was the nation's special guardian — its last line of defense, so to speak. But the association between the king's sexual potency and the land's fertility had a downside, as well. What if the king failed to produce an heir — what did *that* mean for the land? Would it, too, cease to bear fruit and wither away into nothingness?

This was a very real fear for the ancients, a fear that provides the central theme of the grail literature. It is a simple but universal story line: The land is withering up and dying, and an heir must be found — someone who can discover the mystery of the grail and show himself worthy to assume the throne. The king himself has failed to produce an heir and is on his deathbed, yet he *cannot* die until a suitable successor is found. He longs for the day when such a hero, a knight of royal blood and noble heart, arrives to release him of his obligations.

In some tales, the knight is Percival, who appears to have been original hero of the story. In others, it is Gawain, whose most famous adventure involves a contest with the so-called Green Knight. This knight is obviously a fertility god in disguise, for he not only survives a seemingly mortal blow from Gawain, but does so despite the fact that his head has been completely severed. In still other versions of the myth, the destined heir is Galahad, who took his name from the biblical region known as Gilead. This area was known for its healing herbs and spices. And it was for this reason that the prophet Jeremiah had asked in his oracle: "Is there no balm in Gilead? Is there no physician there? Whey then is there no healing for the wound of my people?" [262]

But one question remained unasked.

Just what is the nature of this wound?

It is this question that is addressed in the grail stories, which lament that the king is stricken by a grievous wound and lies confined to his bed in a mystical castle. This place is known as Munsalvaesche, a word that means "mountain of salvation." On the one hand, it might refer to the artificial mountains erected in ancient Egypt, the pyramids that served as the pharaohs' gateway to the heavens. On the other, it might refer to the Temple Mount in Jerusalem, the presumed site of Solomon's holy sepulcher. Perhaps most likely of all, it referred to both.

In the grail stories, however, its location is indefinite — so much so that the valiant knights who seek the place can only discover it with great difficulty. Moreover, once they depart, they seem incapable of retracing their steps to find it once again. All this indicates that it is a place beyond the realm of the living, part of a faerie spirit world to which access is fleeting and customarily denied. One might almost expect to find the hero crossing the archetypal waters of death to reach it.

And if so, those expectations are only mildly disappointed.

When the wounded king first appears, he in fact greets the hero Percival from a boat (or ark) in the midst of a river. The king is out fishing from the bow of his watercraft, an activity that earns him the name by which he will be known from this point forward: the Fisher King. Approaching, the knight asks him whether there is a ford or bridge in the vicinity by which he might cross, but the king responds that no such crossing is available. In this portion of the tale, the king appears to be assuming the role of the ferryman in ancient myth. Although he does not ultimately bear the hero across the waters, he does offer him the hospitality of his castle. One can only wonder whether an earlier version of the tale placed this castle was on the *opposite* side of the river, for it is clearly a mystical place that belongs to another realm.

Whatever the case, the hero accepts the king's offer and is pointed toward the castle. Once inside, he again meets his host, "a handsome nobleman with grizzled locks" who is reclining on a couch.[263] The Fisher King bids him approach and apologizes for not being able to rise and greet him, saying it is difficult for him to do so. As it turns out, he has suffered terrible wounds to his thighs, which have been pierced, leaving him incapacitated.

Why should the Fisher King have been associated with a wounded thigh? For one thing, it is fascinating to note that the Egyptian hieroglyph thought to symbolize the thigh is the image of a headless *fish*.[264] It is also worth remembering the Babylonian myth in which the enraged Enkidu, having slain the bull of heaven, tears off its thigh a flings it at his goddess nemesis.

The bull of heaven was none other than the constellation Taurus, known to the Egyptians as Apis — the animal said to represent the pharaoh. This explains the goddess' anger in the legend. For the goddess in question is Ishtar, known as the queen of heaven and therefore consort of the celestial king. The Apis bull. In symbolic terms, Enkidu has slain not just some mythic beast but the king himself. This symbolism is potent, for it suggests a ritual confrontation between the old order and the new. A young upstart challenges the venerable king of heaven and slays him, ushering in a brave new age. The queen of heaven mourns her fallen consort and vows revenge, foreseeing that her son will one day challenge the usurper and in turn replace him on the throne. This is exactly how the myth of Isis (also called the queen of heaven), Osiris, Seth and Horus played itself out. And it was a theme that would be repeated time and again in ritual and history as the young prince challenged the aging king to a battle for the crown, a fight to the death. In the grail mysteries, the noble knight would play the former role while the Fisher King was cast in the latter.

The nature of the Fisher King's wound — that he has been "pierced in the thighs" — is highly symbolic. For the storyteller, it appears to be a polite way of saying the king has been wounded in his genitalia, rendering him impotent and therefore unable to produce an heir.

At least temporarily.

As a result, not only is the king's health failing, but the land is becoming a wasteland as well. It is, in Egyptian terms, being converted from the garden of Osiris into the wilderness of Seth. Only a valiant knight with a true heart can reverse the course of this great blight, and he can only do so by asking the proper question during the grail procession that is to follow.

There is just one problem: He does not know what the question is, or even that he is supposed to ask it.

He must figure it out himself.

The grail procession that follows provides clear echoes of the Tuatha de Danaan myth, with each of the legendary race's four great "treasures" making an appearance in the ritual. First, a *sword* is given to the hero. Then, a *lance* dripping with blood is paraded across the chamber. There is also a silver platter, analogous to the magical *cauldron*, and the grail itself (which represents both cauldron and *stone*). The unfortunate hero, having been warned previously against the impertinence of asking too many questions, refrains from assuaging his curiosity and keeps his mouth shut. Little does he know that the proper question, which is burning on the tip of his tongue, will free the land from its terrible winter and usher in the newness of spring.

In one version of the myth, it is Galahad who succeeds in healing the Fisher King — living up to his name as the curative "balm of Gilead." By proving himself worthy to succeed the wounded king on the throne, he restores not only the king's health but also the abundance of the land.

An heir has been found, and the aged king may die in peace.

This ancient drama was nothing new to Galahad. It had been played and replayed time and again over the centuries in the form of the wilderness ritual. This re-enactment of the struggle between Seth and Horus culminated in a sacred wedding celebration, the ultimate expression of fertility. It was a fruitfulness that extended beyond the king's bedchamber to the orchards, fields and vineyards of his kingdom. The king and the land were one. And just as the king had vanquished Seth, so he had vanquished the wilderness that Seth personified.

The model for this sacred wedding feast was contained in the text known as Song of Songs. This poetic liturgy, attributed to Solomon himself, celebrated the rite of marriage by equating the king or bridegroom with the mountains of Gilead.[265] It was with this in mind that Jesus would refer to himself as the bridegroom and gain a reputation as the balm of Gilead, destined to heal the wounds of the people.[266] As the new king, this is what he was expected to do.

He also "healed" the new king by, ironically, releasing him from this life. Once an heir had been found, the wounded king was free to die in peace, assured in the knowledge that his realm was in good hands. This is the exact motivation behind the Osiris rituals that took place in the great pyramids. At the center of these rituals was the *djed* column, representing the dead king. The new king, acting as Horus, would set this column upright, symbolically restoring the king to health. No longer would he recline on the couch like the Fisher King;

now he was free to stand tall once more and ascend to the heavenly realm that was prepared for him. The land, too, would be restored as the new shoot sprang forth from the earth.

And so the endless cycle continued.

Even the great king Alexander of Macedon, who subdued most of the known world in a decade of conquest, is said to have taken part in it. The account, though surely legendary, serves to link the Arthurian and Egyptian traditions even more closely. Written several hundred years after the death of Alexander, it was nonetheless being circulated nearly an millennium before the grail romances took written form and centuries before Arthur was said to have lived. This account, a letter attributed to Alexander himself and purportedly sent to his mother, tells the story of a journey Alexander made to the City of the Sun.

This can be none other than Heliopolis, the sacred city of Lower Egypt.

The author then proceeds to describe an altar in the center of the city. This altar, like the step pyramid of Saqqara, had seven steps leading to a horse-drawn chariot driven by a figure of gold and (naturally) emerald. This was doubtless the chariot of the sun, a common feature of solar gods from Apollo to Ra who were said to cross the sky each day by such means. In this case, it must have been the chariot of Horus, the great god of the sun disk who was synonymous with the phoenix. In Egyptian it would have been known by combining the words for "chariot" and "Horus" into a single term: Urit-hor or perhaps Arit-hur.

This charioteer was the king of the Egyptians.

King Arit-hur.

The story, however, does not end there. Apparently seeking to ascend the altar, Alexander is confronted with a bank of fog — a typical symbol not only of the British Isles but of the otherworld — and rebuffed by an Ethiopian "priest of the sun" who demands that he and his company depart. Alexander complies and withdraws with his entourage to a high mountain (a pyramid?), at the top of which is a temple. The description that follows seems to indicate that the occupant of this temple is none other than the Fisher King, a.k.a. Osiris or Solomon: "In the middle of the temple stood a bed, whereon lay a man clothed in silk. I could not actually see his face, but saw his size and strength."

As in the grail legend, the figure is handsome and noble but reclining and apparently *unable to stand*.

Just as a dead man is unable to stand.

One is reminded of the elaborate sarcophagi often associated with Egyptian pharaohs, made to emulate the marvelous chest of Osiris. The case that contained King Tutankhamen's body is perhaps the best-known example, its golden exterior transformed into an idealized representation of the pharaoh. The embodiment of royalty, he is regal and majestic, strong and proud. Yet his true face is hidden beneath the death mask — just as the figure in the mountain temple is hidden from Alexander.

This man's identity as an Egyptian king is confirmed by the presence in the temple of a golden crown suspended from a chain. The benben stone and the phoenix are also present: "A precious stone, which lit the whole temple, took the place of a fire. A golden cage, with a large bird inside, was also hanging from the ceiling." It was this bird that broke the silence, admonishing Alexander in a human voice: "Desist thenceforth from setting thyself up against the gods. Turn back home and do not, through recklessness, hasten thy passage to the heavenly paths." [267]

Another myth involving Alexander also sheds light on the Egyptian connection. In this legend, a brilliant stone from paradise in the shape of a human eye falls into the conqueror's possession. This can be none other than the "eye of Horus" — yet another manifestation of the benben stone. During a series of inquiries as to its properties, Alexander happens upon an aged Jew who tells him a great mystery. If placed on a scale opposite a great quantity of gold, this tiny stone will tip the balance in its favor. Yet if the stone is covered with but a little dust, the scales will tip the other way if only a feather were placed opposite it.

This fable is reminiscent of the Egyptian myth in which the gods were said to "weigh the heart" of the deceased against a feather to determine whether he may proceed to heaven. In Alexander's case, the point is to warn him against the human eye's natural penchant for greed when it comes to earthly treasures. In this legend, Alexander heeds the implicit warning and decides against any further attempt at world conquest.[268]

The two stories appear to have much the same message.

Alexander, who fancied himself (with some justification) lord of the entire world, sought to claim for himself the title of pharaoh as well. But although his armies had cowed the rest of Egypt, the priests of Heliopolis stood firm in their opposition: He was not, after all, of the royal bloodline. He was not the true Horus, but a usurper seeking to secure the Egyptian heritage by force of arms. This, the priests believed, could not be permitted. It was not military might but a noble heart that made one worthy of the throne — a theme that runs likewise consistently through the grail romances. For example, Gawain might succeed in decapitating the Green Knight, but he nonetheless is not the victor in their contest until he submits willingly to a blow from his adversary. It is not pride but humility that wins the day.

Death itself can never be defeated, no matter how powerful the hero. Yet neither can life be cowed into submission. For though one king may die, another will ever rise to take his place, imbued like his predecessor with the noble spirit of Horus. And though a noble knight may fall in battle, it is the death of the valiant — not of valor itself. Others will arise to bear the mantle.

This is the very meaning of the title "chariot of Horus." Just as the chariot was the heavenly vessel that bore the god across the sky, so the body was an earthen vessel that carried the spirit of Horus through this life. At the end of this journey, the chariot driver had no more use for his vessel and therefore set it aside. The king's death therefore paralleled the daily passing of the sun as it slipped below the horizon and into the underworld abyss. During life, each new king bore within him the spirit of Horus — a spirit that passed at death to his successor.

This is why Jesus could make the seemingly audacious claim, "Before Abraham was born, I am." [269] The spirit of Horus was older than Abraham and had been passed from king to king, manifesting itself finally in Jesus. He was the latest reincarnation of all the ancient pharaohs of Egypt, who had lived and died in an endless succession dating back thousands of years. He was the great king Solomon reborn as the phoenix, and he even went so far as to claim for himself Solomon's identity as the sacred "bridegroom" of Israel.

This was the secret of eternal life, a secret obscured by those such as Alexander who selfishly sought immortality as a possession rather than a sacred trust to pass along to the next generation.

This was the message of the grail legends.

It was the message, too, of the Egyptian myths.

And it is a message sadly lost on many ambitious and insecure people who, like Alexander, seek to steal from the temple a treasure that cannot be taken.

XIV

Son of the Dragon

Where does this all leave King Arthur, the man recognized by most as the central character in the grail literature? Each of the brave knights might have his tale, but it is Arthur whom they serve; he and his mystical kingdom of Camelot are what bind their myriad quests and adventures together.

Numerous attempts have been made to locate Camelot, with some researchers claiming to have found the king's fabled court in the extreme southwest of England, others on the east coast, and still others in Wales or Scotland. The fact is that the site of the legendary royal castle is as elusive as that of the Grail Castle — a bit of information that may well provide a clue to its nature. Could it be that Camelot is, in fact, merely another manifestation of the Grail Castle itself? And could it be that Arthur is nothing more than another name for the Fisher King?

These seem like very real possibilities. For one thing, it is Arthur's kingdom that seems to be wasting away under an ever-encroaching blight, and it is Arthur who orders the quest for the grail. Moreover, there is no evidence that Arthur ever fathered a child by his wife,

Guinevere. And the lack of such an heir would, in mythological terms, explain the creeping decay that afflicts the land.

Those familiar with the Arthurian tale will object, however, that Arthur did indeed father a child. According to the most popular version of the myth, he was seduced by his half-sister Morgan Le Fay, who bore him a son by the name of Mordred. The treacherous seed of this incestuous union would turn out to be Arthur's downfall, striking him dead in a battle that effectively ended the age of legends and ushered in the era of science and consciousness.

So it would seem that Arthur was not childless after all. Nor is there any indication that he was ever wounded in the thigh, as the Fisher King was.

Or is there?

To find the answer, it is necessary to once again retreat to the realm of Celtic mythology — the spirit realm of the Tuatha de Danaan and the mist-shrouded barrows of faerie.

There are several indications that the Arthurian myth belonged to this realm from the outset and was only later converted into pseudo-history by men from the era of science who failed to comprehend the language of myth. Morgan's own faerie origins are evident from her title Le Fay. She was in reality a goddess of ancient Ireland, Morrigana, whose name is in fact a title meaning "the great queen" — Mor Righ Anu.

Like Eire and Anat, she was at once a creature of great sensuality and fierce animosity. She was a war goddess often seen washing the clothes or weapons of warriors fated to die. Yet she was also a seductress, using her considerable charms to lure gods and men to her bed. This apparent contradiction reveals her to be yet another goddess of seasonal change, appearing now as a lovely spring maiden and now as a haggard winter crone. Like other seasonal earth goddesses, her natural mate is either the storm god or the solar god-king who calls forth her beauty.

And Arthur, whose very name meant "chariot of Horus," was just such a god-king. His full name was Arthur Pendragon, and the patronymic likewise seems to have originated in Egyptian tradition. It is worth recalling that the pharaohs were anointed with the fat of a crocodile or "dragon." In this manner they became messiahs, a play on words that referred both to the Egyptian word for the beast itself and the verb *msi* meaning "to give birth to." The new pharaoh was therefore considered, in symbolic terms, a son of the dragon.

To this day, the Semitic term for "son of" is *ben* or *ibn*, a word that could easily give rise to an Anglicized name such as Ben Dragon.

Or Pendragon. Indeed, one source prefers the name Bendragon for Arthur's father, whose name is the very similar-sounding Uthr.[270]

The famous name can be broken down from there into three syllables:

➢ Ben, from the Semitic "son of"
➢ Draig from the Welsh for dragon
➢ On, the ancient name for Heliopolis

Using this construction, the name specifically means "Son of the Dragon from Heliopolis." This dragon of Heliopolis cannot have been anything other than the phoenix, the firebird of Horus.

Perhaps the most famous of these dragon kings was Solomon, whose Egyptian name Apophis was that of a giant sky dragon and whose patron deity Seth would evolve into a dragonlord known as Satan. The legendary figure of Arthur carried forth this tradition.

Arthur was also the personification of Horus, who in one version of the myth is himself born *lame in his lower limbs*.[271] The patriarch Jacob, whose stone pillow came to be identified with the grail stone, also was struck lame in this same region when his mysterious divine wrestling partner, Esau in the guise of Seth, touched his hip and threw it out of socket.

As the personification of Horus, it was therefore only natural that Arthur should be portrayed as succumbing to Morgan's wiles. And yet the result of their union is not what it at first appears to be. The tip-off lies in yet another Celtic myth, involving a legendary British monarch named Bran the Blessed, who in many ways appears to be a model for Arthur himself. Like the Dagda, he possesses a magical cauldron of rebirth by which he is capable of raising the dead. And this is, in turn, a prototype of the grail platter — one that serves a central purpose in this particular legend.

The tale begins with Bran having struck a political alliance with the King of Ireland, who is to marry Bran's sister in the bargain. Bran's brother, however, is angry that his sister has been betrothed without his consent and displays his contempt for this arrangement by maiming the Irish king's horses.

In light of this outrageous slight, Bran's only recourse is to placate the aggrieved monarch by offering him the cauldron of rebirth in exchange for his indulgence.

The boon is accepted, and Bran's sister does indeed return to Ireland with her new husband.

She conceives a son by him, but this fails to put an end to their troubles. For the king's foster brothers, still fuming over the disfigured horses, drive the queen from her husband's bed and force her instead to work in the kitchens. The queen is understandably furious at this insult. And she therefore sends word to her brother in Britain, notifying him of her ill treatment at the hands of her new husband's kin. And Bran, equally, chagrined at her situation, responds by sending a naval armada across the straits that separate the two islands.

This is an alarming turn of events for the Irish, who have no navy of their own and indeed are mystified when they see what appears to be a forest growing "upon the sea, in a place where we have never yet seen a single tree." [272] The trees are, of course, the tall masts of ships. And when the Irish king realizes the nature of the threat, he scrambles to somehow avoid an armed confrontation. In an attempt to do so, he quickly abdicates his throne in favor of his infant son — the product of his union with the British princess.

The Irish, however, have plotted an ambush for the British forces. In an apparent move toward reconciliation, the Irish invite their opponents to a meeting inside a certain house. But this is not the friendly overture it might seem. For as it turns out, they have stationed a hundred of their own fighting men around the building, each concealed in a bag ostensibly containing meal. The ruse fools most of the British guests but fails to deceive Bran's brother, who systematically kills each of the hidden warriors as he moves from one bag to the next.

This should be the end of the matter — except for the fact that the Irish now possess the cauldron of rebirth. In the subsequent melee, they succeed in tossing each dead warrior into the cauldron, whereupon they emerge newly invigorated to wreak havoc against the British troops. Does this sound at all familiar? Recall for a moment the tradition that Osiris was depicted as a sack of grain, from which sprouted new life when water was sprinkled upon it. In the same way, the cauldron of rebirth revives the Irish warriors hidden inside *sacks of meal*. Or grain.

In the midst of the fighting, Bran himself is pierced in the foot or leg by an enemy spear and cries out in anguish, "Dogs of Gwern, beware the Morddwyd Tyllion!" [273] Gwern is the name of Bran's infant nephew who has been placed upon the throne of Ireland. But the statement otherwise is puzzling.

What, or who, is the Morddwyd Tyllion?

In fact, Bran appears to have been referring to himself. *He* was the Morddwyd Tyllion. Bran is the one who has been pierced by the enemy spear, and the phrase morddwyd tyllion is usually translated as "pierced thigh." [274]

This is, you may recall, the very nature of the wound that afflicted the Fisher King. His thighs were wounded by an enemy lance, and he was therefore unable to stand upright or father a child. To put it bluntly, he was impotent.

It should be clear enough that the name Mordred is derived from the phrase morddwyd tyllion or pierced thigh. And that Arthur is therefore another manifestation of the wounded Fisher King, who in some versions of the tale is identified by the name Bron. The similarity to "Bran" is obvious.

The similarity to the crucifixion of Jesus is also apparent, for Jesus too was pierced by a spear — the same spear, according to the grail accounts, that later wounded the Fisher King. Unlike the Fisher King, Jesus was wounded in the side. But the word usually translated as "side" in the biblical text is actually the Greek *pleura*, meaning specifically "rib."[275]

This is no accident.

Jesus was considered the second Adam, or Atum. And the very first act of human reproduction had allegedly been accomplished through the efficacy of Adam's *rib*. By piercing this particular body part, the spear symbolically rendered Jesus impotent — the same effect it had on the Fisher King. This suggests that Jesus himself was a manifestation of the Fisher King, a possibility that fits perfectly not only into his own legend but also into the myth of Horus.

Something Fishy

Horus was, of course, associated primarily with the falcon, in which guise he soared across the sky in his magnificent solar vessel. At times, this vessel was depicted as that great Hyksos innovation the chariot. But in other instances, it was seen as a solar "bark" or boat — the very sort of vessel in which the Fisher King is seated when he reveals himself to Percival.

In addition to being portrayed as a falcon, Horus was also seen as a fish. His sacred city of Heliopolis was known to the Egyptians as On, a name that first and foremost meant "pillar" in honor of the obelisk that bore the sacred stone of the phoenix. The word, however, also had a second meaning: "On" was also the Egyptian word for fish, the lesser-known manifestation of Horus.

Why should this have been?

As the sun rose in the morning over Egypt, it appeared to rise out of the waters of the horizon. It would have been only natural for the Egyptians to believe that when Horus disappeared beneath that horizon, he was diving into the waters of the underworld abyss. In doing so, he symbolically became a fish. He then rose again in the morning from these same waters, triumphant over the world of death. This ritual was preserved in the hieroglyph for one of Horus' divine names, a fish that appears to be rising or leaping out of the water.[276] The fish itself is a simple, stylized mark — nothing more than a line creating a loop and doubling back on itself, crossing to form a "tail." It is the very same mark that, when turned on its side, would be used by his followers to symbolize Jesus.

An engraving said to represent Horus even shows him holding a fish over his head as he stands on the back of a crocodile, showing him to be the messiah or son of the dragon.[277] It should come as no surprise that the figure represented in the engraving has also been identified with Jesus, whose most famous symbols are the cross (†) and the fish. And both these symbols were, in turn, hieroglyphic expressions of the Egyptian word *on*. As a pillar, this word was represented by a vertical rectangle surmounted by a cross, the symbolic perch of the phoenix. As a fish, the word was naturally represented by a pictograph of that very creature.[278] And it was this pictograph, in a more stylized form, that came to be used (and still is to this day) as a symbol representing Jesus.

There can be no doubt that Jesus is represented in the scriptural texts as something of a fisher king. In one vignette from his life story, he is described as joining some fisherman in their daily outing on the Sea of Galilee. Directing them to guide their boats to a certain spot, he instructs them to let down their nets, whereupon they haul in "such a large number of fish that their nets begin to break." Their partners then race out to help them, for their boat was so full of fish that it was in danger of sinking to the bottom.[279]

As the fisher king or lord of the fish, Jesus also miraculously multiplies the number of fish available to his followers by turning two of the creatures into enough for thousands to feast on.[280]

Jesus, however, was not the original fisher king.

That honor appears to have belonged to Oannes, a Babylonian

deity who depicted as half man and half fish who was seen as the progenitor of the gods. Evolutionists would doubtless find more than a little to cheer in this symbolism — especially considering Oannes' identity as the first great teacher of mankind.[281] In this regard, he adopted a role identical to that of Osiris, who was credited by the Egyptians as the father of civilization. In other respects, though, he more closely resembled Horus, for he too seems to have been a solar deity who rose from the waters to teach men during the daytime, then descended once again into the deep at sunset.[282] This explained his dual nature as both fish and man, a nature he would share not only with Horus but with Jesus and many others.

The name Oannes is at the root of several recognizable names, belonging to a number of heroes and prophets in the ancient texts. Thence is derived such names as Jonathan and John. It also at the root of the name Honi, which belonged to an enigmatic rain-making prophet who would play a key role in the history of the Jewish nation six decades before the birth of Jesus. The Greek form of his name, Onias, was worn by several Jewish high priests — including one who would be forced into exile and find refuge in a suburb of Heliopolis. And then there is Jonah, in many ways the archetypal fish-man, who supposedly spent three days in the belly of a great fish before journeying to the Babylonian capital.

The connection to Babylon, birthplace of the Oannes legend, is telling. So is Jonah's vocation as a prophet or teacher, the same sort of role accorded Oannes in the more ancient myth. Indeed, Jonah's story seems to have been nothing more than a variation on the Oannes myth. In its original form, it was not even a Hebrew story at all. And this makes it all the more significant that Jesus should have paid it a degree of reverence he accorded no other tale. When pressed for a sign to confirm his authority as a teacher, he boldly asserted that no sign would be provided "except for the sign of the prophet Jonah." [283]

Jesus then went on to compare himself to Jonah. In doing so, he was affirming his authority as a teacher based on the model provided by the archetypal teacher. Call him Jonah or Oannes, it makes little difference. In either case, Jesus was boldly identifying himself as the Fisher King.

The wounded king.

The chariot of Horus.

A participant in the ancient ritual in which the dying king ever gave way to the new king.

The crucifixion was just such a ritual. And, as its horrific nature makes clear, it was not a pleasant ritual by any means. Yet despite the obvious anguish associated with this particular event, Jesus' followers have steadfastly asserted for centuries that it was somehow necessary to the well-being of the human race. Jesus, they have maintained, willingly sacrificed his life for the good of his people.

The obvious question is: Why?

The answer lies in the king's symbolic role as guarantor of the earth's fertility. As the personification of the sun god Horus, he was expected to call forth the seed from the depths of the earth. Yet if he were "wounded" — or impotent — and unable to produce an heir, how could he be expected to ensure the fruitfulness of the earth? A barren womb meant a barren landscape, and this could never be allowed. The cold reality was simply this: No such king could remain on the throne. A suitably virile replacement would have to be found.

And the old king would have to be put out of his misery.

This is the message of the various grail myths. Arthur himself is slain by his own heir, "Mordred," whose name indicates that he is in fact nothing more than the embodiment of his "pierced thigh." His impotence. It is this impotence that causes the wasting away of the once-fertile land, and it is this impotence that leads to his death at the hands of the one who would succeed him to the throne.

The wounded Fisher King's fate is exactly the same. He can only succumb to the sleep of death once a suitable heir has been found, one worthy of replacing him on the throne. The successful candidate is invariably a knight renowned for his prowess in battle. It is this knight who releases the ailing king from his woeful existence (by killing him in combat!) and subsequently takes his place as ruler of the kingdom.

Such stories express the ancient code known as tanistry, under which a young claimant to the throne challenged the reigning monarch's fitness to continue occupying it. This code provided a mechanism by which the virile heir apparent could challenge the old, weak and impotent king to a contest of strength. By dispatching him, he could seize the throne for himself and, in the process, ensure the continued fruitfulness of the land. The virile young champion could then claim the queen as his prize and father a child upon her as a sign of the earth's restored fertility. The king was the land. The land was the king. It is just this sort of tanist ritual that Seth had undertaken in slaying his older brother, the good king Osiris, to seize the throne. It is also what the young Horus had done in turn by defeating his aging uncle Seth in *their* epic conflict.

This tradition is extremely ancient, almost certainly dating back before the dawn of historical records. It appears to be the remnant of an instinctive drive, witnessed among many animal species, in which a strong male emerges from the pack to claim the dominant position — and with it the right (often exclusive) to enter into sexual relations with the females of the group. He thus becomes the "father" of the group until a strong challenger emerges to wrest the privilege from him. Darwinists will recognize this as natural selection in action, and they may take some satisfaction from the knowledge that it appears to have served as a foundational principle for a broad array of religious beliefs.

The Hebrew scribes, for example, appear to have preserved a record of just such a tanist succession in the legend of the prophet Elijah, who was said to have been taken up to heaven on a chariot of fire. This fiery chariot unmistakably identifies Elijah as yet another manifestation of the sun god Horus. Indeed, the Greek version of his name — Elias — is probably related to the name Helios, which not only belonged to a solar deity but also served as the root prefix in for the city of *Helio*polis.

As a solar figure, Elijah is at the center of the myth in question. And yet he is not the only pivotal figure in this tale; equally important is his *successor*, Elisha, who is the only one present at the time of his death.

As the story opens, the narrator reveals that Elijah is about to be taken up to heaven on a whirlwind. There could be no clearer cue that a death scene is in the offing. There is no clear evidence, however, that Elijah himself knows what lies ahead. Intending to go forward on his own, he tells the young Elisha to remain where he is; Elijah himself, meanwhile, prepares to undertake a solitary journey to the far side of the Jordan River. This is the second indication of what is in store, with the narrator using the familiar motif of the river crossing to signify an imminent passage to the spirit world.

Elisha, however, refuses to obey his master — despite two admonishments — and insists upon accompanying him on his journey. Unlike Elijah, the younger man appears to have a good idea of what the future holds, for when a group of prophets asks him whether he knows what is in store, he answers clearly and succinctly: "Yes, I know. But do not speak of it." [284] The prophets seem to be in the dark as to what is about to transpire, but obviously Elisha has a pretty good idea.

Moreover, it is clear that Elisha has a vested interest in keeping this information from his master.

Why?

It appears he is planning to issue a tanist challenge and slay Elijah, thereby (he hopes) taking his place as leader of the people. And it is not long before his intentions become clear in this regard. Elijah, apparently sensing his acolyte's purpose in disregarding his instructions and following him across the river, asks him: "Tell me, what can I do for you before I am taken from you?"

Elisha is not slow to answer, confessing that he seeks a double portion of Elijah's spirit. This appears on the surface of things to be an odd request — unless, that is, Elijah's spirit is actually the spirit of Horus. It is this spirit that passes at death from the monarch to his heir. And it is this spirit that drives the chariot of fire, the heavenly vessel of the great sun god. As a result, it is no surprise to find that the two men's conversation is interrupted by the sudden appearance of just such a fiery chariot that passes between them and takes hold of Elijah, transporting him up to heaven after the manner of Osiris. Elisha's exclamation at this point is telling: "My father! My father!" It signifies that Elijah has been transformed into the heavenly father, Osiris, while Elisha has taken on the role of his son Horus.

According to Hebrew legend, Elijah did not die at all but was translated directly to heaven. And just this sort of end is prescribed for the king in Egyptian lore. The pyramid texts declare to the king, "You have not departed dead; you have departed alive" and implore the deity to "grasp the king by his hand and take the king to the sky, that he may not die on earth among men." [285] Such language all but spells out the fact that Elijah was a priest-king in the Egyptian tradition.

After his master's translation into heaven, Elisha returns to the company of prophets bearing Elijah's cloak — the mantle of his leadership. The prophets, having watched the two men journey across the river, want to know what has happened to Elijah. But the younger prophet is not forthcoming. When they propose sending a search party in retrieve their revered leader, Elisha first attempts to block them and only assents because he is too ashamed (literally, he turned pale) to press the matter.

But why should he have been ashamed?

It was not his fault that Elijah was taken away up to heaven — was it?

The fact is that the two men were the only ones present at Elijah's translation to heaven. Only Elisha knew what had really happened. If he had murdered the old man in a tanist power grab, that would have given him ample reason to be ashamed. And it would have given him a very strong motive to prevent the prophets from searching for the body and discovering the truth. Fortunately for him, their search for the missing prophet would not prove successful; Elisha would be free to assume the position of leadership that Elijah had once held.

This was the nature of tanistry, a practice that took its name from the goddess Tanit.

In Greece, she was known as Diana. And it is in the sacred grove of this great goddess that this sort of drama played itself out time and again.

In this profound ritual, the priest was handed a sword and sent forth into the woodland, charged with standing guard over a single tree. There, he was to be challenged by a young warrior seeking to the claim the tree as his own. It was the symbol of the priesthood and the divine kingship that went with it; the right to be called the consort of Diana herself. [286]

It was, of course, the tree of Osiris. The priest who guarded the tree was none other than the Egyptian high priest or *kher heb*; he was the cherub warrior with the flaming sword whose task was to guard the tree of life in the biblical garden. One day, he would certainly be defeated, for there would come a time when he was no longer young and strong enough to defend the tree. And there would come a time when a brave and noble warrior would issue a challenge he could not meet. This was the inevitable sequel to man's expulsion from the garden.

He would return.

He would defeat the *kher heb*.

He would reclaim paradise.

He would obtain the tree of life.

At first glance, it seems that the Hebrew scribes inexplicably left this sequel out of their accounts. The story of Eden appears to end with Adam being sent into exile, denied access to the tree and immortality. But this was hardly a satisfactory conclusion, and it was only a matter of time before someone decided to write an ending to the story.

That someone turned out to be Jesus and his followers, who cast him in the role of a new Adam destined to undo the damage done by the archetypal first man. If Adam had been exiled, Jesus would fight his way back into the garden. He would slay the priestly *kher heb* — represented in his day by the temple priesthood — guarding the "tree of life" in the center of the garden. This tree was the burial ark of the tree god Osiris, the sacred object that was housed in the center of the temple.

According to one tradition, the cross itself was even fashioned from the wood of the tree of life. It was the gateway to immortality, thrown open once more by a ritual death, never more to be closed again. This was the essence of the mythic ritual that was to become the most pervasive and influential faith of modern times — a myth that nonetheless had roots (so to speak) as ancient as the tree of life itself.

The Guardian

Jesus was the *kher heb* priest standing watch over the sacred tree of life, symbolized by the cross.

As such, he was the divinely appointed guardian of eternity.

This appears to have been the role of the Fisher King from the beginning. In the grail legends, it is he who stands guard over the ephemeral Grail Castle on the mountain of salvation. The pyramid. Or the temple mount in Jerusalem, where the *kher heb* high priest stood guard over the hallowed inner sanctuary, the shrine of the ark that contained the dead king's mummy. In this regard, it is no wonder Jesus' followers would refer to him as the great high priest.[287]

The source of all this imagery appears in a single hieroglyph. It shows a man seated, gazing westward and holding in his hand a fishhook — from which dangles the same stylized fish symbol used to symbolize both Jesus and Horus. This is, undoubtedly, the Fisher King, who is always depicted seated or reclining, being unable to rise unable to rise because of his infirmity. The meaning of this hieroglyph is even more revealing: It is the pictogram for "guardian," and it formed the Egyptian word *sa*.

This seems an awful lot like *sah*, the word denoting Osiris as the constellation Orion.

Sah-Amen was the hidden (mummified) Osiris.

Sa-Amen was the guardian of the hidden Osiris — the high priest, who served in the temple of Solomon. As such, he was also Sa-Amen in another sense: *Sa* (the pronunciation was the same, but the hieroglyph was different) also meant "son." Hence, he was the son of Amen, just as Horus was the son of Osiris. He was the *kher heb* who stood guard at the tree of life, the tree wherein the body of Osiris stood encased.

The king, cut down in by the usurper, had risen again from the earth to become the upright one, alive again though he had perished. And now he ascended to heaven on the celestial ladder of Jacob, a ladder created for him by Horus and Seth.

These gods were the two vertical posts of the ladder. And they were also the pillars of the temple, Horus representing strength and Seth the embodiment of stability. A pink granite statue of the third pharaoh named Rameses depicts his transformation into Osiris, with the dog-headed Seth standing at his left and the falcon-headed Horus at his *right hand*.[288]

Could this very symbolism have been the origin of Jesus' famous declaration that he would be exalted to heaven and sit at the *right hand* of his father? Osiris was Horus' father.

Was Jesus therefore equating himself with Horus?

It would seem so.

He was the son/sun who would come in the clouds of heaven, just as the sun disk Horus parted the clouds for his passage across the sky.

Jesus might die, but as the sun was reborn from its dark abyss each morning, so he, too, would be reborn. This was his destiny.

Many Mansions

But despite such assurances, there was still a great deal of uncertainty among the ancients about their fate beyond the grave. What exactly would happen to them after death? This was the question that gnawed at men two or three thousand years ago as surely as it does at their descendants. Jesus would assure his followers that his death was not a tragic event, but the means by which he would "prepare a place" for them in the afterlife.[289]

"In my father's house are many mansions," he told them. "If it were not so, I would have told you." [290]

This enigmatic saying appears nonsensical on the face of it. Aren't houses and mansions the same thing? Indeed, this wording troubled some translators so much that they chose to translate "mansions" as "rooms." Their decision to do so, however, is unfortunate because it obscures the meaning of the original text. The word translated as "house" refers to an abode or residence, which might be a house or some more expansive entity such as a kingdom. "Mansions" derives from the Greek verb meaning "to stay." It was therefore a place to stay or way station — not a simple room, but not a permanent residence either.

The landscape of the grail romances is littered with such way stations. Heroic knights seem to be forever wandering from one castle (or mansion) to the next, finding a new adventure at each stop along the way. There is the Castle of Belrepeire, the Castle of Damsels, the Castle of Death, the Castle of Pride and the Castle of Wonders. Most are mystical ports of call in a long journey across the barren wilderness that symbolizes the land of death, the afterworld.

The ultimate destination is the Grail Castle of the Fisher King, who represents God the Father. In this context, it is clear that Jesus was not assuring his followers that each of them would get his own abode in heaven; on the contrary, they were all bound for the same dwelling place. A long journey lay ahead of them, yet they could take comfort in the knowledge that many way stations would be prepared for them along the road. Jesus would make sure of it.

In offering this reassurance, he was drawing on imagery explicitly rendered in Egyptian mythology. According to the Egyptians, the abode or kingdom of the father-god Osiris was divided into seven districts. These corresponded to the seven steps on the pyramid of Saqqara and the throne of Solomon, which in turn represented the seven heavenly realms one must pass through after death. Each of these realms was marked by a bright guardian — the sun, moon or one of the five planets visible to the naked eye. And these were specifically seen as fortresses marking the boundary to each successive realm in the kingdom of the dead.

These way stations were specifically referred to as mansions.[291]

The first of these is particularly noteworthy, for it is said to have been marked with three symbols. The first is the familiar *ankh* or cross of life, which is highly significant. But the other two are objects of even greater interest. They are the hieroglyph of the *djed* column, which translates as "stability," and a second vertical pictograph of a staff meaning "power." Here we have the two pillars that stood at the entrance to Solomon's temple/tomb — Jachin and Boaz, whose names signify stability and strength. The temple itself therefore must have served as the first way station or mansion on the dead king's journey through the afterlife.

We also have the explanation for the psalmists' most famous work:

> *Yea, though I walk through the valley of the shadow of death*
> *I will fear no evil, for thou art with me*
> *Thy rod and thy staff, they comfort me* [292]

The rod was the *djed* column of stability at the entrance to the temple, which was flanked on the other hand by the staff, the column of strength. In passing between these pillars, one entered the temple shrine — the valley of the shadow of death. In doing so, one would pass beneath the cross of life inscribed on the cornice, clearly marking this gateway to immortality. This was the place of the tree of life, it proclaimed — the cross of hope and the resting place of Osiris. Here was the first of the many mansions Jesus had promised to his disciples.

It was, in fact, a perfect replica of the first heavenly mansion, precisely constructed to match the design of a celestial temple. Temples in Egypt were also known as mansions, and this particular mansion was particularly significant. It was not merely a crypt, but also a way station.

It was the end, but just the beginning.

XV

In the Cards

By the medieval period, the traditions of ancient Egypt had been all but forgotten. Those who believed in one god and one church had little regard for such polytheistic nonsense. And Osiris, the most widely revered deity in the ancient world, had been relegated to the religious scrap heap along with all the other "idols." His was not merely a competing faith; it was something much more dangerous. If one were to examine it too closely, one might recognize the uncanny similarities between the Osirian doctrines and those attributed to Jesus.

And the Osiris myth predated the birth of Jesus by three or four millennia.

The conclusion would have been inescapable: Jesus must have drawn aspects of his own teaching from the polluted well of pagan idolatry. Some early writers, painfully aware of the similarities, tried to pussyfoot around the problem by attributing them to an ingenious plot of Satan. It was he, they maintained, who had somehow forged a counterfeit of the authentic tradition. But they failed to explain how he could have possibly created such an imitation thousands of years *before* the advent of the genuine article. And, in the ultimate irony, they naïvely failed to realize that Satan himself was not the personification of evil, but merely another god "borrowed" from the Egyptian pantheon.

All this mattered little, however.

The library at Alexandria had burned to the ground, reducing thousands upon thousands of valuable manuscripts to ash and cinder. The works that escaped this horrible tragedy were consigned to other flames born of the same purpose by those in the establishment who sought to conceal the embarrassing truth. Anyone who wished to learn the ancient mysteries was branded a heretic and left to face the prospect of torture or death unless (and sometimes even if) he recanted. Facing this sort of intense pressure, few would dare to investigate the ancient roots of their faith — if they were even aware of them — and none would do so openly. The hieroglyphs that had borne the sacred message of ancient Egypt across the centuries gradually fell out of use. After a time, no one alive remembered how to read them at all, and it is only the relatively recent discovery of the Rosetta Stone that has enabled scholars to once again decipher their meaning.

Yet even in an atmosphere permeated by inquisitions, purges and other heavy-handed methods of intimidation, the old ways were not forgotten. Those intent upon keeping them alive still managed to pass on their knowledge, cleverly embedded in codes known only to those who knew their meaning.

Such coded messages were veiled in the most harmless of guises. A faerie tale. A child's game. A rhyme or song. These were the sorts of things that were passed on from generation to generation, until finally their meaning was all but forgotten by those who could see in the cards only a winning hand and hear in the minstrel's rhyme only an odd phrase that made one chuckle.

Nursery rhymes told of "faeries" who lived beneath the earth and flitted about from tree to hedgerow, engaging in a mischievous game of hide-and-seek with human children. It was a game they always seemed to win, vanishing in the mist at the very moment the seeker turned his head. These faeries, sprites and elves were what remained of the proud ancient god-race known as the Tuatha de Danaan, who had brought their four treasures to the emerald isle in ships from across the sea so very long ago.

Yet echoes of these four treasures remained in the suits of the tarot deck, suits that survive in our own modern deck of playing cards.

➢ The spade is in fact a stylized broadsword, related to the French symbol known as the fleur-de-lis.
➢ The heart was originally a chalice, corresponding to the grail and the sacred cauldron of rebirth.
➢ The club began as a flowering rod and thus can be traced to the staff of Aaron, the bleeding lance of grail lore and the spear of the Tuatha.
➢ The diamond suit originally consisted of "pentacles" or five-pointed stars that must have represented the fiery stone from heaven itself, the grail or benben.[293]

The tarot cards were divided into four suits and another category, which we would call the "face" cards. These latter were known as trumps (i.e., *trumpets*), designed to spread a particular message in the form of a clarion call. And it was this message that the establishment found troubling — so troubling, in fact, that it condemned the trumps as tools of the devil. Eventually, the number of trump cards was whittled down to four, which appear in our modern deck: the king, queen, jack and joker.

But what of the others?

Many were adorned with obvious Egyptian symbolism, the very sort of imagery the establishment considered most alarming. This is hardly surprising, for the cards were often associated with a class of nomadic tinkers and traders who traveled in caravans across medieval Europe. These people were known for their colorful dress and sometimes mischievous ways. Often, they would tell people's fortunes using the tarot deck. These nomads were known as gypsies, a slurred contraction derived from the term *Egyptian*.

The trumps of the tarot included one called Strength, which is portrayed in one of the oldest tarot decks — the so-called Charles VI deck — as a woman embracing a broken pillar. This can only be a representation of Isis mourning her dead husband Osiris, who takes the form of a *djed* column. The name of the card appears to derive from one of the pillars guarding the entrance to Solomon's temple, the boaz or "strength" pillar.

Another trump is the Devil, who is shown in this same deck with donkey's ears. This identifies him as the personification of Seth, whose totem animal was the ass. In his hands, he holds a string of fourteen balls that looks like a snake. It calls to mind the ancient Egyptian legend in which Seth brutally chopped the dead body of Osiris into *fourteen pieces*.

On the card known as the Hanged Man, a youth is seen dangling by one foot from a crossbar suspended between two uprights. This roughly hewn structure looks very much like the sort of wooden framework often used to support a grapevine. The youth therefore appears to symbolize the "vine" that springs forth from the dead Osiris — he is the virile young sun king or Horus. As if to confirm this, he wears a golden collar around his neck that sends forth like-colored threads, radiating outward like the sun's nourishing rays.

The youth is set against the background of a golden sky and a green field, the latter sprinkled with golden grains that appear to be wheat stalks. In his hands, the youth holds two sacks that appear to be filled with gold. Yet the context suggests another possibility. Perhaps, instead, these sacks are filled with golden wheat. Perhaps they are the makeshift mummies of Osiris that were fashioned in ancient Egypt and then watered until grain sprang forth through the mesh, symbolizing the dead king's resurrection.

Other trumps in the tarot deck are similarly revealing. The Justice card shows a woman bearing a sword in one hand and a balancing scale in the other. The former is a familiar symbol of the grail romances; the latter is the sort of scale used to weigh the heart of the deceased against a feather in Egyptian tradition.

On the Sun card, the solar orb shines down upon a flaxen-haired girl who appears to be holding a spindle. This identifies her on one level as the eternal seamstress spinning forth the thread of life. But her "spindle" also looks quite a bit like an archer's bow and arrow draped across her shoulder. This was the weapon of Diana, the goddess of the hunt, who was intimately associated with the sun. Indeed, in Greco-Roman tradition, she was the twin sister of the sun god Apollo. And in her guise as the Celtic goddess Dana — divine mother of the Tuatha de Danaan — she was the consort of Bile, a figure derived from the storm god Baal who (like his fellow storm god, Yahweh) eventually came to be closely linked with the sun. So closely, in fact, that he was seen as synonymous with Apollo.

The Judgment card portrays seven naked figures rising from a wooden chest as two winged angelic figures gaze down from above. The chest links the ritual burial casket with the ancient Ark of the Covenant, which likewise was topped with two winged "angels" — representations of the twin sisters Isis and Nephthys. The card, likewise, depicts the angels as twins, indistinguishable from one another except for the fact they are facing in opposite directions.

Of the four "face" cards eventually included in the modern deck, the most interesting is perhaps the jack. This card appears in the tarot deck as the Charioteer, an axe in one hand and a sheathed sword at his side, set against a golden background and yet another field of grain. The symbolism of the sun chariot and its driver Horus are unmistakable — which is probably why this imagery was excised from the card in its modern form.

As it is, the jack is depicted as a two-headed vertical mirror image dressed in full regalia and holding some sort of weapon — the type varies from one suit to the next. The king in each suit is likewise armed, usually with a sword after the manner of the *kher heb* priest king protecting the tree of life in the sacred grove. The implication?

The cards depict the tanist ritual, in which the prince challenges the aging king to a contest of arms. It is a battle to the death, with the winner ascending the throne and the loser forfeiting his life.

But why should the prince be called a "jack?" What exactly is the derivation of this term?

The name is actually a diminutive form of Jacob. And this makes perfect sense, for the legend of Jacob appears to have served as a model for one of the most critical scenes in the grail romances — the meeting of the wounded king and the noble knight destined to take his place. Like the wounded king of grail lore, Jacob's father is reclining on a bed and barely able to even sit up when his son approaches.[294] Jacob then tricks the old man into blessing him, a gesture by which the dying king symbolically passes of the mantle of authority to his heir.

The reference to the blessing seems natural enough under the circumstances, but it also serves to disguise the violent nature of the encounter. In the tanist ritual, of course, the heir was expected to kill the wounded king. Yet the Hebrew scribes understandably found such a suggestion distasteful. They could hardly permit one of their revered patriarchs to be seen murdering his own father, so they altered the text to eliminate any reference to violence.

Almost.

For the verb "to bless" provides a revealing clue to the legend's original form. In Hebrew, this word is *barak*, which will be familiar to modern readers as the patronymic of an Israeli prime minister and — in a variant form — of an American president. It may, perhaps, be familiar to students of ancient history as well: The great Carthaginian general Hannibal (whose city began its history as a Phoenician colony) wore the variant Barca as his surname.[295] It was this Hannibal who would pose the greatest threat in half a millennium to the armies of Rome, which would not again face so great a challenge until they succumbed to the barbarian hordes. *Barak* is closely related to the homophone *baraq*, which meant "lightning" and was also used in reference to a flashing sword.[296] Such a connection was only appropriate, for the ancients saw lightning as the gleaming blade of the storm god.

Baal ...

Whose consort was Tanit ...

Also known as Diana ...

The goddess of the sacred grove wherein the *kher heb* priest guarded the tree of life with a flaming sword.

In the original form of the legend, Isaac must have drawn his sword to meet Jacob's challenge and been slain by the young "jack" who supplanted him. It is revealing that the name Jacob means exactly that — he who supplants. Just as the young prince Horus killed the old king Seth to claim the throne of Egypt, so Jacob now killed Isaac to supplant his father as clan chief.

As a young man, Isaac had been Horus.

But as an old man, he had come to personify Seth.

This was part of the never-ending cycle that repeated itself time and again throughout the ages. As each king grew old, he *became* the personification of Seth — just as the young king was viewed as the embodiment of Horus and the dead king was seen as Osiris. This would explain why the figure of Aaron plays the part of Seth at one point in the *Exodus* account yet is most closely identified with Osiris.

With this realization, it is possible to put the true nature of the wilderness ritual in stark perspective. When the young heir went forth into the wilderness to do battle with Seth, he was actually challenging the old king to a tanist duel. In many cases, this was no simple ritual enactment — it was a bloody confrontation that left one man dead and the other on the throne. This is what happened when the young Elisha slew his mentor Elijah in the wilderness beyond the Jordan River, then returned having appropriated a "double portion" of his spirit.

There are also indications that Jesus himself went through this transformation. Clues to this are evident in his name, which in the Quran of Islam is given not as Jesus but as Issa. This name is similar to those of three ancient figures who were depicted as personifications of Seth.

> *Isaac*, the old and bedridden patriarch destined to be displaced by his son Jacob. In this context, he is clearly Seth. And his name is said to have meant "laughter," an activity often ascribed to the devil in later tradition. (It is interesting to note, however, that Isaac played the role of Horus during his youthful conflict with the Seth figure Ishmael. Here is clear evidence of his transformation from Horus to Seth as he aged.)
> *Esau*, whose red hair and hostility toward his younger brother cast him even more clearly in the role of Seth. With this in mind, it can hardly be seen as an accident that the devil would come to be depicted as a red-skinned fiend.
> *Issachar*, who is described in no uncertain terms as a "strong donkey," the incarnation of Seth's totem animal. The donkey's piercing bray can be seen as a sort of evil laugh, once again calling to mind the devil.[297]

This final name appears to be nothing more than a variation Isaac. Just as the Hyksos pharaoh Yakob-har became Jacob, so the name Issac-har might have shortened to Isaac by the Hebrew scribes. There is, in fact, evidence to suggest that a pharaoh with a name similar to Issachar ruled during the Hyksos period. One of the kings names from this era Sekerher (or Seker-her), in deference to the god Seker, an ancient guardian of the tombs who later became identified with Osiris. This name, if slurred, could have produced something like the name Issachar.

Isaac for short.

It is worth digressing for a moment to note that other tribes of Israel apparently took their names from Egyptian sources. The tribe of Dan, for example, seems to have derived its name from the legend of Danaus and his daughters, who boarded ships and crossed the sea to escape from Egypt. These daughters of Danaus would enter into Irish legend as the children of Dana, the Tuatha de Danaan. And they would pass into Hebrew lore as Dan, a tribe specifically associated with ships: "And Dan," the prophetess Deborah would ask, "why did he linger by the ships?" [298]

Naphtali is the only tribe described in decidedly feminine terms, as "a doe set free that bears beautiful fawns." [299] Even today, it is a popular name for girls, despite the fact that it is supposed to have been worn originally by a male figure. There may be good reason for this. Phonetically, the name sounds very similar to that worn by the favorite queen of one of Egypt's most powerful pharaohs — none other than Ahmose himself. Nefertari was not only a queen, she also held the distinction of being high priestess of the god Amen and bore the title "wife of god." [300] As such, she became the spiritual mother of the nation — and more, she became matriarch of the royal lineage. Indeed, the royal bloodline seems to have run not through the king directly but through *her*. For every king who held the throne of Egypt for several generations after Ahmose was the eldest son of the pharaoh by a descendant of this Nefertari.

This would explain the description of Naphtali as the doe who bears beautiful fawns. The prefix *nefer* in Egyptian means "beautiful." And the fawns in question were doubtless the sons she bore to her royal husband, princes who would be heirs to the throne of Egypt. One can only wonder whether this woman's true name was Nefer-*tany*, which would identify her as none other than "Beautiful Tany," the Queen of the South who first allied herself with Apophis and later defected to Ahmose and the Thebans.

The Queen of Sheba.

It would make sense, for Ahmose — who pursued the fleeing Hyksos army into Palestine and established sovereignty over the land — to have paid tribute to his favored consort by naming a portion of his conquests in her honor. It would have made even more sense because the suffix *tari* bears a resemblance to *terra* and similar words meaning "land" in a number of tongues. This would have identified the region in question as the beautiful land, a fitting epithet for the rich pasturelands and vineyards to be found there. It was this region, dedicated to the beautiful Nefertari, that eventually made its way into the Hebrew scriptures as the "tribe" of Naphtali.

Just as interesting is the name Asher, which appears to be somehow linked with a wooden cult object known as the Asherah pole. These poles were often set up in "groves" to resemble trees. They always seem to be linked with a goddess of the same name, but this identification raises a serious question: Why would a goddess be represented by such an obviously phallic symbol?

The obvious answer is that she wasn't. Though there is more to this than meets the eye, the Asherah pole probably was never meant to represent a goddess at all, but a male deity somehow associated with the goddess.

The question is, which one?

The fact that the god Osiris was often represented as an erect pillar provides a potent clue — as does the identification of this tree god with a sacred "grove." Once again, the language evokes images of the primordial garden, with the *kher heb* priest guarding the tree of life. This garden with its many pillars was symbolized by the great temple of Solomon, which housed the mummy of the dead king or Osiris. In light of this, one is not at all startled to learn that this very temple at one point is said to have *housed* an Asherah pole.[301]

All of this has a major bearing on the identity of Asher.

When one considers that the letter "s" and the combination "sh" were interchangable in the ancient Near East, it becomes more than plausible that this name could alternately be rendered as Asser. This is virtually identical to the Egyptian name for Osiris, which is Asir. It is fascinating to discover that the great Assyrian (Osirian?) empire of Mesopotamia appears to have taken its name from the same root. Its patron god bore the name Assur or Ashur, as did its capital city, and several its kings incorporated this name into their own.

- Ashur-uballit
- Ashur-dan
- Ashur-nasirpal

➤ Ashur-banipal

The national name Syria seems to stem from the same source. Recalling that *suwr* in Hebrew means "to reign," this would make Syria the land of rulers. As Osiris was the great first king of Egypt, such a designation is only natural. In light of all this, it therefore appears that the so-called tribe of Asher was named for and associated with Osiris himself, just as the tribe of Issachar was associated with this god's nemesis, the storm god Seth.

All of which brings us back to Jesus' association with this same god.

In a shocking bit of graffiti left behind a pillar in Rome, an unknown artist scrawled a crude rendering of a man staring up at a figure hanging on a cross. The crucified individual had the body of a man but the head of an *ass* or *donkey*. Accompanying the drawing are the statement "Alexmenos worships his god" and, in the upper right-hand corner, the letter Y.[302] This letter could have easily stood for Yeshua, the pure Hebrew version of Jesus' name. The graffiti, left there less than two centuries after Jesus' death, appears to depict him as a manifestation of Seth — whose totem animal was the donkey.

This would appear, on the face of it, to be a shockingly derisive scrawl. Seth was, after all, the original version of the great adversary known as Satan. And such a depiction would therefore appear to modern eyes as the basest sort of mockery, an unconscionable attack on Jesus and his followers. But this artist's message was not meant for modern eyes. It was meant to be viewed in an entirely different context, one that viewed Seth not simply as an evil interloper in the world arena but as a key player in the broad scheme of nature.

In ancient thought, Seth symbolized the baser animal nature that had to be subjugated by the spiritual being imprisoned within. This was done, symbolically, by nailing the god's totem animal to a cross. Paul would express this principle eloquently in a letter to his Galatian followers: "Those who belong to Christ Jesus have crucified the sinful nature with its passions and desires. Since we live by the spirit, let us keep in step with the spirit." [303]

Paul sometimes refers to the sinful nature as the *flesh*, a term that allows him to draw an even starker contrast between it and the spirit. This language allows him to ensure that the dichotomy between flesh and spirit is firmly established. The spirit is to be cultivated; the flesh is to be subdued or even slain. It is the flesh that is crucified, not the spirit. The body is, indeed, nothing more than a container for the spirit: "We have this treasure in earthen vessels, to show that this all-surpassing power is from God and not from us." [304]

The vessel itself was not the treasure.

Paul also spoke of the body as a temple, but that did not make the temple itself divine. A temple devoid of God's presence was, after all, of little use to anyone. It was very much like a dead body, a corpse left to slowly putrefy, robbed of the spirit that had sustained it during life. But if this is what happened to the flesh when it was crucified, what then became of the spirit?

Clearly, it went elsewhere.

To find out where, one needs look no further than the Egyptian kingship ritual. It seems that the pharaohs made it their custom to anoint a successor to reign jointly with them as co-regent in preparation for the younger man's accession to the throne. There are even indications that, upon naming a younger co-regent, the elder pharaoh yielded the bulk of his power to his successor.[305] And this makes perfect sense. For in naming his heir, the elder pharaoh became — according to the ritual tradition — the personification of Seth, while the spirit of Horus was transferred to the younger heir apparent. Each successive pharaoh was, beginning with his co-regency, considered the Arit-Hur or "chariot of Horus," the vessel that bore this divine spirit until it was passed along to the next king. Though the body was mortal, the spirit itself was eternal. It therefore stands to reason that, at some point, this spirit must have been passed to Jesus — who, in turn, must have passed it on to a successor.

And this is just this sort of transfer that appears to have taken place upon the cross. It is on the cross that Jesus is depicted as Seth, a purely animal being devoid of the Horus spirit. And it is likewise on the cross that Jesus recognizes the departure of this same divine spirit with his memorable lament, "My God, My God, why have you forsaken me?" Immediately after this mournful cry, Jesus is described as giving up his spirit.[306]

This was the spirit of Horus, which could then have been expected to take up residence in Jesus' successor. In light of this, it is fascinating to note that the man who followed Jesus as leader of his movement was none other than his younger brother James, whose name in Hebrew just happened to be Jacob.

The supplanter.

The jack.

Man for All Seasons

The ancients viewed nearly all their sacred rituals as reflections of a greater heavenly reality. There was a heavenly temple, a heavenly Jerusalem and even a celestial Nile. There were heavenly kings, just as there were kings on earth. And the royal succession, likewise, was nothing more than an earthly manifestation of some greater heavenly reality.

This reality was revealed in the passing of the seasons.

Each year, the sun appeared to be born at the winter solstice and begin its slow ascent to the height of its power at midsummer. Then, having reached its apex at the summer solstice, it began a slow decline that culminated with its "death" in the month we call December. It would then remain at its lowest point on the horizon for three days before starting to rise again — signifying its resurrection or rebirth.

The cycle of the sun god thus mirrored that of the earth goddess, who was depicted in springtime as a virginal beauty and in winter as an ugly old crone or a grizzled she-warrior.

The sun god was the infant Horus at his advent, almost always pictured sucking on his finger like a newborn babe. He was said to have been placed in a manger at his birth (or rebirth) three days after the solstice, our twenty-fifth of December. By midsummer, he had reached the zenith of his power, shining down in all his glory from a fiery throne directly overhead. In this aspect he was the "lord most high" who caused his subjects to declare, "Look, he is coming in the clouds, and every eye will see him." [307] But as the year progressed, his power waned and the sweltering heat of summer gave way to the cool breezes of autumn. This season took its name from Atum, the sun god who also gave his name to Adam and who was equated with the setting sun.[308] By the time winter set in, he was the dying king Seth, ready to be supplanted on the throne by the new Horus to be born at the solstice.

Seth was the god of darkness, and this was his time. Minute by minute he conquered the daylight in this season of shortening days, slowly and methodically expanding his domain as the weakened sun fled toward the southern horizon. The old sun's death and impending rebirth as Horus was celebrated at Rome in the form of the Saturnalia, a seven-day festival dedicated to the god Saturn — whose name is a variant on both Seth (or Set) and Satan. The seven days doubtless corresponded to the seven celestial mansions through which the dead god was fated to pass.

It is clear that the tanist ritual played itself out each year on a celestial scale, with Horus once again deposing Seth and taking his place upon the throne of heaven. It was, in a very real sense, a ritual of the resurrection or new birth. The new Horus-sun was born at the very hour when the world was at its darkest, manifesting itself as "the light that shines in the darkness."

It was at the moment of his birth that "the true light that gives light to every man was coming into the world." [309] These are the words provided by the author of *John*, one of four canonical accounts purporting to describe the life of Jesus. It has often been maintained that this author provides no account of Jesus' birth, yet it is apparent from these quotations that this is simply not the case. True, he forgoes the familiar magi and the manger. Yet in doing so, he is merely bypassing the symbolism and going straight to the heart of the tradition — describing the event in the starkest of celestial terms. As the light, Jesus was none other than the invincible sun, born to conquer darkness and its author, the old king Satan/Seth.

The Horus spirit of the old king was transferred at this sacred moment to the new king. The process took a total of three days — the solstice period of mourning, during which the sun remained at its lowest point on the southern horizon. This was when it remained in its grave, or in the belly of the great primordial fish that lurked beneath the surface of the waters. The spirit's emergence from these waters was a sign of rejoicing, a sign that the celestial king had been "born again" of the water and the spirit.

Birth and resurrection were one.

As the prophet Isaiah would proclaim in an oracle later applied specifically to Jesus:

> *The people walking in darkness*
> *Have seen a great light*
> *On those living in the shadow of death*
> *A light has dawned* [310]

And as the prophet Malachi would write, "the sun of righteousness shall rise, with healing in its wings." [311] This sun of righteousness was Horus, the winged falcon god or phoenix, who rose up on celestial wings from his earthen grave. He was a sun of righteousness for he was upright — the position signifying life to the Egyptians and the position in which the Osirified mummy of the dead king was set to affirm his resurrection.

The mummy played a major part in the ritual of rebirth. And it is for this reason that the infant Jesus was depicted wrapped in swaddling clothes, strips of linen analogous to those used in wrapping a corpse during mummification. It is also why the magi are seen bringing the baby gifts of gold, frankincense and myrrh, each crucial in the mummification process. According to Herodotus, myrrh was among the spices used to fill the abdomen of the deceased after it had been cleansed and washed.[312] Although frankincense was not used in this portion of the process, it also appears to have been employed in embalming. Before wrapping the mummy, the embalmers would smear the underside of the linen strips with "gum" — probably a resin such as frankincense, which not only gives off a pleasant fragrance but is also known to preserve the skin. Gold, of course, was found in abundance in the tombs of the pharaohs and was used to adorn their sarcophagi as well.

The Egyptians referred to the embalming process as the *karas*, and the mummy itself was a *karast*, a word that sounds a lot like christ.[313] Christ or messiah meant simply "anointed one," implying that the embalming process was a sort of anointing for the afterlife. And so it was.

The spices, aloes and resins used in the process effectively anointed the body for its journey to the otherworld. After Jesus' death, this process was followed assiduously by his disciples: "Taking Jesus' body," they "wrapped it, with the spices, in strips of linen," and in doing so created a mummy, which they placed in a garden tomb.[314] This tomb was described as a sort of cave, cut into the face of the rock itself.[315]

All this symbolism was highly significant.

A strong early tradition had it that Jesus was born in a cave. Now, his corpse was laid to rest in the same locale. Birth and resurrection were, again, one and the same. In either case, the cave signified the land beneath the earth — to which the sun descended after its daily journey across the sky. This same drama played itself out on an annual basis, with the sun descending toward its winter "tomb" on the southern horizon before ascending again as the revitalized sun or Horus. The cave was, therefore, a point of both arrival and departure for the sun king.

In a Latin text purporting to tell the story of Jesus' birth, he is described in precisely these solar terms:

The child himself shone brightly round like the sun
And was pure and most beautiful to behold
Since he alone appeared as peace
Spreading peace everywhere…

And this cave was filled with bright light
Together with a most sweet odor
The light was born, just as dew descends from heaven
For its odor is more fragrant than any aroma of ointments [316]

Jesus is depicted in this revealing text as the sun reborn from its winter cave. He is, moreover, identified as the prince of peace — the new incarnation of the sun king Solomon, whose very name means peace. Yet there is a hint even here of what is to come. The "aroma of ointments" bespeaks a time when the sun shall return to its cave in death and be anointed for burial with fragrant spices.

In the account of Jesus' burial, this cave is in the midst of a garden, signifying the primordial garden from which Adam was banished by the sword-wielding *kher heb* priest. In one version of the story, a solitary young man dressed in robes of priestly white attends the tomb of Jesus. He is the *kher heb* appointed to guard the tree of life, the mummified Osiris that Jesus has become.

In another version of the story, two women sit watching over the cave. As the author of *Matthew* has it, "Mary Magdalene and the other Mary were sitting opposite the tomb." [317] In this context, the two women represent the two Egyptian goddesses who spread their wings across the burial ark of Solomon. One was Isis, the mother of life; the other was Nephthys, mistress of the underworld. The latter was the "lady of the castle" who became the grail bearer of later tradition. It was she who watched over the ailing Fisher King's passage into the next life. The former was at once the virgin and the mother, and one of her many names was Meri. As earth goddess, it was her place to watch over the mouth of the cave, which served as the gateway to her domain. The word for cave in Hebrew was *mearah*, a fact that may have some bearing on the presence of a woman named Mary at such a place for Jesus' interment — as well as the legend that Jesus was born in a cave to another Mary. The earth was both womb and grave for mankind, "for dust you are, and to dust you will return." [318]

As the sun died each day when it dipped below the horizon, so it would be born anew in the morning when it ascended once again. The same could be said for Horus, whose most popular title was in fact Horus of the Horizon.

And the same could likewise be said for Jesus.

The popular misconception is that religious leaders chose to celebrate Jesus' nativity on the twenty-fifth of December more than three centuries after his birth. In actuality, this decision had been made for them long before, by Jesus himself or his earliest followers. The earliest stories of Jesus, written within a century of his execution, are replete with clues meant to identify him with the dying and rising sun god Horus. It was not as though later religious leaders simply adopted a pagan holiday to make things more convenient for their calendar; in fact, this "pagan" holiday was significant from the very beginning.

The likelihood that Jesus was actually born on December twenty-fifth is remote indeed. This was, from the outset, a purely symbolic date identifying him as Horus incarnate. Indeed, many have labeled the advent as woefully misplaced in the dead of winter, pointing specifically to the legend that shepherds were the first to hear the news of Jesus' birth. This would have been impossible, they contend, because shepherds would hardly have been out on the hillsides watching their flocks at night in the dead of winter.

It is a valid point.

But the fact is that the shepherds themselves are equally symbolic. And in symbolic terms, the idea that Jesus should have had *two* birthdays — one at the winter solstice and the other during the summer grazing season — is not at all farfetched. Certainly, this was true of Horus.

Egyptian myth makes it clear that Horus is sort of a dual character. Some even went so far as to depict him, in two separate manifestations, as two separate deities. The first was Horus the Younger, the newborn babe born at the winter solstice. In this form, he was commonly portrayed with a finger to his mouth and wearing the mostly shaven head typical of youth in the Egyptian culture. This Horus was *sol invictus*, the "invincible sun" born anew every solstice. But there was also another Horus — Horus the Elder, whose birthday was allegedly in the middle of *summer*. This tradition is tied to the legend of the five epagomenal days, when the five great gods were said to have been born. Horus was born on the second of these, identified as the modern twenty-eighth day of July.[319] At this time of year, the sun was at its brightest and most powerful, having reached its apex at the summer solstice a month earlier. It beat down on the Egyptian desert with a searing ferocity, leaving no doubt that it was king of the heavens. By identifying Jesus' birth with both manifestations of Horus, the scribes were leaving no doubt as to his identity: He *was* the invincible sun, embodying all the power of a king at the height of his power and all the promise of a newborn heir to the throne.

Beyond this, however, there was a specific reason shepherds were chosen as the first to hear the news of this great event.

The birth of Jesus took place on the cusp of a new age, and there is no doubt that his followers — practiced in the Heliopolitan art of observing the stars — recognized this. The stars were crucial because their position in the sky determined the nature of the current age. And this position changed, ever so gradually, over the course of time as the planet's rotational axis changed. It was an immensely slow, cyclical process that no one was likely to notice in a single lifetime. In fact, the entire cycle (known as a precession) took just slightly less than twenty-six thousand years to complete.

That's twenty-six *thousand*.

It is therefore a credit to the astronomers of Heliopolis that they were able to identify and track this phenomenon with an amazing degree of accuracy. As the earth's rotation shifted, the sky appeared to shift as well. Each morning at the vernal or spring equinox for more than two millennia, the same constellation would greet the rising sun. But by the end of this period, the sky would have shifted enough that the sun would appear to rise in a *different* constellation. Because the sun disk was identified with Horus, the constellation in question would also be viewed as divine and particularly associated with the reigning pharaoh.

At the founding of the Egyptian kingdom, that constellation was Taurus the bull. It was therefore natural that, during this period, the Apis bull should have come to be viewed as sacred and synonymous with the king. But this age ended sometime a few centuries before the Hyksos invasion of Egypt, with the rising sun having moved into the constellation of Aries — the ram or sheep. It is worth recalling that the Hyksos were, according to one interpretation of their name, *shepherd kings*. This may have referred simply to their role as semi-nomadic herdsmen, but it may have had astronomical significance, as well.

The biblical scribes referred to their patriarchs time and again as shepherds. And when those who fled Egypt embarked upon their great exodus, they identified themselves by marking their doorposts with the blood of a lamb. Future generations would mark this signal event with a feast they called the Passover, and it is no accident that Jesus should have been crucified during this very celebration. His blood, naturally, came to be identified with the blood of the lamb; his cross was the doorpost to eternity. But there was something even more striking about the timing of the crucifixion: It took place at the end of the age.

By the time of Jesus' death, the sun had begun to rise in a new constellation.

Pisces. The fish.

The death of the lamb put an end to the age of Aries and inaugurated a new age, during which the sun would rise again. Jesus would, like the sun, be resurrected. But he would no longer be the lamb who was slain. He would thenceforth be known as the Fisher King, the sun rising in Pisces. The fish would be the symbol of his victory and the promise of his future reign, a new golden age that would eclipse all that had gone before it, restoring Solomon's grand temple to its status of pre-eminent place in the civilized world. Only one person could do this, and that was Solomon himself, or more precisely the spirit of Horus that had dwelt in the legendary king, transferred now to his rightful heir.

Jesus firmly believed he was that person.

And he would act in accordance with that belief.

STEPHEN H. PROVOST

XVI

Secret Identity

So where does Yahweh, or Jehovah as he is sometimes called, fit into all this? Here is a god who seems to have little relevance to the Egyptian pantheon, whose presence in — and dominance of — the Hebrew tradition appears strangely out of place. He introduces himself first to Moses in the form of a burning bush, declaring himself to be "the god of your father, the god of Abraham, the god of Isaac and the god of Jacob." [320] This introduction is a bit vague for Moses, who presses this disembodied voice to provide a little more information. A name perhaps.

But the deity remains enigmatic, saying merely: "I am who I am."

In Hebrew, this translates as something like *hayah havah*, which can be easily truncated to read yahvah or yahveh. So it turns out that the god's name really isn't a name at all. It is, in actuality, nothing more than a code name that allows the deity to avoid revealing his true identity. The question that therefore arises is: What might that identity be?

When one remembers that Moses is, in fact, Ahmose, the answer isn't hard to guess. It was under Ahmose that the cult of Amen began to gain primacy in Upper Egypt. The pharaoh seems to have attributed a series of military victories to this very god, for he showed his appreciation with a generous endowment to the god's temple at Karnak. This is the same temple of that appears to have served as a model for the temple of Solomon. It was the original temple of Sah-Amen, otherwise known as "the hidden Osiris." Such a connection would explain the historian Manetho's assertion that Moses was, in fact, a priest of Osiris.

It would also go a long way toward explaining Yahweh's reluctance to reveal his true name. He was, like Amen, a hidden deity who refused to show his face to any man. Instead, he appeared to Moses as a burning bush — in a scene chock full of familiar images. The flame that is not extinguished. The bush or tree. Its divine guardian. All of this symbolism calls to mind the image of the cherub (or *kher heb* priest) with the flaming sword who stood guard over the tree of life — yet another symbol of Osiris. It is apparent from all this symbolism that Yahweh was merely a title for the hidden Osiris, otherwise known as Amen.

Out of Seir

This is confirmed by the song of the prophetess Deborah, perhaps one of the oldest pieces of literature in the Hebrew canon. This text includes a reference that seems to identify Yahweh's place of origin as Seir, often identified more specifically as "the mountains of Seir." [321] Here is yet another name that appears to be related to the Egyptian name for Osiris.

Or Asir.

In this context, it appears possible that the mountains of *Seir* were actually the mountains of *Osiris* — the pyramids. And this possibility only grows stronger when one discovers that the region of Seir was populated by none other than that mysterious tribe of people known as the Horites. The similarity of this name to that of Horus bears repeating, as does the fact that Yahweh's dwelling place was a mountain called Horeb — literally "the heart of Horus."

Yahweh's association with a sacred mountain makes perfect sense, for his name bears some similarity to a combination of two Egyptian roots: *dja*, meaning "mountain" and *wa*, meaning "great."

The great mountain. Otherwise known as Horeb or Seir.

The linguistic and textual clues would seem to indicate that Horeb was in fact one of the mountains of Seir, a conclusion bolstered by a Hebrew text that indicates this particular mountain lay at the end of the Seir road.[322] According to legend, it was at Horeb that Moses received the sacred tablets inscribed by the finger of his god. But another tradition held, similarly, that a certain set of sacred tablets had been produced in the land of *Seir*.[323] These were the tablets of stone and clay that had been inscribed by the finger of Seth before the flood — the tablets Solomon was said to have discovered and deciphered. They contained esoteric knowledge and had been deposited "in the middle of the house of his father in the oratory, where he used to pray to the lord." [324]

This oratory appears to be a room of some sort, in this case located in the middle of the house.

Its function is obvious, both from its location and its name.

One at once recalls that the temple's inner sanctuary stood at the very center of the structure ("my father's house," as Jesus would refer to it). And this sanctuary, moreover, was known as the *debir*, a word that stems from the Hebrew verb meaning "to speak." Indeed, *debir* was probably nothing more than a word for oratory — the place where the high priest came to speak, or pray, to the father god Sah-Amen. This was the resting place of the dead king Osiris.

In Palestine, it was the temple of Solomon on Mount Zion. (Though the original may have been little more than a tent structure, later temples were built on this spot by Nehemiah and, later, Herod the Great.)

In Egypt, it was the great pyramid.

One was a temple crypt situated atop a mountain; the other was a temple crypt shaped like a mountain. The distinction is scarcely worth mentioning. Each is identified in ancient tradition as a repository for sacred and magical writings inscribed on tablets by patriarch or deity. Variously attributed to the hand of Noah, Seth, Yahweh, Thoth and Enoch, these sacred chronicles purportedly held the key to a trove of wisdom from an earlier age — wisdom lost to humanity at the time of the flood. It was this wisdom that enticed the medieval crusaders to invade the so-called holy land and reclaim it from its Arab masters. Their stated goal? To recover the site of the holy sepulcher. Yet their prize can hardly have been the burial place of Jesus, whose tomb was reputedly empty in any event. No, it must have the temple of Solomon in Jerusalem, or the site on which it is supposed to have rested, for it was from the temple that the guardian Knights Templar took their name.

This itself was the original holy sepulcher, which had housed the sacred ark or casket of Solomon.

And was not Jesus the bridegroom — Solomon reborn?

There is every indication that knights who traveled to Jerusalem were looking for something, perhaps those tablets of ancient wisdom they believed to have been stored away in the temple's foundations. Others have, with equal diligence, maintained the hope of rediscovering an archive of forgotten science or long-lost knowledge from the bowels of the great pyramid at Giza. This was where Thoth supposedly hid his arcane library, waiting for it to be rediscovered in the proper time.

In the temple of Osiris.

Or the mountain of Seir.

It was the great flood of an earlier age that supposedly had washed away this ancient wisdom, concealing it safely from the prying eyes of men. This was the flood that was said to have destroyed the earth, leaving only a single man and his family to begin the cycle of regeneration. In light of this, one might postulate that the hero of the flood is somehow linked to the mountains of Seir, the birthplace and repository of this forgotten knowledge. And indeed he is. For according to one legend, Noah was told to set forth on his journey through the watery deluge from atop these very mountains: "Make yourself an ark from some wood that does not rot," he was instructed, "and hide in it — you and your children and the beasts and the birds of the sky, from small to large. And set it on upon Mount Sir." [325]

This entire passage is very peculiar. For one thing, why would Noah want to *hide*? The danger, after all, is not from some enemy but from the waters of the flood. For another, why should he set his ark upon a mountain? This would seem to defeat the purpose of building such a vessel in the first place. The point, after all, was not to keep it on dry land until the last possible moment, but to set it adrift upon the waters.

What could the writers have meant?

The truth of the matter is that they were speaking in symbolic terms. The waters were the waters of death, and the "ark" was the funeral casket of the dead king. The forty days was the period of embalming, and Noah was instructed to *hide* because his body was being hidden in the ark or sarcophagus — he was becoming the personification of Amen, the *hidden god*. The mountain was the great pyramid, next to which was buried a great sea vessel equipped to bear him on his long journey over the waters of the celestial Nile to the great constellation Orion.

This was the constellation associated not only with Osiris but also with Gilgamesh, the Babylonian flood hero whose story formed the basis for Noah's adventure. Gilgamesh had sought eternal life. And the name Noah may well stem from the Egyptian word *nhh*, meaning "eternity." (The hieroglyph for this particular word contains a prominent o-shaped symbol, making it conceivable that some would have rendered it as something like *noheh*.)[326]

One God

As Noah was instructed to hide himself, he was therefore doubtless a manifestation of the hidden one: Amen.

And it was Amen whose cult would become pre-eminent with the ascension of Ahmose, attaining under him an exalted position that few gods of Egypt would ever match. Over the course of several generations, his temple at Karnak was steadily built up to become the crown jewel of the nation's religious culture, the focus of its faith. What the pyramids had been to the pharaohs nearly a millennium earlier, this temple was to their successors. Amen became the national god of Egypt, the power behind the pharaoh's throne. The other gods retained their places, but it was Amen who reigned supreme in a system that was not quite monotheism but an unmistakable step in that direction. And further steps would be taken in the ensuing years. Ahmose would show his dedication to this god by naming his own queen as high priestess in his temple, thereby endowing her with the magnificent title of "god's wife." He would name his own son Amenhotep — Amen is joyful — in honor of his patron god, and no fewer than four pharaohs would wear that name over the course of the next two centuries. The second of these would sanction an ode to Amen identifying him in terms that were nearly monotheistic:

> *You are the sole one who made all there is*
> *The unique one who made what exists* [327]

Two generations later, the third Amenhotep would erect a lavish hall supported by an expansive colonnade at the Karnak temple and would be one of Amen's most ardent supporters. Yet at the same time, he would also pay tribute to another deity — Aten, or the sun disk. It was to this god that he dedicated a series of palaces on the Nile's western shore, dubbing the complex "Aten's Splendor." The estates included a mile-long lake, which the pharaoh would frequent aboard a boat that was likewise dedicated to the solar orb. The worship of the sun disk was, of course, nothing new. Amen himself was a sun god, and it was therefore quite natural that the sun disk itself should be seen an object of veneration, as it had been for centuries upon centuries.

But under Amenhotep's son and successor, it would become something much more. This pharaoh began life wearing his father's name, but changed it within five years of his accession to reflect his single-minded devotion to the sun disk. His new name, Akhenaten, meant simply, "he who serves the Aten." The pharaoh even went so far as to equate himself with his patron god, eliciting expressions of adoration from his vassals that depict him in these very terms. Letter after letter from his archives begins with words such as these:

To the king, my lord and my sun god...[328]

This in itself was hardly an innovation. The pharaohs had long viewed themselves as the incarnation of the sun god Horus, and the Aten itself was simply another name for the solar god. What made Akhenaten's religious program unprecedented was not his decision to worship the sun or equate himself with its splendor, but his resolution to do so at the expense of every other god. In a zealous campaign supported by the army of Egypt, he set about proscribing the worship of every other god — particularly Amen. No longer were their names to be mentioned in any royal pronouncement. No longer were their priests to be honored. Henceforth, the pharaoh decreed, the Aten would be the one true god, to be revered and worshiped throughout the land as the sole creator and sustainer of life.

And this was not all.

Akhenaten's rise to power also precipitated a radical change in artistic representation. Gone were the idealistic portraits of the pharaohs and their queens that had been the standard for centuries, from one dynasty to the next. The expressions of serene indifference worn by the statues of previous pharaohs were wiped away in a single stroke to make way for a bold new style. In some ways, it was more realistic. A child might be seated on the queen's knee, giggling and playing innocently with her mother's jewelry. Young princesses were seen embracing each other in a clear display of affection. Faces were adorned with expressions of joy and excitement. In other ways, however, these images were strangely grotesque, exaggerating the curvature of the hips or upper body and elongating the cranium into a melon-shaped oddity. Various theories have been offered to explain this odd style. Some have seen it as the manifestation of a disease known as Frohlich's syndrome, which produces some of the same physical affects. Yet this condition also renders its carrier impotent, and it is clear that Akhenaten fathered several children. Others have viewed the curved hips and overly developed breasts displayed on the pharaoh as evidence that he was a woman masquerading as a man. There is precedent for such a pretense: Only four decades earlier, the queen Hatchepsut had donned a false beard and pharaoh's crown to rule all of Egypt. Yet, again, such a precedent seems irrelevant if Akhenaten actually fathered children — as it seems he did. In the end, the best explanation may be that the pharaoh was tailoring his own features and those of his attendants to mimic the curvature of the solar orb he so ardently worshiped.

Even more important than this abrupt change in artistic style, however, was the political upheaval that accompanied Akhenaten's religious awakening. Not only did he proscribe the worship of Amen, he embarked on an ambitious scheme to transplant the capital itself from that god's seat of worship — Thebes — to a barren patch of land on the east bank of the Nile many miles to the north. Here he designed and began to construct a new capital known as Akhetaten, literally "the horizon of Aten." On this site, he built a new Mansion of the Benben as his primary temple and entertained dignitaries from across the Near East who came to congratulate him on his grand new city.

It would not last.

Completion of the new capital was Akhenaten's crowning achievement, but it was also the beginning of his downfall. The city itself was fast becoming a glorious tribute to the Aten, but the hurried pace and vast scale the project were taking their toll. In order to expedite matters, Akhenaten had pressed a good portion of his army into service, leaving the fighting to vassal princes and mercenaries employed to patrol the distant frontiers. The pharaoh exhibited little interest in conquest himself, and he can hardly have been an inspiration to the veteran soldiers now forced to do menial labor constructing his city — such a task can hardly have boosted morale.

On top of this, the city's very location put Akhenaten at an even greater disadvantage. It put him at a distance from the despised cult of Amen in Thebes, but was this really such a good thing? In such relative isolation, the pharaoh was in no position to keep an eye on the disenfranchised priesthood of Thebes and its supporters, a constituency that doubtless harbored no great affection for the pharaoh. In discarding the ancient gods and replacing them with a single, omnipotent deity, Akhenaten had been taking a great risk. Would the people at large stand for his campaign to uproot centuries of their most cherished traditions?

Surely, he should have known the answer.

So why did he embark on such an enterprise? Perhaps it was simple vainglory, the idea that he would be seen as the son of the only god. Or then again, it could have been a sincere, heartfelt conviction that his actions were truly pious. But there is a third possibility — one that does not preclude either of the other two, but is based upon more practical considerations. Perhaps Akhenaten sought to consolidate his own power by consolidating the power of the gods into a single entity. In doing so, he could supplant the cacophony of competing myth and doctrine emanating from the temples of Amen and Ptah and Khnum and Sobek and the myriad other deities, along with their priests and priestesses. Now there would be but one great god who would speak with a single, clear and resonant voice.

That god would be the Aten.

And that voice would be the pharaoh's.

It was a bold stroke, one that would someday succeed as monotheism at last prevailed in its protracted battle with the forces of ancient tradition. In the short term, however, it was simply too great a shock to be absorbed so quickly. Akhenaten's experiment was destined to fail, his new capital fated to crumble into dust, his name to be erased from history — only to be rediscovered by chance in recent times. Even today, there is no record of what happened to the pharaoh. He simply seems to have faded from history, replaced for a short time by his heir, Smenkhkare, who was quickly succeeded in turn by the famous boy king Tutankhamen — popularly known as "King Tut."

Though there is no account of Akhenaten's final days, there are a few clues as to what must have happened. Shortly after his accession, Smenkhkare yielded to intense pressure from the military and the priests of Amen to abandon the new capital and return to rule from Thebes.[329] Akhenaten himself must have endured the same sort of pressure, in the face of which he steadfastly maintained his devotion to the Aten. With the military chafing under the burden of building the new city, it was probably eager to abandon the project and resume its traditional role as protector of the two lands. And the priests of Amen would have been equally anxious to reclaim their position as spiritual leaders of Egypt. It is not hard to imagine these two discontented factions uniting to overthrow the man who would become known as the heretic king. If they did, in fact, accomplish this, it would explain the apparent willingness of Smenkhkare to abandon Akhenaten's dream. He would hardly have wished to share his predecessor's fate. It would also explain Tutankhamen's decision to incorporate the name Amen into his name — he had previously honored the Aten by wearing the moniker Tutankh*aten*.

Fear can be a powerful motivator.

Despite Akhenaten's failure, he has been honored by history as the first to attempt the great experiment of monotheism. Some have even seized on this distinction to equate him with Moses, also considered an innovator in this regard. This appears to make sense considering that many heroic figures in Hebrew are in fact Egyptian pharaohs in disguise. But Moses' very name seems to indicate that his true identity belongs to a king who was called by the suffix *mose*. And his participation in the great exodus would seem to place him in the Hyksos era, when just this sort of mass departure occurred as the shepherd kings were expelled from Egypt.

The pharaoh Ahmose fits comfortably within both these parameters.

Akhenaten, by contrast, does not.

Yet that hardly means the heretic pharaoh fails to appear elsewhere — in somewhat disguised form — in the Hebrew scripture. One simply has to know where to look. Because Akhenaten lived some generations after Ahmose, one would expect to discover his Jewish alter ego sometime later in the historical record than Moses. And indeed, this is exactly where a king named Josiah can be found.

The similarities between the reign of Josiah and that of Akhenaten are numerous and revealing. Just as Akhenaten proscribed the worship of all but a single god, so Josiah embarked on a whirlwind campaign to establish his patron deity as the sole god worthy of reverence. He appears to have been particularly zealous in tearing down "Asherah poles" — the pillars dedicated to Osiris and his feminine counterpart in Palestine, the goddess Asherah. And he was zealous in departing from the ways of his father, who had paid tribute to the full pantheon of gods.

His father's name?

Amon.

Akhenaten's father was, of course, Amen-hotep. The similarity between the two names could hardly be plainer. The rabbis spoke of Josiah as "a shining model of true, sincere repentance. Though he at first followed in his footsteps of his father Amon, he soon gave up the ways of wickedness and became one of the most pious kings of Israel, whose chief undertaking was the effort to bring the whole people back to the true faith." [330]

This could easily have been a description of Akhenaten, who was considered the "shining" earthly manifestation of the brilliant solar orb. At first, he did follow in the footsteps of Amen, ruling from Thebes for the first five years of his reign and retaining a measure of respect for the priesthood of the favored god. The high priest of

Amen is still mentioned as being active during the fourth year of his reign, and the pharaoh continues to refer to himself as Amenhotep until his fifth regnal year. At this point, however, it seems that something dramatic must have happened, for thenceforth the king and nearly all the members of his court adopt names that pay tribute to the Aten.

He is Akhen-*aten*. His son is Tutankh-*aten*.

His daughters bear names such as Merit-*aten* and Akhesenpa-*aten*.

It is at this point that he decided to move his capital north, and it is at this point that he undertook his systematic campaign to proscribe the worship of every other god — especially Amen. Though he, like his father, revered the Aten before this, his devotion was now both undivided and unconditional. Clearly, something momentous must have taken place at some point during the fifth year of the pharaoh's reign to create this abrupt shift from merely favoring the Aten to worshipping the sun disk exclusively.

The question is: What?

The record offers no direct answer, but it does contain an enticing clue that may hold the key to solving this particular mystery. In his writings on the Aten, the pharaoh would refer repeatedly to his "teaching," evidently a code of worship he believed to be of divine origin. Its contents, for the most part, have not been preserved. But it appears to have condemned not only the other gods but also their graven images — the statues set up in their temples. These were to be replaced by the universal image of a stylized sun disk, its rays stretching forth like arms toward the king and queen, its "hands" warmly caressing them.

Whatever else the teaching of Akhenaten contained, it seems to have been some sort of written document that formed the basis of his belief system. It is possible that he himself authored it. But given the sudden change in his philosophy during the fifth year of his reign, it is perhaps more likely that it came to his attention at that point — and the king, responding to what he perceived as a revelation from the one true god, acted upon it to create the world's first truly monotheistic religion.

Interestingly, this is exactly what happened to Josiah.

It was during this king's reign, in the midst of a building project to repair the temple, that a high priest named Hilkiah discovered a manuscript of great importance closeted away there. The document in question is described merely as the "Book of the Law of Yahweh that had been given through Moses." [331] This description immediately prompts a number of questions — none of which are answered in the scribal texts. Where had it been all this time? Why had no one found it before? It appears to have turned up suddenly, materializing almost out of thin air with no further explanation. And its contents are obviously revolutionary, for Josiah immediately tore his robe and lamented the certitude of divine wrath because the nation had "not acted in accordance with all that is in this book." [332]

This was not some subtle change that is being demanded, but a radical departure. In response, Josiah "stood by the pillar" and renewed his covenant with the one true god. This pillar scene recalls once again the imagery of the *djed* pillar that represented Osiris, but this king was no worshipper of the ancient sky father. Indeed, he instructed his men to burn the Asherah poles dedicated to Osiris and his divine consort, and he placed a ban on the priests installed by his forebears — priests charged with burning incense "to the sun and moon, to the constellations and all the starry hosts." [333] Furthermore, he centralized the worship of his own god, confining the sacred rituals to his capital and depriving the rural priests of their office.

This sounds very much like what Akhenaten did, decreeing that his capital should be the center of worship for the entire country. Like Josiah, he ordered that the images of competing gods be torn down and their names no longer uttered. And like Josiah, he condemned the priests of these gods and those who refused to abandon them to an ignominious fate as national pariahs. This was the nature of the teaching that was found in the bowels of the temple under King Josiah — probably the very same "teaching" that is alluded to in connection with Akhenaten. Josiah attributed this doctrine to the legendary prophet and general known as Moses, and Akhenaten may have likewise ascribed *his* teaching to a long-lost doctrine propagated by Ahmose. What greater authority could he have claimed for his reforms than that of the great liberator, founder of the modern state of Egypt and father of the current dynasty?

But in fact, the document was probably older. Much older.

In searching for its author, it is perhaps worth recalling the legend of the sacred tablets — the stones from heaven that were preserved from before the flood and attributed variously to Noah, Thoth, Seth and Enoch. These tablets, inscribed by the "finger of god," had been hidden somewhere on the sacred mountain of Seir. This much was common knowledge. What the legend failed to divulge, however, was the exact location of mountain where the tablets were concealed. The uninitiated were left to assume that these fabled writings had been closeted away somewhere in a craggy range of hills on the Sinai Peninsula known collectively as Seir. This was the clear meaning of the story on its surface. But those who knew better knew enough to look *beneath* the surface, and these people must have realized that the tablets weren't in the Sinai at all.

They were in Egypt.

In the mountain of Seir — otherwise known as the mountain of Osiris.

They would have known, furthermore, that this was not a real "mountain" at all. It was, in fact, the largest of three massive pyramids that rose from a great plateau to the west of the Nile River. This huge structure and its two companions were aligned with the celestial belt of Orion, the constellation of Osiris, and had been built by a pharaoh who lived nearly a thousand years before Ahmose was born.

The Grand Plan

His name is rendered variously as Khufu (his Egyptian name)

and by his Greek name Cheops, and although he constructed the most impressive monument ever built, remarkably little is known of him. What is known, however, is intriguing to say the least. Manetho, for example, states that he was "arrogant toward the gods." [334] And according to Herodotus, he was a despotic ruler who alienated his subjects by closing down all the temples and placing a broad prohibition on the practice of any religion not sanctioned by the state. Instead, he had himself proclaimed divine and sanctioned the worship of Ra, the sun god.

All this parallels almost exactly the course taken by Akhenaten, who likewise instituted a monotheistic cult dedicated to the sun.

It seems as though Akhenaten somehow inherited the traditions of Cheops.

But how?

Again, the great pyramid holds the answer. A story survives that Cheops sought the wisdom of a sorcerer in building his great monument. Everything about it had to be precise, and the king had gone to great pains in measuring the dimensions of the pyramid and calculating its position in relationship to the stars. To truly accomplish his goal, however, he would need to one final piece of information. It was the sort of information that only a sorcerer could provide, for it touched on the nature of the universe itself, occult knowledge known only to a chosen few.

"It is said," the pharaoh began, "that you know the number of the secret chambers in the sanctuary of Thoth."

But the sorcerer shook his head and demurred. Apparently, he was not one of the chosen few after all. "Please, I known not the number thereof, my sovereign lord," he apologized. "But I know the place where" that information may be found.... "There is a box of flint in a room called Revision in Heliopolis. In that box (you will find it)." [335]

A box of flint.

Flint is a very hard quartz stone, most widely known as a useful tool for starting fires because it gives off sparks when struck against another surface. It has been, from time immemorial, known as a firestone. And what better description for a meteorite that has fallen from heaven, leaving in its wake a trail of fire as it pierced the atmosphere like a phoenix? This is hardly a chance analogy, for the magician's sacred "box of flint" was to be found in no other city than the site of the benben and sacred resting place of the phoenix, Heliopolis.

One cannot fail to recognize the similarities between the box of flint containing sacred information and the Ark of the Covenant, which supposedly contained its own stones from heaven inscribed with hallowed text. It is just this sort of container that the sorcerer was describing. Moreover, it was associated with Thoth, the divine scribe widely credited with having inscribed the secrets of heaven on tablets of precious stone.

These appear to have been the very tablets Cheops sought — and which the sorcerer was unable to produce. The story breaks off at this point, and there is no way of knowing what happened next. But having been supplied with such a crucial piece of information (the location of the tablets), one would be hard-pressed to imagine the pharaoh simply abandoning his quest. Indeed, it is reasonable to assume that he set off at once for Heliopolis to retrieve the sacred tablets and ended up using them as a basis for completing his pyramid.

But what if, when he was done, he didn't return the divine tablets to Heliopolis?

What if, instead, he locked them away in the recesses of his great monument?

This, it appears, is exactly what happened. The traditions are unanimous in associating the tablets with the sacred "mountain" or pyramid, making it quite possible that they were stored there for a certain period. At some point, however, they must have been removed. For Manetho would report hundreds of years later that Cheops had produced a sacred document, a copy of which the historian claimed to have in his possession.[336] He could not possibly have obtained such a copy, however, unless the document in question had been discovered and removed from its hiding place.

Conveniently enough, just such a discovery was made during the reign of Josiah (a.k.a. Akhenaten). It was then that the priest Hilkiah, in the midst of renovating the temple, stumbled across a document known as the "Book of the Law of Yahweh that had been given through Moses." The contents of this book would serve as the blueprint for Josiah's reforms, including his decree that the temples be closed and his sweeping denunciation of the gods.

It is quite reasonable to suspect that just such a message could have come from Cheops, who "closed all the temples" and further succeeded in "excluding his subjects from the practice of their religion." [337] The chance discovery of his sacred book in the recesses of the pyramid temple seems to have changed everything. The superstitious king viewed it as a sign from the heavens and took it to heart, making up his mind then and there to assiduously adhere to its instructions.

As Cheops had done, he enacted sweeping reforms.

But in the end, those reforms would not endure — any more than they had endured for Cheops. In less than a generation, the dream of Akhenaten had been swept aside like the desert sands that buried his abandoned capital. His heir would reign only a short time, but would remain in power long enough to begin the process of forsaking predecessor's wholehearted devotion to the Aten. The priests of Amen regained their influence, and the seat of government moved back upriver to Thebes. When, after a short time, this pharaoh in turn died, his successor Tutankhamen would complete the transition back to the old ways, working vigorously to undo everything Akhenaten had accomplished. Indeed, he would be described on a seal to his tomb as he "who spent his life in making images to the gods." [338]

The very same pattern can be seen upon Josiah's death. His heir, like Akhenaten's, remained on the throne for only a brief interval but failed to continue in the ways of his pious father. Instead, he "did evil" as his ancestors had done, presumably restoring the rural priests to office and re-establishing the Asherah poles in their high places. And his successor likewise continued in this pattern of evil, further distancing himself from the reforms instituted by Josiah.

But just how did the history of Akhenaten become attached to a Jewish king who supposedly ruled some six centuries later and hundreds of miles away? The heretic pharaoh rose to power long after the expulsion of the Hyksos, so his traditions could hardly have reached Palestine by that route. Indeed, most of Akhenaten's legacy was systematically expunged in Egypt shortly after his death, his monuments dismantled and his edicts erased by successors determined to restore the cult of Amen to its former glory.

To the north and east, however, the story was somewhat different. Not only had Akhenaten held sway over the Nile, but he had been lord of Palestine as well. Hundreds of letters from vassal states in the region, uncovered in the ruins of the pharaoh's capital, make this abundantly clear. And just as Akhenaten exercised secular control over Palestine, he doubtless also imposed his unique religious program on his subjects there. This program would have ended, as in Egypt, with his death. But it is unlikely that the restoration of the old ways was pursued with the same fervor in the north as in Egypt itself, and the memory of Aten worship would have therefore lingered in the minds of many who had been "converted" to the heresy.

Akhenaten's ban on the worship of graven images would endure in Palestine, even as statues of the gods were returned to the temple precincts in Egypt. And the innovation of monotheism would endure as well, contending mightily against the rival traditions of polytheism until, at last, it overcame them.

The Adonis Myth

Echoes of the Aten cult may perhaps be preserved in the name Adon, often used by the Hebrew scribes as an alternative form of address for Yahweh. The name that also bears a certain resemblance that of the dying and rising god Adonis, who was fated spent part of the year above ground and the rest of his time in the underworld — a clear manifestation of the solar cycle.

The story of Adonis appears to be closely related to that of the original resurrected god Osiris. Both heroes are closely identified with trees, but whereas Osiris becomes encased in a tree after his death, Adonis springs forth from one at birth. The reason for this peculiar advent is somewhat complicated. It seems that his mother had been transformed into a myrrh tree by the gods, their purpose being to spare her from the murderous wrath of her father.

Why was he so upset? Because she had seduced him in order to conceive the child Adonis.

The woman's name was Myrrha.

One cannot help but see a certain similarity to Mary, who in a different tale would conceive a child by *her* (heavenly) father — a child who, interestingly enough, would be brought gifts of myrrh upon his advent. These connections seem too close to be accidental. Indeed, they may very well have been sprinkled throughout the sacred texts for the express purpose of identifying the latter-day hero as a manifestation of this particular god.

Myrrh was a particularly potent clue, because this spice was crucial to the mummification process. It was used to prepare the fallen king to rise again, quite literally, when his prone casket was set upright in the inner chamber of the great pyramid temple. Myrrh was nothing less than the balm of Osiris, the original mummy, whose consort Isis was also known as Meri. In Egyptian, this name meant "beloved" and was often associated with Amen — reinforcing the commonality that existed between the traditions of that god and those of Osiris.

It seems likely that the high priestess of Amen, whose title was "wife of god," also bore the title "beloved of Amen." In Egyptian, this would have been Meri-Amen, a popular name borne by more than one woman of note in the nation's annals. At some point, it must have become so popular that it transcended national boundaries, finding its way into Palestine as the slightly conflated Mariamne — a name that itself was subsequently shortened further to Mariam or simply Mary.

The myth seems to have come full circle.

But history seldom follows neat circular patterns, and as any traveler who charts a course along the Nile must surely suspect, several twists and turns remain ahead.

The trick will be to navigate them safely.

XVII

Gate of God

Cheops was obsessed.

The pharaoh would not rest until he found the box of flint described by the sorcerer, the box containing sacred tablets attributed to Thoth. Only once he had obtained these tablets could he finish building his great pyramid on the plateau. The urgency with which he sought them made it obvious that they were somehow essential to the success of his project.

But why? What was it about these tablets that made the pharaoh so intent upon finding them?

The nature of the project itself provides the answer. In building his pyramid, Cheops was attempting to secure his own immortality, and he must have believed those tablets were crucial in allowing him to do so. They revealed the number of secret chambers in the sanctuary of Thoth, information that must have been astrological in nature. Thoth was, after all, the god who had set the year at its proper length of three hundred and sixty-five days, having crafted the five "epagomenal" days out of light he obtained in a wager with the moon.

Each of these days was a chamber through which the sun must pass in its annual journey across the heavens. It was a journey that took the golden orb from its mystical "birth" at the new year's dawning to the grave in the dead of winter — a grave from which it would emerge three days later, resurrected to new life as the days again grew longer. This great celestial cycle of death and rebirth was the key to immortality, the pharaoh believed. If he could somehow harness the mystical energy that fueled the solar chariot in its flight across the heavens, he believed, he too could conquer death and rise again like the new year sun.

The tablets contained the information he needed to achieve this great feat.

Yet how did he know this?

The answer can be found in the legend of the archetypal flood hero (Noah), whose story the pharaoh sought to duplicate in the construction of his pyramid. It was a legend Cheops must have known quite well, for he took great care in following it. Not only did he construct an artificial mountain as the place of ultimate refuge from the great flood, but he also buried an ark at the base of it to carry him across the treacherous waters of death. These were two key components in the flood epic. Yet there was a third element that was just as important to the story — an element somehow omitted from the *Genesis* account, but one that was hardly forgotten by other scribes who told the same story. From Cheops' actions, it is easy to guess what it was.

The tablets.

According to some, Noah had buried these tablets before the flood to preserve the divine knowledge imparted in an earlier age. He recognized that he could not simply commit all this sacred material to memory and that it would be lost unless it were somehow protected from the deluge, to be unearthed at some future date and relearned by his descendants.

This tale is told in a Sumerian myth whose hero is a king named Ziusudra, described as the last king in a dynasty before a great flood inundated his lands. It was his story that formed the basis for the epic of Gilgamesh, wherein the hero goes in search of immortality and finds the flood's only survivor living on a magical island across the sea. In this version of the tale, the man who has braved the deluge is identified as Utnapishtim, but it is clear that this is merely another name for Ziusudra. For one thing, his name is more of a description than anything else — it means "he who saw life." This serves to identify him as someone who has died but lives on, a ghost who has somehow succeeded in transcending his own mortality. His myth and that of Ziusudra boast numerous similarities, and the two figures (who are really one and the same) both hail from the same native city or Shuruppak.

In light of such parallels, one would expect the myth of Ziusudra to contain numerous points of contact with the Noah legend. And indeed it does. So similar were their stories, in fact, that the Jewish historian Josephus — in compiling his chronicles of the Jewish people — went so far as to proclaim them the same person. Referring to the writings of a Babylonian who had preserved the legend of Ziusudra, he declares that the author in question "gives us a history of the deluge and what then happened, and of the destruction of man thereby." He then goes on to say that the writer "also gives an account of the ark wherein Noah, the origin of our race, was preserved when it was brought to the highest part of the Armenian mountains." [339]

For Josephus, it did not matter that one writer called the hero Noah and the other named him Ziusudra — to him, they were the same person. But the Ziusudra epic and the story of Utnapishtim contain some information not found in Noah's story. Some crucial information.

In the story of Noah, for example, the floodwaters recede and the ark comes to rest on the mountains of Ararat, whereupon and the hero at last ventures forth onto dry land. Leaving the ark, he builds an altar on the mountain and sacrifices burnt offerings to his patron god. But the story of Utnapishtim relates that the offerings were not made on a mountain at all, but instead "on the top of a hill-like ziggurat." [340]

The confusion isn't hard to understand. A ziggurat was an artificial mountain, but it was also a temple — and as such would have been equipped with an altar. In this light, the true meaning of the text comes into focus. Noah did not land on the mountains of Ararat at all. He in fact *built* an artificial mountain or ziggurat, equipped with an altar wherein he could sacrifice to his patron deity. The ziggurat in question is the temple of the god Ea in Eridu, where the hero ultimately took up residence. One version of the story has the hero declare, "I lived in the temple of Ea my lord." [341]

Who was this Ea?

His name sounds suspiciously like Yah, the shortened form of Yahweh that was in common use among the Hebrews. Such an identification makes perfect sense in light of the flood narratives. It goes a long way toward explaining why the hero built an altar to Yahweh (actually the Elohim, consolidated in later tradition as the single god Yahweh) in the Hebrew version of the myth, but made sacrifice instead to Ea in the Mesopotamian epic.

The fact of the matter is that the two were most likely the same god.

In still older versions of the tale, his name was Enki, the Sumerian god of wisdom and the waters — two prominent elements of the flood myth. The connection with the waters is obvious; the link to wisdom less so. But this is where the sacred tablets come into play. The wise god Enki knew the flood was coming and feared that all the wisdom of ages past would be washed away with the great deluge. He therefore instructed the flood hero to conceal them in the city of Sippar, a city that was also known by another name.

The city of the sun.

This is a fascinating piece of information. It at once makes it abundantly clear why, centuries later, the pharaoh named Cheops would be told to seek the sacred tablets of Thoth in Heliopolis — likewise known as the city of the sun. The two cities were both centers of the solar cult, and both apparently became associated with the myth of the divine tablets inscribed by the god of writing. In Sumer, this god was Enki; in Egypt, it was Thoth. The names were different, but the main structure of the myth survived in both venues.

After the flood, the hero's relatives were instructed to return to Sippar and uncover the tablets that had been hidden there.

But what of the hero himself?

The Mesopotamian myth records that he left the ark with his wife, daughter and the man he had hired to be his captain. After building the altar and making his sacrifice, "he was seen no more." A voice then was heard proclaiming that "because of the great honor he had shown the gods, (he) had gone to the dwelling place of the gods and that his wife and daughter and steersman had enjoyed the same honor." [342] The implication is clear — he has died and been taken to the afterlife as a deified king. And this is confirmed in another version of the tale, wherein the gods grant him "life like a god" and settle him across the sea on the isle of Dilmun, a fabled paradise also known as the land of the rising sun.

One is reminded at once of the mystical island of Avalon to which Arthur retreats after he is mortally wounded in the Grail myths. The imagery of the rising sun speaks the language of the resurrection clearly and eloquently, leaving no doubt that the hero has journeyed to a mystical land of enchantment where he is ever renewed like the golden orb itself. This journey begins immediately after the hero builds an altar and sacrifices to his god, a sequence that is as important as the events themselves. It is almost as if the ziggurat temple that housed the altar was a gateway to the afterlife.

The Tower of Bab-ili.

The Gate of God.

A stairway to heaven.

This was the function of the ziggurat, so it is hardly surprising that the hero should go to "live" in the temple mountain immediately before his departure to the otherworld. The temple was also a shrine, the final resting place of the deified king. The flood hero built it not only to house an altar to his god, but to provide himself with a final resting place — just as Cheops would seek to do with the his pyramid centuries later.

Who Was Enki?

The god Ea or Enki plays a pivotal role in the flood myth. It is he who warns the hero that a flood is imminent and instructs him to build an ark, and it is he who receives the hero's sacrifice when the waters subside. Enki was entrusted with the custody of the mystical canon known as the *me*, the decrees upon which heaven and earth had been founded.[343] As such, he was revered as the original scribe, the inventor of the written word and the wisest of all the Mesopotamian gods.

His memory is preserved in the Hebrew texts with a single reference that is as fascinating as it is brief. The Hebrew scribes of later monotheism had no interest in retaining any reference to a deity they perceived as "another" god, so they allotted him nothing more than a passing reference and demoted him to the status of a man — though it is quite apparent he is something more than mortal. Indeed, he is described as a companion of the Elohim. And the manner in which he ended his time on earth makes his tale even more intriguing: "Enoch walked with the Elohim; then he was no more, because the Elohim took him." [344]

The name Enoch is simply a variation on Enki, with the second syllable transposed from its original *ki* sound to *ik*. Enki is a Sumerian name meaning "lord of the earth" (*en* meaning lord, *ki* meaning earth). But he was seen first and foremost as a master of the waters. He was the ruler of the abyss or *abzu*, the name by which the ancients knew the watery depths of the Persian Gulf.

As the water deity, Enki was the obvious choice to serve as patron god of the flood hero. And it was therefore natural that elements of the flood story should creep into the legend of Enoch. Compare the following two passages, the first by the Hebrew scribes in reference to Enoch and the second by the Babylonian writer Berossos in his account of the flood hero's fate after the waters subsided.

> ➤ Enoch walked with the gods; then he was no more because the gods took him away.
> ➤ After this, he disappeared altogether (and) ... from then on was seen no more. Because of the great honor he had shown the gods, he had gone to the dwelling place of the gods.[345]

In both cases, the hero disappears and goes to dwell with the gods. This is, of course, nothing more than a poetic way of reporting his death. But some whose ears are less attuned to poetry and more inclined to take things literally did just that, assuming that the person in question had simply disappeared off the face of the earth in the twinkling of an eye. This left the door open to all sorts of speculation. What happened to Enoch after he was taken? What did the gods say to him when he walked with them? Could they have imparted some sort of mystical information? And if so, was it possible that this information might have survived?

The myth that identified Enki as the keeper of the *me* provided the answer. These sacred documents must have been the very same tablets preserved by the flood hero at Sippar and later unearthed by his kinsmen. They reportedly contained an account of "the beginning, middle and end of all things."[346] And how could such an account have been obtained but by walking with the gods and making careful note of all they related? This logical conclusion gave rise to a wealth of literature attributed to Enoch, most of it dealing with his alleged ascent through the seven heavens and the record of what he saw there. One such document describes him in terms that would as easily have fit Enki or Thoth: "Enoch, righteous man, scribe of righteousness."[347]

Just as scribes produced writings to pass off as Thoth's famous emerald tablets in Egypt, so they authored works purported to contain the revelations of Enoch. The two figures are even more closely linked by a specific numeral attached to their names — three hundred and sixty-five. Thoth, of course, was responsible for extending the year by five days from its previous standard to three hundred and sixty-five days; Enoch, meanwhile, is said to have lived three hundred and sixty-five *years*. This figure stands out on a list wherein all the other patriarchs mentioned were said to have lived at least twice that long. Aside from Enoch, Lamech enjoyed the shortest life span of the group at slightly less than eight hundred years.

All these figures are, of course, exaggerated. But the mythmakers must have had a reason for deviating from the pattern in Enoch's case, and they must have had a reason for specifying that his age corresponded exactly to the number of days in the solar year. Clearly, they have preserved a connection with solar mythology, and this is only natural considering Enoch's identification with Enki. Although the Sumerian god's home city was Eridu, he was also closely connected with Sippar — the city of the sun — where he instructed the flood hero to bury the sacred tablets.

In Sumerian myth, Enki was the son of the sky god An. The significance of this becomes apparent when one remembers that the Egyptian city of the sun, Heliopolis, was originally known as On or Annu, meaning "pillar." From its inception, it seems to have been a symbol of the sky god. In many ancient myths, the sky god was the primeval male element whose union with the earth goddess was the ultimate act of creation. The phallic pillar paid tribute to this creator deity, who sent rain down upon the earth to fertilize her womb just as a man would release his seed into a woman. Moreover, the ancients believed that the sky was literally supported by a mystical pillar or a series of pillars, which they dutifully represented in the form of actual, physical columns.

This sky god was known to the ancients as An. But in later times, his cult was superseded by that of another heavenly father, Osiris, who dwelt in the sky and was seen as progenitor of the royal house. Whatever one might call this heavenly father, however, it is clear that the pillar of Heliopolis was set up to proclaim his reproductive power and to celebrate the birth of his divine son, the pharaoh.

Enki was the first of these divine offspring, according to the Sumerian myth, and the flood hero who served as king of Shuruppak was one of his heirs. Call him Noah. Call him Utnapishtim or Atrahasis, Ziusudra or Xisuthros.

The names might have changed as the story made its way from Sumer to Egypt and Palestine, but the story itself remained largely the same and survives to this day in no fewer than six variations, including the *Genesis* account. This makes it among the most widely attested of the ancient myths, not to mention one of the most enduring, having survived for some five thousand years.

Noah in China

The names Ziusudra and Xisuthros, two epithets by which the flood hero is known in separate versions of the myth, are obviously similar. But the origin of the name Noah has yet to be fully explained. One possibility, already noted, lies in its apparent relationship to the Egyptian word *nhh*, designating "eternity." It may also be linked to the Hebrew word *nuwa*, meaning "to wander" — and this may have been derived from ancient China, of all places. The Chinese, it so happens, had a flood myth of their own. And this myth recounted the deeds of a heroic figure who bore a familiar name.

Nu Wa.

In the original version of the story, this personage was decidedly feminine. Indeed, she was the goddess who had created mankind in her own image out of clay.[348] But a later variant on the myth depicted Nu Wa as a man, protégé and successor to the first god-king. It was this great king, Fu Xi, who imparted to mankind all the knowledge he would need to thrive upon the earth. He instructed man in the art of music, invented script so he could set his thoughts to paper, taught him to fish and to domesticate animals for food.[349]

This sounds very much like the role played by Enki, the inscriber of the famed stone tablets in Mesopotamian lore. The similarities in the various myths allow one to trace the story back to its origins with relative ease:

- Enki (or Ea) was the patron of the Mesopotamian flood hero.
- Yahweh (or Yah) was the patron of Noah.
- Fu Xi was likewise the patron of Nu Wa.

According to the Chinese tale, the deluge began when a tyrant arose in the final year of Nu Wa's reign. This despot rose up to challenge the fire god in battle, but seeing that he could not prevail against him, he flew into a rage and butted his head against the pillar of heaven (a massive bamboo stalk) and knocked it down. In doing so, he tore a hole in the sky and caused rainwater to pour down upon the earth in a monumental deluge. Mankind was obliterated from all the earth, with Nu Wa's contingent the only survivors. Eventually, Nu Wa managed to repair the damage by patching the hole in heaven. "After this," it was written, "the world was at rest, the heaven made whole and the old things were unchanged." [350]

Interestingly, the Hebrew name for Noah also may be related to the word *nowach*, signifying rest. And the new stability inaugurated by Nu Wa's work in repairing the heavens is likewise expressed in the Hebrew myth, wherein Noah is promised that "as long as Earth endures, seedtime and harvest, cold and heat, summer and winter, day and night will never cease." [351] Or, in the language of the Chinese myth, the old things would remain unchanged.

Just as Noah and his family are the only survivors of the great deluge, so it is also with Nu Wa's group. And the presence of the so-called pillar of heaven reminds one at once of the similar pillar at Heliopolis that served as the nesting place of the phoenix, the bird of fire. In the Chinese myth, it was an epic battle between the proud tyrant and the fire god that helped precipitate the deluge. Could this fire god have been somehow connected to the phoenix, which in

Egypt symbolized the unconquerable fiery sun god Horus?

The parallels are tantalizing.

Just as Horus defeated the storm god Seth, so the fire god of China defeated a tyrant who spawned a great storm.

It is also worth noting that the Chinese had their own legend of the phoenix, which like the Egyptian bird was an avatar of the sun. According to some accounts, it dwelt in the fiery orb itself, and at least one author likened its eye to the radiant solar disk — a reference that recalls the eye of Horus. A Chinese ornithologist called it the principal among three hundred and sixty bird species, citing the number of days in the solar year (minus the five epagomenal days added by the Egyptians). In light of this connection, it was only natural that a certain king should appoint his minister of the calendar under the title of phoenix.[352]

The spread of such traditions to lands as far afield from one another as China and Egypt is amazing. Yet there can be little doubt that these stories are related. Nor can there be any question that the flood story which originated in the east eventually made its way to the land of the pharaohs. At some point, perhaps shortly before Imhotep built the step pyramid of Saqqara, a trade caravan or royal delegation must have brought the tale to Egypt, where it was embraced by a royal house that saw itself as heir to the tradition. The pharaoh Cheops considered himself the latest in an unbroken line of divine kings dating back to the dawn of civilization. He was convinced that he, like the royal flood hero, was the rightful custodian of Enki's wisdom — or Thoth's, to use the god's Egyptian name. And he therefore sought access to it in preparation for his own death and journey across the great watery expanse.

As the flood hero had constructed an ark, he did likewise.

As the flood hero had built ziggurat, so he built a pyramid.

Mountain of Fire

At the apex of the pyramid was the benben stone, symbolizing the famous firebird known as the phoenix that was said to descend upon it in a dazzling spectacle of light and flame. Such an event would light up the pyramid in a blaze of glory, creating a mountain of fire that could be seen from horizon to horizon. And just such a mountain is described in the Enoch literature, set in the midst of the original garden of paradise. In the text, an angelic guide gives Enoch a tour of heaven, and he is stunned by all he witnesses. "He showed me a mountain of fire that was flaming day and night," the author relates. When Enoch questions him about what he has seen, the angel answers him: "This tall mountain which you saw whose summit resembles the throne of God is indeed his throne." [353]

The symbolism of the account is plain. The mountain blazes day and night, a flame that cannot be quenched to serve as a beacon of eternal life. Whose eternal life? The king's. For the mountain itself is a divine throne, fit for a king who has conquered death and has been taken up to heaven to walk with the gods. This was exactly what happened to the pharaoh when he ascended the stairway to heaven as the new Osiris. He walked with the gods, and in fact became one of them, an immortal, just as the flood hero before him had done.

Where did this symbolism come from?

Once again, the origins lie in the flood myth. The myth of Ziusudra reports that the gods rewarded the hero for his devotion to them when they "elevated him to life like a god." [354] It was on a mountain that the hero expressed this devotion by building an altar and offering a burnt sacrifice to his patron god, thus creating a divine eternal flame. The mountain was, of course, really the ziggurat of Enki in Eridu. This was the stairway to heaven by which the hero was, quite literally, "elevated" to godhood. But the storytellers who crafted the legend in its final form didn't know that. Somewhere along the way, the tradition had become garbled: A narrative that had once focused on an artificial mountain began referring to an actual mountain — though exactly *which* mountain was open to some debate.

In the Hebrew text, it was referred to oddly enough as the

mountains of Ararat. A native scribe would hardly have used such a term. Uruat itself meant mountains, and it would have been redundant to say "mountains of mountains." Merely mentioning the Uruat would have sufficed — any reader within a reasonable proximity of the Tigris-Euphrates river valley would have understood the reference at once. But the language of the text appears to demonstrate that the scribe (and his readers) had little familiarity with such things. Evidently, the geography of Mesopotamia was largely a mystery to the residents of Palestine at the time this text was composed.

Or was it?

Is it perhaps just possible, in the alternative, that the phrase has been misinterpreted altogether and the Hebrew scribe is being unfairly portrayed as ignorant?

In light of such questions, the odd phrase "mountains of Ararat" is worth examining. In Hebrew, it translates as *har* ararat. The first word, *har*, was indeed a Hebrew word for mountain, and this is how it has been translated in the text. Yet it has another meaning as well. It is also a name for the Egyptian god Horus, the sun god whose symbol was the phoenix and whose spirit was incarnate in the ruling pharaoh. It was the pharaohs who built the artificial mountains known as the pyramids, so it would make a lot more sense interpret the phrase *har* ararat as meaning not "mountains of mountains" but "mountains of Horus." And such an association with the sun god and his firebird would mark them quite clearly as mountains of fire.

The same principle applies to Mt. Horeb, the sacred mountain where Yahweh confronted Moses in the form of a burning bush that was not consumed. Once again, the motif of the flaming mountain is revisited. And once again, there is some confusion on the part of translators who have unwittingly rendered the text in question redundant. If the prefix *hor* (a variation of *har*) is translated simply as mountain, the phrase at once becomes nonsensical. But if this prefix is recognized instead as a reference to the god Horus, it makes perfect sense.

Finding such material in the story of Moses should come as no great shock, for a careful study of his legend reveals that it contains almost all the main elements present in the flood story.

- ➤ He journeys across dangerous waters in an ark or *tebah*.
- ➤ He is closely associated with a mountain of fire.
- ➤ He is designated as the keeper of sacred tablets.
- ➤ He is a righteous man who inaugurates a brave new world.
- ➤ He is taken directly to heaven rather than dying a natural death.

This final tradition, though not contained in the scriptural account, proved to be quite persistent and was reflected in later apocryphal texts such as *The Assumption of Moses*. As with the Enoch myth, it drew its inspiration from a bit of ambiguity in the canonical account of its hero's death. Though the author of *Deuteronomy* stated in no uncertain terms that Moses was buried, he also left the door open to speculation with the curious statement that "to this day, no one knows where his grave is." [355]

In truth, the explanation for this was quite simple: Moses' grave wasn't in Palestine at all, but in Egypt, where the pharaoh Ahmose was in actuality lain to rest. As a pharaoh, he claimed the flood myth as his inheritance and made sure that his story was told to future generations in terms that were consistent with the language of this timeless epic. In doing so, he was pursuing the very same goal Cheops had striven to achieve a thousand years earlier.

Immortality.

The legendary Mt. Horeb was located in the mountains of Seir — the mountain of Horus among mountains of Osiris. In other words, it was one pyramid standing amidst many.

Interestingly enough, an obscure Arab tradition connects these very mountains with no less a personage than Cheops himself. The pyramid builder was no insignificant monarch. An impression of his signet ring has been found as far afield as Nineveh, the ancient city in

Mesopotamia that plays a prominent role in the legend of Jonah. And his realm extended far to the north and west of his capital, to the rugged desert high country known variously as Uz and Seir in southern Palestine. This raises the distinct possibility that he or his armies were the first to designate the craggy peaks in that region as the mountains of Uz-Seir — Asir or Osiris.

Incredibly, a district known as Asir can be found in the same region, somewhat to the south along the Arabian Peninsula. There one can find the continuation of the same mountain range that rises farther to the north, near the Dead Sea, and stretches south along the seacoast for hundreds of miles, ringing western and southern edges of the peninsula. These are the mountains of Uz-Seir, or Asir. And where the ancient name of Osiris is found, one might also expect to find the names of his consort (Isis) and his son (Horus).

Confirmation of this is found in and around Asir, where several towns share the name Al Issa.[356] The first word is the Arab equivalent of El, the name of the highest god in the Canaanite pantheon. The second is even more intriguing, considering its clear linguistic connection to the god Seth in his various Hebrew incarnations: Esau, Isaac and Issachar. It also bears a close resemblance to Isis, whose actual name in Egyptian was Au Set.

Literally, the great Set(h).

The linguistic maze takes a number of twists and turns at this juncture, but it is worth holding on and going along for the ride. First, however, it is necessary to revisit the original legend of Isis and her son Horus, who was supposedly conceived as the result of a miracle rivaling that of the virgin birth. Legend had it that the young prince was the product of a union between Isis and Osiris — *after* his father had died. This would have certainly been no mean feat for poor Osiris, who according to tradition was forced to rise from the dead in order to conceive an heir. In fact, however, an alternate tradition provides a much more concrete explanation: According to this version of the tale, Isis in her grief was comforted by none other than her husband's murderer, Seth, who became her lover. This raises the intriguing possibility that it was he, rather than Osiris, who was the father of her child.

Such a development would have been fully consistent with the tradition of the tanist ritual, which pitted an aging monarch against a more youthful rival for the throne — and for the hand of the queen.

The latter was, in fact, was the real prize.

It was only through the queen that the fertility of the land could be restored, and it is for this reason that the successful tanist challenger was obligated to lie with her. This obligation is preserved in the Hebrew law code, of all places, in the form of the so-called levirate marriage. Under this law, a man whose brother died without issue was obligated to marry his brother's widow and provide the dead man with an heir. The author of *Deuteronomy* set forth this law as follows: "If brothers are living together and one of them dies without a son, his widow must not marry outside the family. Her husband's brother shall take her and marry her and fulfill the duty of a brother-in-law to her. The first son she bears shall carry the name of the dead brother, so that his name will not be blotted out from Israel." [357]

Here is the obvious explanation for the confusion surrounding Horus' parentage. He was, in physical terms, the son of Seth. Yet in the eyes of the law, he was the son of Osiris — who had died without issue and left his brother with the task of fathering an heir in his name.

The child's parentage was therefore, in a way, uncertain. Was he the son of his true father, or was he in some manner illegitimate? Was he the son of his father in heaven (Osiris) or of a mere mortal (Seth)? It is perhaps something more than coincidence that these same questions would swirl about Jesus, a man identified by some not in reference to his father but to his *mother*: "Isn't this Mary's son?" [358] And Meri was another name for Isis.

Whose name, in turn, bears a resemblance to "Issa" from the place name Al Issa.

Near the mountains of Asir or Osiris.

The name Issa itself appears in the Hebrew texts as a word

simply meaning "woman" and applied to no less a figure than the archetypal mother of humankind, Eve. It appears to be a form of the name Isis, perhaps abbreviated and combined with the Egyptian word *sa*, meaning son. And the son of Isis was none other than Horus, the incarnation of his heavenly father on Earth in the form of the pharaoh. The king. The messiah. The parallels are nothing short of incredible. Add to this the fact that Jesus is referred to in the Quran under the name Issa, and one has rather convincing evidence that he was considered the new Horus.

The region of the Arabian Peninsula known as Asir lies less than two hundred miles from Egypt itself, separated from it only by the straits of the Red Sea. Its proximity would have allowed for easy access by ship, and traders undoubtedly made their way overland as well by way of the Sinai Peninsula, bringing with them the myths and traditions of Osiris, Seth, Isis and Horus — traditions that seem to have taken hold in the land of Uz-Seir. Even today, the memory of this legend is preserved in the region. In the city of Mecca, just to the north of the region known as Asir, there is preserved a black meteoric stone that has been incorporated into the wall of the Ka'ba, the holiest site in the Islamic world. Here is yet another benben stone, the symbol of Horus. It even appears conceivable that the name of the shrine itself appears to have something to do with Egyptian mystical tradition, combining the words for spirit (*ka*) and soul (*ba*).

It is obvious from such clues that the Egyptians had a tremendous influence on the region. According to one scholar, the Arabs have preserved a tradition that refers to the pharaoh who built the great pyramid as "Cheops of Mt. Seir or the land of Uz" and further identifies him, incredibly enough, as the Wizard of Uz. [359] Visions of the famous emerald city depicted in L. Frank Baum's novel and the famous film adaptation immediately come to mind, and rightfully so. For this can be none other than the famous city of the sun, where the emerald tablets of Thoth were locked away. When the pharaoh discovered them and stored them in his pyramid, he became the keeper of their divine secrets and thus was transformed into a wizard.

The infamous "man behind the curtain" in Oz can be seen as a version of the "hidden god" Amen, and the palace in the Emerald City provides a fitting counterpart to the temple and its inner sanctuary. Whether Baum intended any of this is hard to tell. He reportedly patterned his *Wonderful Wizard of Oz* after the Grimm and Anderson faerie tales. And the word Oz supposedly came from a chance glimpse of a label on a filing cabinet: O-Z.

Nevertheless, it is worth noting that he also published (anonymously) a book for adult readers titled *The Last Egyptian* that includes references to a statue of Isis, a slave girl named Nephthys and a high priest of ... yes ... Amen. Baum said he wrote the novel anonymously to avoid hurting his career as a children's writer. But it seems also possible that his references to Egypt might have revealed a source of inspiration for Oz. Or perhaps he simply loved the land, which he visited with his wife after he wrote his first Oz book.

But we digress.

Over time, the actual mountains of Orisis — the pyramids — became confused with the mountains of Uz-Seir in Palestine, and the legend of Moses and the divine tablets was transferred to this locale in yet another example of a tradition whose true origins have been obscured by the seemingly continual process of textual revision and cultural relocation.

This same process was in play during the transmission of the flood story, which has survived in several versions from different epochs. One of these, the epic of Gilgamesh, does not mention the "mountains of Ararat" at all, but instead indicates that the ark ran aground on a mountain called Nisir, traditionally identified with a peak in the nearby Zagros range. (One may notice the similarity between the name Zagros and the term ziggurat.) In fact, however, the mountain's name is probably derived from the root *nisirtu*, which meant "concealed" or "not readily accessible." [360]

Such terminology again recalls the great god Amen, whose very name meant "the hidden one" and whose cult was most closely associated with the pharaohs of Egypt. It also brings to mind the image of the Grail Castle, that mysterious citadel that lay concealed in the mists of a foreign realm somewhere across the waters of a flowing river. This was the same river of mortality that the flood hero had crossed to find the hidden sanctuary on the other side, the temple or castle or mansion that mirrored the artificial mountain in which his body had been lain to rest.

The Grail Castle was the pyramid.

The pyramid was the ziggurat.

The ziggurat was the mountain of Noah.

Its name, Nisir, bears a certain resemblance to the Hebrew word *netser*, usually translated as "branch" or "shoot." This word would be used to announce the coming messiah, the branch that would spring forth from the stump of Jesse, just as Horus had arisen from the petrified body of the ancient tree god Osiris. Some would identify this man as Jesus of Nazareth, a title that supposedly linked him to a tiny village near the heart of Galilee. The only problem with such an identification is the absence of any evidence that such a town existed until three centuries after Jesus' birth. It is much more likely that he was Jesus the *netser*, or perhaps even Jesus the *nisirtu*.

The incarnation of the hidden one, the great god Amen.

Nile to Nottingham

The death of Akhenaten brought with it a return to the old ways. In Egypt, the temples to Amen, Osiris and the other gods were restored, along with their associated statues and *djed* pillars. In Palestine, the Asherah poles were restored to their former places of prominence on the hillsides. These wooden counterparts of the *djed* had been a natural development in the region, where wood was more plentiful and stone less abundant than in Egypt.

Now they returned, once again bearing witness to the risen nature god who emerged from the dead at springtide. In time, they would become all but synonymous with it. On the first day of each new May, a wooden pole would be erected on the city green, around which men and women would dance in a celebration of the greatest merriment. Each participant would take in his hand a strip of ribbon and, as he danced, would gradually entwine it around the great maypole.

A king of May would be chosen, sometimes known as Green George. This curious designation seems somehow related to St. George, the legendary dragon slayer whose day is celebrated a week earlier.

This particular saint is a curious character. As the national saint of England, he is often depicted as a knight in armor riding out, lance in hand, to do battle with a fearsome winged beast. But this caricature only serves to conceal his true origins, for St. George didn't come from England at all — he was a bishop of Alexandria.

In Egypt.

And the tales that formed around him were decidedly Egyptian in character. The dragon he slew was almost certainly Seth, and as its slayer he was associated with the beast's eternal nemesis Horus. Even the name Horus appears to have a certain affinity with the name George, which can be traced through its various forms in different languages:

➢ Georges, pronounced "jhorjh(es)" in French.
➢ Jorge, pronounced "hor-hay" in Spanish.

Both of these names, taken together, appear somewhat similar to the name Horace, which in turn sounds virtually identical to that of *Horus*. All this was part of a natural process that took place over a span of centuries. Egyptian myths made their way via Phoenician trade ships to the British Isles, where they were incorporated into parallel native traditions surrounding the spring fest and subsequently merged with tales about the Egyptian saint.

At the center of it all was the divine vegetation king, a figure responsible for ensuring the prosperity of field and vineyard for another year. As in the pharaonic tradition and stories of the grail, the king and the land were joined at the hip — the monarch's success was measured by the land's fecundity. If the king bore no heir, it was an omen of poor harvests to come. And if he grew old and feeble, the crops might be expected to fail as well; the leaves might lose their luster and tumble from failing branches; the herds might wander miles before finding suitable pasture to graze. A new king would have to be found to replace the old — one young and vital enough to ensure the land's prosperity.

So it was too with the Green Man.

It was his duty to bring the land its fruitfulness; if he failed in this charge, he was rudely cast away. In one locale, St. George's Day was celebrated with a grand procession, at the center of which was a youthful lad covered in birch leaves playing the part of Green George. When this procession reached its end, either the youth himself or an image of Green George was thrown into the river. A song that seems to have been associated with this proceeded as follows:

> *Green George we bring*
> *Green George we accompany*
> *May he feed our herds well*
> *If not, to the water with him* [361]

The song clearly indicates that immersion in the river is Green George's punishment for failing to perform his expected duties. The river, as in so many other traditions, signified death. And the entire ceremony has the feel of a ritual re-enactment of the mysteries of Osiris, who was likewise slain and cast into the river. The Egyptian god-king was also well remembered for having become encased in a tree — just like the Green George youth in his garment of birch leaves.

If the king could no longer guarantee the land's abundance, he would be cast away as Osiris had been and replaced by a new Horus or Green George. Horus was, after all, the shoot of life that sprang forth from the dead body of petrified (mummified) tree-king Osiris. Not only did this concept find its way to the British Isles, it also surfaced in Palestine, where it could be seen quite clearly in Hebrew traditions surrounding the messiah or anointed king: "A shoot will come forth from the stump of Jesse; from his roots a branch will bear fruit." [362]

It was only natural that the king, portrayed as a green *shoot* in the legend, should come to be depicted as a green *man*. His face, peeking mischievously out from a ring of leaves, would adorn a multitude of chapels and cathedrals in the Middle Ages — a seemingly out-of-place pagan visage intruding upon a decidedly Christian world.

But was it?

Or was it the face of the messiah himself, ringed in leaves from the hawthorn plant that was synonymous with the maypole fest? These leaves were gay and festive. Yet they were guarded by rows of long, sharp thorns that protruded outward from the plant to give the unsuspecting passer-by a nasty prick. Turned inward and pressed against the head of a person wearing such leaves, they would have been quite painful. Here indeed, it would seem, is the crown of thorns that, according to legend, was placed upon the brow of Jesus at his crucifixion — the crown of the maypole king.

Players told his story in rhyme and dance each springtime. Traveling from house to house, they would place garlands on the doorframes and the outer sills of window casements in homes across the countryside; then they would act out their spring plays on the village green or in the marketplace, to the delight of those who gathered to watch them. They were called mummers — a term derived from a root meaning "mask" or "disguise" — because they wore just such masks during their charades and skits. Yet perhaps there was another reason, as well. Perhaps they were so named because of their connection to the ritual *mummification* of the maypole or Asherah pole. Just as the dead king Osiris had been masked by strips of linen, so now the people of the village wound strips of ribbon around the may pole. A wooden *djed* column for the modern age.

Such ceremonies were presided over by the two most important mummers of all, the king and queen of May. The king was often depicted as Green George but even more frequently as another familiar character. As famous as St. George's legend was in England (and, for that matter, across Europe), in time another story came to eclipse it in popularity and importance. It was the story of a man who made his home in the greenwood with a band of merry men as his followers; a good-hearted rogue who robbed from the rich and gave to the poor; a peerless archer and a romantic suitor devoted to his lady love Marian. Like King Arthur, his origins are shrouded in the mists of time, and there are no contemporary accounts of his accomplishments. It is therefore nearly impossible to discover what portion of his tale is myth and what is history. Yet that has not deterred a score of generations from toasting his fame and saluting his bravery.

The man's name, of course, is Robin Hood.

The Shire Wood

Sherwood Forest is a real place, on a real map in a real country. Its original name was probably the Shire Wood, a vast expanse of forest, bog and thicket that covered no less than thirty miles at the heart of England. Only later, when it was established as an official hunting preserve for the king and his favorites, did it acquire the more technical title of forest. People caught carrying a bow and arrow in such regions were considered poachers and subject to harsh punishment.

If there was a historical Robin Hood who dwelt in this historical forest, he was doubtless such a person. But there are many indications that would lead one to the opposite conclusion — that he was not a historical personage at all, and that he was in fact a creature of myth. For one thing, there are no contemporary records referring to the man, who is described variously as a yeoman, a wronged nobleman and a Saxon freedom fighter.

He could hardly have been all three.

Nor is it clear exactly when he lived, as some chroniclers place him in the reign of the second King Edward while others say he was active more than a century earlier under Richard the Lionheart. His base of operations is given variously as Sherwood Forest, the village of Barnsdale to the north and the town of Loxley to the west. Indeed, the confusion is such that it is nearly impossible to know when or where this legendary outlaw lived his life.

But perhaps there is good reason for this. Indications are that Robin Hood lived at various times in a multitude of locales — often appearing simultaneously in many of them. How did he manage such a feat? The answer is simple, and it should be quite familiar to anyone who ever marveled during childhood that the jolly red-clad elf with the white beard should make his presence known on every street corner during the holiday season. The fact is, he was not who he appeared to be. Nor was he a single person. *He* was actually *they* — any number of actors suitably plump and appropriately disguised to provide at least some semblance of authenticity.

The aged elf with the fluffy white beard and the bright red coat was the old man of winter himself. He was the aged king, his face lined with creases and his belt struggling to rein in his ample paunch. As the embodiment of winter's cold and darkness, he was Seth — the eternal adversary — feared and reviled in some quarters as "Old Nick," a pseudonym for the devil. Yet he was also an integral part of the season's celebration, a joyous time to celebrate the sun's renewal. During this time, many looked back fondly on the year that was and saw in the old man, not an adversary, but a bestower of generous gifts and a symbol of all they cherished in their memories. How, they asked, could such a kindly figure be so maligned? The answer was that he could not. And therefore they sanctified him, transforming him from Old Nick into Saint Nick, a character who, incidentally, wears red — the color of Seth.

The old king died at the end of every such season. But with his death came the promise that a new king would succeed him in the springtime, a virile young hunter clad in green who would banish the snow and replace it with morning dew; who would call forth the robin to proclaim the new season in song; who would magically restore the leaves to the branches and the green grass to the pastureland.

Just as any number of actors might portray the jolly old king during winter, so also a healthy quantity of performers could be counted upon to play the part of the new king in springtime. In many local festivals, he was Green George; in others, Jack-in-the-Green. But perhaps his most famous guise was that of the roguish forest outlaw known for robbing from the rich and giving to the poor — that impeccable bowman and sheriff's nemesis, Robin Hood. One youth might play the part in Nottingham, another in York and still another in some southern village on the River Thames. On the first of May, Robin was ubiquitous.

He was more than a simple outlaw; he was the King of May, accompanied in most cases by his beloved consort Maid Marian. Echoes of the Egyptian ritual are somewhat faint but may be found if one knows where to look. Robin's traditional outfit of Lincoln green identifies him plainly as a vegetation king, the messianic "shoot" springing forth from the stump of the dead monarch. And Osiris himself is depicted in the maypole ritual and mummers' dance. As the dancers wrapped the Asherah pole in strips of ribbon, Robin presided over the merriment — himself a "mummer" whose face was veiled by a hood.

These dancers were the original merry men.

Or, perhaps, Mary's men.

A recurring theme in the rhymes of these jolly outlaws is their roguish leader's unflagging devotion to a certain Mary. Her identity seems to vary from one tale (or even one stanza) to the next — in some cases, she is the virgin mother; in others, she is Mary Magdalene. In one story, Robin extols the virgin as a man would praise his beloved, calling her "the truest woman that I have ever found." [363] Yet in the same story, he speaks of having founded a chapel to Mary Magdalene in his hometown and expresses a yearning to return there.[364]

The May Queen

Such confusion is hardly unique to the Robin Hood legend.

Throughout Europe, black statues of a mysterious maiden have been revered for centuries as images of the virgin mother. Yet in fact, they may be something altogether different. It is intriguing to discover, for example, that many of these statues are to be found in villages associated with the veneration of the *other* Mary. The Magdalene. The black visage that stares back at the devotee reminds one at once of the dark-skinned Queen of Sheba, the Ethiopian consort of King Solomon who in many ways served as the model for the sacred royal bride. But the imagery probably goes back even further than that.

To the myth of Isis and Osiris.

It was here, in the tragic story of true love rent asunder by the god-king's awful murder, that the black goddess had her origins. She was Isis, sad and mournful. She was Isis, proud and defiant in the face of great privation. The art of Egypt depicted her time and again in the color of mourning, evermore deprived of her husband's fellowship and accompanied only by her infant son Horus. Here is the origin of the Madonna-and-child imagery so familiar for the past two millennia. The black robes worn by Isis accentuated her ashen countenance, and these same robes adorned her priestess as she commemorated the drama of mourning.[365]

This was one of her most familiar aspects, yet still it was one of many. She was known Myrionymos — literally, the goddess of ten thousand (or myriad) names. One cannot help but notice the resemblance between this title and the name of Robin's consort Marian. Nor can one escape its nagging similarity to Mary. And indeed, there is a further connection to be made here, as well. One of Isis' many names was Meri, goddess of the sea.[366] She was the protector of sailors who braved the open water, guiding them safely to their destination if they honored her. The sea itself — known in later times as the *mer* or *mare* — took its name from her, as did the mariners she preserved from storm and shipwreck. This she did by lighting their way in her guise as Sirius, the brightest star in the midnight sky and the last to be eclipsed by the light of morning. The ancient mariners navigated their ships by the stars, and as such found the celestial Isis an invaluable ally. Because of her unparalleled brightness, she was dubbed queen of heaven, another of her myriad names.

It is a title she would share with Mary, the virgin mother.

The connection of Isis to the sea and its vessels was powerful and enduring. The Egyptians built a great lighthouse four hundred feet high and dedicated it to her, its beacon fashioned to complement the beams of her heavenly luminary. So impressive was the Pharos, as it was called, that men deemed it among the seven wonders of the ancient world. It may have drawn its name from two roots meaning "house of Isis," for it shared the island upon which it stood with a temple to the goddess. Standing above the harbor of Alexandria like a fixed star, its bonfire was kept ever burning to help sailors guide their ships to port.

One legend tells of a ritual conducted by the priests of Isis, wherein they would inaugurate the new sailing season by dedicating a ship in her honor.[367] The ceremony involved a great procession during which the ship was launched into the open sea. Yet as queen of heaven and patron goddess of the sea, she not only watched over mortal sailors as they cast their boats adrift on an earthly ocean, she also guided celestial seafarers on their journey across the heavens. Hence her frantic search for her slain husband's ark-casket after it was cast into the waters of the Nile. It was her duty to see his vessel safely to the far shore of eternity, not just as his faithful widow, but in her capacity as the goddess of celestial passage.

She is portrayed in just such terms in the tomb of an ancient king. There, she takes the form of a bird in flight above the mummified pharaoh, holding in one hand the hieroglyph of a sail that signified the breath of life.[368] In the other hand, she holds an *ankh*, the symbol of immortality. It is as though she is providing the ark-casket with the sail as its means to cross the ocean of death and reach the shores of eternal life.

The sail imagery was not limited to this single instance, but endured for centuries and even millennia afterward. During the Roman period, coins were minted showing the goddess with her hand on a billowing sail, in one instance staring at the Pharos lighthouse that had been dedicated in her honor. But although she was the protector of all mortal seafarers, it was her role as celestial keeper of the ark that was pre-eminent. As the goddess of birth, she guided the pharaohs into this world upon her ark — just as the infant Moses was ushered in upon such a vessel in the Nile. As the goddess of death, she conveyed them to the heavenly realm aboard another such vessel, the casket ark of Osiris.

Or Noah.

Or Solomon.

Her dual aspect as birth and death goddess most likely spawned a tradition that she was not one, but two. Thus arose the tradition of the twin sisters Isis and Nephthys, identical in nearly every respect, yet one a goddess of new birth and the other a guardian of the underworld. Together, they were the original "ark angels," serene and confident as they stretched their golden wingtips forward toward one another and stared face-to-face across the sacred Ark of the Covenant. In this pose, they formed an arc of their own, a shape not unlike that of the arching rainbow that welcomed Noah's ark to its final resting place. Such parallel imagery can scarcely be seen as pure happenstance, especially when one considers an ancient relief that has survived from an ancient palace in Mesopotamia, original home of the flood myth. It shows a traditional reed basket boat or *quffa* that looks remarkably like modern representations of Noah's ark. Yet it also bears a striking resemblance to the Ark of the Covenant, for it depicts oarsmen facing one another at bow and stern, arms outstretched toward one another as they pull against the current.[369] Such basket boats were made from reeds and coated with pitch, a method apparently utilized by the flood hero in building his vessel. In one version of the myth, he is instructed: "Let its structure be of good reeds." [370] And in the familiar legend of Noah's ark, he is told to "coat it with pitch inside and out." [371]

The parallel is even clearer with the ark of Moses, which is described as a "papyrus basket" coated with "tar and pitch" and thereafter placed among the reeds along the riverbank.[372]

In the Mesopotamian myth, that river was the Euphrates. In Egypt, it was the Nile. And when the myth of the deluge was transplanted from one place to the other, it was naturally altered to reflect its new surroundings. The deluge of the flood myth was easily transferred to the Nile floodplain, which experienced a deluge of its own each year when the snowmelt from the central African highlands made its way downstream toward the delta. During this time of inundation, the swollen river would overflow its banks, fertilizing the soil on either side of the raging torrent — a midsummer event that marked the beginning of a new year.

As was their habit with such milestones, the Egyptians celebrated this sacred event with a festival — and not just any festival. This was the Apet or Opet celebration, the single most significant festival of the year in Thebes. This celebration became more elaborate as the years passed, expanding from a week and a half to nearly four weeks and involving a huge abundance of supplies: eighty-five cakes, three hundred and eighty-five jars of beer and more than eleven thousand loaves of bread.[373] Reliefs from the period of Tutankhamen depict one of the central rituals of this celebration, the transfer of several golden boats (or arks) from the temple at Karnak to Luxor a short distance away. A grand procession is seen making its way through the streets of Thebes, led by jubilant minstrels ringing in the new year with song and dance. Behind them march a number of white-robed priests carrying poles on their shoulders that support the golden boats themselves.[374]

This was, it turns out, the very same mode of transport used to convey the golden Ark of the Covenant from one place to the next. Interestingly enough, that ark was housed in the temple of Solomon, while the arks used in the Opet festival were kept in the temple of Amen at Karnak. Three arks were involved in this ritual, representing the divine family of Thebes. One carried a likeness of Amen himself, while the other two bore stone statues of his consort Mut and their son Khons. The names of these gods may strike the ear as strange and exotic, but in fact their roles are quite familiar. Indeed, they closely paralleled those of the divine family of Osiris, Isis and Horus.

Amen was Osiris, the unseen heavenly father. His son Khons was portrayed sometimes as a young man and at other times with the head of a hawk — thus identifying him plainly with the hawk-headed god Horus. And Mut, meanwhile, was styled as "queen of the gods" and "lady of heaven." [375] The same epithets were of course applied to Isis, the mother of Horus. Both were famous as great mother goddesses, and indeed the name Mut meant "mother." [376]

The ritual journey of these golden boats through the streets of the capital began the celebration, which culminated in an important ritual inside the temple at Luxor. It was here that the god entered into his "harem." [377] The word evokes unmistakable images of a royal house of sexual pleasures, and one may well be reminded of Solomon's huge assortment of wives and concubines. Indeed, this may not be far from the mark. The ceremony that was celebrated when the ark had reached its destination appears to have been the consummation of a ritual union, during which the pharaoh himself underwent a sort of mystical transfiguration. When he emerged from the inner court or harem of the temple, he was greeted with cheers of adulation from his subjects as they acknowledged this metamorphosis.

Clearly, something significant had happened in the inner courts of the temple. From the records that have survived, it appears that the divine spirit or *ka* had been merged with the pharaoh's mortal body, transforming him into a figure at once mortal and divine. The ceremony is reminiscent of a similar tradition involving Jesus, wherein the holy spirit took the form of a dove and descended upon him, presumably uniting with him in the same manner the divine *ka* spirit united with the pharaoh. This, of course, took place at his baptism — a personal inundation that paralleled the Nile's inundation that served as the backdrop for the Opet festival.

A controversy would rage for some time among Jesus' followers as to whether he had become divine at the moment of his baptism or whether he had been born in that particular state. There was, however, no inherent conflict here — not if one understood the Egyptian traditions on which Jesus' story was based, traditions that were linked closely with the imagery of the Opet festival. In a sense, the pharaoh's ritual union with the *ka* or holy spirit at the festival season only served as confirmation of a process set in motion at the his very conception. This had taken place, according to tradition, when the father god Amen had taken on the likeness of the previous pharaoh and had intercourse with the current ruler's mother.[378]

This woman was none other than the beloved of Amen, or Meryamen, the priestess queen hailed as "wife of god." One sees quite plainly in this tradition the roots of a much later and more famous narrative in which a woman named Mariamne, or Mary for short, conceives a divine child through mystical intercourse with a very similar father god — one to whom prayers were customarily concluded with the single word, Amen. Perhaps clinching the connection is the fact that, in later years, the title "wife of god" fell to someone other than the queen of Egypt — someone who, significantly, was expected to be celibate.[379]

In other words, a virgin.

During earlier times, however, this was not the case. Indeed, it seems possible that the inner precincts of the temple where the pharaoh underwent his ritual transformation at the Opet festival were in fact a sacred bridal chamber where he, in the form of Amen, lay together with his queen in hopes of conceiving a child. In their effort, they would be aided by the divine presence that dwelt in the holy chamber or harem, as it was called. Such a ritual consummation of erotic love parallels the traditions, preserved by the Hebrew scribes, surrounding Solomon and his beloved queen as they entered the bridal chamber.

Or harem.

This ceremonial tryst is described in typically beautiful poetic language by the Song of Songs, attributed to Solomon:

> *When I found the one my heart loves*
> *I held him and would not let him go*
> *Until I had brought him to my mother's house*
> *To the room of the one who conceived me* [380]

Solomon's queen would not rest until she embraced her husband in her mother's house, the very place where she herself had been conceived. From the urgent language, it is obvious that the site itself was extremely significant — even holy. One might reasonably infer that it was a temple sanctuary, an inner chamber perhaps representing the womb of the goddess that had been set aside for the very purpose of royal procreation. And this possibility is only magnified when one realizes that the temple of Luxor was dedicated to the great Theban mother goddess, Mut. It was, quite literally, the divine "mother's house" mentioned in the Solomonic poem. This was the place where men and women of royal blood were conceived. It was the place where the pharaoh, in the guise of Sah-Amen, guaranteed the continuity of the royal line by fathering a child by his beloved.

It made sense that this ritual should have been undertaken at the height of the inundation, because this season alone represented the height of fertility. The king and the land were one, it was believed. And so it was that when the bountiful Nile fertilized the great floodplain on either side of the river, it was assumed that the pharaoh would also be at the height of his sexual prowess. Just as the land would soon spring forth with the fruit of the inundation, so the queen would bear quickly the fruit of her womb.

It was the natural way of things, and so it had been from time immemorial.

After the arks crossed the city from Karnak to Luxor, the ceremony of the Opet continued thereafter for nearly a full month. At the end of that time, the golden boats were paraded back across the city by the same route in a second procession to great fanfare that marked the end of the celebration. It is a celebration preserved not only on the relief of Tutankhamen, but also in the Hebrew scriptures, which describe David orchestrating a nearly identical procession involving the Ark of the Covenant.

In this narrative, David brings together thirty thousand men to bring the ark down "from the house of Abinadab, which was on the hill." [381] The number may be significant, for thirty priests were involved in the procession of the Opet. And the house of Abinadab appears to be important as well.

Who was this Abinadab?

Two men by this name are mentioned in various scriptural accounts, but neither plays a prominent role in the legends surrounding King David. One is his older brother, who is mentioned in passing on a couple of occasions; the other is a son of Saul who is killed in battle with the Philistines. In this particular passage, however, neither of these men is mentioned personally. Only his "house" is specified. The fact that this particular house was situated atop a hill raises another possibility. What if it were not a house at all in the common sense? What if it were, in fact, a house of god or temple.

This makes perfect sense. The name Abinadab means "father of generosity," an epithet that could well apply to a god and one that would have been especially fitting during the season of inundation, when the Nile waters overflowed in their generosity toward the land and its people. This god, this father of generosity, can only have been Amen. As the patron god of Thebes, it was his temple at Karnak whence the golden arks were born during the procession.

As the "hidden Osiris," it was he who was responsible for the Nile inundation. According to legend, it had been his death that resulted in a great flood of tears being shed by the widowed goddess Isis. These tears filled the Nile to overflowing, resulting in the yearly inundation — the beginning of which was always marked by the "night of the tear."

When David removed the ark from its house on the hill, the

ensuing procession was marked by a great celebration. As the ark made its way along the road, "David and the whole house of Israel were celebrating with all their might before Yahweh, with songs and with harps, lyres, tambourines, sistrums and cymbals." [382] The sistrum in particular was associated with Isis and featured prominently in her temple rites. In all, the entire scene sounds like exactly the sort of parade depicted in the Opet reliefs of Tutankhamen, transported by the storyteller to a new setting.

It had come from Mesopotamia to Egypt and now north again to Palestine.

During the course of this long journey, the oarsmen originally depicted at the bow and stern of the *quffa* ark in Mesopotamia gave way to images of the two protective goddesses charged with watching over it. The inundation marked the death of the old year and the beginning of the new. So it was that Isis and Nephthys, the twin goddesses of life and death, came to be the ark's twin guardians. It was Isis, the goddess of the inundation, who brought the ark safely to its earthly shore at birth, signifying a new beginning; her twin Nephthys guided it likewise to its heavenly mooring after death. These sister goddesses made their way into later tradition as two Marys (or Meris), one of whom gave birth to the anointed messiah while the other stood watch at his tomb and assured his ascension to heaven. The first was the virgin; the second was the Magdalene. But like Isis and Nephthys, they were ultimately two aspects of the self-same goddess.

Isis herself was a paradox. As both virgin and mother, she embodied the apparent contradictions seen time and again in fertility goddesses — young and nubile in springtime yet old and decrepit in winter. This principle of duality is captured in vivid language by the writer of a gnostic text known as *Thunder, Perfect Mind*, in which the speaker is obviously just such a goddess: [383]

> *For I am the first and the last*
> *The honored and the scorned*

The whore and the holy one
The wife and the virgin
I am the mother and the daughter
The barren one and her many sons
I am she whose wedding is great
Yet I have not taken a husband

I am the midwife and she who does not bear
I am the solace of my labor pains
I am bride and bridegroom
And my husband it is who begat me

I am the mother of my father
And the sister of my husband
And he is my offspring
I am the slave of he who prepared me

The contradictions laid forth in this monologue reveal the nature of the speaker. Like Isis, she is the sister of her husband; like Mary she is wife and virgin; like the Magdalene, she is whore and holy one. She is, in fact, the personification of wisdom whose virtues have been lauded throughout the ages even as she is derided as a whore. The reason? Because wisdom does not discriminate by class or standing; like a harlot, she is available to any willing to pay the price to have her. This idea is laid forth most famously in the proverb attributed to Solomon, who portrayed wisdom in terms of a street corner prostitute brazenly hawking her wares:

Wisdom calls aloud in the street
She raises her voice in the public squares
At the head of the noisy street, she cries out
In the gateways of the city she makes her speech [384]

Wisdom personified was known as *sophia*, a decidedly feminine name that is at the root of the so-called sophist movement and eventually came into vogue as a proper name. The concept also, incidentally, lent its name to the great Turkish mosque (formerly a cathedral) in Constantinople known as the Hagia Sophia.

In Solomon's proverbs, wisdom is the key to understanding the process of life and death, the gateways to the earthly city wherein her charges dwell in their mortality. She is their mother, expelling them from the womb. She is likewise their lady in mourning, bidding them farewell as they return to the womb of the earth. She is Mary and Magdalene, Isis and Nephthys. She is the mystical grail bearer depicted in some scenes as a comely maiden and in others as a loathly damsel: "Blacker were her face and her two hands than the blackest iron covered in pitch." [385] One was life; the other death. Yet these two damsels, so different at first glance, are in reality but different aspects of the same eternal principle of passage. Could it be that the author, in comparing the blackened skin of the death goddess to the color of pitch, is recalling her role as guardian of the pitch-covered ark?

The French Connection

Isis' role as guardian of the ark helped make her the patron goddess of Paris, the city that was to become the greatest in all of France.

Paris?

This might seem to be a strange place to find the Egyptian goddess, but a glance at the area's geography reveals that it was a natural fit. The city itself was built around an island in the River Seine — site of the famous Notre Dame cathedral or sanctuary of "our lady." There can be little doubt that the lady in question was originally Isis. The site was perfect for her, for it seemed to make manifest the enchanted floating island of ancient lore on which she had hidden her infant son. This son, Horus, would grow up to be king of Egypt, and it is therefore fitting that French kings should have been crowned in the cathedral of Notre Dame.

The island at the heart of the city was the focal point for the entire region, known collectively as the Ile de Paris.

The island of Paris.

It was, in truth, the island of Isis. No fewer than a dozen statues of the black virgin have been found at various locations in the city, images of the goddess holding her infant son and attired in the ashen robes of mourning. One such statue was kept in the abbey of St. Germain des Pres and revered as the Virgin Mary for nearly a thousand years. This icon — "thin, tall, straight, naked or with some flimsy garment" — was no anomaly. For the abbey stood within shouting distance of the sacred island and had been built on the site of a former Isiac temple.[386]

This was her city. Her island.

Its very name brings to mind another island, the isle of Pharos in the harbor of Alexandria where the goddess' great lighthouse and temple had once stood. The wondrous tower with its shining beacon certainly made an impression on the French, whose word for lighthouse to this day is *phare*. But what was the origin of the original name?

Pharos is derived first of all from Egyptian the root *par*, which indicates a house, and secondly perhaps from the goddess' name itself. This name, Au Set or Ast in Egyptian, would yield the name Parast when combined with the initial root. The resemblance to Paris is striking, and it becomes even more apparent when the Greek form of the goddess' name is substituted, creating the compound name Parisis.

A second possibility is that the name is a variation on the familiar royal title pharaoh, originally *par-aa* or "great house." Such a term would certainly have applied both to the lighthouse at one end of the island and the temple of Isis at the other.

This would explain why Isis herself was referred to as "the lofty Pharos (or great house) of light." [387]

She was the tower.

And as such, she was the forerunner of Mary Magdalene — the harlot saint held in such singular esteem by so many villages where black virgin statues have been found. This Mary was one of the few women from her era to be identified using two names, the second of which was a variation on the Hebrew word *migdol*. It is fascinating to note the meaning of this particular word. It is not, as some have supposed, a geographic reference tying the woman in question to a particular village known as Magdala (though such a village did in fact exist). On the contrary, it is a title and a description. And it means "tower."

Like Isis, this particular Mary was called a tower. Like Isis, she wept for her lord at his death and witnessed his ultimate triumph over the grave. And like the goddess, she was particularly associated with sailing and the sea. Legend had it that she embarked after Jesus' death on a perilous journey across the Mediterranean, setting sail in a ship that eventually deposited her on the southern shores of France. There she lived out the remaining years of her life, at last yielding her spirit and being laid to rest in the town of Aix.

This village had been built on the site of natural hot springs — hence its original name: Acqs, meaning "the waters." This made it a perfect fit for the legend of the Magdalene, identified as she was with the sea goddess Isis. As the legend took hold, she came to be revered by the people of the surrounding countryside as *la Dompna del Aquae* or the "Lady of the Fountain." [388] The fountain in question was the hot springs of Aix, whence would stream forth further legends with the passage of time. Among them were the grail traditions, which spoke of a mysterious "lady of the lake" who imparted unto King Arthur the famed sword Excalibur. This woman's title was but a corruption of the French lady del Aquae, or the lady of the waters.

She was the Magdalene reborn.

And this etymology may in turn be connected with yet an older tradition, that of the Theban mother goddess Mut. As Amen's consort, she was the "beloved of Amen" or Meryamen (Mariam), and she held a place in the Egyptian pantheon was quite similar to that of

Isis. Her temple's location at Luxor is also telling, for the name stems from the Arabic word *l'ouqsor*, meaning "the palaces."[389] This word bears a certain resemblance to *l'acqs*, a natural variation on the name of the French town where Mary Magdalene supposedly spent her last days. As the woman who wept at Jesus' tomb, Mary has already been identified as Isis in mourning — the black Madonna Nephthys who served as mistress of the afterworld. And Nephthys' hieroglyph identified her as the grail bearer or "lady of the castle."

Or, perhaps, the "lady of the palace."

The lady of L'Ouqsor or Luxor.

Mut.

As Isis, she was goddess of life and mother of all; as Nephthys, she was the keeper of the tomb. And this dual role was completely in harmony with the dual role of the temple at Luxor itself, which served both as a shrine (or tomb) for the goddess-queen just as Karnak and the pyramids were tombs for the great god-kings. At the same time, however, the temple also housed the sacred bridal chamber where king and queen could consummate their union. The divine Madonna Mut watched over their coupling, the spirit of motherhood ensuring a fertile union.

The lady of the lake served a similar function in the Arthurian cycle. As the sacred harlot and goddess of life, she bestowed upon the impotent king the phallic symbol of newfound virility. The sword. This was its true purpose. The barren land could only be restored if the monarch fathered an heir, and the lady-goddess was giving him the means of doing so. Symbolic? Yes, highly so. But deeply meaningful to those who knew how to interpret that symbolism.

It is no accident that Arthur's consort, the famous Queen Guinevere, appears in the legend as yet another manifestation of this self-same lady of the waters. According to one interpretation of her name, it meant "white wave" — an explicit connection to the sea.[390] She was apparently a member of the Moray or Murray clan, whose symbol is a mermaid staring into a mirror as she combs her hair.[391] Once again, the nautical theme is apparent. In Irish, the word *murreagh* indicates a level, marshy tract of land by the sea.[392] And one cannot help but take notice of the clan name itself, which bears a certain affinity with Meri or Mary.

The comb played a significant role in a story called *The Knight and the Cart*, which recounts the journey of a knight escorting a damsel along the road. In the midst of their travels, they come upon a spring in the middle of a field (the hot springs of Aix, perhaps?), next to which there lay a comb of gilded ivory. Someone had apparently forgotten this comb, which still had within its teeth a lock of hair belonging to its owner. As it turns out, the owner in question is none other than Guinevere, with whom the knight is so smitten that he gingerly removes the hair entangled in the comb's teeth and presses them to his bosom.

It is clear that the knight in the tale is the famed Lancelot, the gallant French hero whose adoration for the queen has become such an integral part of the Arthurian saga. There is good reason for this. For his full name, or title, is Lancelot du Lac — or Lancelot del Acqs.

It appears that he, too, was said to hail from the very same town where the Magdalene was buried.

And there is more.

For the Magdalene, like fair Guinevere, has long been known not only for her association with water but also for her hair. She has long been identified as the sinful woman named Mary who poured perfume on Jesus' feet and wiped them with her long, flowing hair. After her journey to France, one legend has it, she retired to a cave where she dwelt from that time forward — her naked body shielded from the elements only by her plentiful, flowing locks.[393] Her reputation as a sinful woman or a harlot was widely circulated and exploited by critics of Jesus' movement who gleefully painted him as an associate of "tax gatherers and sinners." [394]

Such as Mary Magdalene the harlot.

And his mother Mary, whom they painted as an adulteress in ridiculing the supposedly "virgin" birth.

Sometimes, the portraits of the two women could get a bit

muddled. For example, a rabbi seeking to discredit Jesus would accuse his mother of being not only an adulteress, but (of all things) a women's hairdresser.[395] This is a curious accusation, to say the least. But the rabbi apparently latched onto the Aramaic term for women's hairdresser and associated it with Jesus' mother. The phrase in question is *mgadla nshaya* — the first part of which sounds suspiciously like "Magdalene." [396]

The rabbi should be forgiven his confusion. It would have been an easy mistake to make in dealing with two women named Mary who embodied the two aspects of Isis, life-giving mother on the one hand and mourning widow on the other. In many traditions, the mother of the resurrected god-king also played the role of his lover — a duality found in the myths of Inanna, Isis and many others. Such traditions had a tendency to blur any historical distinctions, so that even today it is often harder to untangle the interwoven strands of tradition than it must have been for Lancelot to extricate Guinevere's precious locks from her ivory comb. There is even strong evidence to indicate that Jesus' mother and his bride both wore the title Mary Magdalene. These two Marys were, in many senses, two sides of the same coin.

One thing is certain, however: Those stands run through the hot springs town of Aix or Acqs south of France, specifically. And it was from France that many popular tales of medieval romance first sprang, making their way across the channel to England just as the Magdalene had, according to legend, made her way across the white waves of the ocean centuries before.

Tales of the grail.

Tales of Lancelot and *la Dompna del Aquae*.

And tales of a young hero and his lady love that came to be incorporated into the legends of none other than Robin Hood.

Back to Nottingham

It may come as a surprise that the story of Robin and Marian originated not in England but in France, and that its hero was only later equated with the legendary archer of Sherwood. The tale survives in its earliest form as a pastoral play by Adam de la Halle titled *Robin et Marion*, composed in the thirteenth century. In it, a shepherdess named Marion remains true to her love Robin by fending off the unwanted overtures of a certain knight.[397] The heroine's occupation is particularly noteworthy, for Mary Magdalene was likewise identified as a sort of spiritual shepherdess — the female counterpart to the good shepherd, Jesus. As the prophet Micah had proclaimed:

> *As for you, O watchtower of the flock*
> *O stronghold of the daughter of Zion*
> *The former dominion is restored to you*
> *Kingship will come to the daughter of Zion* [398]

The phrase "watchtower of the flock" is translated from the Hebrew *migdal-eder*, a name that sounds suspiciously like Magdalene.[399] There can be little doubt that the Magdalene was regarded as the fulfillment of Micah's prophecy and thus also served as a prototype for the heroic shepherdess Maid Marion in the French play. In Irish, her name would have been Morrin — a name later Anglicized as Marion — which literally meant "long-haired." [400] Once again, the connection to the Magdalene is obvious, for her flowing locks were her single most outstanding attribute.

The name Maid Marian, when inverted, produces Mar(ian)maid. Or mermaid. The prototypical lady of the waters and Pharos tower of the flock, shining her beacon far and wide for all to see. She was the shepherdess, and Robin was her consort. He was the green man who embodied the principle of virile young king. He was Horus. And he was Jesus. Even the name Robin could conceivably derive from the Hebrew title *rabban*, a variant of *rabbi* or "teacher" that was used in addressing Jesus.

Robin's legends contain their share of clues as to the famed archer's true identity, beginning with his well-known policy of robbing from the rich and giving to the poor. Jesus was certainly no thief, but he did advocate a similar set of priorities when speaking to a rich man: "Go, sell everything you have and give to the poor. Then you will have treasure in heaven." [401] Robin, like Jesus, has a right-hand man named John. And even his expertise as an archer may owe something to the story of Jesus, who was said to have been a man without sin. The Hebrew word for sin had its origins in the skill of archery — its literal meaning was "to miss the mark." That was something Robin Hood never seemed to do.

The tales of Robin Hood, like the grail romances and the tarot decks, kept alive the ties of Jesus' movement to the ancient traditions — ties that the establishment would go to nearly any length to sever. And it nearly succeeded in doing so, not through the overt suppression of tarot decks or bans on the May festivities, but through the watering down of the legends themselves. Eventually, most people simply forgot how to interpret them. Having been shorn of their original message, the tarot became a relatively harmless pastime indulged in by fortune tellers, charlatans and poker players. The stories themselves, meanwhile, degenerated into little more than quaint faerie tales told to children when tucking them in at night. Bereft of their true meaning, they no longer posed a threat to the established way of thinking.

But the clues were still there for the curious who wondered at their singular nature.

And there were still a few who knew — or could learn — how to read them.

The Persian Messiah

The grand experiment with monotheism that had been born under Josiah had failed — or so it seemed. His death had meant the death of his dream. Without the personal force of his conviction to support such ambitious reforms, there was simply not enough backing to maintain them. His brief reign had not afforded him enough time to create a new status quo. The old gods and their champions remained ever lurking in the shadows, ready to reassert themselves at the first opportunity.

Just as they always would.

But though Josiah's dream died with him beneath the searing heat of the Aten at Amarna, it did not rest in peace. He had established a principle that others would recognize, in time, for its ability to ensure a stable monarchy. That principle was simple: If one god ruled in heaven, there was nowhere else to turn. Paul would put it succinctly when he asked, "If God is for us, who can be against us?" [402] And if that god had anointed the reigning monarch, there was no one else on earth who could oppose him. To do so was to guarantee one's own annihilation.

King James of Britain — the same monarch who would

commission the famous translation of the Bible in the early seventeenth century — would pay tribute to the power of this principle. "The state of monarchy," he began, "is the supremest thing upon earth; for kings are not only God's lieutenants upon earth, and sit upon God's throne, but even by God himself are called kings." The implications of such a statement were obvious, as James was quick to note as he continued. "As to dispute what God may do is blasphemy... so it is sedition in subjects to dispute what a king may do in the height of his power." [403]

This principle would become known as the divine right of kings.

James was hardly the first to recognize it. That honor might well be accorded to a man named Cyrus, who as emperor of Persia invoked this very principle to guarantee his sovereignty over a single vanquished territory. So successful was this program that it not only allowed him to maintain control of the territory in question, but it also succeeded in changing the course of history.

The problem he faced was rather complicated. Five decades earlier, the empire of Babylon had conquered Jerusalem, deposing its king and exporting a large number of its subjects in a forced relocation designed to minimize any further resistance. This included large portions of the upper- and middle-class populations, those deemed most likely to support a new revolt.

They were carted off en masse to Babylon itself, where they were resettled and doubtless told that they would never again see their homeland. This mass of political exiles, however, remained a potent force — one that Cyrus knew he could tap into when he launched his campaign to conquer Babylon.

As it turned out, the conquest itself was accomplished with scarcely a blade unsheathed or an arrow fired. Cyrus, who had already annexed the powerful states of Media and Lydia, was an unstoppable force. His strategy was simple: He would court the allegiance of various officials by promising to respect their gods — something the Babylonian king had failed to do. One of his first official acts was to remove various objects of worship that the king had brought to

Babylon from across the empire, sending them back to the cities whence they had been taken.[404] In showing such deference to the gods of each city and province, he was able to win the support of those who had felt spiritually disenfranchised by the king of Babylon. They opened their gates to his armies, welcoming him as their liberator.

Among these disenfranchised groups were the exiled Judeans, or Jews, who had been brought in exile to Babylon and their progeny. There can be little doubt that they were among those who greeted Cyrus as their champion, and he quickly rewarded them by allowing them to recover their homeland. He did so, however, only on condition. His decree, preserved by the Hebrew scribes in their chronicles, read as follows: "Yahweh, the god of heaven, has given me all the kingdoms of the earth, and he has appointed me to build a temple for him at Jerusalem in Judea. Anyone of his people among you, may Yahweh his god be with him and let him go up." [405]

The divine right of kings could not have been more forcefully stated. The god of heaven had appointed Cyrus to govern every earthly kingdom. And it was by Cyrus' decree that the temple would be rebuilt. The emperor was, in effect, equating his decree with the word of a single god. This was a crucial step toward monotheism. But perhaps even more importantly, the emperor chose to grant the right of return only to those among the exiles who were Yahweh's people. In doing so, he ensured their loyalty to him as the champion of their god and at the same time effectively established a monotheistic state in Palestine.

This loyalty is expressed in no uncertain terms by a prophecy attributed to Isaiah, which describes Yahweh's approval of Cyrus as his anointed one — his chosen messiah or king. According to the prophecy, Yahweh proclaimed of Cyrus, "He is my shepherd and will accomplish all that I please. He will say of Jerusalem, 'Let it be rebuilt,' and of the temple, 'Let its foundations be laid.' This is what Yahweh says to his messiah, to Cyrus, whose right hand I take hold of." [406] Such language is incredible, for it directly abrogates a promise made to David that "Yahweh, the god of Israel, has given kingship of Israel to David and his descendants forever." [407] Even more seriously, it contradicts an explicit command of the Torah that a king "must be from among your brothers. Do not place a foreigner over you, one who is not a fellow Israelite." [408] Cyrus was no Israelite, nor was he a descendant of King David. But his power was such that it was politically expedient to honor him as king, no matter what the ancient texts had to say.

Scribe of God

Despite these obvious contradictions, the sacred texts would play a major role in the program instituted by Cyrus and promoted by his successors. The Persian emperors had established themselves as divinely appointed rulers of Palestine, but they recognized that their hold on power would remain tenuous unless they could codify their status in a sacred document. In short, they had to get it in writing.

The dramatic proclamation of Cyrus' messianic status, attributed to the prophet Isaiah, was a step in this direction. Isaiah himself never uttered these words, but they were nonetheless added to a corpus of the prophet's sayings — no doubt at the emperor's behest. The section of Isaiah's works that contains this particular prophecy has long been recognized as a later addition by a different author, perhaps a propaganda minister for the emperor. Its inclusion in (or intrusion upon) the writings of so august a personage as the prophet lent them an instant air of legitimacy.

But was it enough?

One of Cyrus' successors concluded that it was not. In order to solidify his hold on power, he would have to somehow make Persian supremacy an integral part of the law code itself. He would need his own propaganda minister to rewrite, or at least reinterpret, the ancient writings and ensure the perpetual loyalty of the Hebrews. For this task the Emperor Artaxerxes chose a man known simply as Ezra and commissioned specifically to act as a priest and "scribe of the law of the god of heaven." [409] To him was entrusted "the law of god which is in your hand" and the task of enforcing this law in the territory of Abar-nahara — literally, the land beyond the (Euphrates) river.

Did Ezra himself write or rewrite this law? Certainly his commission as a scribe would indicate that he was up to such a task. And the divine law was said to have been *in his hand*, perhaps a poetic way of saying that the law had been penned by the scribe himself — just as the heavenly scribe had produced the divine codes by engraving them with his finger on tablets of stone. To whatever extent Ezra authored or altered the ancient texts, he most certainly was charged with interpreting them. And as an agent of the emperor, he was charged with interpreting them to the empire's advantage.

The restrictions begun under Cyrus would continue under Artaxerxes. The men of Abar-nahara would worship only one god at only one temple. They were proscribed from mingling or intermarry with foreigners, thus restricting their ability to form any alliance that might pose a threat to the empire's authority. Ezra and his cohort, the imperial governor Nehemiah, were unyielding on this point. Anyone who had married a foreign woman was ordered in no uncertain terms to dissolve the union forthwith: "Separate yourselves from the peoples around you and from your foreign wives." [410] They were forbidden even to speak the languages of nations around them, thus further impeding their ability to negotiate any treaties that might threaten the empire. The punishment for violating the degree against fraternizing were swift and severe. Nehemiah placed a curse on the head of the transgressors, ordered them beaten and had their hair pulled out. He then forced them to swear an oath that they would never repeat the proscribed behavior. [411]

This policy of isolation had been followed consistently since the beginning of the Persian period. When the first exiles had returned under Cyrus, a group of men from the northern region known as Samaria had dispatched a delegation with an offer to help the newcomers rebuild the temple. Perhaps it was simply a goodwill gesture. Perhaps it was something more. But whatever it was, it was doubtless perceived as an offer of political alliance that carried with it the potential for disrupting Persian hegemony over the region. Those in charge of the project therefore rejected it in no uncertain terms: "You have no part with us in building a temple to our god. We alone will build it for Yahweh, the god of Israel, as King Cyrus, the king of Persia, commanded us." [412]

The language left no doubt that they were acting on behalf of Cyrus, who had doubtless forbidden any foreign interference in the project he had sanctioned. Its purpose was not to facilitate foreign entanglements. Quite the opposite: It was designed to put the former exiles further in his debt, solidifying the bond between god and emperor under the principle of divine right.

And it worked.

So successful were the emperors and their propaganda ministers that the monotheistic program they instituted would prevail from that point forward despite numerous challenges from the old gods and their champions. Ezra himself would be lauded as a sort of second Moses, the author of a covenant with the one true god that would endure throughout the ages. The Samaritans, on the other hand, victims of the systematic prejudice that went along with Ezra's reforms, would condemn him in their literature as "Ezra the accursed." [413] There was no room in Ezra's monotheism for the Samaritans and their temple. Henceforth, there would be but one god, one temple, one emperor and one true mode of worship.

Or so it appeared to the casual observer.

But the fact of the matter is that, even after the suppression of rival temples in Palestine, at least one temple of Yahweh remained open for business elsewhere. And it is hardly surprising to find that the site in question was in Egypt. Two centuries before the time of Ezra, a temple to Yahweh had been established on Elephantine, an island situated in the Nile River at the southern edge of Upper Egypt. It served as a citadel of sorts, guarding the frontier against any possible incursions from raiders or armies coming up out of

Ethiopia. In fact, the men who built the temple of Yahweh had been brought there as mercenaries recruited by one or another of the pharaohs to frustrate Ethiopian ambitions in the region.[414] And there they had remained after the war was over, staying faithful to their patron god and building a temple whose physical specifications — ninety feet long and thirty feet wide — and building materials seem to have matched those used in Jerusalem.[415] This temple remained standing for something like two centuries, surviving even when the Persians decided to extend their empire further and became the first foreign power to conquer Egypt since the Hyksos.

The emperor who directed this campaign was Cambyses, heir to the messianic Cyrus, who followed a program in Egypt that resembled the policy his predecessor had established in Palestine. In an effort to squelch any threat of nationalism, the temples to all the indigenous gods and goddesses were despoiled, leaving only a single deity's shrine undisturbed.

The temple of Yahweh in Elephantine.

According to one papyrus scroll, "when Cambyses came into Egypt he found this temple built" to Yahweh. And when his armies invaded, "they knocked down all the temples of the gods of Egypt, but no one did any damage to this temple." [416] Perhaps this was because the Hebrew mercenaries there collaborated with the Persians against their enemies, just as their counterparts in Babylon had when Cyrus invaded that city. But whatever the reason, the temple of Yahweh was spared the destruction visited upon the shrines of the native gods.

In the short term, this was certainly helpful to the Hebrews on Elephantine island, who remained free to conduct their sacrifices at the temple they had built there. But in the long run, it only served to create a feeling of ill will between the Hebrews and the native populace, who must have seen the survival of Yahweh's temple as a grating symbol of foreign imperialism. It was all but inevitable that, at some point, the Persian Empire would weaken and the Egyptians would throw off the foreign yoke. And at the first sign of that weakness, the temple of Yahweh would serve as a prominent target for the Egyptian nationalists.

Their opportunity came when the Persian governor assigned to Elephantine was called away and replaced on a temporary basis by his deputy. The Egyptian residents of the city saw this as their chance to make a statement and incited a riot in the name of the island's patron god, the ram-headed Khnum. The target of this riot was the temple of Yahweh, which was attacked as the deputy governor — perhaps fearing for his own safety — took no action to prevent its destruction.

This created an awkward situation for the Hebrew inhabitants of Elephantine, who found themselves constrained by the very Persian policy that had proven so advantageous to them in the past. It was natural for them to seek assistance in rebuilding their temple from their countrymen in Jerusalem. Yet the Persians had gone to great lengths to isolate the exiles who had returned to Palestine, promoting a strict monotheistic code to ensure that they did not forge any potentially troublesome (for the Persians) alliances with foreigners.

Suddenly, the Hebrews at Elephantine found themselves in that category. Under the code practiced by the former exiles in Jerusalem, the Elephantine temple was an unlawful "rogue" shrine that could not be recognized, much less granted any form of assistance. So when the priests in Jerusalem received the pleas for help from their counterparts at Elephantine, it is hardly surprising that they responded with silence. For two years, the Elephantine priests waited in vain for a response. And in the end, they were forced to direct their appeal instead to the Samaritans — likewise considered rogue worshippers by the Jerusalem priests — and to the secular governor of Jerusalem appointed by the Persian emperor.

This entreaty was, as might be expected, far more successful. The governors of Samaria and Jerusalem sent a joint reply condemning the deputy governor of Elephantine as a "reprobate" for allowing the temple's destruction and authorizing the construction of a new shrine on the same site, along with the resumption of sacrifices.[417] This was a clear victory for the Hebrews of Elephantine, yet it would turn out to be only a temporary reprieve for the temple. Less than a decade after the new building was approved, the Persians' weakness in Egypt became such that it could be exploited as a basis for permanent change. A civil war between two rival claimants to the Persian throne distracted the imperial armies, leaving Egypt vulnerable to insurrection. A revolt was launched to free the country from Persian domination, and its success led to immediate changes at Elephantine. The cult of Khnum, in whose name the temple of Yahweh had been destroyed, was exalted and the Hebrews who had spent the past two hundred years on Elephantine appear to have seen the writing on the wall.

They abandoned the temple site, never to reclaim it, and probably left the island altogether.

That, however, was hardly the end of the Hebrew presence in Egypt.

Far from it.

Indeed, the temple at Elephantine was not the last — or even the most significant — temple to Yahweh constructed in the land of Egypt. That honor would fall to a temple constructed more than two centuries after the Elephantine site was abandoned. It would be built far to the north of the citadel island, in a location that would appear on its surface much more strongly associated with Egyptian religious tradition than with the cult of Yahweh. That location was the city of Leontopolis, the "city of the lions" that stood almost within shouting distance of the most ancient and revered spiritual site in all of Egypt.

Heliopolis.

The city of the sun.

Crisis in Jerusalem

The city was in an uproar.

For years — tradition said it was centuries — the office of high priest had been filled by a son of Zadok, someone from the line of priests founded by a man of that name. The name itself meant "the just one" and served as a reminder of the high priest's holiness. It had first been worn by David's high priest, and just as this king's throne was said to be established for eternity, so Zadok and his sons were fated to serve at the temple altar in perpetuity.

Until now, that is.

The line of Zadok had survived Egyptian imperialism, the Assyrian invasion and even the Babylonian exile. But now it was placed at risk by a new regime under the leadership of a man named Antiochus, the fourth ruler to bear that name in a line of Greek emperors known as the Seleucids. These men had been rulers of Syria and the surrounding region for well over a century when Antiochus claimed the throne, having inherited their empire from Alexander the Great. The general from Macedon — the region just to the north of the lower Greek peninsula — had conquered most of the known world in the course of a single decade. But he had died childless at a relatively young age, leaving his lieutenants to squabble over the pieces of his empire. In the end, they divvied it up into three pieces, with one of them taking Macedon itself and the other two splitting the rest between them.

General Ptolemy founded the Ptolemaic Empire, making his capital in the city his mentor had founded and named for himself — Alexandria in the Nile Delta. The other commander, a man named Seleucus, established his Seleucid Empire with its capital in the Syrian city of Antioch. These two heirs to Alexander's empire had been rivals from the beginning, battling back and forth across the fluid border region that separated them — a region that inevitably included Jerusalem. Whichever side emerged victorious for a particular season, its ruler seemed content to let the people of the city practice their religion as they saw fit. By this time, these people were no longer called Hebrews so much as Jews, a name derived from the ancient tribal territory of Judah that surrounded the capital city. And their religion was well established as the monotheism promoted so successfully by Ezra under the auspices of the Persian emperors. To be certain, the ancient traditions of polytheism imported so long ago from Egypt remained, but these were suppressed by the dominant priesthood and either practiced privately or in the countryside.

As a result of this phenomenon, such rural religion would come to be labeled by the establishment alternately as paganism (from the Latin *pagus*, meaning provincial district) or heathenism (from the Anglo-Saxon word *hæth*, referring to an uncultivated tract of open land). Both terms were considered somewhat derisive. To the Jews at the time of Antiochus, the city was the center of the universe. And the city in question could only be Jerusalem.

This was where the high priest, the son of Zadok, served at the one true temple of the one true god. And this was where the crisis was brewing. The reason? Antiochus, it turns out, was not as reasonable as his predecessors when it came to letting the Jews practice their religion without interference. There were several reasons for this, not the least of which was the emperor's rather inflated ego. He called himself Epiphanes or "god made manifest," a title that his detractors seized upon and corrupted into the similar-sounding Epimanes — meaning "utterly mad."

In so labeling himself, he was doing nothing other than what the Egyptian pharaohs had done for centuries when they claimed to be the manifestation of Horus on earth. Then again, Antiochus' fault lay not so much in alleged madness as ambition, and in this trait also lay one of his greatest strengths. As it turned out, he would need it.

The Spoils of War

The young Antiochus had faced a number of obstacles in his path to power, most of them having been placed there by the father who shared his name. For one thing, he was not first in line to the throne. His father had done him the discourtesy of siring an elder son named Seleucus who claimed that honor, and who would indeed assume the title of emperor when the elder Antiochus died. But this was the least of the young prince's problems. Of more immediate concern was his status as a de facto prisoner of war, a predicament that he likewise owed to his father.

The elder Antiochus had been an ambitious man, too. His reign was long and, for the most part, prosperous enough that he would become known to history as Antiochus the Great. But ambition left unchecked can cause a monarch to overreach, and this is exactly what the emperor had done. Three decades into his tenure, an opportunity presented itself that he considered too good to pass up. It stemmed from a conflict outside his borders that seemed tailor-made for exploitation. King Philip of Macedon, one of the three heirs to Alexander's empire, had stirred up trouble with his program to consolidate control of the Aegean Sea. This program was hardly welcome news to a pair of small independent states in the region — states that stood between the king and his goal of a united Aegean.

Faced with the prospect of being overrun by the superior

Macedonian forces, they had little choice but to send out an urgent appeal for assistance. And they directed this appeal to an emerging power in the Mediterranean region, one they believed just might have the strength to turn back an assault by the king of Macedon. This formerly minor republic to the west had greatly enhanced its reputation by defeating the seemingly invincible Carthaginian Empire under the command of Hannibal — a general of legendary status who, with his army of elephants, had very nearly brought the entire Mediterranean to its knees.

But not quite.

The armies of this seemingly outmatched republic had marched out to meet him and shocked the world by using a mixture of military discipline and superior strategy to defeat the great general. This victory initiated a major shift in power away from Carthage and northern Africa — which would never again approach the level of influence it had achieved under Hannibal and his predecessors — and toward the emerging republic, situated on Europe's most geographically prominent peninsula.

It was also bad news for Philip of Macedon, who had made what appeared at the time to be a shrewd decision in aligning himself with the Carthaginians. In many cases, the art of survival in politics involves winding up on the winning side, and in this, Macedon had failed miserably. Fortunately, it had been a peripheral player in the drama pitting Carthage against the upstart republic known as Rome. As a result, its generals could return home to lick their wounds — a luxury not afforded the Carthaginians. But the long-term ramifications of Macedon's involvement were not yet quite so clear.

They would become so in short order.

It was only a few years after Rome's victory over Carthage that the Macedonian king sought to flex his muscles in the Aegean. The two small city states threatened by this new policy were hardly fools. They knew that the Macedonians had incurred the enmity of Rome just recently by aligning with Carthage, and they were betting the republic would be none too eager to settle the score.

The Romans, still intoxicated with their victory, lost no time in responding to their request for assistance, swiftly proclaiming independence for the Greek city-states under Philip's dominion and backing their words with a decisive victory over Macedon a year later. As it turned out, however, the "independence" bestowed upon the Greeks by their deliverers amounted to little more than exchanging one imperialist (though not yet imperial) regime for another, and it wasn't long before they found themselves chafing under their new Roman overlords just as they had under the Greeks.

Being too weak to fight their way out of this predicament, the city-states therefore had little choice but to repeat the process they had followed so recently and decided to appeal to help from the outside.

This is where the Seleucids came into the picture.

It is difficult to know what Antiochus the Great was thinking. Had he not been paying attention during the Romans' victories over Carthage and Macedon? Did he simply have such supreme confidence in his own forces that he considered such factors irrelevant? Whatever the case, he saw in the Greeks' plea for help an opportunity to expand his own dominion to encompass the entire northeastern seaboard, and he wasn't about to let such an opportunity pass him by. He led his armies on an expedition to Greece and caught the Romans off guard, claiming the territories for himself and giving them their third overlord in less than a decade.

This time, however, the action would not stand. The Romans, surprised by Antiochus' action but hardly willing to concede the day, regrouped and launched a counterattack, expelling his forces from Greece and destroying the fleet of ships he had dispatched to the Aegean. But this was not the end of it. Not content with restoring the previous status quo, the Romans turned their attention to punishing the Seleucid forces for their ill-advised intervention in the republic's affairs, pursuing them into the area then known as Asia — modern Anatolia or Turkey.

Suddenly, Antiochus found himself in a rather desperate

situation. If he stood and fought, he risked his army's annihilation by the clearly superior Roman forces. But if he turned and ran, he might as well cede his entire empire to the republic. Faced with two such jarringly unpleasant alternatives, Antiochus chose the former. He took his stand and took his medicine at the Battle of Magnesia, which ended with the destruction of his forces and an armistice that imposed harsh punitive conditions on Antiochus for his presumptuous actions. According to terms of the so-called Peace of Apamea, Antiochus agreed to:

➢ Cede much of his territory in Asia to the Romans' vassal states.
➢ Cease recruiting men for his armies from Greece and the Aegean.
➢ Dismantle the greater part of his fleet.
➢ Refrain from attacking any friend or ally of Rome.
➢ Surrender his war elephants to the Romans.
➢ And, most significantly, pay an indemnity or fifteen thousand talents.[418]

It was this final condition that had the most direct impact on the younger Antiochus, then merely a prince who stood second in the line to the throne of Seleucia. Not only did the indemnity enrich the republic's coffers, it also ensured that the elder Antiochus would lack the financial wherewithal to rebuild his armies and seek to avenge his humiliating defeat at some future time. This was a bitter pill for the Seleucid emperor to swallow.

And the Romans, who were as adept at business dealings as they were at war, wisely demanded some sort of guarantee that Antiochus would pay the agreed-upon indemnity.

That guarantee came in the form of the younger Antiochus, who would be entertained as a "guest" of the republic until such time as his father's debt was fully retired. He would remain there after his father's death and the accession of his elder brother Seleucus, under whom the indemnity continued to be repaid on the long-term compensation schedule set forth as part of the treaty. During Seleucus' final years on the throne, however, a crucial change was made in the terms of the deal. The emperor arranged to free his brother from Roman custody in an exchange under which his own younger son was sent to take his place.

Upon his release, Antiochus made straightaway for Athens, where he ingratiated himself to the locals with his generosity and made political allies who he hoped would serve as valuable allies in the future. The young prince clearly had every intent of making a favorable impression and moving up in the world, and though it is impossible to say whether he directly coveted the throne at this stage of his career, events soon conspired to place him in a position where he might claim it.

The events in question revolved to a great extent around a man named Heliodorus, chancellor to Seleucus and a man of significant ambition himself. They were precipitated in large measure by the treaty with Rome, which had placed a heavy burden on the empire in the form of the cursed indemnity. The payment schedule was taxing on the imperial treasury, to say the least. And the emperor was constantly looking for ways to generate revenue that might be used to ease this burden to some extent.

Perhaps the most accessible sources of quick cash during the period were the numerous temples that dotted the landscape. The priests who served these sacred houses collected tributes and offerings to their patron gods and goddesses, and in so doing built up substantial treasuries. Because the sanctuaries were considered inviolable, they also served as depositories for wealthy noblemen looking for a safe place to store their valuables.[419]

This logic made sense as far as it went. But the promise of safety that transformed temples into magnets for money, ironically, made them vulnerable to covetous men whose eyes were easily distracted by the glint of all that gold. In this case, those men included Seleucus, who had a debt to repay and discovered in the temple treasuries a convenient source of funds with which to retire it. These temples included the temple of Yahweh in Jerusalem, which would in years to come be made famous for its stash of wealth thanks to a bitterly sarcastic remark from Jesus, who likened it to a "den of thieves." [420]

Two full centuries before that remark was uttered, Seleucus set his sights on becoming one of those thieves. Taking aside his chancellor Heliodorus, he charged the man with conducting a raid on the temple and emptying its treasuries for the good of the empire. The temple's bounty was reportedly four hundred talents of silver and two hundred of gold — hardly enough to make a significant dent in the indemnity, but helpful in making a payment or two.[421] Having received his charge, Heliodorus dutifully complied and set forth on an expedition to Jerusalem to secure the promised bounty and deliver it to Antioch. But once he reached his destination, he was confronted by an obstacle he hadn't counted on. Specifically, the high priest Onias tried to stop him from entering the temple to retrieve the treasure.

Heliodorus, of course, was having none of it. He brushed aside Onias' objections that the funds consisted of money intended for widows and orphans along with private deposits belonging to a certain high-ranking nobleman. Onias could only stand aghast, the color draining from his face, as Heliodorus and his men brazenly forced their way into the temple to take their own inventory of its treasures. So far, everything was going according to the chancellor's plan.

But what reportedly happened next was hardly in the script. As Heliodorus and his bodyguards were preparing to enter the temple treasury, they were confronted out of nowhere with a horseman who set his steed charging straight at them in a fury. The horse rode at Heliodorus, striking him with its front hooves and knocking him to the ground, where he found himself assailed by two young men who — like the horseman — seemed to have appeared out of thin air.

These two beat the chancellor so savagely that he lost consciousness and had to be carried out of the temple on a stretcher.

The horseman and his two cohorts came to be seen in the popular imagination as divine messengers sent to protect the temple. In fact, they were probably members of the temple guard who had managed to get the better of Heliodorus and his men by ambushing them when they least expected it. Onias obviously knew the truth of this, for he feared "that the king might think that Heliodorus had suffered some foul play at the hands of the Jews," and therefore offered a sacrifice in the hope that the chancellor might recover.[422]

Heliodorus did eventually regain consciousness and managed to survive the furious assault. His two assailants, however, couldn't resist rubbing it in a bit when the chancellor at last regained consciousness.

"Be very grateful to the high priest Onias," they admonished him. "It is for his sake that the Lord has spared your life. Since you have been scourged by heaven, proclaim to all men the majesty of God's power." [423] The message was couched in bold references to God and heaven, but its meaning was clear enough: Don't mess with us again, or you'll get worse.

It was a message that Heliodorus apparently took to heart, for upon returning from his failed mission, he sarcastically told Seleucus: "If you have an enemy or plotter against the government, send him there, and you will receive him back well-flogged — if indeed he survives at all." [424]

Seleucus apparently heeded this warning and refrained from sending another deputation to Jerusalem. But he would have done well to listen more carefully to Heliodorus' words, which contained an implicit word of caution against something far more dire. As it turned out, the prospect of another failed raid on the temple was the least of the emperor's problems. In fact, he did have a "plotter against the government" in his midst, one who would in short order arrange for his assassination and attempt to install himself as emperor in all but name, ostensibly serving as regent on behalf of the emperor's young son.

That plotter, as fate would have it, was closer than he could have imagined.

He was, in fact, Heliodorus.

Break with Tradition

While all this was going on, the younger Antiochus was still in Greece making a name for himself. He had spent his time there ingratiating himself to those who counted in Athenian society, offering lavish gifts from his personal fortune to erect temples (in stark contrast to his brother's practice of robbing them) and make other improvements. His generosity was so well known that the citizens appointed him to the office of master of the mint.

When he learned of his brother's assassination, however, Antiochus' life of leisure and celebrity came to a screeching halt. All at once, he was thrust into the thick of a political firestorm from which he would be lucky to emerge alive. It was clear enough to him and his advisors that he, not Heliodorus, was the rightful regent and that he could not simply sit by and watch the scheming former chancellor usurp that role. He therefore made use of his recently made Greek connections and borrowed some troops from the king of Pergamum, using this army-on-loan to dislodge Heliodorus and claim the throne for himself.

Though he nominally shared power with his brother's young son, it was quite clear from the outset that Antiochus was the true emperor. With that mantle, however, he inherited all the problems that had accompanied it under his brother and father — most particularly the indemnity to Rome and the responsibility for paying it. Suddenly, the personal fortune that had been so important in forging connections with the elite in Athens seemed like a pittance in comparison with the outstanding debt. And Antiochus, like his brother and father before him, was forced to investigate potential sources of income that might help him minimize this burden.

In Athens, he had learned that it never hurt to grease a few palms in an attempt to fulfill one's goals. There, he had been the one whose generosity was rewarded. But now, suddenly, the shoe was on the other foot: He was the one who was in need of cash — and in a position to hand out favors and choice titles if the price was right. One such position was the high priesthood of Israel.

Of course, it wasn't supposed to be that way. The priesthood wasn't an office to be bought or sold. It was conferred by Yahweh upon his chosen representative, a descendant of Aaron from the tribe of Levi. But the realities of politics have a way of trumping tradition when push comes to shove, and the combination of money and politics is a formidable one. In this case, the money came from what might have appeared to be an unlikely source — the brother of the high priest, who happened to covet the position for himself.

At the time, the high priest Onias was embroiled in a scandal of his own. For some time, a particularly bitter rival named Simon had been seeking to undermine the high priest's authority, questioning his allegiance to the emperor and urging his removal from office. The logical replacement, of course, would have been Simon or someone of his choosing. Eventually, these accusations became so serious that Onias decided it was best that he travel to Antioch and offer a personal defense before Antiochus. The situation must have seemed particularly dicey for the emperor, who found himself forced to choose between a legitimate high priest tainted by scandal and a rival claimant who seemed motivated by political factors. Neither choice was particularly satisfying, and it was therefore quite fortuitous that a third option suddenly became available in the person of Onias' brother, Jason.

By replacing Onias with Jason, Antiochus could (at least to some extent) maintain the hereditary legitimacy of the office while at the same time removing the taint of scandal that Simon had introduced. It is also quite possible that Antiochus blamed Onias for the attack on Heliodorus that had thwarted Seleucus' raid of the temple. He may even have suspected that the entire story of divine intervention was a fiction concocted by Heliodorus to obscure a more sinister truth — that he had entered into an "arrangement" with Onias to pocket the money himself in exchange for supporting Onias in the priesthood. There is no evidence that such an arrangement was in play, but someone of Antiochus' character almost certainly would have considered the possibility. And considering his brother's demise, he would hardly have been inclined to give Onias the benefit of the doubt.

Such factors would have almost certainly played a role in Antiochus' decision to accept Jason's proposal. But the most important element in the equation was something far baser.

Money.

Jason offered to pay a sizeable sum to the royal treasury in exchange for the right to don the high priestly robes. It was, flat out, nothing but a bribe. And it was quite effective. In short order, Onias was stripped of the office he had held for nearly a quarter-century and saw it transferred to his brother. Jason, for his part, assumed the high priesthood and began making annual payments of three hundred talents to the royal treasury in exchange for the right to retain the office.

This arrangement remained in effect for a few years and seemed to be working rather well despite complaints from pious Jews that the new high priest was too … Greek. Part of Jason's deal with the high priest called for him to promote Greek culture as a means of integrating the region into the imperial mainstream. He therefore promoted Greek institutions such as athletic games, setting up a Greek-style gymnasium in Jerusalem, and advocating a program whereby Jewish nobles could purchase the right to be recognized as citizens of Antioch, the capital, for a mere hundred-and-fifty talents. This program, of course, added even more money to the imperial treasury and served to further ease the burden of the Roman indemnity.

Religious purists hardly approved of such innovations, frowning upon the idea of men parading around naked during athletic contests (as was the Greek custom) and shaking their heads at the efforts of some to hide their circumcision — a badge of honor to the pious —

while competing in such events. In the end, however, it was not the purists who brought about the upheaval that was to shake the region to its foundations. The problem was not naked men competing in athletic events, it was naked ambition on the part of a single man.

This man's name was Menelaus.

Menelaus was the brother of Simon — the same Simon who was captain of the temple and had been responsible for spreading the rumors that led to Onias' ouster as high priest. All things considered, he was hardly a man to be trusted. Yet inexplicably, Jason did just that: He appointed Menelaus as his personal envoy to Antiochus and instructed him to make the annual payment to the emperor on his behalf.

Predictably, Menelaus had other ideas. Upon arriving in Antioch, he promptly set forth a proposal to increase the payment by three hundred talents if the emperor agreed to strip the high priesthood from Jason and confer it instead upon Menelaus.

Antiochus, who seemingly never saw a bribe he didn't like, agreed to the arrangement and did as Menelaus suggested. Ironically, though, Antiochus never saw the money. Menelaus couldn't manage to raise the funds he had promised and, despite threats from the emperor's administration, managed to remain in office without ever making good on his part of the bargain. And he continued Jason's policy of promoting Greek culture at the expense of religious fidelity.

The pious Jews who had chafed at such liberal policies under Jason, a high priest from the house of Zadok, found them intolerable when sanctioned by a man without any legitimate claim to the post. They had a natural champion in Onias, who was still considered by many to be the lawful high priest and who had withdrawn to Antioch in the aftermath of his expulsion from office. There, he had kept a low profile and waited for an opportunity to accuse Menelaus of some impropriety that — considering the man's character — he seemed almost certain to commit.

Sure enough, such an opportunity soon presented itself.

It began as an opportunity for Menelaus, who saw the emperor's absence as a chance to enlarge his own wealth. He lost no time in pilfering some valuable items from the temple and selling them to Andronicus, a corrupt minister Antiochus had left in charge during his absence. This was just the sort of reprehensible act Onias had been waiting for. He therefore determined to blow the whistle on Menelaus' scheming, but not before ensuring his own safety by taking refuge in the temple courts at Daphne, a few miles from Antioch. This was a sensible enough precaution. In the ancient world, a temple sanctuary was just that — a sanctuary. According to the conventions of the day, a person was considered untouchable so long as he remained inside. But perhaps Onias forgot he was dealing with men who had little regard for such conventions. Instead of observing them, Menelaus immediately began making arrangements to rid himself of his longtime nemesis. To this end, he once again enlisted Andronicus, perhaps under threat (implicit or otherwise) that he would expose his collusion in the aforementioned financial deal unless he cooperated.

Whatever his motives, Andronicus did indeed cooperate. Feigning a conciliatory disposition, he approached Onias in the temple with his hand extended in friendship, vowing that no harm would come to him if he left the sanctuary. It was, of course, a bald-faced lie. But Onias, convinced by the minister's false display of camaraderie, abandoned the temple precincts.

His trust earned him a swift death.

When Antiochus returned, he was furious. But although he condemned Andronicus to death for his part in the whole sordid mess, Menelaus got off scot-free (as he always seemed to). Even so, he had inadvertently made Onias not only a hero but a martyr, immortalizing him as a champion of orthodoxy and a symbol of righteousness against the false priest who had replaced him. Henceforth, he would be remembered as Onias the Just, "a good and virtuous man, modest in appearance, gentle in manners, distinguished in speech and trained from childhood in every virtuous practice." [425] And in the war that followed shortly on the heels of his death, the general who led the Jewish rebellion would find his inspiration in the slain high priest.

On the eve of a crucial engagement, this man would see a vision of Onias, "praying with outstretched arms for the whole Jewish community." In it, the fallen priest would turn to the general and indicate a second man, a white-haired man of dignified carriage and an air of authority. This was, it turns out, the prophet Jeremiah, who would present a golden sword to the general with the following words of encouragement: "Accept this holy sword as a gift from God; with it, you shall crush your adversaries." [426]

This sword would become so famous that it would even make its way into the grail romances, wherein the valiant knight Gawain is said to recover it.[427]

But that is another story.

The most important consequence of Onias' death was his elevation to the status of revered patriarch, worthy to stand alongside the immortal prophet Jeremiah and intercede on behalf of the entire nation. This made Onias a more powerful figure in death than he had been in life. Yet his departure from the land of the living left a void that was difficult to fill. For the first time in memory, the high priesthood had fallen into the hands of a pretender and there was no one from the house of Zadok to contest his claim to the office.

Or was there?

Onias, it turns out, had a son.

Fish Stories

Onias was an old name.

The ousted high priest slain at Menelaus' behest was the third such office holder to wear it, but in reality it was much older still. It was in fact the Greek form of a Hebrew name by which he probably preferred to be known, Yohanan or Jonathan. Perhaps his close friends and associates would know him by a nickname such as Honi, Jonah and the still-popular John.

All these names, including Onias, were variants on a very old name that was neither Greek nor Hebrew.

But Babylonian.

Oannes, as we have seen, was a rather strange composite figure, often depicted with the body and head of a fish — but also equipped with the head and feet of a man. This rather monstrous creature also spoke with the voice of a man. It was almost as though the man himself had been swallowed by the fish but had somehow survived, poking his head out from behind the scaly creature and speaking to mankind. Such an image immediately brings to mind the legend of Jonah, the prophet who was swallowed by a huge fish and later disgorged with a mandate to warn a certain city of its imminent destruction. That city was Nineveh, in the heart of Babylon.

The land of Oannes, birthplace of the original myth.

Indeed, Oannes seems to have been involved in a myth almost identical to that of Jonah. In this tale, he was swallowed by the Babylonian goddess Derceto in the form of a giant whale, who subsequently gave birth to him anew.[428] This accounted for his unique fish-man aspect. Despite this rather odd appearance, Oannes was not your typical monster. He was, to the contrary, a creature of great wisdom who was credited with bringing a degree of civilization to mankind. According to the Babylonian legend, Oannes spent his days teaching men the intricacies of writing, mathematics, architecture and the legal code. At night, he would disappear beneath the waves of the ocean, a feat made possible by his amphibious nature.[429]

This daily cycle — during with Oannes provided enlightenment during the day, then retreated to the underworld each night — makes it clear that he was yet another manifestation of the sun god. Just as the Egyptian sun god Horus became a fish as he plunged into the ocean at eventide, so it was also with Oannes. According to tradition, Oannes had taught savage men everything there was to know about civilization. So thorough was his instruction that, it was said, nothing of consequence had been discovered from that point forward. In words attributed to another wise solar monarch, Solomon, there was nothing new under the sun.

As the keeper of ultimate wisdom, Oannes was equated with the wise divinity Enki or Ea.

This made a good deal of sense.

Enki was, after all, the god of the waters who served as mankind's protector during the great deluge. It was he who instructed his favorite to build an ark that would carry him across the perilous waters of mortality to the great land of eternal bliss beyond the sea. He was also the one who produced the great tablets of wisdom — tablets similar to those housed in another ark, the Ark of the

Covenant. And this ark, in turn, has been referred to in Ethiopian tradition as "the belly of the ship." [430]

This phrase strikes a chord for anyone familiar with the story of Jonah, the prophet who supposedly spent three days in the belly of a great fish. The similarity is apparent. And it at once raises an intriguing question: Is it just possible that the fish and the ark are one and the same?

A look at the story of Jonah provides some clues.

The tale begins with the prophet receiving a commission from his patron god to visit the city of Nineveh in Babylon, where he is to warn its citizens of their imminent destruction. Jonah, however, tries to avoid this rather unpleasant assignment by running away, boarding a ship bound for some distant port. This attempt proves futile when "such a violent storm arose that the ship threatened to break up." [431] As the storm sweeps over the ship, Jonah lies below deck in a deep sleep and is only roused when the captain comes to him pleading desperately for his help.

The crew then casts lots to determine the cause of the storm, and Jonah is singled out as the one responsible. Forced to admit that he has been attempting to avoid carrying out his divine commission, he is castigated by his fellow sailors and thrown overboard into the sea. At once the storms cease, and the men thank Yahweh with sacrifices and vows of fidelity.

Jonah, for his part, is swallowed up a the great sea creature.

There can be little doubt that the entire sequence of events is meant to symbolize the crossing of the waters of death. To begin with, Jonah is depicted as sleeping in the bowels of the ship as the fierce storm rages all around him. Sleep was an ancient euphemism for death, and Jonah's presence *inside* the ship recalls that of the "sleeping" pharaoh inside the ark-that-was-a-casket. This symbolism is driven home by repetition, with the scene shifting from the belly of a ship to the belly of a great sea creature. Both are emblematic of the grave, as Jonah himself makes clear in his lament. He declares to his god in no uncertain terms: "From the depths of the grave I called for help and you answered my cry."

> *You hurled me into the deep*
> *Into the very heart of the sea*
> *And all the currents swirled around me*
> *All your waves and breakers swept over me*
>
> *I said, "I have been banished from your sight"*
> *Yet I will look again toward your holy temple*
>
> *The engulfing waters threatened me*
> *The deep surrounded me*
> *Seaweed was wrapped around my head*
>
> *To the roots of the mountains I sank down*
> *The earth barred me in forever*
> *But you brought my life up from the pit*
> *Yahweh my god* [432]

Jonah was dead, but he would be reborn. Just as the fish-man Oannes descended into the sea every evening and emerged again with the morning sun, so it would be with the fish-man Jonah. He would rise again from the depths of the earth, having successfully traversed the perilous waters of death. This potent symbolism of death and rebirth was hardly lost upon Jesus, who was obviously well aware of the meaning behind the myth. Recognizing its significance, he declared that "as Jonah was three days and three nights in the belly of a huge fish, so the son of man will be three days and nights in the heart of the earth." [433] The earth had barred Jonah in, and so would it be with Jesus. But he too would be lifted up from the pit to new life.

Of this much he was sure.

It had happened to Jonah, and it had happened to Noah — both of whom had crossed the waters of death to arrive in a land of new life and fresh beginnings. Indeed, the stories of these two patriarchs are so similar as to suggest that they are perhaps variants on the same mythic original. The theme of crossing the waters of death was certainly constant. Moreover, both great heroes survive a fierce storm by taking refuge in the belly of a great ship. And in both tales, a sacrifice is offered to Yahweh when the storm finally abated.

It is this ship or ark that protects these heroes from the ravages of the sea, just as the funeral casket protected the mummified pharaohs from the ravages of death. The Egyptians took great pains to preserve the bodies of their kings, using elaborate embalming rituals in hopes of maintaining them in a serene, lifelike state. To this end, they were aided in great measure by the arid Egyptian desert, which provided the perfect environment for such preservation. Moisture is the great accomplice of decay, in whose presence microorganisms thrive, breaking down organic matter quickly and leaving only bare-bones evidence of what came before. If, therefore, something is protected from moisture by an arid climate, it is much more likely to be preserved. This is why many papyrus texts buried hundreds or even thousands of years ago in the Egyptian desert have turned up intact (to a greater or lesser degree) beneath the sands. It is also why Egyptian mummies are so marvelously preserved.

Did the ancient mythmakers know about the dangers of moisture to the mummified corpse when they wrote of their heroes being protected from the waters of death? It seems at least possible, if not likely. When a man died, it marked the end of a cycle, the culmination of mortal existence. The Egyptians had a word for this concept, which signified completion or finality. It literally meant "to bring to an end."

That word was, fittingly, *arq*.[434]

Jesus would speak in these very terms when he uttered his famous final words on the cross: "It is finished." [435] Had he spoken in Egyptian, he might very well have voiced the word *arq*. And it would have been appropriate, a signal that he was ready to board the celestial ship and cross the waters of death into heaven. The pharaohs were prepared for this mystical voyage through the meticulous process of mummification — the organs were removed and placed in separate containers; the body was bathed in spices and ointments to preserve it, then carefully wrapped in linen strips. And indeed, this is exactly what Jesus' caretakers would do:

"Taking Jesus' body, the two of them wrapped it with the spices in strips of linen."[436]

Jesus was thus prepared for his journey to the heavens. Although it is nowhere declared explicitly that he made this journey in an ark, there are several indications that he did so. One is a Samaritan tradition involving the messiah, who was known to this particular group of people as the *ta'eb* or "penitent one." He is clearly identified in Samaritan literature as a latter-day Noah, whose calls to repentance would protect Israel from the flood of corruption just as the ark had preserved Noah from the physical floodwaters. And just as Jonah's own calls to repentance would save the sinful Ninevites.

This Samaritan messiah would be named Joshua — or Jesus.[437]

It is also worth remembering that Jesus' tomb was attended by two women named Mary.[438] This is quite telling when one remembers that Meri was another name for Isis in her personification as goddess of the sea, a divine protector who with her twin sister Nephthys had ushered the ark of Osiris into the otherworld. These were the two Meris whose winged figures adorned the mercy seat on the famed Ark of the Covenant.

Despite the lack of any clear allusions to a seagoing vessel in connection with Jesus' death, such veiled references serve to supply the missing pieces. Moreover, the legend states quite plainly that Jesus was "taken" to heaven — implying he was a passenger aboard a vessel *of some sort* — and that his followers watched as he slowly disappeared beyond the clouds.[439] The image shares much in common with the familiar parting sequence repeated time and again throughout history in so many ports of call. The great ship with billowed sail lifts anchor and heads out to sea, bearing the departed loved one slowly away toward the horizon. So it was with the mortally wounded King Arthur when he undertook his mystical voyage to the enchanted isle of Avalon. And so it may have been with Jesus, as well. It seems altogether likely that, in the original version of the legend, he was taken up to heaven in an ark. This was, after all, the mummified pharaoh's traditional vehicle to the stars and it had to preserve him as it crossed the heavenly waters, just as it preserved Noah, Jonah, Moses and other figures who undertook this perilous journey to the heavens.

Notable among these heroic personages was the famed Greek adventurer Jason — whose name was, like that of Jesus, a Greek rendition of the Hebrew name Joshua.

This particular Jason was famous long before the birth of Jesus for his exploits on the open sea and in a series of great adventures. It was he who took center stage in one of the most famous myths, setting out with fifty heroic crewmen aboard a ship known as the *Argo* to recover the prized golden fleece. This had belonged to a magic flying ram created by the god Hermes to rescue two brothers from the clutches of their murderous stepmother. In this, the animal succeeded, though one of the brothers fell off its back during the escape and drowned in the narrow straits of water that linked the Black Sea to the northeast with the larger Mediterranean. Those straits subsequently became known as the Hellespont (Sea of Helles), named in honor of the fallen hero. Despite this misfortune, however, the other brother — whose name was Phrixus — managed to complete the journey, and upon doing so expressed his gratitude by sacrificing the magical ram to Zeus.

This story follows the familiar pattern of the flood myths, in which the hero is carried safely across the waters of death and afterward gives thanks with a sacrifice to his patron god. In this case, the vessel is a magical ram rather than a ship. But this is hardly a concern, for the story serves as a prologue to the more famous epic of Jason and his men, whose journeys were entirely aboard a *ship*. Even more significantly, this ship was known as the *Argo*.

Or ark.

Other similarities to the flood myths surface as the epic unfolds.

At one point, for example, Jason releases a dove to gauge whether it is safe to proceed, just as Noah does in the flood myth.[440] In an early version of the Gilgamesh legend, the protagonist is accompanied by fifty heroes on one of his adventures — the same number of crewmen who signed on with Jason for his journeys on the *Argo*. These companions of Gilgamesh go forth carrying fallen tree trunks, a peculiar image on the face of it until one considers an intriguing possibility: Perhaps these tree trunks served as oars or punting poles for propelling a ship.[441]

A ship such as the *Argo*.

But this is not the end of it, for the legend also reveals that the fifty companions of Gilgamesh hail from the city of Uruk. There is nothing particularly unusual about this, as this was their leader's hometown. Yet there may be something more going on here. One can hardly fail to notice that the name Uruk sounds suspiciously like the word ark, a relationship that seems more than coincidental. It may be recalled that Uruk was home to a great ziggurat or holy mountain similar to the mountain upon which the flood hero's ark supposedly came to rest.

This particular ziggurat was sacred to Inanna, who as queen of heaven served as a forerunner to the Babylonian goddess Ishtar — as well as to Isis. This goddess, it turns out, is linked rather closely with the patron god of the flood hero, Enki — or in the Hebrew tongue, Enoch. (Interestingly, the city of Uruk is sometimes referred to as Unuk, a name that sounds very much like Enoch. And an earlier Enoch in the biblical tradition, the son of Cain, supposedly had a city named in his honor. Could this have been that city?)

It was Enki who created the sacred tablets of divine wisdom known as the *me* and entrusted them to the flood hero, telling him to preserve them during the deluge by burying them in the city of the sun. Because these tablets contained the secrets of the universe, they were coveted by a variety of mortals and deities, not the least of whom was Inanna. She therefore devised a plot to procure them for herself, setting out to call on Enki in a visit that demanded a lavish reception. The god, not one to breach protocol, welcomed her with a sumptuous feast at which there was much drinking and merry-making. As the evening wore on, Enki became inebriated and foolishly agreed to give her the *me*. With the tablets safely in hand, she quickly departed in her boat and returned to Uruk, where she hid them safely away.

The tablets were now in Uruk, probably kept in the ziggurat dedicated to the goddess — just as, in Hebrew tradition, the tablets were stored in an ark housed in a temple.

From Athens to Jerusalem

It is at this point that another major temple of the ancient world comes into play. Situated atop the famous Acropolis of Athens, it stood in the shadow of the more famous Parthenon but was nonetheless notable in its own right. It was dedicated to the first king of the great city, who according to legend had been born under rather extraordinary circumstances.

The blacksmith god Hephaistos had taken a liking to the goddess Athena and, unable to contain his lust, attempted to rape her. She managed to fight him off, but not before he ejaculated on her thigh. Understandably disgusted at this, the goddess wiped the emission from her skin with a woolen cloth and tossed it to the earth — not realizing that in doing so she had by chance impregnated the earth goddess Gaia. The result of this unconventional union was a baby boy, whom Gaia presented to Athena at his birth so that she might raise her as his own.

This story provides an interesting model for the birth story of Jesus, who like the young child in the Greek tale was destined to be king. In fact, there are several points of contact between the two stories. Athena, like Mary, was a virgin or *parthenos* — hence the name of the goddess' famous temple on the Acropolis. Moreover, several early versions of Jesus' birth story situate the event in a cave, indicating that he symbolically sprang forth from the womb of the earth goddess. This is exactly what happened to the young Athenian boy.

But even more interesting is the name of the king in this particular tale: Erechtheus.

It is worth recalling that Erech was the Hebrew name for the city of Uruk, while the suffix *theus* means simply "god." The first Athenian king, therefore, bore a name that meant "god of Uruk." Or perhaps more precisely, *god of the ark*. This latter definition is even more reasonable in light of the fact that Erechtheus was often identified with the sea god Poseidon and has been depicted as a child with the torso of a human and the tail of a fish.[442] This composite figure, of course, is in the tradition of Oannes, the archetypal fish man who is often identified with Enki — the patron god of the flood heroes and the sacred *me* tablets.

No one could better qualify to be called god of the ark.

Further clinching the connection is the goddess Athena's own involvement in the saga of the *Argo*. Once the adventures of Jason and his companions were finished, the goddess reportedly cast the great ship into the heavens, thereby transforming it into a giant constellation. So impressive was it, in fact, that those who study the skies later divided it into three smaller star clusters:

- Carina (the stern)
- Puppis (the bow)
- Vela (the sail)

When pieced together, these three are easily recognizable as a heavenly ship or ark, riding the waves of the heavenly Nile that cascades like a river across the midnight sky. Here is certainly the celestial model for the arks that were buried alongside the pyramids at Giza, the huge stone structures which themselves were laid to align with the constellation known as Orion. On earth as it was in heaven.

If the Greeks who told of the *Argo* recognized the likeness of a ship in this expansive star cluster, the Egyptians — who were master astronomers long before their Hellenic counterparts — most assuredly did, too. And what they must have seen was the ark-casket in which their first king, Osiris, had been lain and cast adrift upon the Nile. His constellation, Orion, stands in close proximity to the stellar ark, separated only by a narrow expanse that includes the brightest star in the evening sky: Sirius. This was the star of Isis.

This particular star was also known as the "dog star." The Greek historian Plutarch, who was not always reliable on such matters, nonetheless provided an interesting analysis of this tradition. He maintained that the Greeks had adopted the term *cyon*, meaning dog star, based on the similar-sounding Egyptian word *cyein*, a verb signifying pregnancy.[443]

This makes sense in light of Isis' dual role as virgin and mother, a role she shared with Athena. In fact, Plutarch makes no bones about the fact that these two goddesses were to be identified with one another.[444] He emphasizes that both were revered for their exceeding wisdom, an attribute they shared with several other women of note — among them the wise street corner harlot depicted in Solomon's proverbs. This imagery of the wise harlot appears likewise in the story of Gilgamesh, who like Osiris is identified with the constellation Orion.

And who hails from Uruk, the city of the ark.

Early on, the storyteller sets the stage for his hero's meeting with the supernatural wild man Enkidu, who is to become his stouthearted companion in the adventures that lie ahead. His name is obviously derived from that of the flood god Enki, further connecting him to the mythic cycle of the ark. And he also appears to be closely identified with the phoenix, for he bursts onto the scene dramatically in the form of a star (or meteorite) fallen from heaven — a veritable benben stone. This is how Gilgamesh describes a dream announcing Enkidu's imminent arrival:

> *The stars appeared in the heavens*
> *The essence of Anu descended toward me*

I sought to lift it
It was too heavy for me
I sought to move it
Move it I could not

The land of Uruk was gathered around it
While the nobles kissed its feet

A large iron meteorite has come streaming out of the sky and landed in the midst of the people. It is of the essence of Anu, the supreme lord of heaven and father of the gods — hence it is the son of god. Such an omen could only signify the arrival of a new king, whose lofty position is confirmed by the rather vivid image of noblemen kissing his feet. As in nearly all ancient epics of this sort, Gilgamesh needs someone to interpret the meaning of his dream. And the person he chooses is significant: It is his mother, "who knows all." [445]

Here the motif of the wise mother makes its appearance. In Egyptian terms, the mother who knows all would have been Isis, who was noted for her divine wisdom. Gilgamesh's mother was Ninsun, likewise a goddess known for this particular attribute. Her name meant "lady wild cow," a title that has a certain amount of resonance when one considers that Isis was often portrayed wearing the horns of a cow on her headdress. Clearly, the two deities had more than a little in common.

Despite their wisdom, neither is portrayed as a harlot.

But Gilgamesh is not the only figure in the legend to seek counsel from a wise woman. Enkidu, it turns out, also has such a woman to guide him — and she *is* specifically described as a harlot. The erotic poetry that follows is reminiscent of that contained in the Song of Solomon to his black-skinned bride.

The wise woman bared her breasts

> *Enkidu took hold of her body*
> *She was not bashful*
> *She welcomed his passion ...*
>
> *For six days and seven nights*
> *Enkidu took her*
> *Every day and every night*
> *He had intercourse with the woman*

Enkidu's sexual exploits with the harlot are described in vivid detail, but they represent something much more than mere physical intercourse. They constitute, in fact, a ritual initiation into the wisdom of the ages. When Enkidu meets the woman, he is a brute savage, relying on his strength alone to defeat his enemies; in the aftermath of their tryst, he is a barbarian no more: "Enkidu became weak, unable to run as before. But his mind was filled with a new wisdom." [446]

This sets the stage for a showdown between the two heroes, who are brought together to meet one another in the streets of Uruk. Their confrontation begins as Gilgamesh tries to enter the city marketplace only to find that Enkidu has barred the gate with his foot. There ensues an epic struggle:

> *Gilgamesh and Enkidu grappled each other*
> *Holding fast like bulls*
> *They shattered the doorpost as the wall shook* [447]

The struggle is inconclusive. Gilgamesh bends his knee and seems to be conceding the contest to his rival, but Enkidu responds by acknowledging Gilgamesh as the rightful king. The entire episode sounds suspiciously like the struggle between Jacob and the mysterious godlike figure who refused to reveal his name — but who seems to have been none other than his twin brother, Esau. Gilgamesh and Enkidu are likewise described as brothers, with the people of Uruk exclaiming of Enkidu, "He is like Gilgamesh to a hair!" [448]

Moreover, Enkidu and Esau both are described as wild men with long hair who are associated with the open country rather than the cities.

Esau
- His whole body was like a hairy garment.
- Esau became a skillful hunter, a man of the open country. [449]

Enkidu
- Shaggy, with hair on his whole body; endowed with head hair like a woman.
- He knows neither people nor land. With the wild beasts he jostles at the watering place. [450]

Even the climax of Gilgamesh's struggle with Enkidu is reminiscent of the Jacob's struggle with the stranger. In the latter account, Jacob is rendered lame when his rival manages to wrench his hip out of its socket. And the Gilgamesh account seems to contain an echo of just such an injury, as it depicts the hero falling to one knee as if rendered lame at the conclusion of the battle. In both cases, however, the apparent loser is the one who winds up prevailing, thus gaining the right to wear the title of patriarch or king.

In the Hebrew legend, Jacob is advised by his wise mother on how to overcome his brother using trickery rather than relying on brute strength. The same sort of advice was probably given to Gilgamesh, who likewise sought the counsel of his all-knowing mother. These women, like the harlot who seduced Enkidu and the feminine voice crying out on the street corner in Solomon's proverbs, were personifications of wisdom.

Or *sophia*.

This was the Greek word for it, a word that appears in a rather unexpected context among the traditions of the Knights Templar —

the medieval order charged with guarding the supposed site of Solomon's legendary temple in Jerusalem, the place where the Ark of the Covenant was originally housed. These knights appear to have held in particular reverence a disembodied head known as Baphomet, a name that has been linked to the Moorish word *bufihimat*, meaning "father of wisdom." [451] But there is something more to the title than meets the eye. The Templars appear to have employed it as a code word of sorts, using a cipher in which the letters in the first half of the alphabet are exchanged for those in the second half — but in reverse order. When a particularly insightful scholar applied this method to the odd-sounding Baphomet, what he came up with was nothing other than the word *sophia*.[452]

This would seem an odd development, to say the least.

All of a sudden, the disembodied male head known as the "father of wisdom" has taken a decidedly feminine turn. But the combination is significant, for it recalls a particularly vivid scene from the Welsh version of the grail legend. As in the other renderings of the tale, the grail is brought forth by a lovely maiden in the castle of the Fisher King. But this particular version is unique for its vivid — and rather ghastly — portrayal of the grail itself. It is not a stone, nor a curved dish nor even the familiar chalice. It is, in fact, a disembodied head.

Or Baphomet.

Both elements of this peculiar name are brought together quite magically in this equally peculiar scene. One is confronted in a single image with the seductive feminine harlot *sophia* on the one hand, as well as the masculine "father of wisdom" depicted as the disembodied head. In visualizing this rather grotesque spectacle, it is striking that the feminine figure appears to have somehow gained power over the masculine keeper of wisdom, depicted in symbolic terms by the head.

How has this happened?

Through trickery, no doubt. Though *sophia* means wisdom, the Greek word also connotes something more — cleverness. Or deception. Hence the term sophistry, which refers to an argument that appears plausible on its surface but which in point of fact is fallacious. It was just this sort of deception that the goddess Inanna used to trick the wise god Enki out of his precious stone tablets. She got him drunk at a banquet, cajoled him into parting with his treasure and fled with the wisdom of the universe safely in her possession. Poor Enki was never able to retrieve the tablets, which thereafter remained in Inanna's possession. Though the story lacks any reference to a severed head, it appears to have served as a prototype in some respects for the Welsh grail legend. And it appears also to have been used as a model for a much more famous story that *does* involving a severed head on a platter.

This is the biblical story of John the Baptist. The elements of the story are all there. As in the tale of Inanna and Enki, the setting is a great banquet — this one in honor of Herod Antipas, the tetrarch of Galilee. The main entertainment is a seductive dancer named Salome, whose performance so pleases Antipas that he rashly declares: "Ask anything you want, and I'll give it to you. Whatever you ask for, you shall have it, up to half my kingdom." [453] He then goes so far as to seal this rash declaration with his word of honor.

The text itself makes no mention of the possibility that Antipas might have been drunk when he blurted out this promise. Yet it is worth reiterating that he did so at a banquet, where ample wine was no doubt flowing. And, moreover, it is hard to imagine any ruler in even a partial state of sobriety uttering such a reckless oath — and in front of witnesses, no less. Antipas himself was known for his cleverness, to the extent that Jesus would label him "that fox." He was therefore obviously the possessor of *sophia*, the cunning sort of wisdom commonly associated with that animal. Yet in this instance, the wine seems to have overcome him, rendering him vulnerable to the charms of the seductress. And so he swore the oath — an oath that, it is said, he immediately regretted. For no sooner had he spoken the words than the maiden demanded her price: She would not take from him half his kingdom, but she would have the head of John the Baptist on a platter. And in doing so, she would become the grail bearer, the keeper of wisdom.

The scene from the grail legend takes place, significantly, in the castle of the Fisher King.

Just how significant is this?

Extremely, it turns out. After all, the Fisher King's very title would seem to connect him at least peripherally with the ancient fish-god Oannes. And this sort of connection should come as no surprise considering the link to John the Baptist, whose name is merely a derivative of Oannes. A very close derivative, at that. In Greek, the two names are so similar that only a single letter separates them — one is Oannes, the other Ioannes. Moreover, the ancient festival of the summer solstice that celebrated Oannes was later adopted as the Feast of the Nativity of St. John.

And Oannes was simply another name for Enki, whose wisdom was stolen from him by the deceitful Inanna at a banquet just as the Baptist's head (the source of his wisdom) was taken from *him* as the result of a similarly clever deception at another banquet.

John the Baptist performed a similar function to that of Enki/Oannes, not to mention Jonah, issuing a warning to flee from the wrath to come and helping those who heeded his admonitions to pass through the waters safely at baptism. The ancient flood was reproduced symbolically through immersion in the waters of baptism, a ritual that like the flood itself was fraught with symbolism. Just as the flood heroes crossed over the waters of death, so did the baptized initiates.

The words of Paul reveal the connection between the waters and the grave, between the ark and the casket: "We were therefore buried with him through baptism into death." [454]

This burial was to be followed by a resurrection, just as the flood heroes crossed the waters into a paradisiacal new life.

Aboard the ark.

Once Enki was dispossessed of his sacred tablets, this mystical journey became the purview of the goddess who succeeded him. In Greek mythology she was Athena, who cast the *Argo* into heaven. In

Egyptian lore she was Isis, who searched for and found her slain husband's casket after it floated away on the Nile, and became its guardian with her sister Nephthys — twin angelic figures whose wings stretched forth across the mercy seat of the sacred ark. It is likewise to be recalled that Isis was considered the special goddess of ships and mariners, seeing them across the waters of this realm just as she guided the dead across the waters of the otherworld.

This was her role as the goddess of death and rebirth.

The importance of her role in this regard is made clear by her connection with the bright star Sirius. Each summer, this star would slip below the horizon for a total of seventy days, reappearing close to the time of the summer solstice. Its reappearance marked the birth of a new year and was an occasion for great rejoicing, for it closely coincided with the beginning of the Nile inundation. It was then that the snowmelt from the highlands to the south began to make its way downriver and overflow the banks of the vast waterway.

It was a phenomenon that could easily be described as a great flood.

And it seems entirely fitting that this great event coincided with the festival of Oannes, the great flood hero from Mesopotamia. The two great rivers of that region, the Euphrates and the Tigris, must have experienced a similar deluge as the winter snows were transformed into raging torrents, and it would have been a simple matter to transfer traditions surrounding this annual flooding a few hundred miles southwest to the Nile valley.

If the floodwaters symbolized the cycle of death and rebirth, so did the rising of Sirius. Indeed, the seventy-day period during which this star remained invisible below the horizon took on immense significance for the Egyptians, who used it as a model in fashioning their traditions of the afterlife. When preparing the dead to cross over to the other side of the celestial waters, they would embark on a process of mummification that lasted "for seventy days — never longer." [455]

Back to the Mansions

The ancient Egyptians divided up their calendar a bit differently than we do, parceling out the year into three seasons instead of four to signify the three distinct flood stages of the Nile. The first was the inundation, during which the raging torrent overflowed its banks and floodwaters covered the normally dry lowlands on either side of the riverbed. This was followed by the "coming forth," when the waters receded and gave way to newly green and fertile land. The third season, the time of harvest, followed.

But this was not the only difference between the Egyptian year and its modern counterpart. The Egyptians also grouped days together differently, creating a week that was three days longer than the one now in use. It can be compared to the modern calendar as follows:

- Modern system — 52 weeks of 7 days each.
- Egyptian system — 36 weeks of 10 days each.

The modern approach has the advantage of more closely approximating the actual length of a solar year, falling just a single day short of its true duration. The Egyptians, on the other hand, cheated a bit by tacking on the five so-called "epagomenal" days. In doing so, they managed to bring their calendar into rough conformity with the span of a single orbit around the sun. It is worth remembering, however, that these extra days were a later innovation, and that before they were added, the Egyptians observed an annual cycle whose length was quite significant in its own right — one that corresponded exactly with the number of degrees in a complete circle.

There was good reason for this. As the earth revolved around the sun, the constellations appeared to rotate in a circular fashion during the course of a single year. By the time the year was done, they had returned to the position they first occupied at the beginning of the cycle. Noticing this, the Egyptians divided up the circular vault of the sky into a number of segments equivalent to the number of days in their ancient year. And these, in turn, they grouped together in larger segments corresponding to their ten-day weeks.

During seven of these weeks, the bright star Sirius dipped below the horizon and became invisible. This was the seventy-day period of mummification, during which the star of Isis was "dead" as it passed through the underworld. These seven weeks were so crucial to the Egyptians that they named the star *Sept*, which would eventually be adopted as the Latin word for seven. A virtually identical hieroglyph, also verbalized as *sept*, was used to designate a thorn.[456]

This may have been one reason Jesus was said to have worn a crown of thorns just before his death — he was being prepared to reign as lord of the underworld, disappearing with the sacred star below the horizon.

What happened during this process?

The ancient astronomers realized that, even though they couldn't see the star, it must be passing through seven celestial regions (one for each week), just as it would have if it were visible. These were the seven houses of the Egyptian zodiac hidden from view in the underworld. And these houses were none other than the seven "mansions" or way stations through which the soul was destined to pass after death — the many mansions of which Jesus spoke and the series of castles encountered on the grail quest. This quest was nothing less than the pursuit of eternal life, at the end of which the soul would rise up victorious just as the bright star Sirius rose again in majesty after its seven long weeks in the underworld.

For the pharaohs, the conclusion of this period signaled the end of the lengthy mummification process. It was then that the ceremony of raising the *djed* pillar was conducted, and the dead king's likeness was set upright in a semblance of new life. This was the ancient ceremony of the resurrection, and it was all based upon the annual journey of the brightest star in the evening sky.

The star of Isis.

Sirius.

Yet this star was not the only one of significance to the Egyptians. In fact, the second-brightest star in the heavens drew the attention of ancient astronomers almost as readily. This was Canopus, located not far from Sirius. Though it was not located in the constellation of Orion, it was nonetheless known as the star of Osiris — and with good reason. As the star whose brilliance was exceeded only by the star of Isis, it was natural that it should be identified with her consort. But there was something even more significant about it, involving its position in the sky. It was located in Carina, the constellation that forms the stern of the great ship known as the Argo.[457] Indeed, as one faces the ship, it is at the very bottom of the hull; in other words, it is in the *belly of the ship*, exactly where Jonah is said to have taken refuge during the great storm. The phrase "belly of the ship" is the same term the Ethiopians used to describe the sacred Ark of the Covenant.

The sacred casket of Solomon, whose crypt is said to have stood at the center of the ancient temple.

It was this very site that was guarded by the Knights Templar, the mysterious group that revered the disembodied head known as Baphomet — or Sophia. As the personification of wisdom, this great lady was Inanna to the Sumerians and the grail bearer to medieval troubadours. To the Greeks she was Athena, and the Egyptians knew her as Isis or Meri.

She was wisdom personified, the proverbial street corner harlot flaunting her wares to any who would have her. A study in contradictions, she appeared as both sensual seductress and maternal guide. One the one hand she was Gilgamesh's all-knowing mother; yet she was also the harlot who seduced his rival Enkidu, infusing him with her wisdom in an act of sexual passion. In later times, she emerged in the form of two Marys — once again the mother and the harlot. One was the mother of Jesus, the other his most notable female disciple, a "sinful woman" named Mary Magdalene whom tradition has long branded as a harlot.

Is it possible that Jesus, like Enkidu, drew his wisdom from this harlot through the conduit of sexual intimacy? Though such an idea might seem appalling to many today, it would have been quite natural in an age when temple prostitution was common and sex was seen as a solemn expression of reverence for the divine. In fact, a text known as *The Gospel of Philip* describes just such a relationship between Jesus and Mary Magdalene. The document, excluded from the canon because of its esoteric nature, was nonetheless written only a few centuries after Jesus' death. It refers to Mary explicitly as Jesus' "companion" and declares that he loved her "more than all the disciples and kissed her on the mouth often." [458] More recently, the piece of a fourth-century papyrus from Egypt surfaced containing the following words in Coptic: "Jesus said to them, 'My wife … she will be able to be my disciple.' " While nothing in this very fragmentary discovery mentions Mary Magdalene directly, its language seems consistent with gnostic texts that mention the Magdalene as a spiritual consort of Jesus and an embodiment of *sophia*. Time will tell whether anything more can be learned from it.

However, hints of intimacy between Jesus and the Magdalene linger even in the accepted texts, where a woman named Mary anoints Jesus' feet with her tears with costly perfume and wipes dries them with her famous long tresses.[459] In bowing her head at his feet, she was placing herself in a position of obvious sexual vulnerability. And this was not the only instance in which she did so; in fact, she is portrayed as sitting at Jesus' feet on another occasion as well.[460] In one account of her ritual anointing, she is not described by name but merely as "a woman who had lived a sinful life." Her identity as such gave rise to the complaint that it was unseemly for such a woman to touch him.[461] And the entire episode seems to have cemented her reputation as a harlot — a reputation that would remain with her down through the centuries.

But Mary's connection with harlotry seems to have predated her actual birth, for it was part of the role that she would assume — that of temple prostitute/priestess.

The prophet Ezekiel would speak of such a person:

You have built your lofty place at the head of every street
You have made your beauty an abomination
And have opened your feet to everyone who passed by
And multiplied your harlotries [462]

The reference to a "lofty place" would seem to indicate a tower of some sort. The Tower of Babel, the sacred temple to Inanna at Uruk where women were wont to seduce male passers-by, fits nicely into this category. But a further connection may be drawn with Mary, whose epithet Magdalene is drawn from the Hebrew word *migdol*, denoting a tower.

The tower would make its way into medieval tradition as one of the trump cards in the tarot deck. On its face stood a solitary female figure atop a castle, her long hair cascading down the high walls of her refuge/prison.[463] The familiar image is that of a damsel in distress, perhaps specifically of the fairy-tale princess Rapunzel, who is imprisoned in a tower and manages a reunion with her beloved through ingenious (though fantastic) means: She lets down her hair so he may climb "the golden stair." This was a nice story to tell children, who would have had no inkling that the original tale was much more adult in nature.

It concerned a long-haired tower harlot — a description that fits Mary Magdalene perfectly. It also, incidentally, fits Isis, who was said to have resuscitated the fallen Osiris by shaking out her hair over him.[464] And just as Isis attended her fallen husband at his death and restoration, so Mary Magdalene filled this role for Jesus, serving as witness to his resurrection by attending to him at his tomb.

There was also a tradition, preserved in the canonical texts, that Mary Magdalene had seven "demons" or spirits driven out of her.[465] Echoes of this tradition are also found in the literature of the Mandaeans, a reclusive group that survives even today in several small communities across the lower Tigris-Euphrates region. This, of course, is the area that once stood at the heart of Babylon. In their texts, these communities pay particular homage both to John the Baptist and a certain Miryai, describing the latter as a "debauched trough." [466]

In other words, a harlot.

The Mandaean texts also speak repeatedly of "the seven," a group of spiritual beings described in no uncertain terms as dead. According to the Mandaeans, in fact, they had never even experienced life.[467] Indeed, the accounts appear to be saying that these seven spirits have been trapped in the realm of the dead from the beginning of time.

This seems a rather curious statement, but there is actually a very simple explanation. The reference to the dead makes it clear that these powers were somehow associated with the underworld, that part of the heavens *below* the earth. This was the region to which the star Sirius descended for seven long Egyptian weeks, passing successively through each of the seven celestial mansions before rising again at the new year. Each of these underworld mansions was guarded by a specific spirit charged with remaining there, forever "dead" and never able to experience the world of life. These were undoubtedly the seven spirits in the Mandaean literature, and the seven demons that had been cast out of Mary Magdalene. Once they had been cast out of her, she was able to (symbolically) return to life.

At one point, Jesus' disciples asked him whether they should forgive their brother a sin seven times.[468]

It was a sensible question.

In assuming the answer would be yes, they were merely tracing that hypothetical path through the underworld that every soul was destined to follow. During such a journey, the seven guardian spirits would each be called upon to "forgive" the newly deceased individual for the sins committed during his lifetime. If each consented to do so, the soul in question was granted a part in the resurrection. Yet if forgiveness was refused, passage would be denied and the soul would remain trapped in the realm of the underworld for eternity. Because of this, the region guarded by the seven was known as the "sinner's dwelling." [469]

Mary Magdalene, however, *was* forgiven. Jesus even caused quite a stir by stating in no uncertain terms to this sinful woman, "Your sins are forgiven." [470] The seven demons were cast out of her, indicating that she had successfully completed this journey to the other side — having crossed the proverbial waters of death. Probably she did so through the ritual of baptism, which not only signified the forgiveness of sins but also represented a process of rebirth. This was the ceremony held in such high esteem by the Mandaeans, explaining their reverence for John the Baptist.

This figure, of course, is said to have baptized Jesus himself.

Much has been made of the fact that Jesus consented to undergo this ritual even though he was (according to established doctrine) free of sin. If the only purpose of baptism was to establish a state of cleansing and forgiveness, Jesus would supposedly have never felt compelled to submit to such a ceremony. Yet he did. The only explanation given in the accepted texts is vague in the extreme. When questioned about his actions, Jesus is quoted as saying: "It is proper for us to do this to fulfill all righteousness." [471] But *why* was it proper?

Because baptism not only cleansed one of his sins, it also demonstrated the initiate's conquest of mortality. In passing through the waters unscathed, he was following the path of the flood heroes who had gone before him — heroes who had attained immortality by making it to the other side, just as the star Sirius had done. It is no coincidence that this star's re-emergence above the horizon marked the beginning of the inundation of the Nile.

The flood.

The two events were intimately connected. And it is also no coincidence that Mary Magdalene should have been chosen to exemplify the completion of this mystical journey through the underworld. The name Meri was, after all, one of the names of Isis.

And Isis was the goddess identified with this particular star.

With all this in mind, one might expect to find Mary Magdalene present in some form at Jesus' baptism. And indeed she appears to be. Perhaps the most significant episode to take place during this singular event was the dramatic appearance of a dove, accompanied by a voice from heaven: "As soon as Jesus was baptized, he went up out of the water. At that moment, heaven opened and he saw the divine spirit descending like a dove and lighting on him." [472]

The presence of the dove is significant for more than one reason. First of all, it recalls the flood hero's use of just such a bird to search for dry land when the waters had started receding. At the moment of the dove's appearance, Jesus was coming up out of the waters just as the flood hero had emerged from the great deluge. The end of this great storm was marked by his release of a dove, which returned to him with an olive branch in its beak, symbolizing the new fertility that survives death through procreation. The theme of procreation is, of course, central to the ark myth (at least two of every species are said to have been loaded onto the craft).

And it is a theme taken up by the author of the wisdom book known as *Ecclesiastes*, which was generally credited to the ark hero Solomon.

> *Do not revile the king even in your thoughts*
> *Or curse the rich in your bedroom*
> *Because a bird of the air may carry your words*
> *And a bird on the wing may report what you say*

> *Cast your bread upon the waters*
> *For after many days you will find it again*
> *Give portions to the seven, yes to the eight*
> *For you do not know when disaster may come upon the land*

> *If clouds are full of water*
> *They pour rain upon the earth*
> *Whether a tree falls to the south or to the north*
> *In the place where it falls, there will it lie*

FORGED IN ANCIENT FIRES

As you do not know the path of the wind
Or how the body is formed in the mother's womb
So you cannot understand the work of Yahweh
The maker of all things [473]

The imagery is clearly drawn from the legend of the deluge, and the writer just as clearly knows its significance. It begins with an account of a bird that is sent forth and returns with a report of news to the king, just as the dove was released by the archetypal king Noah and flew back with a message of new fruitfulness. And there follows an admonition to "cast your bread upon the waters" with the promise that, after many days, you will recover it. This is likely to strike a strange chord with readers, many of whom may be left scratching their heads at the image of some very soggy bread. Clearly, the advice is meant to be taken symbolically.

Just as the Eucharist was so intended at the last supper, when Jesus is said to have broken bread and gave it to his followers with the words, "This is my body." [474]

Could the author of *Ecclesiastes* have been using this very same symbolism?

Consider for a moment the fact that this book is attributed to Solomon, the man identified so closely with the dead king Osiris. It is this god who was symbolized by a sack of grain that, when watered, sprang to life. The grain, of course, was used to make bread — hence the imagery of casting one's bread upon the waters in order to find it again. Jesus translated the meaning of this saying succinctly when he declared that "whoever tries to keep his life will lose it, and whoever loses his life will preserve it." [475]

This is my body.

The bread was the mortal body, contained in the ark that was cast adrift upon the waters as the clouds poured down rain upon the earth. Death was sure to triumph. Yet just as surely would the bread, like the dove in the tale of Noah, be found again. The spirit would inhabit a new body, and the cycle of renewal would continue as the kernel grain that fell to the earth rose up again to be fashioned into another loaf. This was the message of new birth that the author of *Ecclesiastes* extolled as a miracle: "As you do not know the path of the wind, or how the body is formed in the mother's womb, so you cannot understand the work of Yahweh, the maker of all things."

This was what it meant to be born again.

Hence, the imagery of the dove in the story of Noah. In the ancient world, the dove was a sacred symbol of the great goddess, the very embodiment of birth and regeneration. It was identified with Isis, who was often known to take on the form of a bird and was depicted frequently as a woman with wings. And it was also identified with sophia, the feminine principle of wisdom.[476] This is none other than the street corner harlot with whom Mary Magdalene is so closely identified. In reading the account of Jesus' baptism, it is worth remarking that the dove does not merely hover over him — it actually descends and alights upon him and (according to one account) *remains* on him.[477] The imagery of a spiritual union of sorts between Jesus and the dove spirit is obvious, and the sexual overtones are likewise not to be missed. The dove was in fact an ancient symbol of sexuality, perhaps in part because of its haunting coo. On the one hand, its voice evoked the moans of a woman in the throes of sexual passion; on the other, it might have been taken for a pregnant woman groaning as she struggled through labor.[478]

Once again, the dual feminine persona of harlot and mother is present. It is therefore not surprising that a voice from heaven should have accompanied the dove's advent, declaring, "This is my son whom I love; with him I am pleased." [479] The traditional assumption is that this voice came from the Jesus' heavenly father, but this ignores the possibility that the voice was *feminine*. And there seems to be a distinct possibility that it was. Both harlot and mother are present in the dove, and so the voice of a heavenly mother in this context would have been natural. For it was the star of Isis (Meri) that was responsible for guiding the celestial mariner through the underworld and preserving him amidst the flood.

Or baptism.

The dove's coo is often heard as a sign of lamentation, presumably for one who has passed from this life. The mourning dove even takes its name from this association, its doleful cry recalling the sobs of a woman grieving a lost loved one — in the same way Mary Magdalene wept for Jesus at his tomb. The rite of baptism required that one first die in order to be born again, so the dove's presence in three roles as mother, bride and mourning widow was altogether appropriate at Jesus' initiation by John the Baptist.

Given all these links, it is no wonder that the Mandaeans so closely associated John and Mary. Her role as the divine harlot sophia is obvious. As such, she was also the seductively beautiful grail bearer who bore the bloody severed head into the hall of the Grail Castle — just as a young seductress named Salome demanded and received the head of John the Baptist on a platter.

The story would truly be complete if it were learned that Mary Magdalene and Salome were, in fact, the same person.

STEPHEN H. PROVOST

The Willow Queen

That question, however, will have to wait.

For now, it is important to return to the story of Jason and his journey aboard the *Argo*. The purpose of this journey was, of course, to obtain the golden fleece that had belonged to the magical ram. And quite a journey it was, taking the *Argo* and her crew to the edge of the known world and back again. The lengths to which Jason went to obtain the fleece of this single lamb recall a saying attributed to Jesus (whose name was closely related to that of Jason): "Suppose one of you has a hundred sheep and loses one of them. Does he not leave the ninety-nine in open country and go after the lost sheep until he finds it? And when he finds it, he joyfully puts it on his shoulders and goes home." [480]

Whether this parable of Jesus has any relation to the story of the fleece is uncertain, but the voyage of the *Argo* is certainly interesting in other respects. Its destination was, naturally, the land where the fleece had been taken after the flying ram helped Phrixus escape from his murderous stepmother. It was there that Phrixus sacrificed the animal to Zeus, subsequently leaving the fleece in the care of the nation's sovereign, Aeetes. His kingdom of Colchis was well off the beaten path, at the base of the mighty Caucasus mountains on the eastern shore of the Black Sea. So remote was this locale — in an area that is part of modern day Georgia — that it is hard to fathom why it should have been chosen as the setting for such a well-known Greek legend.

But the storytellers had their reasons.

Despite its relative isolation, the land is mentioned by no less a figure than Herodotus. This is the same historian who comments at length on Egyptian culture and religion — and who, astonishingly, proceeds to identify Colchis as an *Egyptian colony*. This is amazing considering the two locales lie close to a thousand miles from one another as the crow flies and are separated either by miles of open sea or by the daunting peaks of the Caucasus. Nonetheless, Herodotus is adamant: "It is undoubtedly a fact that the Colchians are of Egyptian descent."

The historian goes on to assert that the original Colchians were soldiers in the army of a certain pharaoh and supports his hypothesis with several pieces of evidence.

- The Colchians, like the Egyptians, have dark skin and woolly hair.
- Both groups practice circumcision.
- They share a method of weaving found nowhere else.
- Similarities can be seen in their language and culture.[481]

Regrettably, Herodotus is not specific about what these final similarities might have been. Some clues, however, are provided in the legend of the *Argo* and some associated myths. One character who figures prominently in these tales is an enchantress named Circe, who was renowned for her knowledge of herbs. She also happened to be the sister of Aeetes, the king of Colchis. And she lived on an island in a stone palace that stood in the midst of a wood, whence she was known to lure men to their doom with her charms. (Many of them she transformed into animals, though they retained their human intellect.)

Circe's name in Greek meant "falcon," the same bird used time and again to symbolize the Egyptian sun god Horus.[482] This might be taken as a coincidence except for the fact that Circe is identified as the daughter of Helios, the sun god (whose name is at the root of the Greek name for the Egyptian city of the sun, Heliopolis). Her fiery hair identifies her further as a solar figure, as does her name — which was also spelled *Kirke*. It is the basis for the familiar word "circle," which is reasonable enough given the sun's circular shape. And it had a secondary meaning to the Greeks as well: "an unknown stone." [483]

Or perhaps a stone of unknown origin.

This would seem to identify it with the stone that fell from heaven, the flaming benben associated with the phoenix — the mythical firebird that was so closely identified with Horus. Traditions such as this, essential components of Egyptian culture, must have made their way to Colchis with the Egyptian soldiers who settled there. But these traditions changed somewhat with the passage of time, until the falcon was no longer a mere symbol of the sun god but his *daughter*.

The daughter of Horus.

She was clearly a goddess of death, for she abode on an island from which men seldom returned. This island was called Aeaea, which meant "wailing." [484] Furthermore, a cemetery in Colchis was dedicated to her, set amidst a grove of willows. This tree would have been a natural choice for such a cemetery, given the fact that the willow has the appearance of a distraught lady attending the gravesite of her lord. Does this image sound familiar? It certainly evokes the picture of Isis mourning over Osiris — or Mary Magdalene weeping at the grave of Jesus.

But the willow imagery clearly predated the legend of Jesus and the Magdalene, even in Hebrew tradition. Rabbinical tradition preserves the particulars of a ritual known as the rite of the willow branch, which was performed during the Feast of Tabernacles at a place below Jerusalem called Mozah. It was here that men went every year to prepare for the feast by cutting down willow branches, which they would then bring to the temple in Jerusalem. There, they would "set these up at the sides of the altar, so that their tops were bent over the altar." [485] This reinforces the altar's identification with a burial ark, with willow trees set beside it so that they appear to be weeping over it, just as the Magdalene wept by the grave of Jesus.

But what of the place name Mozah?

As it turns out, this was the Hebrew name for a town known to the Romans by its Greek name, Emmaus.[486] It was en route to this town that two followers of Jesus were said to have encountered him after the resurrection. The selection of this site cannot have been accidental. For just as the willow queen Mary wept at Jesus' grave on the day of his resurrection, so the willows of Mozah wept at the altar of the dead king, waiting for him to rise again in the form of the new Horus.

Of Royal Blood

To be a daughter of Horus was to hold a privileged position in Egyptian society. For while ultimate authority rested with the pharaoh, the line of succession passed not through him but through his *queen*. If the royal bloodline were to be preserved, it would have to be through the woman known as "wife of the god" or beloved of Amen, otherwise known as Meri-Amen.

Or Mariamne.

Mary for short.

Perhaps this is why the grail bearer is often depicted as holding a chalice — the one Jesus' was said to have used at the last supper. This was the cup of blood, and the grail bearer was therefore the keeper of the sacred bloodline. If this identification is correct, the tradition dated back to the pharaohs of Egypt and their priestess consorts, the "wives of god," who likewise were keepers of a sacred bloodline.

Only a select few women in all of Egypt qualified to hold such a position. They had to have been members of the royal house, usually sisters or daughters of the reigning pharaoh. And they would naturally have been known as "daughters of Horus." For just as the pharaoh himself was considered Horus incarnate, so his daughters would have been seen as offspring of the god. And his sisters, born of the previous Horus (the pharaoh's father), would have naturally enjoyed the same status. Each was therefore qualified to pass the royal bloodline along to the next generation.

This would have required the sort of incestuous activity that doubtless seems perverse to the modern reader, but was seen as a practical necessity for the pharaohs. There was certainly precedent for it: Osiris and Isis, the first pharaoh and his queen, had also been brother and sister. And the royal line that stretched back, in theory, to these two founding deities had to be preserved. This was the mandate placed upon each new pharaoh, whose ability to father a child ensured that the land would likewise yield its fruit. He therefore took sister, daughter or mother to his bed, conceiving upon her a divine child of pure blood who would be fit to rule the kingdom upon his death.

This policy took firm hold under Ahmose (Moses), who used it to secure the succession for his dynasty. One inscription reveals that his favored queen Nefertari bore the multiple titles: "king's sister, king's daughter, god's wife and chief queen." [487] This indicates that Nefertari was the sister of Ahmose and the daughter of some previous pharaoh. She was also the wife of god, priestess of Amen by whom she was ritually impregnated.

She was therefore the "beloved of Amen" or Meri-Amen.

It can be no accident that the Hebrew texts record the name of Moses' sister as Miriam. As it turns out, she was also his wife.

This connection explains why Miriam is portrayed as conspiring with Aaron against Moses at one point. Aaron was, of course, none other than the Hyksos king Apophis — also known as Solomon.

This northern pharaoh had struck an alliance with the dark-skinned Ethiopians and had married their beautiful matriarch, Queen Tany of Sheba. But about this time, the great civil war with the Thebans broke out, changing the political landscape dramatically. As the conflict progressed, Tany renounced her marriage to Apophis and defected to the Theban side. And she sealed this new affiliation by marrying the Theban king Ahmose. She then became known as Nefer-Tany or "beautiful Tany" and was rewarded with the titles wife of god and beloved of Amen. Meri-Amen.

Despite this, an element of suspicion must have continued to surround her so long as the war continued. She was a political opportunist who had defected once, and the Thebans had to be alert to the fact that she might do so again if the tide suddenly turned against them. This suspicion is probably what lies behind the account of Miriam's alleged conspiracy with Aaron (Apophis) in the Hebrew texts, which declare that at some point Miriam and Aaron began to talk against Moses because of his Ethiopian wife.[488] This is likely a garbled version of what actually took place. The Ethiopian wife was none other than Miriam herself, who would hardly be criticizing her own husband for choosing to marry her. Something is missing from the statement — something that must have allowed for the fact that Miriam and the Ethiopian wife were one and the same. In its original form, it probably read something like this: Miriam and Aaron began to talk against Moses, *and a furor arose* because of his Ethiopian wife.

As punishment for her alleged part in the conspiracy, Miriam is afflicted with leprosy and is described as becoming white as snow.[489] This is a startling turn of events, and one that would seem to confirm that Miriam was in fact the Ethiopian wife of Moses. Why else would the narrator go out of his way to describe her skin as turning white, a development that would not have been particularly noticeable on a light-skinned woman but one that would have seemed quite astonishing in the case of a dark-skinned Ethiopian?

The condition of leprosy symbolized something else, as well. Lepers were routinely ostracized from their communities for fear that their disease would spread and afflict their countrymen. This fear of infection was analogous to the fear that a conspiracy against the government might spread in a similar manner. Miriam's leprosy was therefore probably a sign that some in the community were in favor of ostracizing her because she stood accused of treason. Eventually, however, the issue was resolved when Moses refused to accept the charges against her, petitioning his patron god to "heal" her of her affliction.[490]

Once this was accomplished, Miriam was restored to her exalted roles as wife of the god, king's sister and king's daughter. As she was Ahmose's sister, she therefore also must have been his father's daughter — and that father was Seqenenre, whose death following the dispute over the hippopotamus pool helped precipitate the revolt against the Hyksos.

This would seem to indicate that Seqenenre had married an earlier Ethiopian queen, and that Miriam was the product of that union. As the Queen of Sheba, she would become renowned for her wisdom, yet another figure to be identified with the ancient feminine *sophia*. Not only would she become Solomon's harlot (eventually forsaking him for the Theban prince), but she would appear also in the guise of Bath-Sheba, the naked bathing beauty who seduced David in the Hebrew texts.

Building on the precedent of Nefertari's fame, the title of king's daughter would come to be one of the most coveted in all of Egypt. In later times, it would be bestowed upon the eldest daughter of the pharaoh, who would take the title "wife of god" yet would remain a virgin.[491] She would therefore be the virgin Meri-Amen, whose would rule over a huge estate. As the wife of god, however, she would still have a duty to produce an successor miraculously through the help of the god Amen.

A colonnade depicts just such a miraculous conception, involving the favored wife of the first King Tuthmose (the pharaoh who was the second in the line of succession after Ahmose). The colonnade features a series of engravings that portray the pharaoh in his role as

Amen incarnate breathing the breath of life into the nostrils of his queen, thus conceiving a successor to the throne.[492]

A "virgin birth" was sure to follow.

Back to Colchis

This was the way of things in Egypt, where Horus was the sun god incarnate as the monarch and where the king's daughter was therefore the daughter of Horus. In Greece, the role of sun god was filled first by Helios, who ultimately yielded his position in the pantheon to Apollo. Yet regardless of which god attended the solar orb, the connection with the winged falcon of the Nile remained quite evident.

Apollo's oracle center at Delos was linked specifically with a palm tree, the benu tree of ancient Egypt specifically associated with the phoenix of Horus.[493] The god also stood guard over a sacred stone that had fallen from the sky and was housed in the temple at Delphi, the most famous oracular shrine in the ancient world. Its name stems from the Greek word *delphinos*, which refers to the sea mammal known as the dolphin as well as to the womb.[494] This is fascinating when one reconsiders the myth of Jonah/Oannes, who was reborn from the "womb" of a related sea mammal, the whale. And it helps explain the French title *dauphin*, which likewise means "dolphin" but was applied to young princes who were heirs to the throne.[495]

Messiahs, or sun kings.

Indeed, the French king Louis XIV was specifically known by this title, following in the footsteps of Solomon and the other sun kings who had come before — a lineage that dated back to Oannes. It is a lineage reflected in the famed statue of a boy on his dolphin, originally meant to show the youthful sun god's nativity from the ocean waves, buoyed on the finned animal's back.[496] Oannes, likewise, rose up from the sea each day in his aspect of the sun before returning to the waves at nightfall, being swallowed by the waves just as he himself was swallowed by the giant she-whale or sea serpent.

A close relative of the dolphin.

Even the choice of delphiniums to ring the body of Ahmose — or Moses — after his death may be have been no accident. The bluish flower was named for its resemblance to the sea creature.

This benben-type stone at Delphi was originally guarded by a similarly serpentine monster known as Python, but Apollo (a sun god like Horus and Oannes) succeeded in vanquishing this foul beast and thus became the stone's protector. This serpent was also identified with Typhon, which was the Greek name for the Egyptian god Seth.[497] And just as Horus had defeated Seth, so Apollo vanquished Python.

The connection between Horus and the earlier Greek sun god Helios is, if anything, even more apparent. Helios' name not only bears a certain resemblance to that of Horus, but also to "Elias" — the latter being the Greek version of the name Elijah. This was the prophet most famous for being whisked away at his death in a fiery chariot, a universal symbol of the sun. In like manner, the horses of the sun (who pulled the solar chariot across the sky) were said to be stabled at Colchis, the city of Helios.[498]

Circe was the daughter of this Helios, who reigned as king of the sky. This connection is interesting linguistically, for Helios sounds a lot like the Greek word *helice*, denoting the willow tree with which she was so closely linked.[499] As daughter of the sun king, she would have, in Egyptian terms, worn the title of king's daughter and god's wife Meri-Amen. This goes a way toward explaining her association with the weeping willow, whose long, thin branches mimic the long hair of Mary Magdalene as they descend toward the earth.

Circe's association with the cemetery of Colchis links her to the Magdalene at the grave of Jesus, as well as to the tearful Isis grieving her fallen consort Osiris. Her reputation as an enchantress aligns well with that of the Magdalene as a "sinful woman" associated with the seven spirits of the dead. And her legendary command of herbs and spices further links her with Mary, who helped prepare spices to anoint Jesus' body for mummification.

Again, the link to the cemetery and preparation of the dead is obvious.

But there are other links to be mentioned as well — links that are not as readily apparent.

One involves the name Circe, which, as mentioned previously, served as the root for the word "circle." This in turn served as a root for circumcision, the act of cutting away the penis' foreskin by creating a circular incision around it. Hence the name circum-(in)cision. The foreskin naturally covers the head of the penis unless it is removed, just as a cloud might cover the sun in the daytime sky. By removing the foreskin, one might be said to have symbolically removed the cloud covering the sun. Indeed, the Egyptian hieroglyph for the sun god Ra is a circle with a dot at the center, which looks very much like the uncovered or circumcised male sexual organ viewed from the top.

The act or circumcision itself might well have been conveyed in the language of myth as the sun god's victory over his storm-god rival — a rival often depicted as a serpent such as Python or the Egyptian sky monster Apophis. An obvious question presents itself: Could this particular beast have been chosen because of its resemblance to the penis?

Because Circe was the daughter of the sun god Helios, such an operation as circumcision would naturally fall under her purview. And when one considers the fact that the Egyptian practice of circumcision was also followed in Circe's home region of Colchis, this identification becomes even more likely.

But the enchantress' name seems to have given birth to other words, as well. Among them was the Anglo-Saxon word *circe*, whose spelling was identical to that of the name of Helios' daughter. The meaning of the word?

Church.

It is astounding to consider that this word has its origins in the name of a Greek enchantress, yet this appears to be the case. The old English word *kirk*, which has the same meaning, likewise stems from a variant spelling of her name, *kirke*. This word is mentioned in connection with (of all people) Robin Hood, whose final adventure involved crossing a bridge to an abbey or nunnery known as Kirklees, where he died after having his blood let by a treacherous cousin. On his way, he crossed over dark water via a plank that was guarded by an old woman. This woman apparently was not too happy to meet him, for she pronounced a curse upon him — a curse that one can only surmise was fulfilled at his fatal bloodletting.

This might seem at first a peculiar way to die, especially for a swashbuckling hero such as Robin Hood. But when one recalls that Robin has been cast in the mold of Jesus, it makes perfect sense. Like Robin, Jesus underwent a bloodletting of sorts on the cross, when his side was pierced with a spear and the resulting wound yielded a sudden flow of blood and water.[500] This spear would make its way into the grail story as the weapon borne in the grail procession that dripped blood from its point. According to legend, this blood was collected in the cup Jesus used at the so-called last supper and in some traditions transferred to the grail bearer.

This beautiful young woman then became the keeper of the sacred blood.

There is no surprise here, for the Egyptian queens had likewise become keepers of the sacred *bloodline*. The symbolism is evident. Ahmose had championed a system whereby the succession passed through the consorts of the pharaohs rather than through the pharaohs themselves, who relinquished the kingship at their death. Their consorts, however, retained their royal status. The bloodletting therefore signifies the passing of the kingship from the body of the dying king into the care of his still-living consort, who thenceforth becomes responsible for preserving the succession by giving birth to his heir.

This woman is the Mery-Amen or Mariamne — Marian in the legend of Robin Hood, Mary Magdalene in the case of Jesus.

But though Ahmose appears to have revived the practice of matrilinear succession, he hardly initiated it. Indeed, it appears to be one of the oldest known practices, dating back to prehistoric times.

Early in man's development, it is quite possible that the connection between sex and childbirth was not yet known. The primitive state of learning and the relatively long interval of nine months between intercourse and birth may have obscured the causal relationship, leading ancient tribes to conclude that the woman alone was responsible for perpetuating the family.[501]

Before the male role became evident, the feminine principle appears to have occupied a place of great reverence in both the social and religious life of the tribe. The great goddess reigned supreme as the sole bearer and renewer of life, and prehistoric cultures across a broad swath of territory produced small stone figures of women with full breasts and protruding bellies that suggest pregnancy. It was only when the male role in conception was understood that a corresponding male deity entered the picture as consort to the mother goddess. Yet even then, many cultures across Africa, Europe and Asia retained the custom of matrilinear descent.

In the cradle of civilization that was ancient Sumer, the goddess Inanna (the Sumerian counterpart of Isis) was the one who controlled the succession, conferring royal status on the man of her choice. She was served in this capacity by a handmaiden named Lilith, who had a reputation to match that of the witch Circe and the "sinful woman" Mary Magdalene. Her task in the service of Inanna was simple: She was to go out into the streets of Uruk like the wise harlot of Solomon's proverbs and round up as many men as she could. These she brought to Inanna's ziggurat mountain-temple, where she proceeded to engage them in sexual intercourse.[502]

Again, sex is associated with wisdom.

And wisdom, in turn, is associated with the ark — or at least the city of the ark, Uruk, where the *me* tablets were kept.

The Egyptians had a word for a wise or educated man. They called him an *arqu*.[503] A name that would have applied quite nicely to King Solomon, the Hyksos king of Egypt who was renowned above all else for his wisdom and who (not coincidentally) was intimately associated with a very special ark known as the *aron*. Once again, the wheel appears to have come full circle.

The Wind Spirit

Lilith was almost certainly a priestess-queen in the service of the goddess and was probably seen as her incarnation, just as the "wife of god" in Egypt was seen as the embodiment of Amen's divine consort. Her name is derived from the Sumerian word *lilitu*, meaning a wind spirit or female daemon.[504] This links her to Isis, who was associated with a hieroglyph in the shape of a sail — a symbol that translated as "the wind."

But Lilith had something of a sinister reputation.

Like her fellow enchantress Circe, she was associated with the willow tree, which was known among the druids as the *saille*.[505] The similarity to the word "sail," so closely associated with Isis and her mariners, is clear enough. It was in just such a tree that Lilith was said to perch — a tree that was guarded by a dragon, which was eventually slain by no less a hero than Gilgamesh.[506] The story involved Inanna's attempt to grow a willow tree, which she had hoped to use in fashioning a bed and throne for herself. But before she could realize this goal, her efforts were frustrated by the arrival of the dragon and Lilith, who took to living in the tree.

If this particular legend sounds a bit familiar, it should. For it is virtually identical to the ancient fable involving the Queen of Sheba — with whom Lilith was often identified in ancient lore — and her imprisonment in a similar dragon-guarded tree. It may be recalled that she remained perched in the branches of this tree until she was freed by seven heroes or holy men who just happened to be passing by. Like Gilgamesh (not to mention his later counterpart St. George), these seven heroes slew the dragon. And though Gilgamesh accomplished the deed alone, the number seven still figures prominently in the tale — he slew the dragon using a bronze ax that is seven talents and seven minas in weight.[507]

This theme is so pervasive that it can even be found in the

Western Hemisphere. A Cherokee myth tells of four serpents who tried to kill the sun but accidentally slew his daughter. As a result, seven men with seven sticks were sent to capture her spirit in a box and restore her to life.[508] The motifs of the dragon/serpents, the princess and the seven heroes who come to her rescue are, incredibly, exactly the same. Even the idea that the princess is brought back to life corresponds well to the myth of Inanna, who similarly returned from the land of the dead. The fact that the woman is identified as the daughter of the sun connects her to Circe, who was likewise the daughter of the sun god Helios.

Could these seven men with sticks have been the seven guardian spirits of the otherworld through which the star Sirius, the star of Inanna and Isis, passed on its yearly journey? Such an identification seems at least possible, if not likely. Sirius was the star of Isis, with whom Inanna has been long identified. Both were styled "the queen of heaven," a title aptly applied to the brightest star in the evening sky. And the seven spirits protected this star of the goddess as it passed through the underworld on its annual journey.

In the same way, they protected the "dead" sinner Mary Magdalene until they were cast out, signifying her rebirth.

Lilith, like Mary Magdalene, was portrayed as a sinful seductress or harlot, who resembled her further in that she was covered in hair from head to foot.[509] But she was even more closely associated with the Queen of Sheba in ancient legend, preserved in the Hebrew traditions of the Talmud. It was a connection that fit in every respect. For the queen was, after all, the "wife of god," Mery-Amen priestess and consort to the pharaoh Ahmose, just as Lilith was the priestess of the king-maker goddess Inanna in ancient Uruk.

Their roles were absolutely identical.

And Lilith, like the other enchantress priestesses of her ilk, was a vampire — known for enticing her lovers to her bed and deceitfully drawing out their blood until they perished.[510] Thus she, too, became the curator of the *blood*line or royal succession, as dictated by her goddess counterpart Inanna. With this in mind, it makes sense that the Hebrew scribes should have given Lilith "charge of all newborn children: boys up to the eighth day of life, that of circumcision; girls up to the twentieth day." [511] She not only escorted the old king out of this world by lying with him, but she gave birth to his chosen heir and guarded him up to his infancy.

The mention of circumcision further links her to Circe, whose name bespeaks this ritual procedure. It was a ritual that involved the spilling of blood from the sexual organ, imagery that once again reveals the priestess' role as guardian of the bloodline.

Behind the priestess stood the goddess to whom she pledged her faith.

Behind Lilith stood Inanna.

This was the same Inanna who had deceived Enki into relinquishing his precious *me* tablets, thereby taking upon herself the role of wisdom's keeper. And she was the keeper of something else, as well — the royal succession as it passed from one generation to the next through a line of priestess queens. The question therefore arises: Could these two concepts (wisdom and succession) have been somehow connected, or even identified, with one another? Certainly wisdom has long been considered the most important trait in kings, who traditionally inherit their thrones through their bloodline. And ancient people firmly believed that the spirit of a person coursed through his veins, and with it perhaps the wisdom that made him the sage he was. Further, the bloodline was kept alive through sexual intercourse, which the ancients also associated with a means of conveying wisdom. A notable example of this is the story of Enkidu's seduction by the harlot, who left him weaker but *wiser* after their encounter than before.

Enkidu was a manifestation of the phoenix, the meteoric essence of heaven that fell from the sky. As such, he was obviously an archetypal prince or king of Sumer. His name bespeaks devotion to the wise god Enki, the patron of kings such as the flood hero Ziusudra. And just as Enki was the god of kings, so Inanna was the goddess associated with the priestess-queens whose role it was to guard the royal succession. It was her priestess, Lilith, who seduced would-be monarchs in the temple of Inanna. And there can therefore be little doubt that Lilith or someone very much like her was also the harlot who seduced Enkidu in the legend of Gilgamesh.

This seduction was paralleled in the myth of the god and goddess themselves.

On earth as it was in heaven.

Inanna persuaded Enki to part with the tablets by getting him drunk, presumably on wine, the alcoholic beverage of choice among the ancients. Red wine was commonly associated with blood in many cultures, a link that survived in Jesus' day when he associated his own blood with a cup of wine served at the Passover meal. This wine was the essence of his wisdom and his royal authority, which he was imparting to his followers as he prepared for his imminent death.

This was Enki's gift to Inanna as well.

It was imparted by king to priestess in the ziggurat temple, the false mountain or pyramid that was also the tomb of the kings. As the old king died, the new king took the throne. This was the nature of the ancient wisdom guarded by Inanna and her priestess Lilith. It brought forth life, yet did not shrink from acknowledging death. Both were essential; without either, the eternal cycle would collapse — the royal succession would cease.

And if this were to happen, it could never be revived.

This was the nature of tanistry, always seeking a virile young king to replace the aging monarch and ensure the fertility of the land. In a stroke of cruel irony, it was the harlot priestess who both seduced the king and mourned his death, giving birth to his heir and burying his lifeless body. Whether her name be Mary or Isis, Circe or Lilith, it mattered little. Her task was always the same. The womb of the earth was also the grave, and so it had always been.

Hebrew tradition made Lilith the first consort of the archetypal man-king, Adam. Before Eve was taken from Adam's rib, the rabbis said, he was assigned Lilith as his helpmate. Yet they parted ways when Adam insisted that they consummate their union in a particular manner, with Lilith lying beneath him. She balked at this suggestion, and their disagreement was never resolved. In a fury, she escaped him by uttering the magic name of the highest god. At this invocation, she was able to sprout wings and escape him by flying away.[512]

Her special knowledge of this name connects her to Isis, the only figure in Egyptian lore who managed to learn the name of the divine king Ra (having extorted this knowledge from him in exchange for providing a magical antidote to her venomous snake's bite). Isis was also a winged goddess, and Lilith's act of growing wings to fly away fits well into her sacred traditions. But then the connection between these two figures should come as no surprise, considering that Lilith was the priestess of Inanna, who was but Isis in another guise.

Why should Lilith have refused to lie prone beneath Adam during their lovemaking?

Obviously, she must have preferred that their positions were reversed. She was the queen of heaven made manifest, and as such would naturally have preferred to be on top.

A commentator named Hieronymous equated Lilith with the Libyan queen Lamia, who is shown in one relief naked as she straddles a certain traveler asleep on his back.[513] Or at least the traveler *appears* to be asleep. For sleep was a metaphor for death, and the prone position is the same one assumed by the corpse when placed in its coffin. As repulsive as this sounds, the relief in question did not depict an act of necrophilia but an exercise in symbolism that merged the priestess' two functions — mother of the new king and keeper of the old king's tomb — into a single image. It must have been this sort of representation that gave rise to Lilith's reputation as a night demon or vampire who snuck up on men and robbed them of their souls as they slept on their back.

In many Egyptian hieroglyphs, the dead king is depicted lying in just this manner, having taken on the guise of Osiris and being attended by the twin sisters Isis and Nephthys, the "angels" of the sacred ark. And in many of these scenes, the phallus stood erect as though awaiting a tryst with a night demon such as Lilith.[514] Indeed, one version of the Egyptian legend declared that Isis conceived a child by Osiris *after his death*, suggesting that just such a coupling had taken place.

The Mountain Queen

Darkness fell on two occasions — at night and at death.

So it was that Lilith was a creature of the night. As a harlot, she was a lady of the night. And complicit in her seemingly nefarious activities was the great mother goddess Inanna, the benevolent queen of heaven. It was she to whom the great false mountain was dedicated, and it was she who commanded Lilith as her servant. As such, she was the lady of the mountain. This title is, interestingly enough, applied to a goddess once prominent in the Sumerian pantheon. The goddess in question is a certain Ninhursag, whose name means literally "mountain queen." She is also identified as the half-sister of the god Enki.[515]

This familial relationship would have made her a perfect candidate to ensure the matrilinear succession and the continuance of royal wisdom — something Inanna did when she stole the *me* tablets from Enki. Could Ninhursag have simply been a title for Inanna, who was in a very real sense the "lady of the mountain" in that she presided over the ziggurat temple in Uruk? It would seem so. The goddesses share several traits in common, including their association with the moon, the tree of life and fertility. Ninhursag is even characterized as a goddess of the resurrection, bearing the descriptive title "she who gives life to the dead."[516] Her role is therefore analogous to that of Mary Magdalene, who prepares Jesus for his resurrection by anointing his body with spices at the tomb.

This link between the "lady of the mountain" and the false mountains that were the pyramids (both Sumerian and Egyptian) bears closer scrutiny. It is worth recalling that these pyramids were identified with the so-called "mountains of Seir" in the desert of the Sinai Peninsula. It was to this region, later known as Edom, that

Lilith was banished after the dissolution of her union with Adam. According to the prophet Isaiah, she dwelt there in the form of a screech owl — a bird almost universally associated with wisdom. The Hebrew word for this particular bird was *lilyiyth*. The prophet's brief description of her activities there is worth reproducing:

> *The screech owl will nest there and lay eggs*
> *She will hatch them*
> *And care for her young*
> *Under the shadow of her wings*
> *There also the falcons will gather*
> *Each with its mate* [517]

The prophet's words identify Lilith explicitly as a mother who gives birth, and hence the keeper of a bloodline. And not only this. They also explicitly make mention of falcons, the sacred bird of Horus incarnate as the ruling pharaoh. These falcons (or princes) would gather in the land of Lilith *each with its mate* — in order, no doubt, to conceive children. The prophet must have remembered the ancient traditions of Sumer and Egypt, in which temple-mountains were places of divine conception, though he may or may not have realized the significance of these traditions. This drama played itself out now in the shadow of Seir, the great mountain range that came to be equated with the artificial mountains of the pyramids.

The mountains of Osiris.

But there is still another linguistic connection to make involving this tantalizingly significant place name. It is a connection that involves the star Sirius, which in Greek was known as *Seirios*. This was not only the star of Isis, but that of her alter-ego Inanna as well. Legend had it that Inanna undertook a calamitous journey to the underworld, during which she passed through seven gates — symbolic of the seven long weeks spent by the bright star beneath the horizon. After failing to unseat the mistress of the underworld from her throne, she was summarily executed and her corpse hung on a nail.[518] Only through Enki's intervention was she revived, and then only when she sent her lover Tammuz (also known as Dumuzi) to take her place.

Tammuz was known simply as "the shepherd."

As the lover of Inanna, he must therefore have been a shepherd king — the same title applied to the Hyksos rulers.

Jesus likewise styled himself as a shepherd king. For he was not only a messiah, or anointed ruler, but also the good shepherd. Moreover, he had a disciple named Thomas whose name sounds quite a bit like that of the tragic Sumerian hero Tammuz. The name was also interpreted as meaning "twin" — which led to speculation about whose twin he might have been. One tradition came to the rather astonishing conclusion (at least on its surface) that he was *Jesus'* twin. This would have made him a good shepherd as well, just as his namesake hero was.

The death of Tammuz came at Inanna's command, with the goddess once again fulfilling her role as gatekeeper to the otherworld for the dying king. From her temple, the fallen monarch ascended to the heavens, passing through the seven gates of death just as Inanna herself and her star had done. Perhaps this was the purpose of the narrow shaft carved from a chamber in the pyramids that seems to have been pointed directly at the star Sirius. Perhaps it was meant to convey the dead king's spirit safely through the underworld in the arms of his beloved queen. One may be reminded, at this juncture, of the moving portraits of the crucified Jesus in the arms of his grieving mother, revered as the queen of heaven. How is it that she retained her youthful beauty in these portraits, as though she were scarcely older than the savior himself? Perhaps because the Mary in question was the *other* Mary, his consort the Magdalene. It was she who guided the fallen hero safely through the seven gates of eternity as she conceived a child of his blood, ensuring that the sacred bloodline would continue.

In this context, the act of bloodletting was no act of deceit, but a loving act of continuance performed by the devoted goddess who wept for her fallen god-king. And it fell to harlot-priestesses such as Lilith and Circe to reproduce this act of supreme love and sorrow, enacting the heavenly drama in its earthly form of ritual.

Robin Hood and Circe

It is inevitable that the mythic circle should eventually come around to Circe as well, for she too was known for bleeding her lovers to death. Homer's famous hero Odysseus was well aware of this when he paid a visit to her on her island. According to this legend, Odysseus knew full well that enchantresses such as Circe had the power to "enervate and destroy their lovers, by secretly drawing off their blood." [519] This, of course, is exactly the means by which Robin Hood met his demise. Odysseus therefore admonished her not to plot any such deceit in his case and thus escaped her enchantments.

This is but one of the similarities between the story of Robin Hood's death and the legend of Circe. Indeed, the two traditions show several other points of contact as well. Among them:

- Robin Hood had to cross over dark water to reach the abbey. In the same way, one had to cross water to reach Circe's island.
- Circe lured men to her abode and then dealt with them treacherously, just as Robin Hood's cousin the prioress did in the tale of his demise.
- Circe was an enchantress with a reputation for dealing with spells and magic. In Robin Hood's legend, he is placed under a curse by an old woman who seems very much a witch.
- The name Kirklees is derived from an old English title meaning "church of the wood." Circe was also associated with a wood — her willow grove at Colchis.
- This grove was in a cemetery, a place of death. Robin Hood's death in his story therefore fits the setting perfectly.

Even today, churches are often found adjacent to cemeteries, serving as symbolic gateways to the otherworld just as temples did in more ancient times. Indeed, a grave slab supposedly belonging to Robin Hood could be found in the cemetery at Kirklees. But before he died, our hero was involved in a final battle with an adversary described variously as Red Roger and Roger of Donkesley. This character is obviously an avatar of Seth, whose special color was red and whose totem animal was the ass or donkey — a word that sounds a great deal like the artificial place name Donkesley. (This is supposedly a variation on Doncaster, but if so it is an extremely convoluted one).

If Red Roger was Seth, the Robin Hood must have taken the part of his archrival Horus/Osiris. This much is confirmed by the fact that he is always seen wearing green, the color of Osiris' skin in his aspect as a vegetation god. Then there is the emphasis placed on his bow as a fighting weapon, which is buried beside Robin in the legend of his death. Like the fallen kings of Egyptian lore, it would seem that he was transported to the realm of heaven in the likeness of that constellation sacred to Osiris — the star cluster Orion, which was seen as wielding a longbow.

Though the abbey at Kirklees is nowhere identified with anyone in particular, it is enough to remember that it was a nunnery and as such was populated by women who had taken a vow of celibacy. This they did in imitation of Mary the virgin, who appears elsewhere repeatedly in the Robin Hood legend as an object of special devotion for the hero. Once again, the Egyptian origins of the tale are only somewhat obscured. It is perhaps even more notable that Robin Hood supposedly founded a chapel dedicated to Mary Magdalene, who is to be clearly identified with Circe (the thinly disguised prioress of Kirklees).

Some traditions even identify the prioress as none other than Robin's beloved Maid Marian.[520]

Marian was Robin's consort, just as Mary Magdalene appears to have been the consort of Jesus. This relationship was obscured in later times, with the church taking on the role of the "bride of Christ." Yet the very word "church" is derived from the name Circe, who was so closely identified with the Magdalene. If the *circe* was Jesus' consort, the Magdalene must have been as well.

In the grail legends, the pure hero Galahad is presented as a sort of new Jesus, a sinless knight destined to claim the throne of the Fisher King. His name, it will be recalled, was a variant on the place name Gilead — which the prophet Jeremiah mentions in relation to the daughter of Egypt. Eventually, Galahad would die in the city of Sarras after arriving there in Solomon's ship.

Yet another manifestation of the ark casket.

Clearly, this Sarras is yet another name for the mystical otherworld that awaited those who crossed the waters of death in the ark. It supposedly lay in the direction of the Egyptian realm of the dead, far across the western sea.[521] This was the land of the setting sun, and it is therefore no surprise to find that a temple of the sun had been built there.[522] According to legend, this was the city where the grail itself was kept, secured *in an ark* that stood upon a silver table.[523]

One cannot fail to notice that the name Sarras sounds quite a bit like that of Sirius, the star that descended into the realm of the dead for seven long weeks of every year. Nor is it easy to ignore its resemblance to Sarah, the Egyptian name that meant "queen" or "princess." This makes sense, too, when one considers that Sirius was the star of Isis, the goddess who bore the title queen of heaven.

Some have identified Sarras as the city of Marseilles in southern France, the home region of so many "black virgin" statues identified with both Isis and Mary Magdalene.[524] Legend has it that Mary left Palestine sometime after Jesus' death aboard a ship that landed near Marseilles. This was a fitting port of call considering its history as a city sacred to the Artemis — the Greek counterpart to our familiar goddess Diana of the Romans.[525]

The Cup of Orion

Artemis/Diana was yet another virgin goddess who fits a pattern that is becoming quite familiar. She, too, was said to have been held captive in a tree — often a willow. She was even called *lygodesma*, meaning "willow captive." One ancient coin discovered at the city of Myrrha depicts her in a tree guarded by two axe-wielding *cabiri*.[526] These were rather mysterious figures who are mentioned in the tale of the Argonauts, where they are portrayed as guardian spirits who spare sailors from the dangers of shipwreck.[527] They are depicted as residing at Colchis, the Egyptian colony on the Black Sea.

And their protection of mariners would link them, in Egyptian terms, to Isis, the patron goddess of navigators.

The original black virgin.

Diana was a black virgin, as well. And as such she was openly hostile to her suitors, slaying them if they dared venture too close to her. This links her even more closely with royal harlot priestesses such as Lilith and Circe, who were said to seduce their lovers only to slay or bewitch them. The most famous of these suitors was, of course, Orion. It was he whom she shot with her arrow from her island as he strode through the waters approaching the shore, then sent up to heaven as the famed constellation.

The image of the hero seeming to walk on water is, of course, familiar. Jesus would make it famous in a legend probably meant to re-enact this very myth.

In Orion's case, however, the ancients attributed this marvelous feat to his great height, which enabled him to stride across the sea without drowning — supposedly, the waters only reached his shoulders at their greatest depth. Once again, the hero is crossing the waters of death. All that appears to be missing from the story is an ark.

Or is it?

In fact, the picture of Orion's head and shoulders rising above the waves at the sea's deepest point recalls the ability of a boat itself to stay afloat. The vessel, too, manages to ride the crest of the ocean, even appearing to "walk" across the water at its greatest depth.

Apparently, Orion *was* the ark. And there are a number of linguistic clues that confirm this was the case.

The first has already been mentioned: It is the Hebrew word for ark, *aron*, which sounds an awful lot like the name Orion. But that's just the tip of the iceberg. Orion's claim to fame was as an archer, a word that until this point was unlikely to cause so much as a second thought. Yet now it seems suddenly remarkable that the syllable anchoring this word (so to speak) is arch or arc, which of course also denotes the mystical ship used to cross the waters of death. And it is just as remarkable to note that this particular hero's weapon of choice was the bow, another word with definite nautical implications. The bow of the ship was the place where the port and starboard components of the hull came together in a somewhat rounded point, creating the much the same curved shape assumed by the archer's bow when its string is pulled taut.

Orion was not just an archer. He was an *arker*.

As intriguing as all this is, however, the linguistic coup de gras is yet to come. It involves the Greek word for ark — which doesn't appear to be related to much of anything at first blush.

But appearances, in this case, are quite deceiving.

The word in question is *kibitos*, which is used in reference to both Noah's ark and the Ark of the Covenant in the Greek translation of the Hebrew scriptures known as the Septuagint. This word is based on the root word *kibos*, which also serves as the source of the similar-sounding word *kiborion*.[528] A bit of close scrutiny reveals that the second half of this word is identical to the name of the hero Orion, while the prefix sounds vaguely our familiar word "cup." And there's good reason for this. In fact, the word *kiborion* would enter the modern lexicon slightly altered as ciborium, a term that might not be familiar to some but which will be clearly recognizable to Catholic eyes. For it is employed in the ritual language of the church to designate the covered receptacle that contains the sanctified wafers used in the Eucharist — a receptacle that takes the shape of a cup.

The wafers, of course, are meant to represent the physical body of Christ in the mystical ceremony.

The cup therefore serves as a sort of burial casket for the metaphorical body of Jesus, performing the very same function the sacred ark did for the ancient pharaohs. Cup and ark are entirely interchangeable. Both are simply variations on the ancient vessel of the flood heroes, meant to convey them to the heavens. The tragic Greek hero Orion provides the critical link, and Orion was simply another name for the archetypal Egyptian king Osiris.

It is therefore to be expected that somehow, some way, a further Egyptian association remains to be uncovered.

Once again, the word *kiborion* holds the key. It is also a name for the lotus or water lily that grew so plentifully on the Nile. As the tide rose, the flower itself would break free from its stem and be carried away on the current like an … ark. At its center was a round mass of concentrated, yellow pollen surrounded by several thin, golden tendrils radiating outward. The impression it leaves is that of a brilliant sunburst, the golden orb and its rays springing forth in all its glory from the midst of the delicate petals. It is no wonder that the lotus was thought to bear the image of the sun god, the supreme king of all the heavens.[529]

As the sun rose anew each morning and was reborn each winter solstice, so the lotus was viewed as an eternal symbol of rebirth.

Or resurrection.

The lotus was the ark and the cup, an identification that almost certainly gave rise to the rather odd Greek tradition that the sun god Helios sailed back to his home port each evening in a great *cup* that circled the world-encompassing ocean.[530] Helios' home port was Colchis, destination of the Argonauts in their quest for the golden fleece (the original version of the lamb that was slain) and home of the willow cemetery identified with the enchantress Circe.

Once again, the mythic circle has returned to its point of origin.

Avalon

Before leaving the realm of the willow priestess, it is worth paying a call on that mysterious mage from grail lore known as Merlin, reputed to be the wisest man in all the world.

Almost as famous as his protégé King Arthur, Merlin is often depicted in the popular imagination as an aged man with white hair and a flowing beard whose dress is typically a long, dark cloak speckled with stars and crescent moons. This was exactly the sort of robe worn by the ancient high priests of Heliopolis in Egypt, whose main preoccupation was the study of the heavens.[531] Such regalia was supposedly typical of people like Merlin, who were known by trade as wizards. The term is derived from the Middle English *wisard*, which originally meant nothing more than "wise one" or "sage."

This would have made Merlin, in Egyptian terms, an *arqu*.

Merlin's tale begins with his alleged birth to a nun impregnated by a daemon. This story is, of course, rather fantastic. As the tale evolved, it was understood as a dark counterpoint to the miraculous conception of Jesus but, even more importantly, it probably hearkens back much further. The word daemon originally had no negative connotation, but merely referred to a creature of the spirit world — a fairy, ghost or even a deity.

In this light, Merlin's origins mirror those of the ancient Egyptian kings, who were conceived of a "virgin" priestess-queen and the great god Amen in human form. The ceremony in the temple at Luxor ensured the continuance of the royal bloodline through the so-called wife of god. It was she who was crucial to the succession. The identity of the father was less important — he could be practically anyone, so long as he came to her in the guise of Amen. (Such a tradition proved very convenient to usurpers and conquerors, who could graft themselves onto the royal line by fathering a child upon the queen.)

This tradition continued in Merlin, whose mother was a nun — and hence a sacred virgin. The ramifications of this are quite interesting, for if Merlin was the product of an ancient ritual designed to preserve the royal bloodline of the pharaohs, it stands to reason that he himself was a member of that bloodline. In other words, Merlin was not merely a wizard; he was a king. All of which makes his participation in Arthur's destiny all the more understandable.

According to legend, it was Merlin who arranged for Arthur to take the throne. Indeed, he orchestrated the future king's very conception in a manner that once again followed the Egyptian model. It didn't matter who the father of the king was; but the mother was essential. Hence, Merlin devised a scheme that allowed a certain Uther Pendragon to assume the form of the Duke of Cornwall for the purposes of bedding the duke's unsuspecting wife — just as the god Amen assumed the form of the pharaoh as he lay with the priestess-queen at Luxor.

The result, as in Egypt, was a future king.

Arthur.

Eventually, Merlin would orchestrate Arthur's rise to power by arranging for him to remove a sword embedded in the stone and establish the famous fellowship of the Round Table. But in the wake of these accomplishments, fortune was destined to take a sudden and painful turn for both the venerable wizard and youthful monarch he had raised to the throne. And for both men, fortune took a decidedly feminine form. In Arthur's case, she arrived as his half-sister Morgan Le Fay (sometimes known as Morgause), yet another enchantress in the mold of Circe and Lilith.

She is involved in several notable stories involving grail figures, one of which in particular is relevant here. In it, Merlin lets Arthur in on a little secret: The sword Excalibur is powerful indeed, he tells him, but its scabbard is more potent still — because it protects whoever wears it from losing any blood.[532] This is quite an amazing statement. One might expect to find such properties in a shield or breastplate, but in a scabbard? How would that protect anyone from losing blood?

Clearly, Merlin's advice was not meant to be taken in any practical sense, but rather, symbolically. The sword's phallic qualities have already been mentioned. And if the sword represented the male sex organ, it stands to reason that the scabbard must have symbolized the uncircumcised foreskin. The ritual act of circumcision caused the spilling of blood, which was impossible so long as the foreskin — or scabbard — remained intact. Morgan's role as the priestess of the circumcision (a.k.a. Circe and Lilith) is made abundantly clear when, during the course of the tale, Arthur hands her this magical "scabbard" for safekeeping.

Eventually, in other tales associated with the legend, he would succumb to her charms and lie with her — the result of their tryst being the deceitful Mordred, who would be the king's undoing. In lying with his half-sister, Arthur was doing nothing untoward. He was simply following the Egyptian precedent established in legend by the great king Osiris and adhered to so religiously by Ahmose and his successors, preserving the pure bloodline through familial conjugation.

Not only was she Arthur's sister, but Morgan was also a sister of a different sort. According to one account, she was "put to school in a nunnery, where she learned so much that she was a great clerk of necromancy."[533] In other words, she was a sister in the sense that she was a *nun*. Just as Merlin's mother had been, she was sworn to remain a virgin and give herself only to the divine male. This is very much the sort of devotion expected of nuns nowadays, but it seems that there was originally a physical component to their duties. These "sisters" were sisters of the king, just as Isis had been — and they were also his consort.

As in Egypt, these sisters devoted themselves only to divine male. Amen.

If that divinity took on physical form in the person of a king or conqueror, this was to be expected. In the case of Sister Morgan, it happened to take the form of King Arthur. There was nothing odd or unexpected about this. It was part of a ritual passed down for hundreds — even thousands of years.

Another part of this ritual was the tanist challenge in the sacred grove of the goddess. Just as Morgan was following accepted custom in seducing her half-brother Arthur, so their son Mordred was adhering to the same set of traditions when he challenged his father in battle. There was nothing particularly devious in such an act. On the contrary, it was exactly what was expected of the tanist prince (Horus) when he considered himself ready to supplant the aging monarch (Seth) as the *kher heb* or guardian priest-king in the grove of Diana.

Merlin's traditional garb of long robe studded with stars identifies him as just such a *kher heb* priest in the tradition of Heliopolis.

Because of this, Merlin too was fated to be undone by an enchantress similar to Morgan. According to a prophecy he himself had uttered, he was fated to fall in love with the sorceress variously known as Nimue, Neneve, Vivianne or Niniane, a figure who would so intoxicate him as to prove his undoing. Of course, Merlin didn't need to be particularly prescient to forecast such an event. Every king was destined to die at some point and be lain in the sacred cemetery attended by the priestess-queen who would take him to her bosom in the guise of mother earth. In Merlin's case, Nimue would bewitch him with her magic and imprison him in the trunk of a great oak tree.[534]

Obviously, Nimue was yet another manifestation of the enchantress seen elsewhere as Morgan, Lilith or Circe. And Merlin here played the part of the dead king Osiris, who likewise was entombed in the trunk of a tree. It was but the final phase of the pharaonic cycle, which began with the season of the young king Horus and continued through that of the aging king Seth to its completion in the season of the dead king.

Osiris.

This cycle corresponded to that of the so-called triple goddess, who likewise manifested herself in three phases — maiden, mother and crone. Such distinctions doubtless had their origins in the three seasons of the Egyptian year, which were reflected in both the sun and the earth. The former represented the male principle of strength, as personified in the blazing sun; the latter exemplified the feminine principle of stability to be found in the terrestrial deity of motherhood.

(Strength and stability were, it will be recalled, the names of the two great pillars on Solomon's temple.)

As the year passed, the male and female principles evolved with the seasons:

- ➢ In spring and early summer, the sun blazed down with all the glory of the new king, while the earth brought forth the bounty of its maidenhood.
- ➢ In late summer and early fall, the sun's strength began slowly to wane and the earth nourished her people with life-giving water like a mother.
- ➢ In winter, the sun seemed to perish in the darkening sky and the earth grew cold and barren like a crone.

Merlin's legend focuses on the second of these phases, when he personified the aging king, mature and full of wisdom yet declining in strength as he neared the end of life. This was the Seth period, and it is therefore no wonder that Merlin was often portrayed in terms familiar from Seth's mythology. Like other Seth figures such as Enkidu and Esau, he was extremely hairy — so much so that his appearance was said to have alarmed his parents at birth. Further connecting him with these Seth avatars, he was also associated with the wild lands and was considered a shepherd of wild animals.[535]

Moreover, in his later life (the Seth period), he was said to have retired to an island with his pet boar — a totem animal of Seth.[536]

It was during this period that he met the enchantress Vivian, who would seduce him into teaching her his magic, just as Inanna had persuaded Enki to relinquish his tablets of wisdom. As servant of the goddess, this was her role. She was Circe, Lilith, Morgan, the sacred harlot and Mary Magdalene. And she was someone else as well: As it turns out Vivian just happened to be the famed Lady of the Lake.

As such, she must have hailed from the city of Aix in southern France — the city so intimately associated with Mary Magdalene. This was the city of the waters or *l'acqs*, whose name sounds so much like that of *l'ouqsor* or Luxor, the temple of the goddess in the Egyptian capital. It was in this very temple that kings were divinely conceived by the god upon the priestess, thus preserving the royal bloodline in the same sort of ritual that would produce both Merlin and King Arthur.

And this French city also appears to have had another name. Arc.

It was this name that was born by a certain virgin who hailed from this very town and who would be burned at the stake on charges of heresy in the fifteenth century: Joan of Arc. The heresy charge was, most likely, warranted. For she appears to have modeled herself after the virgin priestesses of old whose tradition was so strong in her home region. She became, as they were, the scourge of all men — unwilling to give herself to any of them and slaying them instead in a savage fury. This was just what the goddess Diana or Artemis had done to her would-be lovers, including the unfortunate Orion, who was keeper of the ark.

Joan was, in a sense, the new Circe.

For Circe was almost certainly an archetypal priestess of the willow goddess Diana, just as Lilith was the earthly handmaiden of Inanna. Joan was only the latest in a long line of priestesses — some legendary and some historical — to serve the great divine virgin. Among them was Niniane or Nimue, the seductress who sealed the great wizard's fate in a tree.

She was the daughter of a certain Dionas (a masculine form of the name Diana) who was reputed to be the godson of this very goddess. At one point, she is said to have granted him that his firstborn female child would be so greatly coveted by "the wisest man that ever lived" that he would teach her "the most part of his wit and his cunning," withholding nothing from her.[537] Just as Enki had not withheld the *me* tablets from Inanna — a goddess whose name shares a certain resonance with that of Diana.

Niniane/Nimue is elsewhere identified as a huntress, a crucial attribute of Diana's character.[538] One commentator concluded that Niniane was a Chaldean name, linking it to the Babylonian region that once included the kingdom of Sumer.[539] This would seem to make sense in light of the fact that Niniane is a near-anagram for the name Inanna. And its variant, Nimue, may even be a feminine form of Nimrod, an ancient figure in Hebrew lore with a reputation as a "mighty hunter" of Babylon.[540] Though mentioned only briefly in the Hebrew scriptures, it is apparent from the information provided that he was no insignificant figure. For starters, he is said to have been the founder of Nineveh, destination of the flood hero Jonah. (Interestingly, Nimue is also known by at least two variant names: Niniane/Nimue which sounds an awful lot like Nineveh, and Vivianne, which also has a certain resonance with the biblical city's name.)[541]

The hero Nimrod is said to have ruled a kingdom that included several prominent Mesopotamian cities, including the city of Erech.

Or Uruk.

This was, of course, the home city of Gilgamesh. And in fact, Nimrod was often identified not only with this particular hero but also with his constellation.

Orion, the arker.

It would seem from all this that Nimrod must have been a flood hero in his own right, and the placement of his story appears to offer at least a hint of this — his short biography is the first significant piece of information (only a brief genealogical table intervenes) to appear following the story of Noah. Though the precise derivation of his name is uncertain, it closely resembles a Hebrew place name that means "clear waters." The singular version of this name was Nimrah, and the plural was Nimrim. The latter was a few miles south of the Dead Sea, in the desert of wastes of Edom — the very same wilderness to which the screech owl priestess Lilith fled after parting ways with Adam.

The name "clear waters" not only fits well with the legend of the ark hero, who had to cross the waters of death to achieve immortality, it also recalls the name *acqs*, which likewise meant "the waters." This was, of course, the homeland of Vivian/Nimue, who was known as the lady of the lake.

The name of Nimue's father, Dionas, recalls the Greek god of the vine Dionysus who was often equated with Osiris (Orion) in ancient lore. It also bears a close resemblance to that of the exiled Egyptian prince Danaus, who fled with his fifty daughters across the sea in a great ship or ark. This man and his daughters eventually landed in the city of Argos — which just happened to be the home of the Argonauts.

And it is worth noting that, just as there were fifty daughters of Danaus, so there were also fifty Argonauts.

The Fortunate Isle

During their voyage home, Jason and his crew were forced to stop at Circe's island of wailing near the mouth of the River Po to be purified by the enchantress. Had they failed to do so, the legend declared, they would have been fated to wander the seas in perpetuity.[542] The enchantress thus emerges as a crucial figure in the flood hero's quest to cross the waters of death and arrive in the paradise that lies on some far shore.

This paradise is almost always depicted as an island. In Mesopotamian lore, for example, it is known as Dilmun and is described in the following terms: "The land of Dilmun is pure; the land of Dilmun is clean." On this island, "the sick-eyed says not, 'I am sick-eyed' " and "its old man says not, 'I am an old man.' "[543] This description of the island as a place of purity and healing corresponds neatly to later descriptions of that more famous mythic isle.

Avalon.

There, another enchantress held sway. In this case, it was

Arthur's half-sister Morgan, who filled the role of Circe in the legend of the great king. This was the same Morgan who had used her skills at sorcery to seduce the unsuspecting Arthur, later bearing him a son named Mordred. It was this would-be usurper who challenged Arthur's authority in a tanist struggle that left the king gravely wounded. And, ironically, it was to Avalon — the so-called fortunate isle ruled by the "great queen" Morgan — that he was sent to recover from his wounds.

His journey there by boat, or ark, reveals that he was not merely wounded but in fact slain. Nevertheless, Morgan holds out hope that he can recover and someday return to rule his kingdom. She stretches him out on a "golden bed" and examines his wound extensively, finally declaring that he might one day be restored to health if he is allowed to remain with her for an extended time so that she might apply her healing arts.[544] The mention of healing connects Avalon directly with the legend of Dilmun. Nevertheless, Morgan's promise to restore the fallen king seems to be little more than a ruse designed to keep Arthur in her power, a suspicion apparently confirmed by the fact that he has yet to return to Britain.

Or has he?

When viewed in an Egyptian context, it is clear that Morgan is simply filling the role of Isis/Nephthys and attending the embalming of the mummified king Osiris. The golden bed referred to in the text can be nothing but the gilded mummy cases (or arks) in which the pharaohs were laid to rest. When she spoke of applying her healing arts, it was a euphemism for the embalming process that prepared the dead king to "rise again" as the *djed* column and participate in the opening-of-the-mouth ceremony that confirmed his new life.

Meanwhile, the spirit of the king passed from the *arit-hor* or chariot of Horus to the new king, who then took the reins of this great solar vehicle as the new manifestation of the sun god on earth. As the spirit of Horus passed to his new mortal body or chariot, the *arit-hor* indeed returned from the mystical isle to its earthly kingdom. Thence Horus became in every respect the once and future king, the famed title bestowed upon Arthur. It was Morgan's job as guardian of the sacred bloodline to ensure that this transfer took place and guide the fallen king to his new place in the heavenly realm as Orion.

This latter task is most likely reflected in the name of Morgan's husband, who plays a role in various other aspects of the grail cycle. He is not, of course King Arthur, whose tryst with Morgan is described as decidedly outside the bonds of matrimony. But he nonetheless bears an immediately recognizable name — Urien, which is a virtual homonym for the great constellation Orion. As consort of Urien, Mogan therefore takes on the role of the goddess Diana, the tragic would-be consort of Orion.

This parallel is confirmed decisively in Celtic myth, wherein Morgan is referred to by the name Morrigana. In this context, she is seen seducing less a figure than the great leader known as the Dagda. This incident seems to parallel her seduction of Arthur, but it is even more significant in revealing her nature as an avatar of Diana. How so? Because the Dagda was none other than the leader of the fabled Tuatha de Danaan — the people of Danaus or Diana who had crossed the sea in an ark of their own to settle on the shores of another fortunate isle.

Ireland.

Its location due west of Britain made it only natural to identify the emerald isle with the paradisiacal Avalon. The west was the land of the setting sun, signifying the daily "death" of the sun god, and was equated by the Egyptians with the land of the dead. On top of this, Ireland's reputation as a lush and verdant land must have made it seem like a garden — perhaps even the first garden planted at a place called Eden in the ancient Hebrew myth.

The story of Eden is most famous for its tale of creation and temptation involving a fruit tree. In the original tale, the fruit itself is left unnamed. Yet a tradition quickly evolved, and has persisted ever since, identifying the fruit specifically as an apple. It is therefore interesting to find that the island of Avalon was also known as the "island of apples."[545] This tree was one of two in the garden, the other of which was the so-called tree of life guarded by the cherub with the flaming sword, just as the royal *kher heb* priest guarded Diana's sacred tree in the tanist ritual. The fruit of this second tree was not named, either, but it may well also have been an apple.

Consider, in this respect, the grail story known as *Erec and Enide*.

The title itself should cause a few raised eyebrows, for the hero's name is yet another tribute to the Erech-Uruk-ark linguistic family that seems to be popping up so regularly. The heroine's name, meanwhile, is almost an anagram for that of the goddess Diana. Considering this goddess' connection to the ark hero Orion, it is no wonder that Erec and Enide are matched as consorts in this particular tale, which culminates in a great contest between the hero and another knight. It is a contest that takes place in, of all places, an apple orchard guarded by a champion sworn to slay all who enter.[546] Erec vows that he will be the first to defeat this great champion known as the red knight, who stands watch over the enchanted garden at the behest of a certain maiden. Being a hero, he of course does so, and as his reward blows a great blast on the horn that he has captured as his prize.

This episode incorporates several mythic themes set forth elsewhere. It is obviously, at its core, a tanist ritual challenge in the sacred grove of Diana. The red knight wears the color of Seth, identifying him as the aging king with whom the new champion does battle. His mistress is the goddess herself, at whose bidding he fights off challengers to his position. He also corresponds to Red Roger, the foe Robin Hood vanquishes in his final battle at the priory — or nunnery. The theme of the nunnery seen in the stories of Merlin's mother and Morgan again reasserts itself in the Robin Hood tale, wherein the great archer bleeds to death.

These nuns were the sacred sisters sworn to save their virginity for a mystical union with the god-king.

Just as Isis, the sister of Osiris, had become his bride.

The red knight's mistress in the tale of Erec was undoubtedly just such a "nun." In the course of the tale, Erec discovers her sitting on a silver bed.[547] This is a very significant detail. The word for silver in French is *argent*, which in turn derives from the Greek *argyros*. Both words contain the familiar prefix arg-, as in argonaut. It is, in other words, an ark word. And it is also at the root of one author's name for the queen of Avalon. The text in question deals with the death of King Arthur, who is quoted as saying: "I will fare to Avalun, to the fairest of all maidens, to Argante the queen, an elf most fair, and she shall make my wounds sound; make me all whole with healing draughts." [548]

In other versions of the myth, this was Morgan's job. So Argante must have been another name for Morgan.

But there is more to be said here.

The root arg- referred not only to the ship; it also meant "bright." On a knight's coat of arms, it was often depicted as white, signifying purity. This concept brings to mind at least two possible connections. The first involves the paradisiacal isle of Dilmun, the counterpart to Avalon, which is specifically described in Mesopotamian lore as "pure." The second recalls once again the concept of the pure virgin, in connection not only with the priestess nuns but also with the goddesses they served. Diana was considered a virgin; so was Isis.

Moreover, Isis was also the goddess of healing and embalming, the natural resident of an island where mortal wounds were "healed."

She was also bright.

Indeed, her star Sirius was the brightest in the nighttime sky, appearing white as it shone down but flickering like silver as it sparkled in the heavens. This star, which descended into the otherworld for seventy days each year, would naturally have been the star associated with the mystic island of Avalon. Or Dilmun. Or perhaps even the small, *white* island in the harbor of Marseilles — the city identified in the grail literature as Sarras.

It was to this seaport that the messianic grail hero Galahad traveled in what must have been yet another voyage aboard a sacred ark that crossed the waters of death. There would be no reviving him, not with the healing arts of Circe, Morgan, Argante or any other enchantress. The best she would be able to do was to prepare his corpse for burial, just as Mary Magdalene — the saint of Marseilles and southern France — sought to do with Jesus. The situation recalls vividly the lament of the Hebrew prophet Jeremiah:

> *Go up to Gilead and get balm,*
> *O virgin daughter of Egypt*
> *But you multiply remedies in vain*
> *There is no healing for you* [549]

Though the daughter of Egypt mourned for her fallen king, her healing arts could not revive him. She was Isis and he Osiris.

She was Diana and he Orion and Morgan to his Arthur. She was Mary Magdalene, and he was Jesus. She was Marian; he was Robin.

And always, the saga continued.

Stephen H. Provost

The author writes about American highways, mutant superheroes, mythic archetypes and pretty much anything he wants. A historian, philosopher, novelist and veteran journalist, he lives on the Central Coast of California. And he loves cats. Read his blogs and keep up with his latest activities at stephenhprovost.com.

Appendix

Timeline

Ancient period
(dates approximate)
2630 – Accession of Djoser, pharaoh who commissioned the step pyramid
2550 – Accession of Cheops, builder of the Great Pyramid at Giza
1730 – Accession of Hammurabi, lawgiver and king of Babylon
1720 – Hyksos era begins in Egypt
   Abraham pharaoh
   Subsequent Hyksos pharaohs include Jacob, Benjamin and Solomon
1550 – Ahmose defeats Apophis in Theban uprising
   Moses and the exodus to Palestine
   New Kingdom begins
1480 – Thutmose III conquers Megiddo
1350 – Akhenaten institutes monotheistic worship of the Aten

Age of empires
814 – Carthage founded in North Africa as Phoenician colony
776 – Rome founded
586 – Fall of Jerusalem to Babylonian forces
538 – Conquest of Babylon by Persian emperor Cyrus
525 – Persian conquest of Egypt
458 – Return of exiles to Jerusalem under Ezra
410 – Jewish temple at Elephantine destroyed, later rebuilt
404 – Egyptians launch successful war for independence
   Likely date of ultimate destruction for temple at Elephantine
333 – Alexander defeats the Persians
323 – Death of Alexander; empire eventually broken into three parts
   Kingdoms ultimately set up in Macedonia, Egypt and Syria

Maccabean period
202 – Romans destroy armies of Carthage under command of Hannibal
188 – Peace of Apamea, obligating the Seleucids to pay reparations to Rome

175 – Accession of Seleucid emperor Antiochus Epiphanes
174 – High priest Onias III slain
167 – Abomination set up in the temple at Jerusalem
164 – Temple cleansed
161 – Onias IV establishes Jewish temple in Leontopolis, Egypt
160 – Judas Maccabeus killed in battle
152 – Judas' brother Jonathan becomes high priest
134 – John Hyrcanus begins tenure of three decades as high priest
103 – Alexander Jannaeus proclaimed king and high priest

Herodian period

67 – Death of Queen Alexandra sparks civil war for succession
65 – Death of Honi the Circle-Drawer
63 – Pompey enters the temple in Jerusalem
    Beginning of Roman control in Judea
  47 – Herod appointed governor of Galilee
  44 – Assassination of Julius Caesar
  40 – Roman Senate names Herod king
  37 – Herod's armies take Jerusalem
Herod marries the first Mariamne
  31 – Octavian (Augustus) defeats Antony and Cleopatra at Actium
  29 – Mariamne executed on Herod's orders
    5 – Divorce of Herod and the second Mariamne
  Mariamne's eldest son, also named Herod, stricken from Herod's will
  4 – Joazar appointed high priest for first time
Joazar replaced as high priest
Birth of Jesus
Death of Herod; kingdom partitioned among three sons

Common Era (C.E.)

  6 – Archelaus removed as ethnarch; Roman prefect installed in Judea
    Census under Quirinius, governor of Syria
    Tax revolt orchestrated by Judas the Galilean
    Joazar made high priest by acclamation for a second time
    Joazar removed from office
  14 – Tiberius succeeds Augustus as emperor

18 – Joseph Caiaphas appointed high priest
26 – Pontius Pilate appointed prefect of Judea
34 – Philip the tetrarch dies childless
   Probable marriage of Jesus to Salome (a.k.a. Mary Magdalene)
35 – Execution of John the Baptist at Machaerus
36 – Crucifixion of Jesus at approximate age of forty
   Joseph Caiaphas removed from high priesthood
37 – Caligula succeeds Augustus as emperor
41 – Claudius succeeds Caligula
49 – Jews expelled from Rome because of riots at the "instigation of Chrestus"
54 – Nero succeeds Claudius
58 – Paul arrested after first riot in the temple, placed under Felix's protection
60 – Porcius Festus succeeds Felix as procurator
   Paul appeals to Caesar in Rome
62 – Martyrdom of James (Stephen), the messiah and brother of Jesus
67 – Jews declare independence from Rome
69 – Accession of Vespasian to emperor
70 – Roman forces retake Jerusalem
73 – Fall of Masada, last remaining stronghold of Jewish resistance
132 – Bar Kochba revolt begins; Jews declare independence from Rome
135 – Rome crushes Bar Kochba revolt

Bibliography

Akenson, David Harmon – *Surpassing Wonder*, Harcourt Brace, New York, 1998

Aldred, Cyril – *Akhenaten, King of Egypt*, Thames and Hudson, London, 1988

Allegro, John M. – *The Dead Sea Scrolls and the Christian Myth*, Prometheus Books, Amherst, N.Y., 1984

Alon, Gedaliah – *The Jews in their Land*, Harvard University Press, Cambridge, Mass., 1980

Baigent, Michael and Leigh, Richard – *The Dead Sea Scrolls Deception*, Touchstone, New York, 1991

Baigent, Michael and Leigh, Richard and Lincoln, Henry – *Holy Blood, Holy Grail*, Dell Publishing, New York, 1982

Baigent, Michael and Leigh, Richard and Lincoln, Henry – *The Messianic Legacy*, Dell Publishing, New York, 1986

Baring, Anne and Cashford, Jules – *The Myth of the Goddess*, Penguin, London, 1993

Barker, Kenneth – *NIV Study Bible*, Zondervan, Grand Rapids, Mich., 1995

Barnstone, Willis – *The Other Bible*, Harper and Row, San Francisco, 1984

Bauval, Robert and Gilbert, Adrian – *The Orion Mystery*, Three Rivers Press, New York, 1994

Begg, Ean – *The Cult of the Black Virgin*, Arkana Penguin Books, New York, 1996

Best, Robert M. – *Noah's Ark and the Ziusudra Epic*, Enlil Press, Fort Myers, Fla., 1999

Bialik, Hayim Nahman and Ravnitzky, Yehoshua Hana – *The Book of Legends*, Schocken, 1992

Black, Jeremy and Green, Anthony – *Gods, Demons and Symbols of Ancient Mesopotamia*, University of Texas Press, Austin, 1997

Bonwick, James – *Irish Druids and Old Irish Religions*, Dorset Press, 1986

Bowersock, G.W. – *Roman Arabia*, Harvard University Press, Cambridge, Mass., 1983

Brown, Raymond L. – *Death of the Messiah* (two volumes), Doubleday, New York, 1994

Bruce, F.F. – *Israel and the Nations*, InterVarsity Press, Downers Grove, Ill., 1997

Bruce, F.F. – *New Testament History*, Doubleday, New York, 1969

Budge, E.A. Wallis – *The Book of the Dead*, Gramercy Books, New York, 1999

Budge, E.A. Wallis – *Egyptian Language*, Dover Publications Inc., New York, 1983

Budge, E.A. Wallis – *Legends of the Egyptian Gods*, Dover Publications Inc., New York, 1994

Bunson, Margaret – *A Dictionary of Ancient Egypt*, Oxford University Press, New York, 1991

Campbell, Joseph – *The Hero With a Thousand Faces*, MJF Books, New York, 1949

Campbell, Joseph – *Occidental Mythology*, Arkana Penguin Books, 1964

Charlesworth, James – *Old Testament Pseudepigrapha* (two volumes), Doubleday, New York, 1993

Clark, R.T. Rundle – *Myth and Symbol in Ancient Egypt*, Thames and Hudson, New York, 1959

Clark, Rosemary – The Sacred Tradition in Ancient Egypt, Llewellyn Publications, St. Paul, Minn., 2000

Coghlan, Ronan – *Book of Irish Names*, Sterling Publishing Co. Inc., New York, 1989

Collier, Mark and Manley, Bill – *How to Read Egyptian Hieroglyphs*, University of California Press, Berkeley, 1998

Collins, John H. – *Apocalypticism in the Dead Sea Scrolls, Routledge*, New York, 1997

Colum, Pedraic – *Nordic Gods and Heroes*, Dover Publications Inc., New York, 1996

Coogan, Michael David – *Stories from Ancient Canaan*, Westminster Press, Louisville, Ky., 1978

Crane, Frank – *Lost Books of the Bible and the Forgotten Books of Eden*, William Collins, 1926

Crossley-Holland, Kevin – *The Norse Myths*, Pantheon Books, New York, 1980

Crosson, John Dominic – *The Birth of Christianity*, HarperCollins, San Francisco, 1998

Crosson, John Dominic – *The Historical Jesus*, HarperCollins, San Francisco, 1991

Crosson, John Dominic – *Who Killed Jesus?*, HarperCollins, San Francisco, 1996

Currid, John D. – *Ancient Egypt and the Old Testament*, Baker Books, Grand Rapids, Mich., 1997

Davidson, H.R. Ellis – *Gods and Myths of Northern Europe*, Penguin, London, 1990

Davidson, H.R. Ellis – *Myths and Symbols in Pagan Europe*, Syracuse University Press, N.Y., 1988

De Boron, Robert – *Joseph of Arimathea*, Rudolf Steiner Press, London, 1990

De Santillana, Giorgio and Von Dechend, Hertha, *Hamlet's Mill*, David R. Godine, Boston, 1977

Doherty, Earl – The Jesus Puzzle, *Canadian Humanist Publications*, Ottawa, Canada, 1999

Durant, Will – *Christ and Caesar*, MJF Books, New York, 1971
Eisenman, Robert and Wise, Michael – *The Dead Sea Scrolls Uncovered*, Element Books, Rockport, Mass., 1992
Eisenman, Robert – *James the Brother of Jesus*, Viking Penguin, New York, 1996
Ellis, Ralph – *Jesus, Last of the Pharaohs*, Edfu Books, Dorset, 1998
Eusebius – The History of the Church, Penguin Books, New York, 1965
Ewing, Upton Clary – The Prophet of the Dead Sea Scrolls, Tree of Life Publications, Joshua Tree, Calif., 1993
Finegan, Jack – Handbook of Biblical Chronology, Hendrickson Publishers, Peabody, Mass., 1964
Finegan, Jack – *Myth and Mystery*, Baker Books, Grand Rapids, Mich., 1989
Fox, Robin Lane – *The Unauthorized Version*, Alfred A. Knopf, New York, 1992
Frazer, James – *The Golden Bough*, Wordsworth, Ware, Hertfordshire, 1993
Freedman, David Noel – *Anchor Bible Dictionary* (six volumes), Doubleday, New York, 1992
Freke, Timothy and Gandy, Peter – *The Jesus Mysteries*, Harmony Books, New York, 1999
Frend, W.H.C. – *The Rise of Christianity*, Fortress Press, Philadelphia, 1984
Fricke, Weddig – *The Court-Martial of Jesus*, Grove Weidenfeld, New York, 1987
Friedman, Richard Elliott – *Who Wrote the Bible?*, Summit Books, New York, 1987
Gadalla, Moustafa – *Historical Deception: The Untold Story of Ancient Egypt*, Tehuti Research Foundation, Greensboro, N.C., 1999
Gardner, Laurence – *Bloodline of the Holy Grail*, Element Books, Boston, 1996
Gardner, Laurence – *Genesis of the Grail Kings*, Element Books, Boston, 2000
Gardiner, Alan – *Egypt of the Pharaohs*, Oxford University Press, New York, 1961
Ginzberg, Louis – *Legends of the Jews* (four volumes), Johns Hopkins University Press, Baltimore, Md., 1998
Goodman, Martin – *The Ruling Class of Judaea*, Cambridge University Press, New York, 1987
Goodrich, Norma Lorre – *The Holy Grail*, HarperCollins, New York, 1992
Goodrich, Norma Lorre – *Merlin*, HarperCollins, New York, 1988
Goodrick, Edward W. and Kohlenberger, John R. III – *Zondervan NIV Exhaustive Concordance*, second edition, Zondervan, Grand Rapids, Mich., 1999
Gould, Charles – *Mythical Monsters*, Senate, London, 1995

Graves, Robert – *The Greek Myths* (two volumes), Penguin, London, 1960
Graves, Robert and Patai, Rafael – *Hebrew Myths*, Greenwich House,
    New York, 1983
Graves, Robert – *King Jesus*, Noonday Press, New York, 1946
Graves, Robert – *The White Goddess*, Farrar, Straus and Giroux,
    New York, 1948
Green, Joel B. and McKnight, Scot and Marshall, I. Howard –
Dictionary of Jesus and the Gospels, InterVarsity Press,
    Downers Grove, Ill., 1992
Green, Roger Lancelyn – *Tales of Ancient Egypt*, Puffin Books,
    New York, 1967
Greenberg, Gary – *The Bible Myth*, Carol Publishing, Secaucus, N.J., 1996
Greenberg, Gary – *101 Myths of the Bible*, Sourcebooks Inc.,
    Naperville, Ill., 2000
Guest, Charlotte E. – *The Mabinogion*, Dover Publications,
Mineola, N.Y., 1997
Hancock, Graham and Bauval, Robert – *The Message of the Sphinx*,
    Three Rivers Press, New York, 1996
Hancock, Graham – *The Sign and the Seal*, Touchstone,
New York, 1992
Harrington, Daniel – *The Maccabean Revolt*, Michael Glazier,
    Wilmington, Del., 1988
Helms, Randel – *Gospel Fictions*, Prometheus Books,
Amherst, N.Y., 1988
Hengel, Martin – *The Zealots*, T&T Clark Ltd., Edinburgh, 1989
Herm, Gerhard – *The Phoenicians*, William Morrow and Company,
    New York, 1975
Herodotus – *The Histories*, Penguin, London, 1996
Holt, J.C. – *Robin Hood*, Thames and Hudson, New York, 1989
House, H. Wayne – Chronological and Background Charts of the
    New Testament, Zondervan, Grand Rapids, Mich., 1981
Jacobs, Joseph – *Favorite Celtic Fairy Tales*, Dover Publications Inc.,
    New York, 1994
Johnson, Paul – *A History of Christianity*, Atheneum, New York, 1980
Jung, Emma and von Franz, Marie-Louise, *The Grail Legend*,
    Princeton University Press, N.J., 1998
Kane, Matt – *Heavens Unearthed*, Golden Egg Books, Altoona, Pa., 1999
Keller, Werner – *The Bible as History*, Barnes and Noble Books, New York, 1995
Kemp, Barry J. – *Ancient Egypt*, Routledge, New York, 1989
Kirsch, Jonathan – *The Harlot by the Side of the Road*, Ballantine Books,
    New York, 1997
Kirsch, Jonathan – *Moses: A Life*, Ballantine Books, New York, 1998
Klingaman, William K. – *The First Century*, HarperCollins, 1990
Knight, Christopher and Lomas, Robert – *The Hiram Key*,
    Element Books, Rockport, Mass., 1998

Knight, Christopher and Lomas, Robert – *The Second Messiah*,
    Element Books, Boston, 1998
Kramer, Samuel Noah – *The Sumerians*, University of Chicago Press, 1963
Layton, Bentley – *The Gnostic Scriptures*, Doubleday, New York, 1987
Leeming, David Adams – *The World of Myth*, Oxford University Press,
    New York, 1990
List, Robert N. – *Merlin's Secret*, University Press of America Inc., Lanham, Md.,
1999
Lockhart, Douglas – *The Dark God*, Element Books, Boston, 1999
Lockhart, Douglas – *Jesus the Heretic*, Element Books,
    Rockport, Mass., 1997
Loomis, Richard Sherman – *The Grail*, Princeton University Press,
    N.J., 1991
Maccoby, Hyam – *The Mythmaker*, HarperCollins, San Francisco, 1986
Mackillop, James – *Oxford Dictionary of Celtic Mythology*, Oxford
    University Press, Oxford, 1998
Martin, Ralph P. and Davids, Peter H. – *Dictionary of the Later New
    Testament*, InterVarsity Press, Downers Grove, Ill., 1997
    Mason, Steve – Josephus and the New Testament, Hendrickson
Publishers, Peabody, Mass., 1992
Massey, Gerald – *The Historical Jesus and the Mythical Christ*,
    The Book Tree, Escondido, Calif., 2000
Matthews, Caitlin and John – *Ladies of the Lake*, Thorsons, London, 1992
Matthews, John – *The Druid Source Book*, Blandford Books, London, 1997
Matthews, John – *The Elements of the Grail Tradition*, Element Books,
    Rockport, Mass., 1990
Matthews, Victor H. and Benjamin, Don C. – Old Testament Parallels,
    Paulist Press, New York, 1997
Mead, G.R.S. – *Gnostic John the Baptizer*, Kessinger Publishing, Montana
Mead, G.R.S. – *Simon Magus*, Kessinger Publishing, Montana
Meyer, Marvin W. – *The Ancient Mysteries*, HarperCollins,
    San Francisco, 1987
Moffett, Samuel Hugh – *A History of Christianity in Asia*, Vol. 1, Orbis,
    Maryknoll, N.Y., 1998
Morenz, Siegfried – *Egyptian Religion*, Cornell University Press, Ithaca,
    N.Y., 1960
Morford, Mark P.O. and Lenardon, Robert J. – *Classical Mythology*,
    Longman, New York, 1985
Nadich, Judah – *The Legends of the Rabbis*, Vol. 1, Jason Aronson Inc.,
    Northvale, N.J., 1994
Nodet, Etienne and Taylor, Justin – *The Origins of Christianity*, Liturgical
    Press, Collegeville, Minn., 1998
Pagels, Elaine – *The Origin of Satan*, Vintage Books, New York, 1995
Patai, Rafael – *The Hebrew Goddess*, Wayne State University Press,
    Detroit, 1990

Picknett, Lynn and Prince, Clive – *The Templar Revelation*, Touchstone, New York, 1997
Pritchard, James B. – *The Ancient Near East*, Vol. I, Princeton University Press, N.J., 1958
Quirke, Stephen – *Ancient Egyptian Religion*, Dover Publications Inc., New York, 1992
Rabinowitz, Jacob – *The Faces of God*, Spring Publications, Woodstock, Conn., 1998
Redford, Donald B. – *Egypt, Canaan and Israel in Ancient Times*, Princeton University Press, N.J., 1992
Regula, DeTraci – *The Mysteries of Isis*, Llewellyn Publications, St. Paul, Minn., 1996
Richardson, Peter – *Herod*, University of South Carolina Press, 1996
Roberts, Alexander and Donaldson, James – *The Ante-Nicene Fathers*, Vol. VIII, Eerdmans Publishing, Grand Rapids, Mich., 1986
Rohl, David M. – *Pharaohs and Kings*, Crown Publishers Inc., New York, 1995
S, Acharya – *The Christ Conspiracy*, Adventures Unlimited Press, Kempton, Ill., 1999
Salibi, Kamal – *Who Was Jesus?*, I.B. Tauris and Co. Ltd., London, 1998
Sarna, Nahum M. – *Exploring Exodus*, Schocken Books, New York, 1996
Schneemelcher, Wilhelm – *New Testament Apocrypha* (two volumes), Westminster/John Knox Press, Louisville, Ky. 1991
Schonfield, Hugh – *The Essene Odyssey*, Element Books, Rockport, Mass., 1984
Schonfield, Hugh – *The Mystery of the Messiah*, Open Gate Press, London, 1998
Schonfield, Hugh – *The Passover Plot*, Element Books, Rockport, Mass., 1965
Shaw, Ian – *The Oxford History of Ancient Egypt*, Oxford University Press, New York, 2000
Smith, Morton – *Jesus the Magician*, Seastone, Berkeley, Calif., 1998
Spence, Lewis – *Ancient Egyptian Myths and Legends*, Dover Publications Inc., New York, 1990
Suetonius – *The Twelve Caesars*, Penguin, London, 1989
Starbird, Margaret – *The Goddess in the Gospels*, Bear and Co., Santa Fe, N.M., 1998
Starbird, Margaret – *The Woman with the Alabaster Jar*, Bear and Co., San Francisco, 1993
Steiger, Brad – *Worlds Before Our Own*, Berkley Publishing, 1978
Stewart, Desmond – *The Foreigner*, Hamish Hamilton, London, 1981
Stone, Merlin – *When God Was a Woman*, Harvest Books, Orlando, Fla., 1976
Strong, James – *Strong's Exhaustive Concordance*, Crusade Bible Publishers Inc., Nashville
Tacitus – *The Annals of Imperial Rome*, Penguin, London, 1989

Tacitus – *The Histories*, Oxford University Press, Oxford, 1997
Tatar, Maria – *The Classic Fairy Tales*, W.W. Norton, New York, 1999
Temple, Robert – *The Sirius Mystery*, Destiny Books, Rochester, Vt., 1998
Tenney, Merrill C. – *New Testament Survey*, Wm. B. Eerdmans, Grand Rapids, Mich., 1985
Thiering, Barbara – *Jesus and the Riddle of the Dead Sea Scrolls*, HarperCollins, San Francisco, 1992
Thompson, R. Campbell – *Semitic Magic*, Samuel Weiser Inc., 2000
Thompson, Thomas L. – *The Mythic Past*, Basic Books, 1999
Tresidder, Jack – *Dictionary of Symbols*, Chronicle Books, San Francisco, 1998
Ulansky, David – *Origins of the Mithraic Mysteries*, Oxford University Press, New York, 1989
Verbrugghe, Gerald P. and Wickersham, John – *Berossos and Manetho Introduced and Translated*, University of Michigan, 1996
Vermes, Geza – *The Dead Sea Scrolls in English*, Penguin, New York, 1995
Vermes, Geza – *Jesus the Jew*, Fortress Press, Philadelphia, 1973
Visalli, Gayla – *After Jesus*, Reader's Digest Association Inc., Pleasantville, N.Y., 1992
Von Eschenbach, Wolfram – *Parzival*, Penguin Books, New York, 1980
Walker, Barbara – *Woman's Dictionary of Symbols and Sacred Objects*, HarperCollins, San Francisco, 1988
Walker, Barbara – *Woman's Encycolpedia of Myths and Secrets*, HarperCollins, San Francisco, 1983
Ward, Kaari – *Jesus and His Times*, Reader's Digest Association Inc., Pleasantville, N.Y., 1990
Webster's Dictionary of the English Language Unabridged, Encyclopedia Edition, Publishers International Press, New York, 1977
Weston, Jessie L. – *From Ritual to Romance*, Dover Publications, Mineola, N.Y., 1997
Whitson, William – *The Works of Josephus*, Hendrickson Publishers, 1987
Willis, Roy – *Dictionary of World Myth*, Duncan Baird, London, 2000
Witt, R.E. – *Isis in the Ancient World*, Johns Hopkins University Press, Baltimore, 1971
Wolkstein, Diane and Kramer, Samuel Noah – *Inanna*, Harper and Row, New York, 1993
Wylen, Stephen M. – *The Jews in the Time of Jesus,* Paulist Press, New York, 1996
Yonge, C.D. – *The Works of Philo*, Hendrickson Publishers, 1997
Young, George M. – *Goddess on the Cross*, Capall Bann Publishing, Freshfields, England, 1999

1. John 20:13
2. Roger Lancelyn Green, *Tales of Ancient Egypt*, p. 11
3. John 1:9
4. Green, *Tales of Ancient Egypt*, p. 10
5. Green, *Tales of Ancient Egypt*, p. 23
6. Lewis Spence, *Ancient Egyptian Myths and Legends*, p. 137
7. Gen. 3:4-5
8. Gen. 3:7
9. Gen. 12:10-20
10. Donald B. Redford, *Egypt, Canaan and Palestine in Ancient Times*, p. 108
11. Gen. 21:8-10
12. Gen. 16:12
13. Gen. 2:5
14. Gen. 27:22
15. Gen. 28:13-14
16. Gary Greenberg, *The Bible Myth*, p. 233
17. Gen. 27:41
18. Gen. 28:1
19. Gen. 27:29
20. R. Campbell Thompson, *Semitic Magic*, p. LVI
21. Gen. 31:53
22. Gen. 6:1-4
23. Gen. 32:1
24. Gen. 32:3
25. Gen. 32:26
26. Gen. 32:26
27. Gen. 32:30
28. Gen. 33:1
29. Gen. 33:9
30. Gen. 33:15
31. Gen. 36:2, 19, 25
32. Gen. 37:8
33. Gen. 39:6
34. Gen. 39:7
35. James B. Pritchard, *The Ancient Near East Vol. 1: An Anthology of Texts and Pictures*, p. 15
36. James B. Pritchard, *The Ancient Near East Vol. 1: An Anthology of Texts and Pictures*, p. 13
37. James B. Pritchard, *The Ancient Near East Vol. 1: An Anthology of Texts and Pictures*, p. 15
38. James B. Pritchard, *The Ancient Near East Vol. 1: An Anthology of Texts and Pictures*, p. 15
39. John 13:33
40. John 3:14
41. 1 Cor. 11:24
42. Herodotus, *The Histories*, 2:148
43. David M. Rohl, *Pharaohs and Kings*, p. 347
44. Gen. 42:2
45. Gen. 42:4
46. Gen. 41:49
47. Gen. 47:21
48. Gen. 42:9
49. Gen. 44:9
50. Prov. 16:18
51. 1 Kings 10:21
52. 1 Kings 11:3
53. 1 Kings 10:26, 22
54. 1 Kings 10:23-24
55. Thomas L. Thompson, *The Mythic Past*, p. 166

[56] Sir Alan Gardiner, *Egypt of the Pharaohs*, p. 163
[57] Donald B. Redford, *Egypt, Canaan and Israel in Ancient Times*, p. 120
[58] Gardiner, p. 163
[59] Redford, p. 120
[60] Redford, p. 122
[61] Redford, p. 109
[62] Margaret Bunson, *A Dictionary of Ancient Egypt*, p. 71
[63] 1 Kings 11:42
[64] Redford, p. 122
[65] James H. Charlesworth, *Old Testament Apocrypha, Vol. 2*, The Life of Adam and Eve, p. 294
[66] Ex. 31:18
[67] Nah. 1:3
[68] Ps. 83:15
[69] Jer. 23:19, 30:23
[70] Zech. 10:1
[71] Job 38:1, 40:6
[72] Job 36:30-31, 33
[73] Prov. 1:7
[74] Judges 8:33
[75] Ex. 19:16
[76] Judges 5:4-5
[77] Michael David Coogan, *Stories from Ancient Canaan*, p. 21
[78] Ps. 48:2
[79] 2 Sam. 23:3-4
[80] Matt. 6:29
[81] Louis Ginzberg, *Legends of the Bible*, Vol. IV, p. 157
[82] Lewis Spence, *Ancient Egyptian Myths and Legends*, p. 291-2
[83] Ginzberg, p. 159
[84] Werner Keller, *The Bible as History*, p. 108
[85] Keller, p. 109
[86] Christopher Knight and Robert Lomas, *The Hiram Key*, p. 134-135
[87] Gardner, p. 166
[88] Bunson, p. 159
[89] Gardiner, p. 167
[90] Ibid
[91] Ibid
[92] Gardner, p. 168
[93] Gardner, p. 167
[94] Philo, *On the Life of Moses*, 1:27
[95] Eusebius, *Preparatio Evangelica*, 9:27:4-6
[96] Ex. 1:12-14
[97] Ginzberg, Vol. II, p. 272-4
[98] Ginzberg, Vol. II, p. 285
[99] Ex. 34:29
[100] Ex. 33:20
[101] Gen. 1:2
[102] Shabaka inscription 1:55
[103] Gen. 2:24
[104] Gen. 2:7
[105] R.T. Rundle Clark, *Myth and Symbol in Ancient Egypt*, p. 37
[106] Rundle Clark, p. 40-41
[107] Deut. 5:2
[108] Bunson, p. 9
[109] Ex. 4:24-26
[110] Ex. 3:1-3
[111] Rundle Clark, p. 248
[112] Rundle Clark, p. 247

[113] John 1:1-5
[114] John 5:46
[115] Rundle Clark, p. 246
[116] Lewis Spence, *Ancient Egyptian Myths and Legends*, p. 106
[117] Ex. 2:19
[118] Ginzberg, Legends of the Jews Vol. II, p. 286-7
[119] Bunson, p. 8
[120] 1 Kings 10:1
[121] Song 1:5-6
[122] Ant. 8:165
[123] Matt. 12:42
[124] Ginzberg, Vol. II, p. 283
[125] Lynn Picknett and Clive Prince, *The Templar Revelation*, p. 328
[126] 1 Kings 7:8
[127] Ean Begg, *The Cult of the Black Virgin*, p. 31
[128] Herodotus, The Histories, 2:73 (p. 112)
[129] Num. 12:1
[130] Graham Hancock, *The Sign and the Seal*, p. 18
[131] Redford, p. 128
[132] Pritchard, *ANET*, p. 5
[133] Pritchard, *ANET*, p. 7
[134] Deut. 1:25
[135] Num. 13:23
[136] Num. 13:33
[137] Gen. 6:4
[138] 1 Sam. 17:10
[139] Rev. 16:16
[140] 2 Sam. 10
[141] Neh. 11:1
[142] Gayla Vasalli, *After Jesus*, p. 73
[143] 2 Sam. 24:21
[144] Moustafa Gadalla, *Historical Deception*, p. 149
[145] Pritchard, *ANET*, p. 177
[146] Num. 10:35-36
[147] Ex. 25:8
[148] Jos. 4:11
[149] Budge, *Book of the Dead*, p. 316, 599
[150] Gen. 15:15
[151] 2 Chron. 34:28
[152] Budge, *Book of the Dead*, p. 94
[153] Redford, p. 128
[154] Redford, p.128
[155] Anchor Bible Dictionary, Vol. II, p. 703
[156] Ex. 14:3
[157] Ex. 14:25-28
[158] Ex. 16:3
[159] Ex. 17:3
[160] 1 Cor. 15:22, 45
[161] Josh. 10:12-14
[162] Ps. 78:49
[163] David Rohl, Pharaohs and Kings, p. 288
[164] 2 Chron. 3:15-17
[165] Christopher Knight and Robert Lomas, *The Hiram Key*, p. 102
[166] Ex. 13:21
[167] Plutarch, History of Isis and Osiris 15
[168] Josephus, Against Apion 1:265
[169] Ex. 17:15

[170] Anchor Bible Dictionary, Vol. I, p. 1
[171] Herodotus, *Histories*, 2:4
[172] Greenberg, *The Bible Myth*, p. 233
[173] Mark P.O. Mumford and Robert J. Lenardon, *Classical Mythology*, Third Edition, p.277
[174] James B. Pritchard, *The Ancient Near East*, Vol. 1, p. 66
[175] Gen. 6:19
[176] Pritchard, The Ancient Near East, Vol. 1, p. 70; Gen. 8:6-11, 20
[177] Graham Hancock and Robert Bauval, *The Message of the Sphinx*, p. 35
[178] Gen. 8:4
[179] Gen. 10:10
[180] *Anchor Bible Dictionary*, Vol. II, p. 572
[181] Gen. 11:7
[182] Gen. 11:4
[183] Robert Bauval and Adrian Gilbert, *The Orion Mystery*, p. 121-22
[184] Heb. 9:4
[185] Num. 17:8
[186] Pyramid Text 632, quoted in Bauval and Gilbert, *The Orion Mystery*, p. 222
[187] Koran 10:92
[188] E.A. Wallis Budge, *The Book of the Dead*, p. 248
[189] Pyramid Texts 11-13, quoted in Bauval and Gilbert, *The Orion Mystery*, p. 205
[190] 1 Kings 11:7
[191] Epic of Gilgamesh, Tablet VI, quoted in James B. Pritchard, *The Ancient Near East*, Vol. 1, p. 54-5
[192] E.A. Wallis Budge, *Book of the Dead*, p. 248
[193] Gilbert and Bauval, *The Orion Mystery*, p. 147
[194] Matt. 16:19
[195] Norma Lorre Goodrich, *The Holy Grail*, p. 30
[196] Gen. 4:12
[197] Gen. 4:14
[198] Gen. 4:15
[199] Mark 15:36
[200] Matt. 12:20
[201] Gen. 50:3
[202] Ex. 34:28
[203] 1 Kings 1:38
[204] Gen. 2:13
[205] Laurence Gardner, *Genesis of the Grail Kings*, p. 2
[206] John 3:3
[207] Zech. 9:9
[208] 1 Kings 1:40
[209] Matt. 28:2
[210] Gen. 25:20
[211] Gen. 26:34
[212] Acts 7:23
[213] Josh. 14:7
[214] 2 Sam. 2:10
[215] Judges 3:13, 8:28
[216] 2 Chron. 16:13
[217] 1 Chron. 29:27, 9:30
[218] Song 3:11
[219] R.T. Rundle Clark, *Myth and Symbol in Ancient Egypt*, p. 118
[220] John 12:24
[221] Luke 20:9-15
[222] Matt. 13:30
[223] R.T. Rundle Clark, *Myth and Symbol in Ancient Egypt*, p. 102
[224] Matt. 9:38
[225] Coffin Texts 4:269, quoted in R.T. Rundle Clark, *Myth and Symbol in Ancient Egypt*, p. 118-119

[226] John 15:1
[227] Gen. 3:4
[228] Gen. 4:22
[229] Gen. 2:9
[230] *Anchor Bible Dictionary*, Vol. II, p. 806
[231] *Anchor Bible Dictionary*, Vol. IV, p. 511
[232] Ex. 16:4
[233] Ex. 16:33-34, Heb. 9:4
[234] R.T. Rundle Clark, *Myth and Symbol in Ancient Egypt*, p. 118
[235] John 6:32-33, 35
[236] John 6:54
[237] Acts 2:13
[238] James Frazer, *The Golden Bough*, p. 380-381
[239] Gen. 49:10-11
[240] James Frazer, *The Golden Bough*, p. 380
[241] Gos. Pet. 10
[242] Is. 14:12
[243] Is. 14:12-15
[244] Michael David Coogan, *Stories from Ancient Canaan*, p. 111
[245] Norma Lorre Goodrich, *The Holy Grail*, p. 271
[246] Wolfram Von Eschenbach, *Parzival*, p. 239
[247] Robert Bauval and Adrian Gilbert, *The Orion Mystery*, p. 203
[248] Graham Hancock, *The Sign and the Seal*, p. 68
[249] Wolfram Von Eschenbach, Parzival, p. 239
[250] 1 Clement 12:6
[251] Mark 12:10
[252] Wolfram Von Eschenbach, *Parzival*, p. 239
[253] Graham Hancock, *The Sign and the Seal*, p. 58
[254] John Matthews, *The Elements of the Grail Tradition*, p. 51
[255] Budge, *Egyptian Language*, p. 62
[256] Robert N. List, *Merlin's Secret*, p. 44
[257] Roger Sherman Loomis, *The Grail*, p. 51
[258] Budge, *The Book of the Dead*, p. 622
[259] Gen. 28:18
[260] Emma Jung and Marie-Louise von Franz, *The Grail Legend*, p. 83-84
[261] Gen. 28:13, 14
[262] Jer. 8:22
[263] Roger Sherman Loomis, *The Grail*, p. 31
[264] Budge, *Egyptian Language*, p. 70
[265] Song 6:5
[266] Roger Sherman Loomis, *The Grail*, p. 106
[267] Jung and Von Franz, *The Grail Legend*, p. 105
[268] Loomis, *The Grail*, p. 213
[269] John 8:58
[270] James Mackillop, Oxford Dictionary of Celtic Mythology, p. 424
[271] Plutarch, *The History of Isis and Osiris*, 19
[272] *The Mabinogion*, p. 22
[273] John Matthews, *Elements of the Grail Tradition*, p. 17
[274] John Matthews, *Elements of the Grail Tradition*, p. 17
[275] John 19:34
[276] Mark Collier and Bill Manley, *How to Read Egyptian Hieroglyphs*, p. 160
[277] Gerald Massey, *The Historical Jesus and the Mythical Christ*, p. 25
[278] E.A. Wallis Budge, *Egyptian Language*, p. 80, 69
[279] Luke 5:6-7
[280] Mark 6:38-44
[281] G.R.S. Mead, *The Gnostic John the Baptizer*, p. 17
[282] Massey, *The Historical Jesus and the Mythical Christ*, p. 21

[283] Matt. 12:40
[284] 2 Kings 2:5
[285] Pyramid texts 134d and 604e-f, quoted in Siegfried Morenz, *Egyptian Religion*, p. 39
[286] James Frazer, *The Golden Bough*, p. 1-2
[287] Heb. 4:14
[288] David Rohl, Pharaohs and Kings, p. 13
[289] John 14:3
[290] John 14:2
[291] Budge, *Book of the Dead*, p. 268-9
[292] Ps. 23:4
[293] Margaret Starbird, *The Woman with the Alabaster Jar*, p. 115
[294] Gen. 27:31
[295] Rober N. List, *Merlin's Secret*, p. 234
[296] Job 20:25
[297] Gen. 49:14
[298] Judges 5:17
[299] Gen. 49:21
[300] Cyril Aldred, Akhenaten, *King of Egypt*, p. 135
[301] 2 Kings 23:6
[302] Timothy Freke and Peter Gandy, *The Jesus Mysteries*, p. 52
[303] Gal. 6:24-25
[304] 2 Cor. 4:7
[305] Cyril Aldred, Akhenaten, *King of Egypt*, p. 172
[306] Matt. 27:46-50
[307] Rev. 1:7
[308] Bunson, *A Dictionary of Ancient Egypt*, p. 38
[309] John 1:5, 9
[310] Is. 9:2
[311] Mal. 4:2
[312] Herodotus, *The Histories*, 2:86
[313] Gerald Massey, *The Historical Jesus and the Mythical Christ*, p. 98
[314] John 19:40-41
[315] Mark 15:46
[316] Wilhelm Schneemelcher, *New Testament Apocrypha*, Vol. 1, p. 466
[317] Matt. 27:61
[318] Gen. 3:19
[319] DeTraci Regula, *The Mysteries of Isis*, p. 103
[320] Ex. 3:6
[321] Gen. 14:6
[322] Deut. 1:2
[323] Bentley Layton, *The Gnostic Scriptures*, p. 73
[324] Charlesworth, *Old Testament Pseudepigrapha*, Vol. II, p. 294
[325] Layton, *The Gnostic Scriptures*, p. 72-3
[326] Collier and Manley, *How to Read Egyptian Hieroglyphs*, p. 155
[327] Aldred, *Akhenaten, King of Egypt*, p. 243
[328] Pritchard, *The Ancient Near East*, Vol. 1, p. 266
[329] Bunson, *A Dictionary of Ancient Egypt*, p. 249
[330] Ginzberg, *Legends of the Jews*, p. 283
[331] 2 Chron. 34:14
[332] 2 Chron. 34:21
[333] 2 Kings 23:5
[334] Gerald Verbrugghe and John Wickersham, *Berossos and Manetho Introduced and Translated*, p.134
[335] Bauval and Gilbert, The Orion Mystery, p. 46, 252
[336] Brad Steiger, *Worlds Before Our Own*, p. 117
[337] Herodotus 2:124
[338] Cyril Aldred, *Akhenaten: King of Egypt*, p. 295

[339] Josephus, *Against Apion*, 1:130
[340] Robert M. Best, *Noah's Ark and the Ziusudra Epic*, p. 166
[341] Atrahasis Epic, fragment RS 22.421, quoted in Best, *Noah's Ark and the Zisudra Epic*, p. 27
[342] Syncellus, *Chronological Excerpts*, 55, in Verbrrugghe and Wickersham, *Berossus and Manetho*, p. 50
[343] Roy Willis, *Dictionary of World Myth*, p. 69
[344] Gen. 5:24
[345] Syncellus, *Chronological Excerpts*, 55 in Verbruggen and Wickersham, *Berossos and Manetho*, p. 50
[346] Best, *Noah's Ark and the Ziusudra Epic*, p. 70
[347] 1 Enoch 15:1
[348] Roy Willis, *Dictionary of World Myth*, p. 148
[349] Willis, *Dictionary of World Myth*, p. 80
[350] Robert Temple, *The Sirius Mystery*, p. 291
[351] Gen. 8:22
[352] Charles Gould, *Mythical Monsters*, p. 368-70
[353] 1 Enoch 24:2, 25:3
[354] Ziusudra 257, quoted in Best, *Noah's Ark and the Ziusudra Epic*, p. 258
[355] Deut. 34:6
[356] Kamal Salibi, *Who Was Jesus?*, p. 142
[357] Deut. 25:5-6
[358] Mark 6:3
[359] Steiger, *Worlds Before Our Own*, p. 117
[360] Best, *Noah's Ark and the Ziusudra Epic*, p. 42
[361] Frazer, *Golden Bough*, p. 126
[362] Is. 11:1
[363] *A Gest of Robin Hode* 249, quoted in Holt, *Robin Hood*, p. 19
[364] Holt, *Robin Hood*, p. 50
[365] DeTraci Regula, *The Mysteries of Isis*, p. 54
[366] Regula, *The Mysteries of Isis*, p. 77
[367] Ean Begg, *The Cult of the Black Virgin*, p. 62
[368] R.E. Witt, *Isis and the Ancient World*, p. 39
[369] Best, *Noah's Ark and the Ziusudra Epic*, p. 96
[370] Atrahasis fragment CBS 13532,7, quoted in Best, *Noah's Ark and the Ziusudra Epic*, p. 94
[371] Gen. 6:14
[372] Ex. 2:3
[373] Barry J. Kemp, *Ancient Egypt: Anatomy of a Civilization*, p. 206
[374] Hancock, *The Sign and the Seal*, p. 290
[375] Spence, *Ancient Egyptian Myths and Legends*, p. 143
[376] Bunson, *A Dictionary of Ancient Egypt*, p. 180
[377] Morenz, *Egyptian Religion*, p. 89
[378] Kemp, *Ancient Egypt*, p. 207
[379] Stephen Quirke, *Ancient Egyptian Religion*, p. 97
[380] Song 3:4
[381] 2 Sam. 6:3
[382] 2 Sam. 6:5
[383] *Thunder, Perfect Mind*, quoted in Willis Barnstone, *The Other Bible*, p. 595
[384] Prov. 1:20-21
[385] Begg, *The Cult of the Black Virgin*, p. 87
[386] Begg, p. 209
[387] Witt, *Isis and the Ancient World*, p. 272
[388] Gardner, *Bloodline of the Holy Grail*, p. 129
[389] Hancock, *The Sign and the Seal*, p. 293
[390] Rohan Coghlan, Ida Grehan and P.W. Joyce, *Book of Irish Names*, p. 24
[391] List, *Merlin's Secret*, p. 329
[392] Coghlan, Grehan and Joyce, *Book of Irish Names*, p. 111
[393] Picknett and Prince, *The Templar Revelation*, p. 68

[394] Matt. 11:19
[395] Morton Smith, *Jesus the Magician*, p. 62
[396] Hayyim ben Yehoshua, *Refuting Missionaries, Part 1: The Myth of the Historical Jesus*
[397] Holt, *Robin Hood*, p. 160
[398] Micah 4:8
[399] Margaret Starbird, *The Woman with the Alabaster Jar*, p. 50-51
[400] Coghlan, Grehan and Joyce, *Book of Irish Names*, p. 28
[401] Mark 10:21
[402] Rom. 8:31
[403] King James I, *Works*, Ch. 20, On the Divine Right of Kings (1609)
[404] F.F. Bruce, *Israel and the Nations*, p. 92
[405] 2 Chron. 36:23
[406] Is. 44:28-45:1
[407] 2 Chron. 13:5
[408] Deut. 17:15
[409] Ezra 7:12
[410] Ezra 10:11
[411] Neh. 13:25
[412] Neh. 4:3
[413] Bruce, *Israel and the Nations*, p. 111
[414] Bruce, *Israel and the Nations*, p. 107
[415] Hancock, *The Sign and the Seal*, p. 439
[416] Hancock, *The Sign and the Seal*, p. 445
[417] Bruce, *Israel and the Nations*, p. 109
[418] Bruce, *Israel and the Nations*, p. 128
[419] Bruce, *Israel and the Nations*, p. 128
[420] Luke 19:46
[421] 2 Macc. 3:11
[422] 2 Macc. 3:32
[423] 2 Macc. 3:34
[424] 2 Macc. 3:38
[425] 2 Macc. 15:12
[426] 2 Macc. 15:13-16
[427] Loomis, *The Grail*, p. 188
[428] Barbara Walker, *Woman's Dictionary of Symbols and Sacred Objects*, p. 392
[429] Verbrugghe and Wickersham, *Berossos and Manetho*, p. 44
[430] Hancock, *The Sign and the Seal*, p. 291
[431] Jonah 1:4
[432] Jonah 2:2-6
[433] Matt. 12:40
[434] Budge, *Egyptian Language*, p. 88
[435] John 19:30
[436] John 19:40
[437] Mead, *Gnostic John the Baptizer*, p. 21-22
[438] Matt. 27:61
[439] Acts 1:11
[440] Willis, *Dictionary of World Myth*, p. 26
[441] Temple, *The Sirius Mystery*, p. 135
[442] Temple, *The Sirius Mystery*, p. 281-282
[443] Temple, *The Sirius Mystery*, p. 100
[444] Plutarch, *Isis and Osiris*, in Budge, *Legends of the Egyptian Gods*, p. 211
[445] Gilgamesh, Tablet II, in Pritchard, *The Ancient Near East* Vol. 1, p. 46
[446] Gilgamesh, Tablet II, in Victor H. Matthews and Don C. Benjamin, *Old Testament Parallels*, p. 20-21
[447] Gilgamesh, Tablet II, in Pritchard, *The Ancient Near East Vol. 1*, p. 50
[448] Gilgamesh, Tablet II, in Pritchard, *The Ancient Near East Vol. 1*, p. 49
[449] Gen. 25:25-27

450 Gilgamesh, Tablet I, in Pritchard, *The Ancient Near East Vol. 1*, p. 42
451 Michael Baigent, Richard Leigh and Henry Lincoln, *Holy Blood, Holy Grail*, p. 82
452 Hugh Schonfield, *The Essene Odyssey*, p. 164
453 Mark 6:22-23
454 Rom. 6:4
455 Herodotus, *The Histories*, 2:86
456 Budge, Egyptian Language, p. 71, 74
457 Pamela Forey and Cecilia Fitzsimons, *An Instant Guide to Stars and Planets*, p. 13
458 Gos. Philip, 32, 55
459 John 12:3
460 Luke 10:39
461 Luke 7:37
462 Ex. 16:25
463 Starbird, *The Woman With the Alabaster Jar*, plated insert
464 Walker, *Woman's Dictionary of Symbols and Sacred Objects*, p. 313
465 Mark 16:9
466 Mead, *Gnostic John the Baptizer*, p. 63
467 Mead, *Gnostic John the Baptizer*, p. 40
468 Matt. 18:21
469 Mead, *Gnostic John the Baptizer*, p. 56
470 Luke 7:48
471 Matt. 3:15
472 Matt. 3:16
473 Ecc. 10:20-11:4, 6
474 Mark 14:22
475 Luke 17:33
476 Starbird, *The Woman With the Alabaster Jar*, p. 168
477 John 1:32
478 Jack Tressider, *Dictionary of Symbols*, p. 67
479 Matt. 3:17
480 Luke 15:4-6
481 Herodotus, *The Histories*, 2:104-5
482 Robert Graves, *The Greek Myths Vol. 1*, p. 115 (28.5)
483 Temple, *The Sirius Mystery*, p. 148
484 Graves, *The Greek Myths Vol. I*, p.157 (42.3)
485 Bialik and Ravnitzky, *Legends of the Jews*, p. 182
486 *Anchor Bible Dictionary*, Vol. 4, p. 925
487 Aldred, *Akhenaten*, p. 137
488 Num. 12:1
489 Num. 12:10
490 Num. 12:13
491 Aldred, *Akhenaten*, p. 136
492 Aldred, *Akhenaten*, p. 139
493 Temple, *The Sirius Mystery*, p. 196
494 Walker, *Woman's Dictionary of Symbols and Sacred Objects*, p. 372
495 Tressider, *Dictionary of Symbols*, p. 66
496 Walker, *Woman's Dictionary of Symbols and Sacred Objects*, p. 372
497 Graves, *The Greek Myths*, p. 80 (21.2)
498 Temple, *The Sirius Mystery*, p. 218
499 Gardner, *The White Goddess*, p. 173
500 John 19:34
501 Merlin Stone, *When God Was a Woman*, p. 11
502 Gardner, *Genesis of the Grail Kings*, p. 122
503 Temple, *The Sirius Mystery*, p 243
504 Graves and Patai, *The Hebrew Myths*, p. 68
505 Graves, *The White Goddess*, p. 165
506 Begg, *Cult of the Black Virgin*, p. 34-35

[507] De Santillana and Von Dechend, *Hamlet's Mill*, p. 440
[508] Matt Kane, *Heavens Unearthed*, p. 27
[509] Begg, *Cult of the Black Virgin*, p. 37
[510] Begg, *Cult of the Black Virgin*, p. 35
[511] Num. Rab. 16.25, quoted in Graves and Patai, *The Hebrew Myths*, p. 66
[512] Begg, *The Cult of the Black Virgin*, p. 37
[513] Graves and Patai, *The Hebrew Myths*, p. 68
[514] Graves and Patai, *The Hebrew Myths*, p. 171
[515] Gardner, *Genesis of the Grail Kings*, p. 63
[516] Anne Baring and Jules Cashford, *The Myth of the Goddess*, p. 190
[517] Is. 34:15
[518] Willis, *Dictionary of World Myth*, p. 105
[519] Graves, *The Greek Myths Vol. II*, p. 359 (170.k)
[520] Caitlan and John Matthews, *Ladies of the Lake*, p. 125
[521] Matthews, *The Elements of the Grail Tradition*, p. 6
[522] Jung and Von Franz, *The Grail Legend*, p. 106
[523] Matthews, *The Elements of the Grail Tradition*, p. 105
[524] Goodrich, *The Holy Grail*, p. 37
[525] Begg, *Cult of the Black Virgin*, p. 54
[526] Begg, *Cult of the Black Virgin*, p. 54-55
[527] Graves, *The Greek Myths Vol. II*, p. 225 (149.d)
[528] Begg, *Cult of the Black Virgin*, p. 51
[529] Clark, *Myth and Symbol in Ancient Egypt*, p. 239
[530] Willis, *Dictionary of World Myth*, p. 93
[531] Hancock and Bauval, *The Message of the Sphinx*, p. 194
[532] C. and J. Matthews, *Ladies of the Lake*, p. 59
[533] Malory, quoted in C. and J. Matthews, *Ladies of the Lake*, p. 60
[534] James Mackillop, *Oxford Dictionary of Celtic Mythology*, p. 329
[535] Jung and Von Franz, *The Grail Legend*, p. 363
[536] Mackillop, *Dictionary of Celtic Mythology*, p. 329
[537] C. and J. Matthews, *Ladies of the Lake*, p. 110
[538] C. and J. Matthews, *Ladies of the Lake*, p. 111
[539] Norma Lorre Goodrich, *Merlin*, p. 210
[540] Gen. 10:9
[541] C. and J. Matthews, Ladies of the Lake, p. 109
[542] Morford and Lenardon, *Classical Mythology*, p. 439
[543] *Enki and Ninhursag*, quoted in Best, *Noah's Ark and the Ziusudra Epic*, p. 74
[544] Geoffrey of Monmouth, *Vita Merlini*, quoted in Matthews, Ladies of the Lake, p. 64
[545] Geoffrey of Monmouth, *Vita Merlini*, quoted in Matthews, Ladies of the Lake, p. 63
[546] Stanley Applebaum, *The Mabinogion*, p. 187
[547] C. and J. Matthews, *Ladies of the Lake*, p. 138
[548] Wace and Layamon, *Arthurian Chronicles*, quoted in C. and J. Matthews, *Ladies of the Lake*, p. 90
[549] Jer. 46:13

www.ingramcontent.com/pod-product-compliance
Lightning Source LLC
Chambersburg PA
CBHW070732170426
43200CB00007B/504